Almost a Century

by
Alfred Harold Honikman

First published by Dog Ear Publishing
4010 W. 86th Street, Ste H
Indianapolis, IN 46268
www.dogearpublishing.net

ISBN: 978-159858-388-5

This book is printed on acid-free paper.

Printed in the United States of America

INTRODUCTION

When discussing events of long ago, family and friends urged me to write my memoirs. I was sixty-five when I retired from architectural practice and turned my thoughts to the day when we would move to the United States to live nearer my sons and grandchildren. That goal was blurred in 1978 by my wife Deena's illness and untimely death.

In 1980, I married Sylvia and shortly after, retired from all public offices in favor of extensive travel with my new wife. We visited Santa Barbara, stayed in the 'New Horizons' apartment that I'd purchased five years earlier. We both loved the environment and the many available on-site amenities that included a 9-hole golf course. Despite our deep attachment to Cape Town, we decided to make 'New Horizons' our future home. It was about 2 miles from the home of my son Terence and his wife Jane and two children. It was also a few hours flight to Florida to my elder son Basil and his Linda following his appointment as Professor of architecture at the University of Miami. We returned to Cape Town in September 1981 to prepare for our final departure. It was not easy! Apart from the necessary material adjustments, there were several sad farewells to our families and life-long friends and - not least - to the city to which we were both deeply attached.

Since then, my focus on developments in South Africa has been marred by distance. Twenty-one return visits in as many years offered little relief. However, it was clear that events were of considerable significance! So much so that many of the tasks to which I once devoted so much time and energy, appeared insignificant - relatively unimportant! That was not a very comforting thought! Had it come earlier, it may have had a disruptive influence. Coming when it did, it served to give my perception of events a more balanced perspective.

These memoirs tell of conditions and developments in my native South Africa during most of the twentieth century. They are not an historic survey. They do scant justice to the wonders of the country or the complexity of the problems it faced. I had lived in the far south - in Cape Town - where conditions, emotions and sentiments were very different from those in the hinterland. It is appropriate, therefore, that the reader be given another perspective - one that reflects the Government's point of view as reflected in Maurice Tyack's foreword to his book *SOUTH AFRICA - Land of Challenge* - published by France Inter Presse, Maurice Tyack, C.P. 541, Lausanne, Switzerland.[1] His foreword reads as follows:

> *As a French writer, I have always been excited by South Africa, where I found more than a place in the sun. It is a land singularly gifted by nature with myriad assets – dazzling flora, abundant fauna, immense mineral riches and, above all, many extraordinary and varied people. Its history is enthralling, teeming with restless adventure, dramatic events and momentous discoveries. Anywhere in the world so wealthy and desirable a land would have become an area of contention, competition and rivalry. It is therefore not surprising that South Africa's past was tumultuous. Today too, it remains one of the most controversial countries on earth, admired on the one hand, envied and hated on the other. Few countries have been the focus of so much attention and criticism, or the subject of so much debate and acrimonious argument. South Africa both to its people and outsiders is an absorbing subject, full of contradictions, puzzles and challenges. It is a country that is never static but is continually changing and developing, always surprising, stimulating and thought-provoking.*

> *This book, in text and pictures, is an attempt to portray the fascination of South Africa - the possibilities, problems, achievements and aspirations of this many-sided land which is at once complicated, naïve, paradoxical, virile, bull-headed, cruel, hospitable, solitary, but above all, very beautiful and unspeakably dear to its diverse peoples.*

In 1998, when my previous book, *In the Shadow of Apartheid*, was published, friends commented that 'it gave too remote a glimpse' of the impact that conditions in South Africa had made on my personal life. They were omissions of which I was not entirely unaware. In a sense, they were deliberate. My purpose was not to write an autobiography but primarily to describe some of the grim events in South Africa prior and subsequent to World War II. I focused on the injustice and incredible inhumanity of the apartheid syndrome, on some of the steps taken to improve on and entrench in perpetuity the massive benefits already enjoyed by the white ethnic minority, and to ensure that the vast African majority would remain subordinate. I wanted to show that the attempt to reconstruct the nation's political and social infrastructure for the exclusive benefit of the minority ethnic group, however skillfully administered, was doomed to failure and was likely to have significant repercussions within the country and beyond its borders.

This book seeks to make good some of the omissions. I will attempt to describe my personal reaction to the ever-changing influences that took place during my seventy years in that God-gifted country. I will try to explain why I did what I did and failed to do more! I will refer to the lofty dreams of Afrikaner nationhood thwarted by politics and the ill-conceived doctrine of apartheid - an ideology that dominated every aspect of life in South Africa for 48 years and culminated in a bloodless revolution that marked the final eclipse of white domination in Southern Africa.

With unquenchable gratitude, I dedicate this book to the six people who added so much meaning and happiness to my life:

My parents, whose way of life, love and care remained an inspiring light throughout my life, and whose lofty principles still guide me;

Deena, my first wife, whose love, grace and bountiful gifts made our home an exquisite family haven for forty-two glorious years;

Sylvia, who, for the last twenty-one years of her life, added grace, beauty, companionship and meaning to my every day;

My sons, Basil and Terence, in gratitude for the purposeful, honorable lives they lead, for their compassion and understanding that enriched my life before and after my lights began to dim.

No man could wish for more.

CHAPTER 1

HE LEARNED THE HARD WAY!

My parents, both born in England, were children when their families migrated to South Africa in the 1880s. The story of Dad's boyhood made a profound impact on me - one that I have felt deeply throughout my life. His father Ephraim, born near Warsaw, Poland, wanted to be a doctor. His parents could not afford to send him to college so he started his career as a medical aide. He was a young man when he left Poland to settle in Leeds, England, where he married Bertha Feinhols. With their young son Hyman, they moved to Sheffield where Dad was born in 1872, as was his younger brother Simon seven years later. Dad was thirteen or fourteen when his schooling in Liverpool was interrupted! His family - mother, father and three sons, moved again - this time to South Africa. They settled in Montague, a small town about 100 miles from Cape Town. Dad learnt to speak Afrikaans - the language of the district. Economically the family faced difficult times! Dad, then about 15 years of age, set out to fend for himself and, if possible, contribute to his family's wellbeing. He told us of his train journey to Cape Town and his arrival at 'the great terminal station'. His sole possessions were the clothes he wore and six ostrich eggs!

From the station, he walked up Plein Street, entered shop after shop trying to sell the eggs and so earn a little money. By the time he reached the top of the street, he had sold four! He was tired, bought a loaf of bread and a tin of jam. At the top - at the Roeland Street intersection - a kind-hearted lady allowed him to sleep in her barn. The next day he called on the shops that he had missed the day before. He successfully disposed of the remaining two eggs. He gratefully accepted the offer of a job as 'shop assistant' and was given blankets and a pillow and allowed to sleep in the adjoining storeroom! His career had started! He wrote to tell his parents that he had found a job!

Although his formal education had been restricted, Dad set about educating himself. Many subjects interested him, especially arithmetic and literature. As children, we were often amazed at his ability to memorize passages from famous works, particularly of Shakespeare from whom he said he 'learnt a great deal!'

Both my grandfathers died before I was born. I knew them only through the life-size portraits that graced the walls of our home throughout my childhood. Impressed by the deep-set eyes and somber appearance of Dad's father Ephraim, I was eager to hear more about him. Dad explained that it was quite soon after he found his first job that the rest of his family came to live in the city. His father (Ephraim) occupied a small cottage in Canterbury Street about a quarter mile from the barn where Dad had spent his first night in the city. It was also a short distance from the city prison known as the Roeland Street jail.

Ephraim had an acquaintance who had been incarcerated in the Roeland Street jail. It distressed him. He was convinced that the man was innocent of the crime for which he had been arrested! One night - it was dark, cloudy, drizzling slightly - Ephraim took a hamper of food for the prisoner. He knocked on the heavy prison doors and waited! He knocked again and again! A storm developed. The rain came down in sheets. He tried to protect the hamper with his jacket! He got drenched to the skin. Minutes later (seemed like hours) the doors screeched open. Through the gap barely inches wide, a warden asked: "Wat wil jy he?" (What do you want?) His father took the hamper from under his jacket, gave it to the warden and told him whom it was for. Shivering with cold, he made his way home. He developed pneumonia (often fatal in those days) and died on July 31st, 1888. My dad was then sixteen years of age.

Subsequently Dad took to insurance. He first represented the Norwich Life Insurance Company and later received an appointment with Sun Life of Canada. There he found his mark. Shortly before the outbreak of the second Boer War (1899-1902) Dad visited the Transvaal Republic where he obtained an interview with President Paul Kruger[2]. They conversed fluently in Afrikaans - a language spoken only in South Africa. The President asked him how it was that he, "a young Englishman", was able to converse in Afrikaans. Dad explained that his boyhood friends in Montague were all Afrikaners. The President seemed pleased with the reply – his manner very amicable. Dad explained that the purpose of the visit was to interest the President in life insurance and to explain its potential long-term benefits to government personnel and how such insurance was being administered in other countries. He also described the advantageous terms offered by his Company. The interview, as Dad described it, ended with his having "secured insurance policies covering the lives of senior members of the Transvaal Police Force." The Company lauded Dad on his success!

MY FATHER, IJ "CHASER" HONIKMAN

Many years later - 20 years after Dad died, I learned the full story. In September 1960 - in my capacity as Deputy Mayor - I had occasion to call on the then Manager of Sun Life in connection with one of the city charities. As I entered his office he extended a very warm hand of welcome and asked: "Mr. Deputy, were you perhaps related to the late I. J. Honikman?" "Most certainly," I replied, "He was my father!" The manager ushered me into the adjoining board room commenting: "It is not a very common name - I thought there might be a link. I have something to show you!" He pointed to several bulky portfolios that lay open on the table and said: "These are some of the records of Sun policies negotiated towards the end of the 19th century. This particular batch contains the policies of the entire Transvaal Police Force! They were obtained by your late father during a visit to President Krueger before the outbreak of the Boer War!" Turning over page after page, he pointed to Dad's bold familiar signature and commented: "An incredible achievement - You can be proud!"

At the start of the century, Dad decided that the time had come for him to launch out on his own. He set himself up as an Estate Agent and opened an office at 14 Burg Street. He was 28 years of age when he fell in love with my mother Henrietta (Hetty) Aaron. She was a very handsome lady a year older than he. They were married in 1901 by the Reverend A. P. Bender, in the 'old synagogue' (now a Jewish museum) overlooking the beautiful oak-lined Government Avenue in Cape Town. For a while, they too lived in a rented cottage in Roeland Street. By 1904 they had two children, Ephraim and Sybil. Their home was too small for a growing family. Dad bought a plot in Kloof Road, Tamboers Kloof, then a much sought-after residential area about a mile from the city center. Architects Black and Fagg were commissioned to design a new house - a lovely home which he named "Epherton" in honor of my grandfather. That was the family home for 15 years. In 1906, my sister Beatrice was born and, 2 years later, my brother Maurice. I followed in 1910 and on the 9th of March 1912, Rita, the sixth child, was born.

MY FAMILY

When I was a child, Mother was ever busy with domestic chores. With six children, a husband, an aging mother and a large home, she had time for little else. Two servants (maid and manservant referred to as 'the boy') relieved her on many menial tasks but they too had to be catered for which added to Mother's duties. In addition there were always visitors - mainly cousins and aunts - for dinner especially on Friday nights. In those days, neither the radio nor TV was available to attract one's interest. Occasionally Mother would relax at the piano, play patience or German Whist with my dad. In later years (after Dad died) when her children were old enough to fend for themselves, Mother blossomed! She had a happy disposition and was in great demand, especially by her grandchildren. She lived with Sybil in Kenilworth at Kenmain Gardens - a group of 36 apartments on the Main

Road Kenilworth. It was the last project designed by my firm[3] before war broke out in 1939 when the partnership dissolved. Sybil, who never married, was a botany teacher at the Observatory Girls High School. Mother died in 1955. She was 85.

MY FAMILY. L to R: ALF, BEATRICE, I.J., EPHIE, MAURICE, SYBIL, HETTY AND RITA

A POWERFUL INFLUENCE

Dad was a very strong personality - a powerful influence on me! He was scrupulously honest, immaculate and thorough in everything he did and expected the same level of integrity and thoroughness from his children! Ambitious for us, he was somewhat of a disciplinarian. I remember one night - I was ten years of age, tired, ready for bed, when Dad decided to examine my homework. I was completing a page in my 'writing' exercise book when he looked over my shoulder! He did not like what he saw! He pointed to letters that were sloping inconsistently and squeezed at the end of the lines! I was made to write the page over and over again until it was neat and to his satisfaction. It was very late - seemed like early morning, before he relented!

Dad was always urging us to be thorough, exhaustive and neat in everything we undertook. He often told us: "half-heartedness is doomed to failure" and "if it is worth doing, it's worth doing well!" He told an impressive story of the time when he was an insurance representative. A rumor was afloat that a very large Johannesburg organization was considering a 'new deal' - one that included insurance coverage for each of its several hundred employees! The rumor caused a stir among insurance representatives. Each one wished that the business could come 'his way' - that he would be the lucky man! The Head of the firm had been in London and was reported to be aboard one of the *Castle* liners returning home. Ingenious plans were devised to capture his business. Dad pondered! He knew that many of his colleagues would seek an interview with the Head! Some would immediately contact his Johannesburg office and make the 'earliest possible' appointment after the Head's return to work! Others would seek to interview him on his arrival in Cape Town and attempt to interest him in one or other of the proposals his company had to offer. To Dad, those ideas, appealing as they appeared on surface, were not good enough! Instead Dad formulated tangible alternative insurance proposals which he described in a carefully worded letter and put it in an envelope addressed to the Head. He then sought an interview with the Cape Town Harbor master, presented him with the document which he explained 'was extremely important and should reach the Head *before* his arrival in Cape Town!' The Harbormaster explained that, each Monday morning, immediately he received the signal that the ship had been sighted, he would board the pilot ship and speed out to meet the incoming vessel, make for the bridge and pilot it into harbor! That was his duty - "there could be no justification for delay!" He regretted, therefore, that he could not undertake to deliver the document; "but," he added, "if you would like to join me on the pilot ship, you could deliver the document in person - but you will have to be here before six!" Dad could not have wished for a better answer! Early Monday morning Dad was in the Master's office in good time, to deliver the letter in person. He had a long interview with his 'prey' before the ship had entered port - well in advance of any of his competitors! As the ship drew alongside the wharf, he spotted two of his contemporaries on the quayside! They were obviously surprised (and disappointed) to see Dad on board in the company of the man they were waiting to meet!

Dad, as I understand, was nicknamed "Chaser" by his friends. They, I gathered, were impressed by the way in which he was said to 'never to miss an opportunity' but 'chased' exhaustively after every opportunity as it arose. The name stuck and that was the name by which he was addressed by his friends years later. Chase became our second son's middle name, his son Stephen's middle name is Chase, and now my great-grandson Rylan's middle name is Chase. It has become a meaningful family tradition.

Dad's intuition and thoroughness often proved highly rewarding! He had quite a stack of similar stories to tell! Of course I was aware at the time that his purpose was to give his children lessons in 'initiative', 'thoroughness' and 'tidiness'! Years later, I realized how invaluable those lessons had been! As an adult I often paused to wonder how my dad would have responded to the particular event or circumstance that confronted me. It gave me a sense of confidence when I felt sure that my decision was precisely the one that Dad would have taken. There were occasions that I could trace my conclusion or attitude to a particular lesson or principle that I had learnt from my father.

Dad died more than six decades ago. His memory and influence remain alive!

CHAPTER 2

EARLY IMPRESSIONS

The first emotional experience that comes to memory was when my mother told me that I was old enough to go to school! I was not yet six years of age as I listened to her explaining that, in future, each week from Monday to Friday, I was to accompany my brother Maurice to and from school. The Tamboers Kloof Preparatory School in Belle Ombre Road, off Kloof Nek Road, was within walking distance - about half a mile, from home.

The first event at school to impact my memory was when my kindergarten teacher explained that the year of my birth, 1910, coincided with the birth of my nation. That fact, presented with apparent seriousness, left me feeling that my birth and the birth of my country were interrelated and thus of related significance! It left me somewhat puzzled and for a while tended to limit my perception of the outside world. 'Nothing of significance' seemed to exist beyond the confines of "Country and me!"

I remember the day I received my first school cap. It carried an emblem bearing the letters *T.K.P.S.* representing the name of the school. At tea-break, one of the older boys took my cap, pointed explicitly to each of the letters and with apparent earnestness announced that they represented: "T for Teach, K for Kaiser, P for Proper and S for Sense" and added: "Teach Kaiser Proper Sense – the blighter!" "Who is the Kaiser?" I asked. "He is king of Germany – a terrible country! They invaded Holland and Belgium and are now killing our soldiers in France!" That was my awakening to the outside world! From then on, *'my country'* ceased to be the 'safe, joyful haven' that had appeased my infant mind. My perception of *life,* such as it was, had been shaken! Until then, I don't think I fully realized that *'my country'* was the *'only world'* I knew. It disturbed me to find that it was but a small part of a vast world of many lands, oceans and peoples! I had yet to learn that my country was an important part of the British

Empire which was 'the greatest empire in history'. That new 'awareness', more than anything else, would serve to lessen the fears and insecurity that I felt as a child as some of the grim realities of World War became known to me! Only then, as my 'vision of the world' broadened, and I became aware that there were people, places and cultures beyond the confines of 'my country', that there were times when there was no WAR! Only then did a kind of 'restless uncertainty' slowly disappear - only then, was I was able join in the fun - to laugh with other boys!

I was seven years old when I joined the Wolf Cubs. Our Pack used to meet at the home of the cub mistress, Miss Grey, on the east side of New Church Street – a 10-minute walk from my home. I remember how proud I was of my first green uniform and of my first star presented weeks later. Warm was the 'glow of achievement' that I felt one afternoon when the Pack was called to attention and I heard the cub mistress call my name. I was one of two cubs who had won a second star!

Miss Grey's brother Wallace, a big fellow, was already a Scout. Occasionally he was present at our cub meetings. His uniform had many badges and impressed me! I longed for the day when I too could be a Scout.

A weekend cub camp was organized and I was excited when my parents said I could go! There were eight of us - six cubs, Miss Grey and Wallace. We all met at 'Kloof Nek'. That is the name of the saddle between the Kloof Corner, the western escarpment of Table Mountain, and the towering pinnacle of Lion's Head. It was also a popular meeting spot for mountaineers.

In the glen, on the Camps Bay side of the saddle, among the Pines and Silver trees, not far from Lord Charles Somerset's Shooting Box, we pitched our two tents - under the watchful eye of Miss Grey! I felt embarrassment when she knelt beside me and took my hand to examine my thumb. I had bashed it with the mallet while driving a tent peg into the ground! For me it was great fun, sitting around the camp fire enjoying hot sausage rolls, potato chips and coffee - my first experience away from home! As the sun set, Miss Grey and Wallace told us yarns and led us in songs that we had learnt at previous meetings - always ending with "God Save the King"- then our national anthem! Inside one of the tents, Wallace showed us how to chop up the ground surface to make it comfortable for sleeping. We split up. Three younger cubs joined Miss Grey to her tent while the rest of us rolled out our ground sheets and blankets. I slept next to Wallace.

Early next morning I was awakened by a ticklish sensation on my forehead. When I opened my eyes I was alarmed and horrified at what I saw! Wallace was fast asleep. A large scorpion had stepped off my blanket onto his! It crawled onto his neck from the collar of his pajamas. I knew the scorpion to be deadly poisonous. Petrified, my immediate impulse was to push it off. Instinctively I held back. The insect turned, moved off his face onto the blanket and onto the ground. Wallace, unaware of what had occurred, yawned, rubbed his neck and exclaimed: "Good morning!" He seemed undisturbed when I told him what had happened. He looked around, glanced below his ground sheet and turned over to sleep! The worrisome intruder had vanished! Maybe it was I who had intruded on its domain!

CUTS

One morning during my second year in kindergarten school, the bell had rung and I was way behind a group of children scurrying back to class. Miss Luckhoff, the teacher on duty, called me. "You're dawdling," she exclaimed, "did you not hear the bell?" Before I could respond, she instructed me to report to the Principal – something all the children dreaded!

Miss Gilfillen the headmistress was known to be very strict! Timidly, I tapped on the door. It opened. She stood there holding a thin bamboo cane. "And what brings you here young man?" I explained. "You will learn not to dawdle when the bell rings – turn around!" I received two cuts behind the knees. They hurt! It was during the war! Endless stories about 'our enemies' the 'terrible Germans' produced an impression in my mind that there was no person worse than 'a German'! Miss Luckhoff was known to be of German descent and I was convinced that was the real reason for my reprimand! Some time elapsed before I was willing to admit - even to myself - that I was not only dawdling at the time, but was thinking of how I could escape attending that particular class.

AN AWESOME REVELATION

After dinner one evening, my dad took me out onto the verandah. He pointed to a bright full moon that had begun a partial eclipse and explained how the Earth's shadow fell across the moon. The night grew darker; momentarily my wonderment turned to fear! Dad quickly assured me that it would not last long – that the full moon would soon return in all its glory! Slowly the shadow passed. I stared at the expanse of twinkling stars! Then, with Dad's help, I became aware of the 'vast Universe' that surrounded me! I pondered over it for days. For a long time my vision of 'that Universe' remained blurred but it was ever awesome and increasingly wonderful! Everything seemed to have changed - in a way that I am unable to describe.

CHILDISH FOLLY

One afternoon brother Maurice and I were walking home together from school. We had just crossed Kloof Nek Road, when I noticed that my shoe-lace was undone. As I bent down to do it up, I handed Maurice my overcoat to hold. I then noticed that the lace of the other shoe was loose! I proceeded to attend to that too. Maurice thought I was taking far too long. He exclaimed: "Hurry up!" Impatiently he put my coat on the pavement and started to walk on. Stubbornly I refused to pick it up and followed him down the hill. At the corner, Maurice went into the bookshop to collect our parents' weekly papers ("Answers" and "Pearsons"). Wondering about my coat, I looked back to the spot where we had been standing. The coat was not to be seen! We returned home without it!

Maurice gave mother the papers. She looked towards me and asked: "Alfie, where is your coat?" I explained that Maurice put it on the pavement and I would not pick it up. Mother was infuriated and uttered "I'll tell your father!" She lifted the telephone from the hook and I heard her call the number: "Central 1679." She signaled us to scram.

When Dad got home he asked us to explain our conduct. No explanation satisfied him. He said that we had behaved like two 'spoiled children'! He went on to say that there were many children who were cold and wet because their parents could not provide warm winter coats like the one we were willing to cast aside, that we were "both stupid, thoughtless and naughty." We were told to turn face downwards over the side of the bed. With his razor strop, Dad gave us each two whacks on our bottoms! Maurice got up and went out of the room. I remained and yelled loud and clear! That brought Dad back to give me one more for my trouble!

Later I realized that it was my ego, more than my hind-quarters, that had been hurt. I became aware that there were less privileged people in the world, countless children in dire need of warmth - and much else! I had learnt a lesson! I was still a boy when I was made aware that fate had put me on the better side of a line dividing the 'haves' from the 'have-nots'! Less dramatically, in later years, I learnt that fate had also put me on the more favored side of an ethnic line - that the vast majority of our people on the other side dwelt in dire poverty!

In time, I became aware of the extent to which the nation was steeped in ethnic cleavage! It distressed and appalled me to witness 'race' and 'color' being deliberately exploited for political purposes and for the material advantages it secured for the privileged white minority. It worried me intensely as I learnt that the actions of the Government had brought 'my country' into contempt by the civilized world.

FAMILY TIES

In addition to my five siblings, there were nine cousins on my father's side all living in Cape Town and eleven on my mother's side, of whom three lived in the Cape, five in the Transvaal and 3 in German South West Africa. In 1915, my cousin Joey Cohen, the eldest of all the cousins whom we had never met, arrived from Johannesburg. He was wearing the khaki uniform of a soldier! He explained that in a few days time - he was not sure when - he would have to report to the Castle for duty. From there he and his squadron would march to the harbor to board a troop-ship en route to England and thence to 'Flanders, the battle fields of France!' Intently, I listened to stories about his training - the conquest of German South West Africa by the South African army led by General Smuts[4] and the surrender of the German army in South West Africa, There, in what was then 'enemy territory', my cousins Rosy, Ada and Gena Phillips lived with their parents. Keetmanshoop was a small town not far from the Kalahari Desert. Joey told us that our cousin Ada had developed spinal meningitis and was taken (before the outbreak of war) to Germany for treatment. The hospital where she was being treated was commandeered by the German army! All civilian patients were moved. Somewhere in Germany, cousin Ada was 'lost'. Tirelessly her distressed parents strove to find her. Uncle Phillip contacted embassies and international merchants in search of some means of communication with his daughter - all no avail. That was my introduction to some of the realities of War - to the horror devastation, and unspeakable suffering it entailed.

Ada was subsequently found in Britain. She had been 'exchanged' for a German officer prisoner-of-war and was in the care of the British Red Cross organization. She was among the children in a press photograph that was widely published in Britain. The photograph bore the caption "HELP THESE POOR CHILDREN". My cousin Joey, who at the time was recovering from temporary blindness through shell-shock and was recuperating in another hospital in Britain, was given a newspaper and made to read the caption! He immediately recognized his cousin Ada whom he had met on a visit to Keetmanshoop. He apparently ejaculated: "That's my cousin Ada!" The hospital authorities took up the matter and Ada was soon reunited with her family.

ACT OF UNION

The year 1910 was of immense significance for my country. It was the year that the British Parliament introduced the Act of Union by which the old Boer Republics, the Transvaal and Orange Free State, were united with the British colonies of the Cape and Natal, to form a single self-governing country - the Union of South Africa. It was a moment of great rejoicing - at least for those with British affiliations. That included the majority of citizens of the Cape and Natal and embraced many Afrikaners who had lived under British rule over the past century. Most of the population hoped that the Boers (loyal to the old defeated republics of the Transvaal and Orange Free State) would regard the Act as a token of reconciliation. Indeed it was so regarded by many of the Boer leaders who felt that progress and peace were inseparable. They decided to bury the hatchet and collaborate with the British in the task of building a new nation.

In the Transvaal and Orange Free State, conditions were very different. There, to many Afrikaners, the memory of the concentration camps[5] and the losses they suffered during the Boer War produced a deep bitterness that lingered on for decades. Many fostered a deep-rooted hatred of the British. Defeat had not destroyed their dream of an exclusive Afrikaner nation 'uncontaminated by foreign British influence'. That dream ran counter to the spirit of the 'Union' and to the dominant national goals. It had been the source of a long bitter political division that prevailed for the better part of the century. (It was eclipsed only in 1994 by a bloodless revolution – one that produced an all-embracing democracy and marked the end of white domination. It also brought an end to the bitterness and injustice of apartheid and smothered the flame of Afrikaner nationhood.)

In 1910, the 'new' country adopted the motto "Union is Strength" (Eendraght Maak Maght). It represented the lofty hopes of a young nation founded in the year of my birth. As I recall 'Het Volk' (the ruling Party of the old Transvaal Republic) merged with the British Unionist Party of the Cape. Together they formed the new South African Party. Under the leadership of General Louis Botha, the Party, with strong public support, felt that it was their destiny to carry the 'New' nation into the future. Botha accepted Britain's invitation to serve as the Union's first Prime Minister. Second in command was another Boer War General, Jan Cristiaan Smuts (Deputy Prime Minister). With them sat another Boer War General - J. B. M. Hertzog[6]. They, and other prominent leaders of the old Republics, sat side by side with John X. Merriman, Sir Abe Bailey, Sir Thomas Watt, Ernest Oppenheimer, Patrick Duncan and other staunch British leaders of the old Cape Colony.

When I first heard about these episodes in the history of my country, I was still in junior school and they appeared to be little more than passing events in the political parade. Years had yet to pass before they made a meaningful impact on me. I was still at school and there were other interesting and more enjoyable events to attract my interest.

In 1918, my father was elected to represent our ward as a City Councilor. An amusing story he told at the time was that on election day, soon after entering the Long Street polling station, he was face to face with a Malay gentleman who appeared bewildered and lost. Apparently he had never been in a polling station before. Not knowing where to turn, the poor man looked to Dad with a worried plea in his eyes. Articulating every syllable, he exclaimed slowly: "I want to vote for Mister Ho-Ne-Ke-An." Amused, (and with much delight) Dad showed the stranger to a polling booth.

OSTRICH FEATHERS

Before the outbreak of the World War I, ostrich feathers became fashionable.

In all the capitals of Europe and America, affluent ladies adorned their hats and skirts with plumes of ostrich feathers. A lucrative trade developed; ostrich farmers of the Cape flourished. Dad seized the opportunity to participate in the feather trade and, as a second string to his bow, he became an ostrich feather merchant. The trade grew into a 'boom' - interrupted in

1914 by the outbreak of World War I. As children we enjoyed the stories of his buying missions to the ostrich districts of the Cape. Each trip lasted 4 or 5 days. Dad would buy selected plumes, have them sorted, graded, packed, and shipped to London's feather market. He returned home at week-ends to tell us of his adventures. Vividly I recall his trips to Oudtshoorn and Worcester, his friendship with farmer Willem Naude and his brother David whose beautiful home "Excelsior" he had visited. (Years later, a chance incident took me there! That's another story for later.)

THE INFLUENZA EPIDEMIC

1918 witnessed the end of World War I - the cruelest, most devastating of all conflicts in human history. Celebrations everywhere were marred by the advent of the Influenza epidemic – a plague that lasted long and left no country untouched. It accounted for the loss of more lives than the war just ended!

In our part of town, almost every household was affected. Of the eight members of my family, only my eldest brother Ephie was affected. He had a fairly mild attack and was back on his feet within a few days. The rest of us, though free of infection, were not uninvolved. In those grim days, hot lemon water was regarded a good antidote for 'flu' and people were encouraged to drink lots of it. Dad resumed his trips to the country districts, not for feathers, but to return with cartloads of lemons! As children we were required to distribute the lemons to the homes of affected families in the neighborhood. We were told to knock on doors, inquire if lemons were needed and to deliver a bag of six or seven lemons to each affected household. We were warned repeatedly that, in no circumstances, were we to enter the houses or accept gifts or any form of remuneration. Everyone was aware of the risk of infection. I called on countless homes and was never asked to enter. Occasionally I was asked to wait while the lady went back saying that she had some sweets for me – which reluctantly, I was bound to refuse!

HOLIDAYS BY THE SEA

During the first half of the twentieth century Muizenberg was probably the most popular seaside resort in South Africa. It was situated on the False Bay coast about fifteen miles from the heart of Cape Town. There the beach of soft white crystal sand, totally unmarred by obstruction or any form of pollution[7], extends eastward for 20 miles from the boulders at the foot of the mountain towards Somerset Strand. Safe bathing and relatively warm waters of the Indian Ocean made the resort particularly attractive to parents with young children. They would flock there particularly during the six weeks school holiday in the summer months of December and January. A commuter train covering the 25 miles from the city center to the British Naval base at Simonstown, passing through most of the residential suburbs, gave locals ready access to Muizenberg and the other unique False Bay resorts of St. James, Kalk Bay and Fish Hoek.

As children we all had a special longing for summer. Dad usually rented a house in Muizenberg for December and January to coincide with our six weeks holiday from school. The house we occupied in December 1918, named "Godelming", was double-storied, situated about a mile from the village and about half a mile from the most popular part of the beach. It was there Maurice, Rita and I would meet our friends each morning to swim, surf, play and sunbathe. Our older siblings met their friends elsewhere nearby. Our spot was sheltered from the sea breezes by two long rows of gaily-colored bathing booths.

SHIPS THAT PASSED BY NIGHT

One morning, lying face down on my surfboard, basking in the sun, fingers tracing idly through the sand, I struck something hard and metallic! It had a serrated edge! Curiously I brought it to the surface. It was a coin - a half-crown piece! Whoh! I had never had so much money – 5 times my weekly pocket money! Perhaps there was more! Spontaneously my fingers returned to the spot. Within seconds they struck another smaller coin - a shilling piece. I was elated. Now, with the shilling I had already saved, I had accumulated four shillings and sixpence - seven times my weekly pocket money! "What could I buy with that?" I wondered!

I showed my discovered treasure to Maurice and Rita, got dressed and quietly walked away. I made for the village center. In a shop window on the Main Road, my eyes focused on a complement of four miniature white battleships. How I longed to have them! Their price was marked '5 shillings and sixpence' - an amount well beyond my means - a shilling more than I possessed! Sadly I walked my way home. If I saved all my pocket money, it would be two weeks, before I would be in a position to buy them! I decided to do just that! A week went by. Came Monday! Maurice and I been given our pocket money and were in the 'tuck shop' together. Maurice bought some licorice and a cone of ice-cream. He seemed puzzled that I was not buying anything. I told him that I had put my sixpence away – "saving to buy the ships". No comment! He gave me a piece of his licorice.

I was worried that the ships might be sold by the time I had saved enough money! One day Mother asked me to run upstairs and fetch her book from the table beside her bed. As I lifted the book, I spotted a coin on the carpet. It was lying behind the leg of the little table. I thought: "Mom must have dropped it." I picked it up intending to give it to her with the book. It was a shilling piece! The thought flashed to mind: "With it and my saved pocket money, I would have enough to buy the ships!" I gave Mother the book - said nothing about the coin I had found! I went back at the shop - excited to see the ships were still there! I bought them!

For days afterwards, every time I handled my prized acquisition, I felt uneasy and unhappy! The shilling weighed on my mind. I should have told Mother! I felt awful! I knew that I had done wrong! It marred my interest in the ships! I did not want to see them again! Each time I went to my toys, the ships 'stared at me!' I put them aside – I really didn't want to see them again!

One afternoon a neighbor's boy - friend of my sister Rita - was playing with the ships on the carpet! I watched for a moment. Hesitantly I asked if he would like to have them - to take them home. Rita was aghast! She knew how I had craved for them and exclaimed: "Alfie what are you doing!" I heard myself utter meekly: "I don't want them anymore!"

The 'shilling incident' weighed on my mind for a long while. My attempts to rationalize - *'after all I was only seven at the time'* - did not appease my conscience! I felt ashamed! I never told my family of the inci-dent - let alone my mother and she never uttered a word about it. Perhaps she never knew!

Over the years, I never spoke about the incident - not until now! I was too ashamed. I tried to make amends in one way or another - don't know that I ever succeeded!

CHAPTER 3

THE BIG MOVE

My grandmother Katie Aarons (Mother's mother) lived in Johannes-burg with her elder daughter Leah and her husband Elkin Cohen. Their circumstances were by no means affluent and, on a few occasions, I heard Mother remark: "I wish she could live with us!" At the time, that was not possible. "Epherton" had already become too small for our growing family of eight. I was ten years of age when Dad spoke of a new house in Oranjezicht that he had purchased. A disturbing thought flashed to mind: "Are we about to abandon our home and neighborhood!" My concern gave way to excitement as Dad explained that "Oranjezicht" was a beautiful res-idential area on the lower slopes of the mountain. He went on to say: "You will have a lovely view of Table Bay and the City - the house will be large enough for us all - including Grandma!" The thought of having Grandma with us produced a warm sense of anticipation that we all shared. That goal, Dad explained, could not be realized for several months as our new home was being extensively altered and enlarged.

"LONGWOOD"

"Longwood" was so named because it reminded my parents of Napoleon's place of exile on the Island of St. Helena. They had recently called there during their return voyage from Britain after visiting their birthplaces in Sheffield and Birmingham. It was one of the few homes in the country designed by Sir Herbert Baker[8]. Dad commissioned architects Walgate and Elsworth (they were Baker's representatives in the Cape) to design extensive alterations and additions to the house with the proviso that 'its distinctive character be preserved'. The architects did an admirable job. Two elegant gables remained untouched. One fronted on Montrose Avenue, the other faced west and towards Forest Road and Lion's Head. The origi-nal design included a wide verandah and an open pergola supported on slender white Doric columns that extended for the entire frontage. The per-gola was removed and replaced by a flat roof that gave protective cover to the verandah and formed an expansive balcony with access from the children's bedrooms on the upper floor. Above each column was a boxed teak post with a black twisted wrought-iron protective railing between. We all loved the balcony! It commanded an unbroken vista of Lion's Head, Signal Hill, the city center, the broad expanse of Table Bay and the mountains of Melkbosch Strand beyond.

A large new dining room occupied the open area on the south side of the house (between the kitchen wing and the study) and gave added character to the house. Particularly attractive was the way in which the arched window heads intercepted the lofty vaulted ceiling. A fireplace with a wide teak mantle-piece mounted on beautiful teak columns marked the east-end of the room. Above the dining room was a large south-facing balcony accessed by two steps from the bedroom corridor. It provided a close and awesome view of the upper gorges of Table Mountain.

The property, surrounded by a random sandstone wall, had a frontage of about 170 feet on Montrose Avenue and extended from Forest Road to Hilton Road. The elevated level of the site on which the house was situated was about 100 feet in depth and had a level graveled play area east of the house.

The lower portion narrowed in depth to about 15 feet on Hilton Road. A stone-arched entrance on Montrose Avenue was used to provide pedestrian access to and from the old tram terminal at the corner of Upper Orange Street a few hundred yards away. Soon after the house was purchased, the tramline was extended along Montrose Avenue past "Longwood" to a new terminal shelter some 100 yards west of Forest Road. Informed that the extension was imminent, Dad instructed the architects to incorporate a new gateway and entrance to the house from Forest Road. It proved to be a boon to us and to our visitors who still commuted by tram. (The motor car was a rare commodity in those days). The new entrance was a boon also to the tram drivers and conductors! Quick access to the new terminal made it possible for Mother to provide the men with afternoon tea and cookies - something she did frequently. For the men, the refreshment was a welcome relief at the end of their long eight-hour shift.

"Longwood" was a prototype of Cape-Dutch architecture. The architect responsible, Sir Herbert Baker, was one of its greatest exponents. Our big move to "Longwood" took place in the spring of 1920. I was too young to be aware of the complex problems my parents must have faced having to pack for and move a family of eight. It must have been a trying ordeal. The event, however, was one of considerable moment for all the family. For me particularly it was one of great significance.

When I first entered the house I was amazed at the size and number of living rooms downstairs. In the lounge I recall gazing at the two teak columns and wondered how a craftsman obtained such an even entasis[9] and still kept the columns round! Someone drew my attention to the wood carver's careful chisel marks on the ceiling beams and explained that they had been 'hand-hewn'! In the new dining room, the lofty semi-vaulted ceiling seemed particularly beautiful. When I first walked through the house, I was intrigued that, in addition to the wide carpeted stairway near the entrance, there was a second narrow service stair - at the other end of the house! All manner of mischievous possibilities ('Hide and Seek' and the like) flashed to mind!

I was only ten years of age. The focus on aspects of 'building construction' with reference to 'architectural character' triggered an enduring interest and, eight years later, may have contributed in some measure to my choice of 'architecture' as a career.

Maurice and I were allotted one of the two large bedrooms upstairs; the other was for Beatrice and Rita. Ephraim (then 17) and Sybil (15) were each given their own single room. The third was reserved for our grandmother. "Gran", as she was affectionately known to us children, arrived from Johannesburg weeks later. She was then eighty-five, wrinkled and had a slight limp. She was an interesting personality, had a delightful sense-of-humor and, from the moment of her arrival, endeared herself to everyone - not least my father and her grandchildren. Her dress was always neat and formal. Her skirts touched the floor - the custom those days for women of her age. We kids soon discovered that beneath the outer skirt were several petti-skirts that were of special interest to us as kids! They contained pockets in which she harboured packets of goodies, particulaly "popkies" (jelly babies) of which she seemed to have had an endless supply! We all loved them! Often in the afternoons back from school, we would confront Grandma with a request: *"Got any popkies, Gran?"* She would turn away responding: *"Go on mit you"*. But she would delve into one of her petti-skirts to produce the sought after goodies which she handed to us. With a twinkle in her eye, she would add: *"Don't tell your mother!"* When occasionally we greedily asked for more, additional 'popkies' never failed to appear!

In all the years she was with us, I never knew her to be ill. If she ever felt 'off color', she never showed it. She was always pleasant - a great source of joy to us all and to her many visiting grandchildren.

Upstairs there was another large room with a low ceiling above the Study - the 'box room' – used primarily for storage. It served also as my hobby room or 'workshop' as I preferred to call it.

THE CELLAR

The ice-chest - (in those days the refrigerator had not yet been invented) - was placed in a lobby outside the inner kitchen door and obstructed another door that I assumed gave access to a deep unused cupboard below the service stair. We had been in the house a few months when I decided to investigate! Flashlight in hand, I managed to push the ice-chest aside and opened the obstructed door. It was no cupboard! It was dark and clammy! There was another stairs leading down! I worked my way through countless cobwebs and ventured down in search of 'the unknown'! I 'discovered' a large basement under the breakfast room. It must have been ages since anyone had been there! In one corner on the floor, was an old-fashioned black top hat covered in dust! I thought: 'Must be a relic of the Boer War!' Then I spotted two black wrought-iron gratings! They were beautifully shaped! I thought they would look well in the lounge hearth. The rest were old clothes - valueless junk! Suddenly I heard my mother's voice: "Who's down there?" I replied: "Coming - It's only me." I took the gratings and returned up the stairs. Mom, appalled at what she saw, declared: "Look at you – you're filthy! Go and have a bath and wash your hair." I closed the door, put the ice-chest back in place and went to the bathroom. When I saw the color of the water and the cobwebs floating on the surface, I understood Mother's concern. I took the gratings into the yard, scrubbed them clean and put them in the lounge fireplace. I thought they looked very handsome but they evoked no comment and apparently remained unnoticed until Dad came home! He spotted them and asked where they had come from? When Mom explained that I had found them in the basement, Dad was delighted! He commented: *"They look good! Thank you, lad – they're splendid!"* From then on, they remained part of the lounge furniture. I had been given a great boost!!

The dining-room furniture was unique. It was all of mellowed, hand-carved Flemish oak made in Belgium. It was very special! It had been brought from 'Epherton' and was resplendent in its new setting. Mother told me that, when Dad was contemplating the purchase of "Longwood", he made a careful note of the all the dimensions and subsequently labored with the architects, to ensure that there was an appropriate setting for each piece! The large sideboard had two sculptured figures supporting upper glass cabinets and occupied most of the north wall. The suite included a separate display cabinet, a desk *cum* bookcase and a two-tiered dinner wagon. All fitted neatly in niches that seemed to have been specially designed for the purpose.

The table had a two-inch curved, molded and delicately carved edging - the object of constant admiration by visitors. When fully extended, it was large enough to seat sixteen people. Maurice and I were quick to observe that it was also ideal for table tennis - provided Dad would permit it! Indeed he did – after which the dining room was the scene of countless games and the focus of attraction to my brothers, cousins and friends for many years. I remember my concern the first time we played. To attach the net posts to the table, the metal brackets had to be widened to fit over the sculptured edge. The risk of damage was obvious! I was concerned "What would Dad say if the carving got chipped?"

I regarded Dad as a strict disciplinarian! It was only a few days earlier that I had to sit up with him till long after midnight writing and rewriting a page in my copybook until he thought it was flawless and neat enough!

Through constant usage, the table edge showed very distinct signs of wear. Attempts to conceal it failed. There was no question that Dad had spotted the damage but he never commented! He too had matured with time! He was obviously happy and relieved that his kids chose to have their fun at home in preference to possible mischief outside.

For our first ten days at "Longwood" we were without lounge furniture. It was on order with D. Isaacs & Company - the most reputable furniture manufacturer in the city. When in due course the furniture arrived, I could not believe my eyes! Each piece seemed a work of art beautifully executed! Of classic design, by Mappin & Webb, all were of highly polished Stinkwood[10]. Two tables, two small side tables and ten chairs - all looked extremely well on the large deep crimson Persian carpets. We were all delighted. My parents made sure that it all arrived in time for Maurice's bar mitzvah celebrations in January 1921. Two years later I performed my own bar mitzvah in the same synagogue as Maurice after being tutored by the same Mr. Cohen.

JUNIOR SCHOOL

We younger children saw little of our eldest brother 'Ephie'. He slept in the adjacent room, was eight years my senior, had his own friends and probably regarded his brothers as 'two kids'! When occasionally he was with us, he was inclined to tease. It irritated me intensely! He was keen on singing. Despite the double wall separating our rooms, his high pitched voice was disturbing! We were sure he was trying to emulate Richard Tauber (a well known tenor in those days).

Maurice and I went to SACS (South African College School) - about a mile down hill from home. I was in Standard 3 and he in Standard 5. Our ages were only two years apart but our interests seemed entirely different. We slept in the same room but tended to go our separate ways. I thought he considered me 'too young' for him and his friends. We walked to school together but invariably returned home separately! Maurice was far more serious-minded than I, more obedient and far less inclined to mischief! I regarded him as 'mother's favorite' and that tended to separate us. Dad, on the other hand, always immaculate, strict and thorough in everything he did, seemed to have a particularly soft spot for me. Smiling, he often looked my way and repeated the words: "bread and butter daddy" which, I was told, was the first intelligible comment I ever uttered. When I was a little older he would jovially address me as "Alphonsque' - a playful derivation of 'Alfred'. It developed into "Phonsque" and that nickname prevailed for the rest of my life at home.

Soon after our move to "Longwood", Maurice went twice a week to the home of a Hebrew teacher for training prior to his bar mitzvah. Printed invitations were sent out to celebrate the occasion. For several days prior to the event, the postman delivered gifts for Maurice. They included two gold-banded fountain pens, gold cuff links, pen & pencil sets, leather wallets, cloth-bound volumes of the works of Shakespeare, Byron, Keats, Shelley - you name it! We counted no fewer than one hundred and ten such gifts from acquaintances, many of whom we had never met!

The ceremony took place in the beautiful Gardens Synagogue - an historic landmark of the oak-lined Government Avenue.

Responding to the Cantor's call, Maurice mounted the bema[11], where he read the Blessings and sang a portion of the Torah all in Hebrew! Later during the service, he stood on the marble steps in front of the Ark and recited a long prayer of gratitude, devotion and promise. He turned to look up to Reverend Bender who, from his high pulpit, blessed Maurice, lauded him for his performance and implored him to perform his newly attained manhood duties with dignity, honor and devotion to family and country! I was very impressed and wondered: "Would I do as well in two years time?"

The following afternoon and evening "Longwood" was agog with visitors. Family and friends gathered from far and near. Maurice was the recipient of countless accolades - well deserved. He was also the envy of his friends as they gazed in awe at his many gifts that had been assembled in the study. Maurice seemed totally unruffled. He had performed admirably! For me, the occasion was overwhelming – an ordeal I shuddered to contemplate!

VILLA RITA

Because of the big move to "Longwood" towards the end of 1920 we missed our usual sojourn in Muizenberg that year. Dad, knowing how much we all enjoyed the holiday months at the sea, bought a pair of semi-detached cottages there in Hansen Road. He named one "Hettonia" after my mother; the other "Villa Rita", after my young sister. "Hettonia" was leased but "Villa Rita" was reserved for our annual visit in December 1921.

Our new abode was in the heart of the village. There were many playmates. Several of the families living opposite were from the city and were known to my parents. They, like we, were spending the warm summer months by the sea. The Kossuths lived almost directly opposite. Their main home, also in Forest Road Oranjezicht, was a few blocks from "Longwood". The children, Doris, Fred and Gertie, were contemporaries of Beatrice, Maurice and Rita and were already known to us. Next door to the Kossuths were the Friedlanders on one side and the Setzens on the other. The Levitans were but a few doors away. They included four children: Pauline, Eileen, Constance and Eustice. Eustice was about my age. He was not very friendly and was always in mischievous trouble.

SMOKING!

After lunch one-day Eileen asked me to join them on a stroll across the sand dunes. She was several years older than I and I suppose I felt flattered that she should ask me. I gladly joined them. We walked. Not very far from home, we rested on a white sand mound partly covered with the 'sour fig' growth - a prolific feature of the area. The figs, cone-shaped and about half-inch in diameter, looked like large red crumbled berries. They emitted a thick sweet juice that we kids enjoyed. We sat chatting and sucking figs.

I watched Pauline and wondered why she was rubbing her hands together! It turned out that she was crumbling dry fig leaves that had become parched in the sun! She opened her bag, took out some folded pieces of newspaper and a box of matches. She wrapped the crumbled leaves in the paper, folded it into the shape of a cigarette and licked the edge. She then put it to her lips, struck a match and lit the end!

Twice she puffed, coughed lightly each time, blew out smoke and handed it to me. "Try it," she said. It seemed childish to refuse! I put it to my lips and drew a breath! It had an unpleasant taste, was hot on my throat and made me cough! I gave it back. Pauline laughed, puffed again and threw the smoldering concoction away. Days later I wondered what it was about smoking that adults seemed to enjoy. I wanted to try again!

I knew the names of only two brands of cigarettes: "Pinhead" and "Flag". I was aware that cigarettes could not be sold to children under the age of 16. However, I went to a small Indian shop in the next street, crossed my fingers and asked: *A packet of 10 Flag please - for my uncle!*" Seemingly unconcerned, the shopkeeper handed me the packet saying: "Fourpence please." There may have been a twinkle in his eye that I hadn't noticed!

I cannot recall what happened after that. Obviously I intended to keep the packet hidden from my family but it must have been found for I never saw it again! Too much intervened for me to care!

MY BROKEN ARM!

The windows on the north side of the house overlooked a narrow paved service lane that provided access from the street to the kitchen entrance at the rear. Some two or three feet below the windows was a narrow plastered ledge about two and a half feet above the paving.

I must have been a pretty mischievous child! It occurred to me that if a member of the family saw me enter one of the rooms from the corridor, I could close the door, and 'disappear' - out of the window, climb along the ledge and into the window of the adjoining room! One day an opportunity arose to do just that! I was with Sybil in the corridor. I entered one of the rooms and closed the door. The room was empty! Soon, I thought, Sybil would be wondering what had happened to me! I opened the window sash and looked out. No one was in the lane! Through the window I climbed and clung to the window frame while my foot reached down to make contact with the narrow ledge. The ledge sloped a little and seemed rather too narrow but I was bent on completing my 'escape' from Sybil. Clinging to the bare wall, I tried to make my way along the ledge! I slipped and crashed down, landing on my right arm against the bare paving! The pain was excruciating. I ran into the house screaming - holding the damaged forearm against my chest. The next thing I remember was that I was on my parents' double bed; my elder brother had tied one end of a cord to the brass bed head and was seeking to tie the other end to my wrist! Apparently he felt it to be important that my arm be straightened and conceived of the idea that when I turned the stretched cord would do it for me! Needless to say, more yells prevented that from happening! The doctor came. He proceeded to bind my arm in its bent position, firmly to my chest making quite sure that I would be unable to move it! He turned to my parents: "He will have to keep it in that position for a few weeks." Looking towards me, he added: "Try and not move it lad."

Over the next few days, I heard occasional references to the accident. Sybil's comment that 'it was a stupid thing to do" angered me. I listened tight-lipped. I was probably reluctant to concede that she was right!

A few days elapsed when my father came home for lunch, accompanied by a different doctor. I was sitting at the table in the dining room when the doctor removed the bandages and had a good look at my arm. Dad was next to me and Mother looked on over his shoulder. I remember my fear when I heard the doctor explain: *"It is important that the arm be straightened - if he is ever to use it again!"* Tears filled the eyes of both my parents. Dad nodded acquiescence.

The doctor put a folded towel on the table, took my right hand in his, and gently placed my elbow on the towel. He looked to my parents and said: "I will need your help!" I was scared stiff! Dad, through his glassy eyes, looked to me. His moustache fluttered as he said: "It's going to hurt young man - be brave!" Mother grasped my shoulders while the doctor slowly lifted the arm away from my chest. He then put the palm of his hand under my elbow, grasped my wrist and said "Sorry, lad"! That is all of the incident that I can remember.

When I awoke, I noticed that my arm was in a straightened position and was in splints, bandaged and strapped to my waist. In due course it healed and was back to normal!

Frequently over the years, I have had occasion to look back on the incident with tremendous gratitude to my parents for having called in a second doctor and, not least, for their acceptance, however painful, of the advice that the arm be re-fractured. I am ever conscious of the fact that were it not for that, my choice of architecture as a career - one that I pursued happily and successfully for more than forty years - would not have been an option available to me.

CHAPTER 4

JUNIOR SCHOLE

JUNIOR SCHOOL

1919 was a memorable year for me. In addition to the big family move to our new home in Oranjezicht, I was elevated from preparatory to junior school and was now a scholar at SACS! I felt proud to be at real boys' school, one that was said to be the oldest and most famous in the country! It was years before I grasped how extremely privileged I was!

At SACS I admired most of my teachers. I regarded the headmaster, Mr. Kipps, with awe as I did Mr. Heynes, the part-time gym Instructor. He was also head of the Gordons Institute, a well-known gymnasium in the city. I remember also Miss Kynoch with much reverence, and not least Miss Sparrow of whom I was particularly fond.

The Principal and most of our teachers were disciplinarians. In retrospect, I can only admire the tactful, gracious way that most of them exercised their authority over a bunch of unruly kids. Most of the boys regarded them with respect and esteem. There was one single exception.

'BULLY' SMITH

It was 1922. I was 12 years of age and in Standard 4. Mr. Smith was the Afrikaans (second language) teacher. The boys usually referred to him as 'Bully Smith". My dislike of the man was intense and remained so long after I had left school. (As I recall he was the only person for whom I ever felt a strong personal aversion.) Its source may be traced to a single incident.

Smith was a hulk of a man, tall, thick set, heavily featured, ginger-haired! There were 36 boys in our class, all more or less of the same age.

Our classroom had four lines of double desks, four seats in depth with a short line of 3 single desks against the two side walls. The lines were separated by aisles each about two feet wide. I sat in the third row on the first aisle. My desk mate Tom Somerville sat to my right on the second aisle. No one sat in the rear desks on the side walls - unless sent there in punishment for some misdemeanor.

One afternoon our Afrikaans lesson was due to commence and we were waiting for Mr. Smith to appear. He expected us to have our readers ready and open to the right page when he entered. I opened the desk flap, took out my reader and placed it on the desk. Tom said that he had left his book at home. Instinctively I slid my book toward the center of the desk, to a position that seemed comfortable for us both to read. Mr. Smith entered the room, greeted us with a customary jerk of the head and took his seat at the head table. "Where were we?" he asked. "Page 76, Sir," was the loud response. Smith signaled to one of the boys to start reading. He then rose from his seat and commenced to pace slowly up and down the aisles, as was his custom. With a shoulder tap and crisp comment: "Next", he would signal which boy was to commence reading. As a rule he would interrupt only to correct pronunciation or to request a translation. When he reached my aisle, he walked briskly towards the rear, turned and halted behind Tom. He addressed us and asked: *"And whose book is that?"* I replied, "Mine, Sir." He touched Tom's shoulder and asked: *"And yours, young man?"* Somerville replied: *"I forgot it at home - Sir!"* Angrily Mr. Smith replied: *"You don't forget books in my class and don't share them!"* With that, his heavy hands fell on our heads and bashed them together! Tom fainted and fell to the floor. I was a bit dazed and don't remember what happened after that.

A day or two went by; seepage started from my right ear and the side of my head was tender to touch. On my return to school, the boys told me that I had sprawled across the desk and was taken out. Tom remained absent for a while; I do not remember his return.

Reluctant to disclose that I had been punished, I never mentioned the incident at home. My parents remained unaware of it! I have often wondered if it was the source of the hearing problem that has troubled me through the years!

MISS SPARROW

"General Assembly" was the final school event of the year. It took place at the end of the fourth term, a few days before Christmas and marked the beginning of our six weeks annual vacation. The venue was the gymnasium shed - large enough to accommodate the entire school of about six hundred boys and staff, all of whom were expected to attend. A few boys from different classes would be called upon to present chosen works of merit and an address by the Principal would conclude the proceedings.

I was twelve years of age and in Standard 5. As I was leaving school one day, I was confronted by Miss Sparrow. Touching my shoulder, she asked: "Alfred, what have you learnt for "General Assembly?" Dumb-founded, I shook my head indicating a negative response. She added: "I nominated only one other in your class and that was two weeks ago. There is not much time left. Please learn something - if not, I'd be disappointed." I was unaware that I had been nominated - probably inattentive at the time, but the last person I wanted to disappoint was Miss Sparrow!

At home I opened my book of poems in search for one that I felt would be appropriate for Assembly. My attention focused on "King Haakon's Last Battle". I had never read it before and it moved me! I read it again and again until I knew it all by heart. With the book closed, I slowly rehearsed it aloud and repeated the procedure every day following, until I felt sure I could say it flawlessly.

When the day came, each class, led by its teacher, was marched to Assembly and seated on the floor facing the platform. The teachers stood at the back, a row behind the boys. The Principal and vice-principal sat to the right of the platform. At eleven a.m. the school bell rang loudly and the vice-principal explained the procedure that was to follow. He concluded by calling out the name of one of the pupils. The lad rose, stepped onto the platform and read an essay that he had written - an interesting story well written and loudly applauded. The next lad announced recited a poem - seemed to rush it through; I had some difficulty following. He was loudly applauded! A third lad was called. He stepped forward, held up an attrac-tive wooden pot-stand that he had made in the woodwork room. He passed it to a lad in the front row. It seemed a splendid job - made me wish that I could produce work like it. Suddenly my name was called. Nervously I walked to the platform and faced the assembly. Never before had I con-fronted so large an audience! I thought of Miss Sparrow, felt sure she would be listening intently and I was eager to please her. I felt myself trembling! Nervously I looked to the headmaster and blurted out: - *"King Haakon's Last Battle"*, and proceeded to recite:

All was over,
Day was ended
As the foemen
Turned and fled.
Gloomy red
Glowed the angry sun descended
While round Haakon's dying bed
Tears and songs
Of triumph blended,
Told how fast
The conqueror bled.
'Raise me' said the king.
We raised him
Not to ease his desperate pain
That were vain.
Strong our foe was
But we faced him.
'Show me that red field again'
Then with reverent hands
We placed him
High above the bloody plain
Silent gazed we,
Mute we waited
Kneeling 'round, a faithful few
Staunch and true.
Whilst above with thunder freighted
Whilst the boisterous North wind blew
And the Carrion bird unsated
On slant wing
Around us flew......"

It went on, but that is all that I can now remember. I apologize to the author, for possible errors and for forgetting his name. At the time, I knew it all.

Towards the end of my recitation, I looked over the boys' heads towards the teachers. Tears ran down Miss Sparrow's face! "Did I blunder?

Had I disappointed her?" I wondered! Other boys performed after me. The assembly ended with a brief talk by Mr. Kipps. He wished the staff and the boys a joyful Christmas and concluded: "School dismissed!"

The boys scattered in all directions. I returned to my classroom to collect my school bag before going home. On the way, Miss Sparrow stopped me and said: *"Alfred, I'm proud of you. You were splendid!"* She bent over and kissed my brow. Overwhelmed and confused, I touched my cap and said: "Happy Christmas, Miss Sparrow!" Excitement surged through my veins! Now, eight decades later, as I relive the occasion, I still hear her voice! The same emotional experience surges through my veins!

THE SABBATH

On Saturday mornings, soon after we'd moved to "Longwood", I began to accompany my dad and brother Maurice on the easy down-hill walk to the Gardens Synagogue about a mile north of home. I was ten or eleven years of age when I recall staring up in wonderment to the magnificent dome above the central bema and at the colorful glazed mosaic décor that faced the concave walls flanking the Holy Ark. The elevated teak pulpit and its beautiful curved teak stairs fascinated me. From its elevated position the minister could be seen by every worshiper - the womenfolk in the galleries above and the men below. What intrigued me were the voices of the choir that came from behind a brass grille above the Ark! A yellow curtain on the other side of the grille concealed the choir from worshipers. Occasionally a gap would appear in the curtain and in it I spotted the twinkling eye of a choir boy! He was taking a glimpse of his audience!

On each visit I noticed something new in that beautiful building[12]. It took my attention while the rest of the congregants were consumed by the ritual.

BIGOTRY

After service my dad usually continued down the oak-lined Avenue to the city while Maurice and I accompanied friends to their nearby homes before starting the up-hill trek home. On one occasion, I was walking with Dubby Gesundheit to his home in Schoonder Street. On the way, I remembered that my mother had asked me to call at the Mill Street pharmacy for a bottle of cough mixture. I was carrying my prayer book in one hand and tallis in the other, so Dubby kindly carried the parcel of cough mixture. As we neared his home, Dubby's father (he was standing on the balcony) called out sternly: "Dubby - come upstairs!" Dubby ran ahead. When he returned he was somber! Later he explained that he had received a sound thrashing for having carried a parcel on the Sabbath! I felt I was to blame for letting him carry my parcel. I apologized but I never understood what 'crime' Dubby had committed to justify such punishment! That evening Dad explained that some very religious people considered it a form of labor to carry parcels on the Sabbath and thus in conflict with the belief that *'on the seventh day thou shalt rest!'* I felt appalled as I could see nothing sinful about carrying a small parcel.

MORE BIGOTRY

I was ten or eleven years of age when I joined my brother Maurice at private Hebrew lessons. The lessons were for an hour and took place in the study at home from two-thirty on Saturday afternoons. Our Hebrew master was Mr. Rabinowitz.

One Saturday after service, I joined my friend Harry Jacobs to his home in Tamboers Kloof. It was about 3 miles from my home and in a completely different direction. We lunched and played together. It was after 2 when I suddenly remembered that my Hebrew lesson was due to commence at two-thirty! There was no way I could make it home in time! I ran all the way down to Orange Street, boarded a tram and arrived home about ten minutes after the lesson had started. I rushed into the study. Maurice was reading. I apologized for being late. The teacher, a heavily set man, looked up. He was angry! He told me to fetch the bible. I went to the bookcase in the adjoining room, removed the only bible I knew of. It was a volume containing both the Old and New Testament. I took it to Mr. Rabinowitz. As he paged through it, his anger mounted. Suddenly he got out of his chair and stared at me! His eyes seemed to bulge from their sockets! He opened the book and with both heavy hands, he ripped he book in two! Without uttering a word he went out of the room and out the front door! I followed! He struck a match and burnt the section containing the New Testament! I was dumbfounded! I had learned that very religious people would not ride, write, tear paper or strike a match on the Sabbath; yet to our (presumably religious) teacher none of that seemed to matter! Apparently, to him there was nothing wrong with lighting a match, burning a bible, destroying property that was not his! He was willing to do all that on the Sabbath with incredible bitterness and anger - all of that for the strange satisfaction of having destroyed a book that did not comply with his brand of religion!

I was appalled and angry! In fact I regarded his behavior with a contempt that developed into a strong disrespect for the man! It was a disrespect that was never appeased even in later years when I learned that there were people of other faiths who committed far more hideous crimes in the name of 'religion'! The thought worried me! *'What was it that induced people, in pursuit of 'goodness', to perpetrate such evil?'*

CHAPTER 5

LAST YEARS AT SCHOOL

I felt proud to be at SACS. Founded in 1828, it was the most highly esteemed school in the country! That reputation may be attributabed to the fact that many of the teachers were known to be Oxford graduates!

My four High School years covering standards 7 to 10 started in January 1924. The school was totally separated from the Junior school. It adjoined the Hiddingh Hall campus of the University. It was part of an extensive complex of buildings situated between Government Avenue and Orange Street to the west. The main building faced Orange Street and adjoined the Hiddingh Hall campus of the University. It had two floors of classrooms overlooking three sides of a quadrangle. On the fourth side were the school hall and cloakrooms. Steps from the quadrangle led down to 'Rosedale', one of the school residences overlooking a large sports field. The standard 7 classrooms were in a new two-story whitewashed building linked to but architecturally out of character with the stone-faced main building.

My last few years at school were filled with new experiences! Some were exciting, some extremely sad - all deeply impressive. Incidents occurred that left me in little doubt that the most undisciplined and mischievous period of one's life is between the ages of 14 and 17! In retrospect, I must acknowledge that some of those incidents were attributable to my own behavior. Some were inexcusable but cannot escape the record!

Let me tell you about some of those incidents and of the masters who, in a sense, were party to them.

MR. HUTTEN

Our curriculum included four entirely new subjects: Latin, Chemistry, Physics and Geometry. I enjoyed them all save for Latin! Mr. Hutten was our Latin master. The boys soon discovered that he was hard of hearing and had a very bad memory. For homework regularly once a week, we were required to study two or three numbered paragraphs from our Latin reader and then to read and translate them during the following lesson. On entering the class-room, it was Mr. Hutten's habit to greet us with a regular: "Good morning" followed by two throaty grunts: "ugh, ugh, where were we?" A few lads got together (I was not among them!) and decided that when next the teacher asked that question they would take advantage of his poor memory and call out the number of a paragraph that we had learnt for the previous week's lesson! If that worked, they figured it would enable them to skip future homework. Most of the other boys heard about the plan and were warned 'not to let on.' When the next Latin class was about to start, I waited! Hutten entered and posed the usual question: "Where were we?" There was a loud response from different parts of the classroom: "Paragraph Sixteen, Sir!" The ruse worked! For the rest of the lesson, paragraphs 16 to 20 were read and translated without difficulty and to the teacher's obvious satisfaction. For the rest of the term the lessons started with paragraphs 16 or 17 at the whim of those who initiated the plan. The numbers changed only when the 'culprits' so decided. The ruse was repeated time and again throughout the year. Mr. Hutten never caught on!

Needless to say our progress in Latin was minimal! In any event it was a subject that did not appeal to me. In Standard 8, with the approval of my parents, I switched to 'German'. Other boys in that class had started in Standard 7. To help make up for lost time, my parents arranged for extra lessons after school at the home of our German teacher Herr Schluter. His home was not far from school and I went there twice a week. He was a congenial and patient teacher whom I liked immensely. I enjoyed the lessons! Within months, I was conversing in German, his home language with a fair measure of fluency.

MR. ROLAND

Mr. Roland, our Chemistry master, was one of the younger teachers. Unlike many, he was by no means 'authoritarian". His manner was gentle, 'dreamy' at times, but always friendly. He was well liked by the boys.

One Saturday evening, a neighbor friend and I had been to an early show in town. It was over at 8 p.m. Making for home, we walked to a tram stop near the corner of Wale and Long Streets. The sound of song from a small gathering of people near the corner drew our attention. It stopped as we approached. It was a street meeting of the Salvation Army. In the center, were four or five uniformed officers. One was addressing the gathering. Among them was Mr. Roland! I was surprised! A measured smile appeared to acknowledge our presence! We waited, thinking that he too may speak! Before that could happen, our tram appeared. We left. In the tram my friend remarked: "That's the kind of chap he is – always wanting to do good!"

In the chemistry laboratory a few days later - I had just lit the Bunsen gas burner in preparation for set experiment, when Mr. Roland came by. He asked if I would care to see him after school. Of course I agreed. When the bell rang at five past three, I made for the lab. Mr. Roland told me about the 'wonderful work being done by the Salvation Army.' He said that he'd be happy to introduce me, if I cared to join! I was really not interested but explained that my Art and German classes after school made it impossible!

MR. HANTON

Mr. Hanton, our Standard 8 physics master, was a short, stocky, red faced, congenial teacher. He was in his fifties, generally well liked despite occasional outbursts of anger that some of the boys associated with 'that schnapps' that he was said to enjoy occasionally between lessons. (I have no idea if there was any truth in that assumption.)

In his class one day we were confronted with a problematical formula that Mr. Hanton tried hard to explain - without success! There was utter silence! Obviously exasperated, Mr. Hanton cleared a portion of the board, rewrote the formula and began explaining anew. Within minutes the problem became clear - I saw the light! With a loud "O yez!" I broke the silence. A few boys laughed. Mr. Hanton didn't think it funny! He turned and faced the class. "Who said that?" he demanded. I raised my arm: "I, Sir!" He was furious! *"Outside!"* he shouted and pointed to the door. The command left no room for discussion! It meant that I had to stand outside the classroom for the rest of the lesson. I had no choice but to obey!

Minutes later Mr. Baxter the headmaster appeared. He was on one of his routine walks around the school.

MR. BAXTER

Generally known as Billie Baxter, he was held in high esteem by the boys and by all who knew him. His posture was always erect and stately, his dress immaculate! He was said to be a firm disciplinarian. Punctuality was his hallmark. He arrived at school at the same time every morning, entered the quadrangle at precisely two minutes to nine. So precise was he that boys were often seen to check their watches to ensure that were correctly set!

On the one occasion that I was made to stand outside the classroom, Mr. Baxter was on one of his routine walks around the school. He asked me why I was missing my lesson. I explained what had occurred. He opened the door, stepped inside and spoke briefly to the teacher. On his return he pointed across the quadrangle and directed me to his office. I obeyed and waited knowing that I was in serious trouble! When he arrived, he opened the door and ushered me in. He held a thin bamboo cane in his hand, looked at me sternly and said: "Honikman - the boys were concentrating. Your comment was an uncalled for intrusion. You must learn to control your exuberance. Bend over!" I received two swipes across my buttocks! It stung! I bit my teeth and waited!

Mr. Baxter went to his seat and addressed me: "That hurt, did it not?" I confirmed that it did. His tone changed. He beckoned me to sit down. Courteously I said I'd rather stand. I guess he knew why! Glancing at a document he had taken from his filing basket, he remarked: "I see you live in Montrose Avenue - not far from my home. Would you care to visit me this afternoon at four - we could have a cup of tea and chat together?"

"Thank you, Sir, I'd like that!" The bell rang. Another session had begun.

"Very well, Honikman - see you at four!"

Sharp at 4 that afternoon I knocked on his door in Belmont Avenue. Mrs. Baxter met me at the door with a cordial smile: "My husband is waiting for you." She led me to his study. He welcomed me! Relaxed in his own home, he seemed a different man from the austere gentleman I thought I knew. He put me at ease and asked if I had any problems at or outside school at which he might be of assistance. I could think of none. Mrs. Baxter brought in a tray of tea and fruitcake. "Milk or lemon?" she asked. I choose milk. "He likes his lemon!" she said. She poured our tea and left. Mr. Baxter referred briefly to cricket and rugby and inquired about my after school activities. He asked if I had any thoughts about a career. I said that I had no firm plans but that architecture had caught my interest. He said he too had once considered architecture as a profession but decided that he was 'not constructive or imaginative enough'. It was after five when he said: "I think I have kept you long enough. If you have problems or ever wish to resume this chat, you know where to find me." He got up, shook my hand and accompanied me to the front door.

I was aware that there were more than 360 boys in his care. I felt privileged to have been asked to his home. More than that, I was impressed. I had always admired him 'at a distance' as it were. He was after all, the headmaster - a stately, immaculate figure! Now, I had met him at a more intimate level. My admiration had become intimate, personal and permanent.

MR. GRIFFITHS

Mr. Griffiths, vice-principal and esteemed matriculation English master, was a much-loved personality. He was one of several Oxford graduates teaching at SACS. I met him for the first time in January 1926 when I entered Standard 9. He stood before the class gently shaking his head, waiting! When we were all seated and quiet, he addressed us: "Boys, welcome to......" We glared at one another; we could not understand what he was saying! His diction was dominated by a strong Oxford accent, totally foreign to us. Within days, however, the problem passed. We became accustomed to the accent and most of us enjoyed the English classes more and more as the months went by.

'Griff' (as he was known by the boys) was a great English scholar. His unique grasp of the language became increasingly apparent particularly at literature class. Two lessons a week were devoted to our set work, Shakespeare's "Merchant of Venice". I have a vivid recollection of the occasion when one of the lads had been called to the front of the class to read Portia's famous speech. He was rushing through it without pause or emphasis. Griff interrupted. A reprimand seemed certain! Instead he said: "Young man, be seated" and continued to address the entire class: "Boys, *language* is the principal means by which man communicates with man. For centuries it was the only means. Of all languages, English is the richest, the most expressive! It merits our respect. Shakespeare mastered it as no other!

With it, he painted many glorious pictures and left us a heritage of unparalleled beauty!" He started to read Portia's famous words: *"The quality of mercy is not strained."* He put down the book and slowly continued the speech by heart: *"It droppeth like the gentle rain from heaven upon the place beneath. It is twice blessed."* Slowly he articulated each phrase. With appropriate gestures for emphasis, he continued ... *"but mercy is above the sceptered sway; it is an attribute of God himself."* The class was spell bound! For me, I think, it was a moment of change, not only in my appreciation of the English language, but in countless other ways!

Regularly at 3:05 p.m. a bell resounded through the school to mark the end of the school day. At that time the masters alternated for weekly 'cloakroom duty' to ensure that the boys dispersed in orderly fashion. It was my custom to hurry to the cloakroom, grab my hat and run to catch my home tram that usually reached the school stop at that time. On a particular occasion, as I entered the cloakroom and rushed past a few hats that were lying on the floor, I heard my name resound through the room! It was the voice of Mr. Griffiths! He called: *"Honik...my friend, come hither!"* Pointing to the floor, he said: *"Stand before me here on that straight line. The next time I see thee pass a hat that is lying on the floor, I'll smite thee hip and thigh - Get thee gone!"* I picked up the hats, put them on pegs and ran! I felt disturbed that I had displeased a master whom I liked and admired. The next day, as I entered the cloakroom, I saw Griff standing in the background. Carefully I bent down, picked up two or three hats and placed them on pegs. Observing my improved behavior, Mr. Griffiths signaled for me to appear before him. With a benign smile, he said: *"Honik... my friend, come hither!"* Shaking his head affirmatively, he commented: *"No need this time to toe the line! It is gratifying to note that my words of yesterday were words of wisdom! Get thee gone fond friend; get thee gone!"*

Such remarks (reminiscent of Shakespeare) were characteristic. I have enjoyed repeating the story. It troubled me that Mr. Griffiths always seemed to abbreviate my name! I thought: 'Maybe, when voices drop, I do not hear all that well" and I wondered: 'Was my hearing impaired?" I quickly dismissed the thought!

On our very last day of school, Mr. Griffiths gave our class a short farewell talk. Encouragingly he referred to some of the problems we were likely to face in the years ahead and wished us success in our careers. Before concluding, he called three names: "Carl Birkby[13], Alf. Honikman and Jim Cuthbert" and asked us to stay behind after the class was dismissed.

As the rest of the boys scattered, the three of us moved to the front row. Mr. Griffiths pulled up his chair. Facing us he said he would like to tell us why we had been called: He added: *"Quite early in my life, I discovered the exquisite beauty in the English language. For me, it was an awakening call - a key to immense happiness! I chose 'English' as a career! Then, as a teacher, the urge to help pupils find that key became paramount. Over the past year, you three satisfied that urge. Your progress told me that my efforts were not in vain!"* There were tears in his eyes. He rose, shook our hands and said: "Thank you, boys - God be with you! Good luck and good bye!"

SCHOOL PALS

Looking back, I realize that most of the boys at school were mere acquaintances - pals in passing! There were a few exceptions whom I could claim to be 'close' and fewer still whose friendship was meaningful and continued through the years. Of the latter, one stands out in my memory! Maurice Walt was referred to as Morrie! Before the friendship thawed, I envied him. He was a brilliant scholar - seemed to take every subject in his stride and always vied for first or second place in the class. What attracted me to him was his modesty. He never asserted himself. In fact he seemed totally oblivious to the fact that his clear-thinking brain was a gift of nature! As a scholar, I was no match for him! Nonetheless, as the months and years went by, a close friendship developed. He lived in the upper part of Kloof Road[14] not far from my old preparatory school but some distance from "Longwood"'. That did not mar the friendship. Morrie had two older sisters, Janie and Freda, both charming girls whom I liked immensely. My brother Maurice was particularly drawn to Freda. There was another brother Frank and a baby brother Alec.

OUDEKRAAL

One of the few occasions that Maurice and I were able to go on outings together was in 1927. It was early one gorgeous sunny Sunday that I packed my haversack, and found my way to Kloof Nek to meet Morrie Walt and his two sisters, Freda and Janie, for a hike to Oudekraal. Four or five others joined us. Single file we set out along the Contour Path to a point beyond Camps Bay. From there we made our way down onto the Chapman's Peak Road. It was still early and traffic was not too heavy so we hiked two abreast, on to Oudekraal. There we rested and picnicked on the beach in the shade of the enormous boulders - typical of that part of the coast. It was a glorious day of good cheer and wonderful fellowship – never to be repeated!

DISASTER

Family Walt, like many other city dwellers, were spending a few months in Muizenberg. Mrs. Walt and her two daughters came to spend a day in the city. Each had her own chores to attend to and went in different directions. Before parting, they arranged to meet again on the station platform in time to take the 5:32 express train back to Muizenberg. It was the fastest and most popular of the many daily commuter trips between the city and seaside. Its normal time for the 15-mile journey was 27 minutes! The train was about to leave; apparently the three did not spot one another as arranged. All boarded the train in different compartments. The train gathered speed; approaching the Salt River station two miles from the city, it left the rails and crashed! Coach mounted coach; bodies were strewn far and wide. The chaos was unspeakable! Hundreds were injured! As I recall, seventeen lives were lost! The three bodies of that lovely Walt family were found among the debris - far from each other! In a flash, Mr. Walt and his three sons lost the only women in their lives! Their grief does not bear description! My memory of that tragic event has not dimmed!

Months went by. A newly built house in Montrose Avenue, opposite the east end of our "Longwood" property, became a children's hostel under the direction of Mr. Memel. There was a tennis court attached to the house. We met Mr. Memel soon after his arrival and Maurice and I were occasional tennis guests. One morning Maurice and I were there, when my friend Morrie Walt appeared. He came to see his baby brother Alec. Alec was still in a pram! He had been placed in Mr. Memel's care soon after that dreadful Salt River accident! Maurice and I greeted him as old friends but he seemed to be in a state of shock! We asked him to join us at home for lunch but he declined – shaking his head. He was in deep distress - seemed to be in another world! His harrowing experience had taken a heavy toll!

BICYCLES

We were a family of six children each of whom 'inherited' the bicycle of our elders. Beatrice had Sybil's bike, Maurice had Ephie's and, when I was ten, I was given Beatrice's! It concerned me that it was a 'girl's bike'! It had no horizontal bar! (No boy relished the thought of having a 'girl's bike'!) My dad spotted my embarrassment! He took a broomstick, cut it to

the desired length, scooped out the ends, blackened it with shoe polish, rubbed it till it shone like metal and bound it neatly in the desired horizontal position. My embarrassment was appeased - but not for long! The new bar soon worked loose. 'No way would it be seen as a 'man's bike!' Again Dad came to the rescue!

FAMILY TAKAI

Mr. Memel soon left the area. His house was occupied by a Japanese family, Mr. and Mrs. Takai. They became friendly neighbors and had two daughters both born in Cape Town. (I can recall the name of one of them – Mariko.) The family came to live in Oranjezicht to be near the St. Cyprians School which the two girls attended. Mr. Takai was a keen tennis player and Maurice and I were often guests on his court. His Company, "The Mikado", was a firm of importers from Japan. The store was in Burg Street in the heart of the city. It was there that my dad bought my first *man's* bicycle for which I recall he paid the handsome sum of five pounds! I well remember the incident because of its importance to me. The (girl's) bicycle that had caused me so much embarrassment was abandoned! Dad had appeased my ego!

WAR!

In 1939, soon after the outbreak of war, family Takai returned to Japan! We did not see them again - not until twenty-five years had elapsed. That is another interesting story - the subject of a later chapter!

A DISTURBING PRANK

The Good Hope Seminary Girls' School in Hope Street, about a half-mile from SACS, was regarded as our 'sister school'. It was the school attended by my sisters. Soon after I entered the High School, I learnt of an 'annual event' that had occurred towards the end of the school year. A group of senior boys would collar a lad whom they considered to be the 'least popular', bind his arms with rope and march him off to our sister school. There he was tied to a netball post, jeered at, and humiliated before all the girls. It was something that I personally had never witnessed - but when I was told about it, it struck me as something mean and ruthless! I hoped that it had been banned. However in my last weeks at school, I was told that such event had in fact occurred the previous day - the victim: a nearby friendly neighbor! In some ways he was 'different' from other boys

- perhaps a little strange, but in no way did that justify the humiliation he must have suffered. Hopefully such behavior has long since been banned.

THE MOTOR CAR

We had been in our Oranjezicht home for six years when builders were busy erecting a double garage at the far Hilton Road end of our site. The Oranjezicht tramcar was then the family's only means of transport to and from the city. Private motor cars were still a rare commodity. I was aware that Dad once had a car. I was too young to remember it. Dad said it was a 'Humber - reputedly a good car but more trouble than it was worth!' Dad explained that the petrol tank was at the rear and invariably the car would splutter and come to a standstill. The slight incline of Kloof Road was too steep for the petrol to gravitate to the engine. To meet the problem, Dad's driver had to remember to enter Kloof Road in reverse to ensure that the angle towards the carburetor was downward. Now, Dad explained that problem had been overcome by the invention of the 'vacuum tank' – a small metal cylinder that was located under the bonnet of a car and above the level of the engine. Because of the vacuum, petrol was 'sucked up' from the rear of the car and allowed to gravitate down to the engine. The garages being built at the far end of our garden were to be completed before the new year when Dad was thinking of another car!

GREAT SURPRISE

In January 1926, Dad came home all smiles! When he came in, he took Mother's hand and led her outside saying: "I have a surprise for you." Intrigued, Maurice and I followed. Outside the front gate in Forest Road was a new blue brightly polished Vauxhall sedan. A uniformed driver doffed his cap and opened the rear door. Dad beckoned Mother to enter and said: "Hetty - this is the family's new-year gift!" Mother took my hand, ushered me in. Dad followed. Maurice sat next to the driver. We drove around a few blocks, down Molteno Road, along Belvedere Avenue and back up Orange Street and Montrose Avenue. I remember listening intently as we turned up-hill. There was no spluttering! The car ran beautifully! Dad had made sure it was fitted with a vacuum tank! On our return home Mom and Dad got out; Maurice and I accompanied the driver to the new garages where he parked the car. He handed Maurice the keys, saluted and crossed the road to the nearby tram stop. The keys were returned to Dad who explained that until we got our licenses, a driver would be available when-ever the car was needed. Dad, Maurice and I proceeded to take driving lessons. I was included as 'next February I would be 17' - the minimum age for a driver's license. Ephraim was away - a boarder at the Elsenberg Training College in Stellenbosch. Girls did not drive in those days.

During the following weeks we all continued to commute by tram as before. Each Sunday, however, we went on drives to Muizenberg and along Chapmans Peak to Hout Bay and into the wine country – always a hired driver at the wheel.

WORCESTER

At that time that Dad decided to visit an old friend, Willem Naude, in Worcester. We set out early one Saturday morning. Mother, Dad and my aunt Eva sat at the back, the chauffeur and I in the front. We had been on the road for nearly two hours and had passed through Wellington and reached the restaurant at the top of the Hex River Pass. There we stopped to stretch our legs and partake of some light refreshment. The chauffeur had driven all the way and I, having completed my course of driving lessons, volunteered to relieve him. Dad thought otherwise – said I should not drive before I actually obtained my license. Instead he took the wheel, the driver next to him. We were on our way, and soon found that the downward drive on the Worcester side of the Pass was a rough unmade gravel road. Driving is on the left in South Africa. We were declining slowly. The road ahead seemed clear but the surface became increasingly corrugated. Dad was driving slightly to the right of center where it was less bumpy. An oncoming vehicle appeared not too far ahead. Correcting his position, Dad turned sharply to the left to give the approaching vehicle ample clearance. The turn he made was a little too sharp! We crashed into a heavy boulder in the mountain embankment! We were all very shaken, some bruised but otherwise unhurt. The vehicle passed us and stopped. It was a large van carrying some members of the Worcester rugby team for a match in Paarl. Two young men approached us and offered to help. Dad was now out of the car. The driver had taken over but the car could not be moved! Severely damaged, it had to be abandoned. The teamsters kindly offered us a lift. To accommodate all five of us they packed themselves on each other's laps and drove us some fifteen miles to the Paarl railway station. There they declined Dad's offer of reimbursement of expenses and drove off to play the game. We waited a while before a train steamed in, to return us to the city whence we returned home by tram.

Dad reported the accident to insurance and to the Vauxhall garage. The car was towed back to the workshop where it remained for several weeks. The chassis had been badly bent, radiator, headlight and mudguard severely damaged. Several weeks later the car was returned - like new! It was hard to believe that it had been in a smash.

Willem Naude died not long after. It distressed Dad that he had failed to see him. Another adverse effect of the accident was that Dad chose never to drive again! The only satisfaction that Dad derived was the receipt of an ex-gratia[15] check payment that came from the insurance company. It was for the cost of repairs - a sum of one hundred and seventeen pounds[16] - an enormous amount in those days – nearly half the cost of the car when new! All family driving was left to Maurice and me.

CHAPTER 6

ESTEEMED NEIGHBORS

The move to 'Longwood" was a milestone in my life and that of my family. Although I was ten at the time, I recall how distressed I was to find that our new home was located too far distant for me to continue my cub membership or to join Wallace Grey's scout troop! However, I joined the 11th Cape Town Scout Troop who met about half a mile from home! Soon I discovered also that my new environment provided new friends and an array of interesting and intriguing neighbors.

THE COULTERS

In Forest Road, directly opposite our front gate, was the entrance to the residence of Mr. C.W.A. Coulter - tall, elegant, highly esteemed English-speaking solicitor. He was also our Member of Parliament, representing the 'Gardens Constituency'. He was a member of General Smuts's[17] South Africa Party, keenly supported by my parents.

The Coulters had one child - Tom. We were not close friends. He was a year or two younger which made quite a difference at that age! They had a tennis court and I was an occasional guest. I enjoyed tennis - thought it a 'great game', but an 'intimate friendship' never developed. I seemed to sense an 'air of superiority' about the family - no doubt a figment of my imagination! 'Mutually respected neighbors' probably best describes the relationship.

THE MALANS

Diagonally opposite "Longwood" was an undeveloped quarter-acre plot, part of the home of the Malan family - Afrikaners of Huguenot descent. Their double-storied Victorian house, situated on the lower part of the site, faced Belmont Avenue and, like "Longwood", overlooked the city and Table Bay.

The head of the household was Mr. F.S. Malan. At that time he was Minister of Mines in the Cabinet of General Jan Cristiaan Smuts. There were three children, an older brother and sister and Berry who was about my age (14). We became friends. Both members of the school Mountain Club, we spent many outings together on Table Mountain. The usual gathering place of our group of young mountaineers was Kloof Nek and from there, we would hike along the contour path to the starting point of our chosen climb. There were a variety of popular climbs on all faces. All were classified by the Mountain Club of South Africa. The easier climbs up the many ravines were designated 'A' and 'B', the more difficult rock climbs, 'C' to 'F'.

Advisedly, inexperienced climbers would not dare venture up the mountain unaccompanied by an experienced climber. The western face overlooking Camps Bay, known as the 'Twelve Apostles', offered many climbs in all categories.

For my first climb to the summit, Woody Ravine was the route chosen by the leader of our group. The only rockwork encountered was near the top. It presented no difficulty but the experience made an indelible impression. Sitting on a granite boulder, looking down between my knees, there was something about the panorama that enchanted me. A single glance embraced the entire village, the white sweep of sand along the coast, the roofs of the hotel, the hot sea water baths and the many homes scattered along the lower slopes. The picture stayed with me. It acquired a quality I hadn't experienced before. Something more than a 'magnificent landscape', it conjured up all kinds of idealistic thoughts and ideas, totally unrelated to the pleasure-bound purpose of the moment, which was simply to enjoy an outing in the open air!

I often revisited that experience in later years. It seemed to be a turning point – when my general attitude and perspectives underwent change! For me, it was an indefinable but crucial moment! Some might say that I was merely 'growing-up', abandoning the bliss of boyhood. It was more than that – something I am not qualified to explain!

The easiest climb of all was 'Kasteelspoort'. It was the one usually chosen for visitors and beginners. Woody Ravine and Woody Buttress were two of the more popular climbs. I was about fifteen, no longer a beginner, when mountaineering became the first of my chosen Sunday occupations. My siblings were not keen on mountaineering. Most of the lads in my group were members of "SACS Mountain Club". We would meet at 7:30 or 8 on a Sunday morning to spend the day in the open. We were invariably led by an experienced climber who would choose one of the many 'rated' climbs best suited to our experience. For those occasions, Mother never failed to provide a nutritious hamper of sandwiches and fruit that she had prepared the previous day.

FAMILY IMMIGRANTS

As a Boy Scout and proud member of the Eleventh Cape Town Troop, I was occasionally required to perform minor duties about the house. When Mother wanted a letter posted to her cousin Ester who lived in Birmingham, England, she would say: "Alfie, be a good scout, take this to the letterbox." On one occasion, she explained the letter was to Cousin Ester's daughter Ida and her husband Leonard. "They have decided to leave England, to come to live in Cape Town. They know no one else here and I do want them to know how welcome they will be!" I had never met 'cousin Ester' or any of her family but the news interested me because I had heard a lot about Ida's brothers Harold, Sydney, Adolph and Lionel[18] of whom the family were immensely proud!

Soon after Ida and Len's arrival, they bought a house in Molteno Road less than a half mile from "Longwood". It was also only a few doors from the home of Mrs. Du Toit where I attended two-hour art classes once a week. Almost as often I would call on Ida. The visits became almost routine after the birth of their only child – Elizabeth. When Ida was called to the telephone or had some other chore to attend to, she would say 'keep an eye on the baby'. That became another "scout duty" – one that I was happy to perform! It made me feel that I was being useful and that my visits were not unwelcome intrusions.

Ida seemed interested in my activities, particularly when I told her of my excitement at having met General Smuts (he was then Prime Minister) at Mac Clears Beacon at the top of the mountain. When I said that we planned to climb Woody Ravine the following Sunday, Ida exclaimed: "Good - I'll bake you some sausage rolls!" It seemed like a passing comment which I dismissed, but while packing my haversack early Sunday morning, Mother handed me a white cake box saying: "You need to pack this - Len brought it for you yesterday." The box contained a dozen light brown delicious-looking pastries. They were the sausage rolls! Ida had not forgotten!

Berry met me at the corner at 7 that morning. Together we walked to the far (east) end of Montrose Avenue and commenced our hike through the woods to Kloof Nek where we had arranged to meet four other members of the Club. By 8:30 we were all on our way, walking single file along the narrow contour path to our first resting point well below the Ravine. It must have been nearly an hour before we reached the steeper reaches adjacent to the buttress. From there on, the gradient, though not dangerous, called for the use of all four limbs! It was past noon when we reached the summit and found a fairly even patch on which to settle for lunch. A small campfire provided hot water for coffee. One of the lads spread out a ground sheet over the scrub and onto it our hamper contents were emptied. All eyes seemed to focus on my white box! I opened it, but chose to start on a cheese sandwich that Mother had prepared. The other lads fancied the rolls! When my turn came to sample them, there was one solitary roll left! I guessed it was intended for me! It was so good - like no other mountain fare I had ever tasted! Obviously, my pals thought the same!

A week or so later I was on one of my usual visits when Ida asked if I had enjoyed the sausage rolls. I said: "It was delicious!" "Why 'it'," asked Ida, "I thought I did a dozen!" "Yes, you did indeed, but the other lads took a fancy to them - I was left with one!" "We'll make good the next time!" said Ida. Thereafter, my sausage rolls increased in number - but they were never enough! There were appetites that could never be appeased!

My kinship with Ida and Len grew close and continued over the years and left me feeling distressed when they finally decided to move to Port Elizabeth. Their move occurred soon after my marriage in 1936 when I decided to commence my architectural practice in Cape Town. It was a time when the entire world was suffering the repercussions of the worst economic depression in history. Like many others, I was struggling desperately to make ends meet! It was at that crucial moment that Len engaged my services to design a new shop-front for his furniture store – Maynards, on Main Street Port Elizabeth. I realized that it would be far easier, cheaper and more convenient for him to employ a local architect or shop-fitter. His gesture, at a time when conditions were perhaps harder for him than they were for me, is not forgotten! Our kinship never waned! Its warmth has prevailed through succeeding generations - despite the years and continents that separate us.

THE FENHOLS

Nathan Fenhols, a cousin and protégé of my father, was a frequent visitor to "Longwood". His wife Doris, of whom I was very fond, was a gracious and artistic person. They too lived in Molteno Road - half way between "Longwood" and the Marks' new home and I would call on them occasionally on my way home from art classes. They had two attractive children, Roy and Berenice. They were of a younger age group than we and we saw little of them. I was about fifteen years of age when Doris asked me if I would design a cover for a cushion that she wished to embroider for her lounge. She must have thought, because I was taking art lessons, that I could draw! I was flattered and reluctant to tell her that I had never done anything like it! She said that she would like the theme to embrace 'Egyptian figures' and to cover an area of approximately 21" x 12". I could not say: "No." Doris was the last person I wanted to disappoint! I accepted the challenge and went home concerned and distressed, for I had no idea how to confront the issue.

At the time there were press references to Howard Carter's discovery of the tomb of Tutankhamen - a Pharoah who reigned (circa) 1400 B.C. Little was known about him other than that he had died at the age of 18. The treasures found in Thebes with his remains included a gold mask of his image and his solid gold coffin! I scanned the papers, looked-up 'Egypt' and 'Pharaoh' in the Encyclopedia Britannica and vainly searched for characteristic pictures of Egyptian women. Nothing seemed remotely appropriate. One afternoon after school I ventured down to the National Library in Government Avenue. With the help of the librarian, I found pictures of an old stone tablet and frieze of Egyptian maidens in characteristic pose. I made a few sketches and went home and drew it up on a two-foot sheet of cartridge paper. I showed it to my mother. She thought it suitable, so I took it over to Doris. I waited for her reaction. She spread the drawing against the back of the couch, looked at it from one angle then another and exclaimed: "That's terrific, Alfred!" She gave me a hug and kissed my brow and so relieved my concern! It was not long before I realized how rudimentary the drawing must have been and that Doris was just being extremely gracious.

PARENTS ABROAD

It was about April/May 1926 that my parents decided to take a 3 months trip abroad. Only in later years did I realize the immense pre-arrangements that must have confronted them prior to departure. They obviously could not leave my grandmother, aged 90, and six children to fend for themselves and run the large household that was "Longwood" at the time! Grandma chose to stay with her elderly sister and niece in their little cottage in Buitengraght Street. Sybil, Beatrice and Rita were all accommodated at the Good Hope Seminary Boarding School; Ephraim boarded at the Elsenberg Agricultural College Stellenbosch where he was studying and Maurice and I stayed with Dr. and Mrs. Harry Cohen whose home was within walking distance of the UCT campus and School. We were all settled in our temporary abodes a day or two before our parents set sail.

All went well while they were away – but when they returned, we all had difficulty recognizing my dad! He had shaved his moustache! That, coupled with the loss of a little weight, rendered him almost unrecognizable! It took us all quite a time to become accustomed to the 'new look'! It was hard to believe that a moustache could make that difference!

1927 MID-YEAR VACATION

Our summer holidays were usually spent in Muizenberg. My brothers and I had never been outside the Western Cape. During the mid-year vacations, mid-winter rains usually kept us indoors. This year, my parents felt it was time for change - for us - and possibly for them too!

They arranged for Ephraim, Maurice and me to spend 2 weeks in Johannesburg where we could stay with my aunt, uncle and cousins Joey, Elsie and Beattie Cohen - the three oldest of 17 maternal cousins.

For the three of us it was a great experience. Johannesburg, a bustling city thriving on gold and dominated by mine dumps, was full of interest. Our cousins went out of their way to give us a good time. Joey, fully recovered from his grim wartime experience in France, had been very active. He arranged a visit to the City Deep Mine. There we were all given yellow raincoats and helmets that we were required to wear before entering a large metal cage that took us deep into the bowels of the earth. We walked through long damp tunnels lit by occasional electric light bulbs; trolleys filled with debris ran on a narrow rail in the opposite direction. We reached a large chamber; several Africans with flashlights on their helmets were on a scaffold, hammering at the rock above them. We retraced our steps to the elevator shaft and were soon above ground, rubbing our eyes adapting to the natural light of day!

With Elsie, Beattie and friends we enjoyed tennis parties, drove out to Germiston, spent a day picnicking on the bank of the Vaal River and walked on the causeway of the magnificent Hartebeespoort Dam.

For the three of us, it was a great holiday - our first taste of life outside the confines of the Cape Peninsula.

POLITICAL INTRUSIONS

I saw very little of Berry's brother and sister. They were much older! Still less did I see of his father F.S. Malan. He, I assumed, was deeply involved with the affairs of State. The 1927 General Election witnessed the defeat of the S.A. Party. It was only then that F.S. and Takai would join us occasionally for a game of Bridge. Even then, his mind often seemed elsewhere! One morning, I was waiting at the tram stop opposite "Longwood" when Mr. Malan appeared. He stood by me but seemed totally unaware of my presence! I greeted him a hearty "Good morning." He turned, raised his eyes above his glasses and asked: "What is your name?" With deflated ego, I replied: "Remember, Sir, I'm Berry's friend - we all played bridge together last night?"

The defeat of General Smuts and the S.A. Party was attributed to a pre-election Pact between Nationalist and Labor Parties. The Pact was widely referred to as an "unholy alliance!" Sheer political expediency had brought two bitterly opposed racial elements into one camp. What a blessing that might have been had it been so motivated!

F. S. Malan and the rest of his Smuts's Cabinet colleagues were in opposition. The new Prime Minister, General J.B.M. Hertzog, had in his Cabinet die-hard anti-British adversaries such as Generals Kemp and Beyers. It was said that their sentiments were so bitter that they refused to utter a word of English. Now, in Parliament, they were in the same aisle seated side by side with Colonel Creswell, Mr. Madeley and Mr. Boydell, three English-speaking Labor Party members of the Cabinet, who could not speak a word of Afrikaans!

In the following months, after lectures, I would often stroll down Government Avenue to listen to deliberations in Parliament. Sitting in the public gallery, gazing down at the assembly of 150 of the nation's chosen representatives, my first impression was one of awe! The very stern looking Speaker, with his long white curly wig seated several steps above the level of the rest of the chamber, made an impressive spectacle! Beneath him sat the 3 Clerks of the House in their (shorter) white wigs. The 24-carat gold mace was placed ceremoniously on the central table to signify that the House was in session - an impressive spectacle!

TABLE BAY SWIMMING

Frequent Sunday mountaineering trips were my favorite week-end pastime. They were with different groups of climbers. Occasionally some were of mixed ages and included Mr. Levine and Mr. Gerber (in their fifties) and their daughters Gertie and Ethel. Gertie was a student at the Technical College. She was my age. We became close friends and frequently met after classes to go swimming off the Pier[19]. The Pier, a broad handsome concrete promenade of classic design, was once the pride and joy of Cape Town. It extended from the foot of Adderley Street out into the Bay. It widened and embraced an open-air amphitheater, a popular venue for the City's symphony orchestra. At the far end of the pier was a lighthouse tower from which a professional swimmer once made a spectacular 50-foot exhibition swallow dive into the sea. Below the amphitheater were a few bathing booths. It was not a popular bathing resort, the water in Table Bay being notoriously cold. It was a convenient nearby venue, however, for Gertie and me to meet, which we often did in the afternoons after classes.

RETURN TO MUIZENBERG

One Sunday I accompanied Gertie on a visit to her friend Tillie (Matilda) Sonnenberg at her home "Zandwyk" on the Beach Road Muizenberg. It was the first of many such visits - the beginning of a wonderful companionship that centered on Tillie. It continued for many years and witnessed a strong attachment between Tillie and Mike Comay. Mike was considered one of the most brilliant students at the University!

We saw little of Tillie's older brother Richard or of three younger sisters. Each had their separate group of friends and "Zandwyk" was a popular haven for them all. On rare occasions we caught a glimpse of Tillie's father Max Sonnenberg - often seemingly deep in thought. He was M.P. for South Peninsula, a member of Smuts's South African Party and we assumed he was pre-occupied with 'affairs of state'. The day came soon after a visit abroad that he opened a small office (above the Waldorf café in St. Georges Street) and started a new business that he named "Woolworth's SA Ltd." It troubled me when I read later that he was confronted with litigation for the alleged wrongful use of the title 'Woolworth's'! Against him was the large overseas conglomerate by that name! I felt much relief later to learn that he won the case, and was free to retain the name as it had never before been registered in South Africa. 'Woolworth's SA' grew rapidly; he opened large departmental stores in all the major cities of the country.

The Sonnenberg home was one of only five or six on the Beach Road waterfront. It had an unbroken vista of False Bay. Nothing but beach of pure white sand lay between the road and the water's edge some 200 yards away. On countless occasions we children could be seen running across those sands with our surfboards and plunging into the waves of the Indian Ocean.

Our swims in Table Bay ended abruptly one afternoon when Gertie informed me that she was about to become engaged to one Sydney Berman – a promising young lawyer - a few years my senior!

I continued to see Mike - more frequently than before although most of his time was spent on the Rondebosch campus. He was a year or two my senior and I - no match for his brilliance! His fame was that in the two previous academic years, he received 'A' grade passes in every subject he wrote! His manner was ever modest. I liked that. His home was in George some 200 miles from Cape Town, and he was resident at "College House", a University hostel in Breda Street. It was within walking distance of "Longwood" where he was a frequent and welcome visitor.

THE UCT QUARTERLY MAGAZINE

At night we reviewed contributions to the UCT quarterly magazine of which Mike was editor. It was he I believe who had me appointed Art Editor! He alone was responsible for the exceptionally high standard of the production. My job was to find art and architectural students willing to produce art-works for reproduction. I had been unsuccessful! Mike would not take 'no' for an answer. As d-day approached for the submission of proofs, he urged me to 'do something about it!' He said: "If you can't find anyone else, you should fill the breach." Eventually the challenge found me sitting in the quadrangle doing a wash perspective of the Hiddingh Hall[20]. I was not very pleased with the result but Mike insisted that it be included. Fortunately the printing process obscured most of the blemishes! On another occasion, I went up onto the flat roof of the new 10-story Hotel

Assembly in Queen Victoria Street. I did a black and white sketch of the steeple of the old St. Georges Cathedral[21] - an important landmark in the heart of the city! That, I thought, was a more successful effort! Then at Mike's urging, I showed an original charcoal drawing that I had titled "Highways of Tomorrow". It was a 'futuristic' portrayal of roads in the sky - something that could never materialize! I thought it was a rather clumsy composition but Mike 'insisted' that it be published. It was my last effort as art editor.

In the following weeks, Mike and I spent many nights quietly 'swotting' together!

THE END OF A ROMANCE

During the September vacation Mike was back home when I had a surprise call from Tillie! I thought: "She surely knows that Mike is away!" She came straight to the point: "Alfie, don't get a shock, but would you care to join me at a dance at Kelvin Grove Saturday week?" I was puzzled, 'why me?' Tillie had been a wonderful friend and I a frequent guest at her home - I could not dream of refusing her. I thanked her and accepted, but I felt uncomfortable – 'something was amiss!'

That Saturday night, (to save me a double journey to and from Muizenberg) Tillie's brother Dick brought her to Kelvin Grove. We met in the club entrance. We had only one dance when Tillie gently tugged at my arm and said: "Let's walk!" We stepped out onto the stoep[22] and into that beautiful Newlands garden. It was a glorious starlit night. We strolled awhile in complete silence! I wondered what was on her mind. I thought of Mike: *'How much he would have liked to be in my place.'* Tillie pointed to a bench among the rose patch. We sat. Minutes of tense silence broke when Tillie asked: "Alf, do you think a girl can be in love with two men at the same time?" I was flabbergasted - speechless for a moment! Then I replied: "I don't think so! She has to be honest with herself and then with them - however difficult that may be!" Tillie then explained that she had been seeing quite a lot of Bertie Stern, that she 'felt for him as she had for Mike.' I responded: "Tillie, only you can decide! It seems that you have chosen Bertie. If so you will have to confront Mike and attempt to explain - it won't be easy!" She pondered a while! "Yes," she said, "I will have to tell him but it's not easy." I felt deeply for Mike. We were close friends! I knew how attached he was to Tillie and I shuddered at the devastating blow he was about to suffer!

On Mike's return from George, he went straight out to Muizenberg unaware of what was in store for him! His visits to my home continued but he got little done! Instead of swotting, he would telephone "Zandwyk," not to speak with Tillie as in the past, but to Betty, her younger sister! The conversations were long! He probably felt that was the nearest he could get to Tillie and clearly Betty lent a sympathetic ear!

At the end of the year, his emotional distress took its toll! His exam results were depressing! For the first time ever, he failed one subject and obtained two 'B' passes in the others, instead of his customary 'A's in every subject.

After that, Mike finally married a UCT graduate in architecture. They migrated to Israel and we lost touch completely. Later I learned that 'his brilliant mind had gained him great prominence' in his new country! We met again thirty-three years later. In 1963, I was on a visit to the United States when we met very briefly. He was then the highly esteemed Israeli ambassador to Washington - deeply preoccupied with the affairs of state.

CHAPTER 7

A GLIMPSE OF THE DESERT

1927 was my last year at school. I expressed the wish to visit my cousins in South West Africa[23] during the June vacation. That was midwinter and it was usually raining at the Cape at that time of the year. Because there was little opportunity for mountaineering or any form of outdoor recreation, my parents felt that the dry desert would do me good! They agreed that I could go.

The journey lasted two days and three nights. I was in the dining saloon while the train steamed through the rich farmlands of Paarl and Wellington and slowly puffed its way through the Hex River Mountain pass. Two lads joined my table. They were returning home to Windhoek. For dinner we all appeased our appetites on delicious baked sole for which the Cape is famed! I returned to my 2nd Class compartment. Four other passengers were already in bed. I climbed into my upper bunk and listened to the repetitive clatter of the wheels on the track below! Soon I was deeply asleep.

There was a tap on the door. It opened. The lights went on. A voice shouted "coffee!" A waiter in his stark white jacket stepped across the compartment and opened the shutters. The distant horizon, silhouetted against a crimson sky, told me that it was early morning.

I spent that day and the next reading, chatting, strolling up and down the corridors - anything to fill time! The Karroo was bleak! Accustomed to the pastures on the Western Province, I scanned the landscape in search of life! Instead there were endless miles of red-brown earth, dry scrub and a leafless tree! A distant whitewashed homestead rushed by!

A stop at the De Aar junction provided some diversion. A few passengers had reached their destination. Others alighted to stretch their legs while the engine was uncoupled and replaced. Facing the line was an old two-story Victorian hotel painted green! The stationmaster said it was a meeting place of politicians after the Boer War. A siren sounded and we were on our way.

We reached Keetmanshoop early next morning. My cousins Rosy and Gena were at the station to meet me. With them was their cousin Clifford whom I met for the first time. He kindly took my suitcase and led us to a car. It was my uncle's five-seated Chevrolet sedan. The number-plate bore the letters 'K15'. The roads were graveled. The traffic consisted of a few horse-drawn carts, an ox-wagon and a few cars. Within minutes we were in the main street; the only tarred street in the town. Tall elegant Herrera women in their lofty turbaned headdress made a singularly impressive sight. Their upright poise gave them an air of elegance - so unlike the Bantu women of the south.

The car turned a corner and stopped. We were 'home'! My Aunt Riddy was on the stoep waiting. She came out, greeted me warmly and escorted me to my room. The house, in keeping with the neighborhood, was a modest single story structure. Attached was a corner shop - my Uncle Phillip's general dealer's store. Uncle joined us at lunch and outlined a 'program of activity' that he suggested might keep me occupied for the week that I was to spend with them. It included 'an evening at home' and another 'with the Schweppes - life long friends' and 'a day on a friend's farm out in the desert'. "That will be on Thursday. We'll be going in two cars." Uncle looked to me and added: "That's it - unlike your great city, there is not much doing in this dorp!"[24]

Thursday proved to be the highlight of my visit. At 8 a.m. the Schweppe's car arrived outside the front door. It was a strange looking brown vehicle - its carriage high above the ground. They referred to it as the 'Unic'! I think its correct name was "Unicorn" - I can't remember! Inside sat Mr. and Mrs. Schweppe, their daughter Sylvia (home from school) and her friend Marge. Cliff arrived with the 'Chev'. My uncle, aunt and cousin Gena sat at the rear and I was invited to sit in the front with Cliff.

Our car led the way! Two or three turns and we were out in the desert! Endless miles of dry brown dusty sand – nothing else in all directions! I thought: "This is far worse than the Karroo - the heart of the Kalahari could not be worse!" It was dry, desolate and featureless. Our road was nothing more than two deep spoors[25] in soft sand. They stretched on ahead as far as one could see. Our speed was painfully slow. The needle of the speedometer hovered between 12 and 15 miles per hour! Cliff commented: "That's as fast as we can go; it may harden later."

Behind us, we were churning up a heavy cloud of dust that masked all sight of the second car! The three passengers at the rear all had their eyes shut. Suddenly the car stopped! Cliff got out saying: "It's boiling!" With a cloth in hand he slowly unscrewed the radiator cap. Steam and water spurted out. He went to the back of the car and took a canvas water bottle from the trunk. "What is happening?" asked my very worried aunt. The second car arrived. Cliff, covered in dust, went across to explain. He returned, emptied the water bottle into the radiator, replaced the cap and the convoy was back on spoor!

It was after midday when distant structures came into view. Minutes later we were at our destination and welcomed by a chorus of chickens as they scattered in all directions. We parked the car in the shadow of three solitary trees near the gabled end of the main homestead. Behind the homestead were several outbuildings and, in the distance, a 'Veekrale'[26].

As Cliff got out of the car, I moved up into his seat. A young Afrikaner boy appeared. He stopped in his tracks five feet away! Starry-eyed, he gaped in wonderment! Maybe he had never seen a motor car before! He stared at the headlights and screamed: "Oe...Oe"[27] Mischievously, I pressed the hooter! The lad jumped and ran - not stopping until he reached the *veekraal*. He looked over his shoulder - seemingly relieved that 'the strange animal with a noisy bark' had not followed him. The poor kid had been badly frightened! I felt guilty and a little ashamed!

Late that afternoon before leaving, Cliff wisely drained and refilled the radiator. Mr. Schweppe said that he would lead the way back - *'our turn to take the dust!'*

Less than half way home, again the engine stalled. The car was at a standstill! Twice Cliff tried the starter. No response! We shouted after the leading car. No response! As the dust settled, we watched it 'disappear' into the distant dunes! My uncle, Cliff and I got out of the car. Cliff went to the rear, removed a stick and inserted it into the petrol tank. He exclaimed: "Plenty – half full!" We were alone in the heart of the desert - absolutely nothing as far as the eye could see, but sand! My aunt started an uncontrolled hysterical laugh! I had never heard anything like it! It sounded frightening! My uncle gave her face two measured smacks in quick succession. The hysteria stopped. Cliff tried the starter again - still no response! Suddenly I recalled what it was that induced my dad to buy the Vauxhall! It was because it was fitted with a vacuum tank[28] capable of drawing the petrol upward to the level above the carburetor. It satisfied him that, when confronted with a slight gradient, the problem he had encountered with the old 'Humber' was unlikely to recur! When I was learning to drive, the working of the 'vacuum tank' was explained to me. I remembered that it could work only if air could enter the petrol tank! For that to happen, a small hole was provided in the cap to the petrol tank! It occurred to me that the Chev. (a fairly new model) may perhaps be similarly equipped! I rushed to the back of the car. There was a small hole in the center of the petrol cap! That told me there was indeed a vacuum tank! I removed the cap, put it to my mouth and blew as hard as I could - to remove any dust that might be blocking the hole. I replaced the cap and shouted: "Cliff - try again." He pressed the starter only once! The engine started immediately and ran smoothly! Cheers and claps from the back of the car hailed me the 'the hero of the day!' We were on our way!

We reached the village by seven. It had been a long, tiring, memorable but interesting outing.

Back on the train three days later, we had reached the foot of the Hex River Mountain. After the brown scrub of the Karroo, green pastures were balm to the eyes! The clean dust-free air tasted like champagne! Within hours, the sight of Table Mountain told me I was nearing home - 'back in civilization'!

I had enjoyed the hospitality of family and friends. The glimpse of life in the remote, desolate regions of southern Africa intrigued me and no doubt broadened my vision - but I was sure happy to be back in a sophisticated dust-free part of the world!

A BUILDING VENTURE!

At home there was a lot of excitement and considerable discussion about a proposed city building project. I asked my dad what it was all about! He said: "I knew you'd be interested." While I was away in South West Africa, he and his friend Mr. Allswang had attended a public auction sale of a city property site in Queen Victoria Street which they had purchased on behalf of a company they'd named "Hotel Assembly Limited". Dad proceeded to sketch the site on a note pad. It struck me as narrow and awkwardly shaped! I asked why they had bought such an odd-shaped property! He said it was indeed unusual; the portion facing Queen Victoria Street was only 30 feet wide narrowing to about 12 feet near the center, but widened to about 50 feet over a considerable area fronting Keerom Street. He explained that property in the central city area seldom came onto the market; the overall area was substantial; he and his partner had consulted an architect and were satisfied that the narrow area near the center could serve as a practical link between the wider areas at both ends. Dad added: "The property is near both the botanical gardens and Parliament. We felt it was ideally situated for a first class hotel - one that the owners named "Hotel Assembly!" Subsequently I learnt that architect Grant[29] had approached Dad at the sale, congratulated him on "a splendid purchase" and added that he "visualized a tall stately edifice of which the city would be proud!" In due course, Grant was commissioned and by the year-end, building operations were under way.

My school days were drawing to a close. Around the table at home, there was some discussion about what I intended to do with my life! I was told that soon I would have to make up my mind! I was in a dilemma! I did not know where my capabilities lay. 'Did I want to be an artist?' I knew I was not good enough and dismissed the idea! Someone suggested 'electrical engineering!' because I had been tampering with simple electrical experiments. I could not see myself as an electrician and my imagination did not go beyond that! I lay awake thinking about it! Plans of the "Longwood" alterations and the shape of the gables designed by Sir Herbert Baker came to mind. I kept thinking about that awkward city site and how it would be resolved!

When Dad again broached the subject of my career, I told him about my recurring thoughts and my dilemma. His response was: "You've always been interested in buildings and drawing - why not give architecture a try?" I had never drawn a plan but the idea stuck! I could think of no direction for which I had any particular bent. I doubted that an aptitude for drawing and painting was any indication of the career I should follow! I wondered if my fascination in 'buildings' was any indication or was it merely a superficial interest induced by the ventures of my father. After endless indecision, I finally enrolled for the long five-year course of architectural study at the University. That was at the beginning of 1928.

CHAPTER 8

FIVE GLORIOUS YEARS: 1928 – 1932

The University of Cape Town started the 1928 academic year on its beautiful new campus on Rhodes Drive Rondebosch about six miles from the heart of the City. The site, a legacy of Cecil John Rhodes and situated on the eastern ramparts of Table Mountain, overlooks the broad expanse of the Cape Flats and commands a magnificent panorama of the Hottentots Holland range some forty miles away. The student residences and many of the faculty buildings recently completed were occupied for the first time. The faculties of Fine Art and Architecture continued to operate in the city.

The Department of Architecture formed part of the Michaelis School of Fine Art, which was incorporated into the University. Temporarily the School was housed in the old St. Cyprians School buildings in Annadale Street. I went there to register and was directed to the office of Mr. Percy Thatcher who explained that the Bachelor and Diploma courses were identical except that the latter called for a thesis to be submitted after completing the final exams. He added that the Diploma was recognized by The Royal Institute of British Architects and entitled graduates to practice anywhere in the British Empire! I registered for the Diploma course!

I knew only one student at the School - Hetty Le Roux. She was a fourth year student of sculpture, a friend of my sister Beatrice and an occasional visitor at "Longwood". Her elder brother Hendre was our family dentist whom I had to visit more often than I liked.

At the end of the year the Michaelis School moved to the Hiddingh Hall campus and occupied the four-story building that had been vacated by the Medical faculty - now part of the new main university campus on the Rhodes Estate in Rondebosch.

The School was headed by Professor John Wheatley[30], an accomplished artist. The Architectural Branch occupied the entire fourth floor. It was headed by Mr. Gregory, a talented architect and Prix de Rome scholar who had come from England. He was our Design Instructor, the only full-time officer in the Architectural Department. The others, all part-time lecturers, were architects and engineers practicing in the city.

Curricula posted on the notice boards gave me a glimpse of what was in store over the years ahead. I made a note of what it contained:

Year 1: Design; History of Architecture; Building Mechanics; Life-Drawing; Anatomy
Year 2: Design; History of Architecture; Building Mechanics; Building Construction; Architectural Rendering
Year 3: Design; Building Mechanics; Building Construction
Year 4: Design; Building Mechanics
Year 5: Design & Practical

For several months, our 'Design' work was limited to the study and drawing of the classical columns: Tuscan, Doric, Ionic and Corinthian and to the method by which the entasis is drawn. 'History of Architecture' introduced us to some of man's primitive dwellings and to the ruins of ancient Greece; 'Anatomy and Life-Drawing' to 'proportion' as pertains to the human frame - all were considered important aspects of the early training of an architect! Much of the work had to be done at home. Dad offered his study at "Longwood" for the purpose. He employed a carpenter to construct a large teak drawing table for my exclusive use. It occupied the entire south wall of the study and was fitted with large sliding trays to accommodate my drawings. It was there that I spent most of my 'off-college' hours for the rest of my college years.

At the beginning, much of the architectural course struck me as being 'too academic'. I was impatient to get on with the 'design of buildings' which was my understanding of what 'architecture' was all about! Remarks to that effect, when my dad inquired how I was enjoying my new work, evoked the response: "Perhaps you should get some practical experience! What about taking a job during the summer vacation?" That, I thought, was easier said than done and replied: "There is nothing I can offer that could induce any practicing architect to employ my services - not even a few ostrich eggs!" No doubt Dad recognized the source of my comment. He smiled and said: "You won't know unless you try!" 'Herbert Baker' was the

first name that came to mind but he was in England! The only other architectural firms whose names were known to me were Walgate & Elsworth,
L.F. McConnel and W.H. Grant. I telephoned their offices and made an
appointment to interview Mr. Grant a few days later.

I went there armed with drawings of the four orders, my 'History of
Architecture' sketchbook and a water-color painting that I had done at art
class! Mr. Grant received me cordially. I told him that I was a first year student of architecture hoping for some practical experience during the long
vacation. He had a quick look at my work and said: "Interesting! - work in
the office is very different! However, if you would like to come here for
two months, your salary will be ten pounds a month!" I was happy to
accept and tried hard to conceal my excitement. Mr. Grant took me into the
drawing office and introduced me to his staff: Mr. Stewart, Mr. Herringer,
Miss Collins, his secretary, and Ron and said that I would be 'joining the
team in January'.

VLADIMIR MEIROWITZ

At the start of the third term, Professor Wheatley sent for me and asked
if I would volunteer to assist Meirowitz on two or three afternoons a week.
He explained that the suggestion was not part of my curriculum, that
Meirowitz had been commissioned to design and execute the "Liberman
Doorway" a major consignment, at the new South African National
Gallery[31] and required a "drawing assistant!" I felt honored and agreed.

It proved to be an important and memorable decision! Meirowitz's studio was on the ground floor. When I reported for duty, he was sitting on the
floor amidst large sheets of drawings. He held a stick of charcoal in his
hand. His blackened fingers beckoned me to sit beside him. With his left
hand, he shook mine and pointed to the drawings on the floor. They were
joined together by strips of adhesive tape. "This," he said, "is the Monu-
mental Liberman Door. These full-size drawings are nearly complete.
From them, I will carve the history of the exodus of the Jews from many
lands until their arrival in the Cape 200 years ago. From them, you will prepare scaled drawings with as much of the detail as possible."

I had never done anything like it! It was a challenge! Observing my
dilemma, he pointed to a drawing board and T-square on a nearby table and
said: "You can do it! You'll be there and I'll be here, if you need me!" He
got up and took me to two large logs of wood in the corner of the studio.

He stroked one as though caressing a child, and said: "This is part of a batch of flawless teak carefully chosen from the forests of Burma!" The work was finicky! When Meirowitz came to see what I was doing, he erased a little here and drew a little there, trying to reshape something that I had drawn. Suddenly he stopped, shook his head and muttered to himself: "I must not do that - a pencil can't do a chisel's job!"

My understanding of different aspects of art, I learnt from him. I admired the man. He was forthright, kind, self critical and extremely painstaking. He worked tenaciously. His wife Eva was a frequent visitor to the studio. When he introduced me to her, he said: "She is the artist - I'm the wood carver!"

A close kinship developed with them both. When my drawings were completed, he remarked that he was 'way behind schedule!' Turning to his wife, he added: "The artist has agreed to do the door panels! I'll be carving the frame, lintel and over-panel with all that history."

The final result was a magnificent achievement. The doors are encompassed in a very broad convex surround, the left side of which depicts in intricate detail the Israelites in the land of Egypt, the Temple of Jerusalem in flames and the expulsion of the Jews from Spain. Shown also are Hebrew figures in Holland; a ship with emigrants symbolizing their departure from Europe; and a Cape homestead to symbolize their arrival in South Africa which culminates the frieze.

The right side shows a willow tree and the waters of Babylon; a camel in the desert; a dome of medieval Germany; Jews in the dress enforced by medieval laws; and Russian emigrants boarding a ship. All is in deep relief, also culminating at the top with their arrival in South Africa (symbolized by the gable of a typical Cape Dutch farmhouse).

Two large door panels depict an African girl and an African warrior. The lower panels show two Cape Malay hawkers, one carrying bunches of grapes, the other fish, on typical long bamboo rods borne across their shoulders.

To a discerning eye, two very different techniques are clearly apparent - the bold hand of the master and the fine craftsmanship of his wife the 'artist'.

The Liberman doorway is an important part of the Gallery's permanent collection. It is a monument to two very fine artists and a tribute to Hyman Liberman, the first Jewish mayor of Cape Town whose generosity made it all possible.

YEARS LATER

In 1941, I had been in practice for a few years when Meirowitz called and said that he had heard I was building a new house in Rondebosch and would like to see it! It was then all but completed! We met at the site and walked through the house together. Before leaving, he pointed to a 15-foot wide expanse of blank wall that extended for all but the full height of the west (entrance) façade! He asked if I would get the builder to put up an eight foot high scaffold, as he 'would like to return in the morning and use that area for a piece of sculpture!' Intrigued and fascinated, I directed the builder accordingly.

Early next day, Meirowitz was up on the scaffold working in cement with trowel and other tools I had not seen before! He had designed and was busy executing a large sculptured panel embracing a Tee square, set squares, compasses and other architects' instruments - all beautifully executed. Interestingly, it was not a flat relief; it consisted of interwoven planes, ingeniously convex and concave to produce a play of shadows that gave the composition a 3-dimensional effect! I was delighted with it as were my family and friends. When I asked Meirowitz what I owed him, he answered: "Don't be insulting!"

Soon afterwards, Meirowitz and his wife moved to Ghana. He had been appointed to head an art school to '*foster and develop the indigenous arts*' of that country.

We kept in touch. In Ghana, he developed a malignant form of malaria and died in 1945. He was 45!

Eva moved to London where I met her again in the fifties and once more (circa 1960) when she was visiting friends in Cape Town. The City Council was then building a new civic center in Claremont, a southern suburb. That, I thought, 'might provide an opportunity for the City to obtain another example of her work.' I telephoned the City Engineer. He consulted the City Architect to find that the services of a sculptor were indeed required. Eva Meirowitz was commissioned to carve a relief in wood of Lady Anne Barnard for a door in the foyer of the new Center. Thus it was that the city was enriched with a second example of her skill.

The unique quality of her work, always the object of generous tribute by her husband, had been overshadowed by the accolades showered exclusively on him for his masterly achievement. This time it was she who received the recognition that was her due.

MY FIRST JOB

In due course I reported for duty with Mr. Grant! I was given a place in the drawing office. It was not long before I realized that I knew nothing at all about the practical side of architecture. I was really of little value to the office! Ron (the office assistant) was given a variety of mundane chores but never worked at the drawing board. He was directed to show me how to make blue prints and ammonia prints. I would help him carry the printing frame and roll of drawings up to the roof of the building and expose them to the sun. A lot of time was spent doing just that! Occasionally, I was asked to color-up a drawing or to copy some full size door details but never to prepare an original! I looked in wonderment at the intricate drawings prepared by Bob Stewart and Herringer. Bob showed me some of the drawings that he had done for the Hotel Assembly! They were plans, elevations and sections! They seemed far too intricate and minute in detail for me ever to reach that level of proficiency! I felt despondent!

The two months passed slowly. I had done so little that could be called 'architecture'! I never knew if the few drawings I did were ever put to a useful purpose and I wondered why had I been given the job! 'Had I obtained it on my own credentials?' 'Did Mr. Grant feel under some kind of obligation to my father because of the hotel?' Those depressing thoughts recurred time and again until eclipsed by the events that followed days later!

AN UNEXPECTED BOOST

On my return to Varsity to start the second year of my course, I was again called to Professor Wheatley's office. He said that the Architectural Branch had need of the services of a 'Student Demonstrator', that such a post had been added to the establishment and asked if I would be interested! I could not believe my ears! "Sir - I'm only in my second year - what would I be expected to do"? He said that the matter had been dealt with at a Staff meeting where it was decided that I should be approached. He added that I would be required to guide first year students in their work - 'particularly in Design and Building Mechanics', that the job carried a salary of 'only five pounds a month' but that I would no longer be required to pay fees! I was flabbergasted and probably looked dubious! "Don't worry - you'll do fine, if that's agreeable to you." I heard myself saying "Thank you, Sir - I am honored." He rose, shook my hand and said: "That's it then - good luck."

Excitement and uncertainty mingled! "Had there been some mistake?" I brushed the thought aside. Then I wondered: "How would I perform - what could I show first-year students? How do I tell my parents?"

When I got home, Mother was in the kitchen. She was busy rolling dough on the table. The moment did not seem opportune to give her my news. I waited! When Dad arrived, he was in a jovial mood. "How's 'Phon-sque[32]?" he asked. I replied I was fine but had something to tell him. "What is it, son?" Not feeling quite sure of my ground, I said that I'd been offered a job as Student Demonstrator. Dad smiled broadly. His eyes brightened. "Congratulations! That's splendid! Have you told your mother?" At dinner Dad looked to Mother and said: "Have you heard about Phonsque?" Every-one at the table looked up. "He's been appointed Student Demonstrator in his faculty." "Excellent," said Sybil. (She had recently obtained her BA degree in 'Education' and was a qualified teacher.) All began to clap. I broke the applause: "Dad, I forgot to mention - Professor Wheatley said that I would receive a monthly salary of five pounds and would not have to pay any more fees!" "My word - what a nice bonus!" said Mother and added: "We're proud of you, son!"

I had received a great boost - felt embarrassed and puzzled! Across the table Grandma wiped tears from her cheeks. I was obviously still too young to understand the emotion that prompted them.

Thirty-five years had yet to pass before I realized fully the nature of the emotional impact that that moment must have made on my parents and par-ticularly, my dad! In 1962, after graduating in architecture, our elder son Basil left home for London. Ten years later our younger son Terence left for Stanford University in California to study aeronautics. In the midst of his studies the following year, he wrote home saying that he had been appointed Assistant to Professor Dr. Hoff, that his salary more than covered his fees and living expenses and that I should terminate the quarterly allowance that he had been receiving from my bank! Then I knew precisely how my father felt that evening thirty-five years earlier!

RUBIN STUBBS

My leaning towards mathematics, geometry in particular, probably accounted for my initial interest in Building Mechanics. My awareness of its importance in the practice of architecture is attributable solely to our lecturer Rubin Stubbs. His principal occupation was that of engineer-in-chief to the Reinforcing Steel Company, a South African firm well-known to architects. Although only a part-time lecturer at the university, he taught all first to fourth year students and devoted much of his time to the Faculty and its students.

I HAD A PROBLEM!

During my first year, Stubbs's voice sounded resonant and clear. At his lectures, my seat was to the extreme left of the second row. At the start of the second year, I realized that I was not hearing everything - particularly when he faced a diagram that he had drawn on the blackboard. None of the other students appeared to have that problem! I moved to the right of the front row. The problem diminished considerably but it appeared again when helping the younger students with their work. I realized then that my hearing was affected. However it did not seem serious enough to worry about.

Stubbs was a brilliant engineer, clear-headed, articulate and painstaking. He was also patient and extremely kind, and was the object of admiration by all. My personal regard for him was immense. Contact with him ceased during my sojourn in Johannesburg (1932-35), resumed on my return to Cape Town only to be broken again with the outbreak of War (1939-45). Thereafter it continued for many years. Like most practicing architects in Cape Town, I consulted him frequently on a variety of structural issues. As I became increasing involved in public affairs, so more of my practice responsibilities were delegated to senior members of my staff. Personal contact with Mr. Stubbs ended.

One night, years later, I met his wife at a public meeting in Rondebosch. I learnt that that they had come to live not far from my home. Soon after, my wife and I received an invitation to a Christmas party at their home. I was delighted to resume contact with Rubin, somewhat older, but little changed.

The invitation was repeated the following year. When we arrived, Mrs. Stubbs welcomed us and said that Rubin was "not too well" and would not be attending! Later I learned that he had undergone gender transformation. He passed away soon after. Widely revered, he gave much to so many.

LEONARD FORBES MC CONNELL

McConnell, practicing architect and part time design assistant, was a congenial personality and an inspiring influence on first and second year students. The esteem in which he was held became quite awesome when it was learnt that he had won the nation-wide competition for the design of the new South African Mutual Building on Church Square, Pretoria.

In 1929, at the start of my second year at architecture, it became clear that, of all the subjects in our course, Design was by far the most critical. We learnt that if one did exceedingly well in all subjects and failed in Design, one could not graduate as an architect. At different lectures we met ex-students who had completed the course, but had not made the grade in one or more of the subjects! Of them, the largest number, those who had failed to pass the crucial Design examination, were employed as assistants in different architects' offices.

Terence Orpen, a fourth year architectural student, and I had become friends. He had accepted an appointment in McConnell's office for his fifth year practical and was already working part time. "Mac" (as we all knew him) had told him that he would be working on the drawings for the 'Old Mutual'. I envied him! Economic conditions generally were at a low ebb and jobs were hard to come by. The 'Old Mutual' was a prestigious and a large project in those days. I decided to approach Mac to see if he was likely to need a second assistant during the summer vacation. The result was that I was offered a job for two months at the end of the year at a monthly salary of 20 pounds. I was elated and concerned! I realized that I had been of little value to Mr. Grant in his office and wondered whether I had advanced sufficiently since then to do better the next time round! For some time, I harbored the thought that it was not my ability but possibly my father's connection with the Hotel Assembly that had induced Mr. Grant to offer me the job, that he felt under some kind of obligation to my father! That uncomfortable feeling persisted until I told my parents of my inter- view with Mr. McConnell. 'Mac' was familiar with my work at college and my dad had never met him! I felt a sense of relief knowing that I had obtained the promise of a second job of my own accord - entirely without Dad's possible influence!

RELAXATION

With the added time given to my job as student demonstrator, I found I was devoting more night hours to my own work. Dad was pleased that I had arranged for a job during a second long vacation. He felt that I had been working 'pretty hard' and suggested that I should relax a little. 'Take a night off occasionally," he said. I told him that my friend Sonny Emdin had invited me to a dance two weeks hence at their Hotel Belvedere in Muizenberg but that transport was a problem. Thoughtfully, he responded: "You have your license now, why not take the car?" That, I guess, was the answer I was waiting for!

My friends Albert and Brenda Bertish had also been invited to the dance. We arranged to go together. That night I drove the Vauxhall as far as their home in Newlands and from there, Albert drove us to Muizenberg in their car. The dance was a fun party which is all I remember of it, except that it was there that I met May Wolfe - a most attractive girl of about my age! She had a captivating smile and her English accent fascinated me! We danced together a few times. She lived in Simonstown; her father served in the Admiralty and their home was in the naval dockyard. I knew it to be an extensive walled-in area under British jurisdiction with heavily guarded iron gates and required a permit to enter. May assured me that did not apply to personal visitors - that I only had to mention their name to the guard, and he would open the gates and let one through. "Try it sometime – it's that easy." After that, I visited May on a few occasions. The heavy cast iron gates, about 10 feet high, bore the letters: 'GV Rex Imp'[33]. As May had said, when I mentioned her name, the gates were opened and the car was 'saluted' through. I met her parents and her younger sister Eileen.

A DANCE AT LONGWOOD!

A few weeks later my parents agreed to hold a dance at "Longwood" to reciprocate the hospitality extended to Beatrice, Maurice, Rita and me. (My eldest brother Ephraim was away; Sybil - ever studious, was not inter-ested!). May Wolfe was the first on my list of friends to be invited. The 20 miles distance from Simonstown could, I thought, present a transport prob-lem. I told her that Sonny Emdin and Albert Bertish were to be invited and I felt sure that one of them would be happy to bring her. So it was. Sonny filled the breach. When the day came, most of the furniture was removed from the lounge and dining room; the sliding doors between the two were opened wide and everyone danced joyfully to the music of a professional pianist whom Mother had engaged for the occasion. May looked radiant! Everyone thought so - not least Albert! I could not help but notice how often he danced with her! It was a fun evening everyone seemed to enjoy. It was after midnight when the guests dispersed. By noon the next day, normality was restored at "Longwood".

A few weeks later I met May again at a dance at the Bertish home in Claremont. After that I never saw her again - for the next twenty-four years!

I cannot explain why we lost touch. Was it my work at Varsity that consumed my interest or was I reluctant to vie with Albert? I will never know for sure. I failed to ask May when we met again twenty-four years later.

DURBAN

My having obtained the promise of a vacation job seemed to give my parents a lot of satisfaction. It also gave me the confidence to 'tell' them that I planned to take my first boat trip to Durban during the June vacation. No longer did I feel the need to 'ask'! They were unaccustomed to such 'assertiveness' by me! I awaited their reaction – with apprehension! Mother smiled and looked at Dad. He responded: "That sounds great - good to be independent." They seemed as pleased as I was!

From my bed I could see the white mast at the top of Signal Hill where a hoisted flag signaled the approach of an incoming steamer. Early every Monday morning the flag told that the mail-ship from England had been sighted and the harbor pilot was on his way. Within minutes the ship would appear from behind the Hill and make its entry to the old Victoria basin. The next day it would leave again for Port Elizabeth, East London, and Durban and not infrequently sail on to Lorenzo Marques and Beira before returning to Cape Town. At 4 p.m. every Friday, it would depart again on its return voyage to Southampton frequently to stop at St. Helena en route. The full coastal trip would take three or four weeks. I had been to the Union Castle office in Adderley Street and purchased a ten-day return ticket to Durban aboard the *Windsor Castle* - one of the Union Castle's commodious weekly mail-ships. The trip allowed for a three-night break in Durban for which I reserved a room at the recommended Hotel Edward on the waterfront – the hotel rate was twelve shillings[34] and six pence per day!

Early on the Monday morning before my departure, I looked towards the mast on Signal Hill. When I saw the flag go up, I knew my ship had arrived! Next morning after breakfast, Dad handed me an envelope and said: "You're on my way, Maurice will drive you to the boat. Have a good time; take care and open this in your cabin!"

The ship seemed enormous! I signed on at the desk. A steward took my bag, saw me to my cabin, unlocked the door, opened the porthole and said: "Will that be all, Sir?" Forewarned that he would expect a tip, I complied. "Thank you, Sir. Have a good trip." I looked in at the dining hall and lounges and stepped onto one of the decks when a voice on the intercom announced: "All non-passengers ashore. The ship is due to depart promptly at eleven - all ashore!" Back in my cabin, I unpacked my bag, sat on the bed and tore open the envelope Dad had given me. It contained four five-pound notes with a message that read: *"Dear Phonsque, enjoy the trip. You deserve it! We are proud of you! Travel safely. God bless! Your devoted father, I.J.H.*

I MEET MR. MILLER

The outward trip was uneventful except that on our first night out, I met a Mr. Michael Miller at the dinner table - an incident that years later proved to be of considerable interest. After dinner we strolled around the deck together. He inquired about my occupation. When he heard that I was in architecture, he commented casually: "You probably noticed our new (OK Bazaars) building going up in Adderley Street. I said I had indeed, that his building was directly opposite my dentist's window in Stuttaford's building - that building activity or the lack of it, was not an unwelcome distraction from the action taking place inside my mouth! Looking puzzled Mr. Miller asked what I meant by: *'the lack of it'*? I explained that I had often dealt with his contractor (The Lewis Construction Company) during the war. They were always keen competitors for army contracts that I had handled and that it puzzled me how they could afford to employ the number of laborers whom I often saw sitting idle on his job for long periods of time! Mr. Miller said he was not at all surprised! He said that after the war, it was difficult to find dependable builders willing to commit themselves to 'lump-sum' contracts. For that reason the Adderley Street contract was on a 'cost plus 10% basis'. He realized such contracts destroyed the incentive for builders to ensure maximum efficiency; in fact they profited by mounting labor costs! He added: "We've since learnt a lesson – to avoid lump sum contracts in the future!"

BASKET TRANSPORT!

The rest of the time aboard was spent relaxing at deck games and at the pool. The next day was spent ashore in Port Elizabeth. We sailed through the night. When I awoke, the ship had cast anchor outside East London. Passengers wishing to go ashore were asked to assemble on the open deck. I had never been to East London so I joined them. Passengers, six or seven at a time, were directed to enter a large flat-bottomed cylindrical basket (about 3 feet in diameter and 6 feet tall) and were hoisted by crane up, out, and onto a tug that took us to the quayside. The basket - a form of transport that I experienced for the first (and last) time!

The following day we were in Durban, an interesting attractive city, crowded with visitors. I spent most of my time in the sea. When not so occupied, I walked along the waterfront, took a bus trip into the lush green Valley of a Thousand Hills – exquisitely beautiful! In the few hours down town - only a few minutes by bus from the waterfront, the stone memorial in honor of those who fell in World War I attracted my attention. The inscription registered in my memory: *"Except a grain of wheat fall into the ground and die, it abideth alone; but if it lives, it bringeth forth much fruit."*

I enjoyed my stay in Durban and hoped to return one day. It was mid-summer. A light dusk continued long after dinner. Strolling on the water-front one evening, I noticed that of the several hotels, there was one near the back of the Edward that seemed quite new! I looked in at the foyer, took a pamphlet from the counter and inquired about the tariff: "Ten shillings a night!" That, I reckoned was 20% less than the Edward! My sense of econ-omy nudged me: "I must remember that for next time!"

The return trip was on the *Edinburgh Castle,* a more recent addition to the Castle fleet. Aboard I met several young people of whom one was a girl about my age. She was introduced to me as Rentia 'Naude', a Huguenot[35] name well-known in South Africa. I asked her if she knew the Naudes of Worcester. She frowned and said: "Why do you ask - I'm from Worcester." I told her of our recent accident on the Hex River Pass on the way to old friends of my father - one Willem and his brother David who lived on a farm "Excelsior"! "I can't believe it," she exclaimed: "David is my father, Willem my uncle – 'Excelsior' is my home!" Excitedly, she took my hand, drew me to a group of her friends and proceeded to tell of the 'remarkable coincidence!'

The incident marked the beginning of a friendly group who gravitated together often during the voyage. I do not remember all the names. I recall Connie, apparently a close friend of Rentia, Dr. Sennet, a stomach special-ist of Cape Town - much older than the rest of us and Madeline Heuyssen, a girl about Rentia's age. We played deck games, dined and danced and chatted together. One of the ship's officers invited us to a tour of the engine room and a few of us arranged to meet him at the purser's office that after-noon at three. Led by the officer we took the elevator down to the bottom deck, thence along a corridor to a door marked "Private - no entry". The officer opened the door and asked us to follow him and not mind the noise! It was deafening. The engines seemed enormous, the room extensive. We stopped. The officer, raising his voice above the din of the engines, shouted: "From here, down a few steps, then it's single file all the way; hang on to each other's waist and watch your step!" We were led along a narrow steel gantry that wound its way among the engines and other con-traptions such as I had never seen before. Everything was immaculate and obviously well cared for. Here and there we stopped for explanations - dif-ficult to hear in the din! We gazed in admiration at two bright steel shafts each about nine inches in diameter; they were turning so fast and shining clean that their revolving movement was hardly visible. In snake-like for-mation we moved on. I was last in line, Madeline in front of me. Suddenly she grasped my hands, lifted them from her waist and placed them firmly on her breasts and held them there! I was too startled to remember what happened then. Within seconds we were at the end of our tour, thanking the officer for a memorable event! I never saw Madeline again!

Early on the morning of our arrival at Cape Town, a few of us were up on the bridge watching that splendid view of Table Mountain. Rentia turned to me and said: "I hope we will meet again. You must come to the farm one week-end." That was nice of her! I asked: "When do you return?" She said her train left at four that afternoon so I suggested we might spend some time together.

Maurice was waiting at the quayside! I introduced him to Rentia and Connie. He took Rentia's suitcase and we strolled to the Vauxhall together. The car looked very smart - newly polished. I explained to Rentia that this was the car that had crashed on its way to Worcester. I told Maurice about Rentia and the remarkable coincidence. Maurice was running late for a lec-ture so he drove to the Hiddingh Hall campus and asked me to take over.

Dad had never driven since the accident. Maurice and I were the only ones in the family who had driving licenses, and all family driving was left exclusively to us. As the two girls had time on their hands before their train left for Worcester, I thought it would be nice, if the car was available, to show them some of Cape Town's many scenic drives. I drove home to see my mother and introduce them to her. The Naude coincidence fascinated her. She served us morning tea and scones, and sent us on our way.

It was a glorious day. We drove along De Waals Drive, walked through Kirstenbosch Gardens to Lady Anne Barnard's Bath, and lunched at Constantia Nek. The girls wanted to do some shopping, I drove them back to town to Stuttafords - their chosen departmental store in St. Georges Street - a stone's throw from the railway station. There we parted! "Would we ever meet again?" That thought probably passed through all our minds.

Months later I had a note from Rentia telling me that her father had died! My father, who rarely revealed his emotions, reacting to the news commented sadly: "I'm sorry we never made it!"

Some time passed. Rentia invited me to spend a week-end on the farm and to bring a friend if I so I wished. Henry Nankin accompanied me. For two restful days we went on long walks, picked delicious grapes in the rich vineyards at "Excelsoir" and at night, played chess or chatted.

There was also time to ponder! I was to have had a glimpse of a scene that probably was once familiar to my father - when he strove to fend for the needs of his large family.

GASOLINE

We called it petrol! There were few service stations in those days. Dad had an account with Mobil Oil Company. About once a month Maurice and I took it in turns to drive about three miles to the Mobil warehouse in Woodstock where we would load the car with about ten 2-gallon cans of petrol to last us a month or more. I remember the price in those days was a shilling[36] a gallon! (about one-ninth of today's price!)

IN THE OFFICE

At the end of the year, my work was a great eye-opener. Mr. McConnell was far more than an 'employer'; he was a patient instructor and a lovable personality. He introduced me to some of the realities of architectural practice! He did so in a manner that seemed to put some of his skill into my fingers. Within a week, I was doing plans and elevations, half-inch and full size details - all real architectural work that (unlike my previous office experience) was put to useful purpose! I worked alongside Terence Orpen. Two years my senior, he was the only other assistant in the office. He was always helpful and gracious – a prelude to a long close friendship.

The two months went quickly by. My salary for the second month was increased by ten pounds! McConnell actually thanked me for my services! He added: "You'll be doing your Intermediate this year. It's an important milestone. Good luck – and by the way, if you'd like to come here again at the end of the year, the job is yours!" I was elated, thanked him profusely and without hesitation, accepted the offer.

CHAPTER 9

HIGHLIGHT OF MY YOUTH

My brother Maurice, while studying for a Bachelor of Commerce degree at the University, was also working as an accountant in my father's office. In addition to his Estate Agency business, Dad ran a small wholesale woolen business for which he employed Mr. Gilmore as traveler-salesman. Gilmore was inclined to be a little shabby in his dress. He struck me as one who never 'quite made it' and it was my impression that Dad employed him out of sympathy. Gilmore appeared a little older than Dad. He was an interesting character and a bit of a philosopher, always pondering over trivia. The woolen office was next to the Estate Office in Dominion House. I was there looking for material for a new suit and Gilmore was helping me choose. I had come from the studio having been at the drawing board for a few hours. Gilmore noticed that my finger-nails were blackened with graphite! Shaking his head as though in profound thought, he exclaimed: *"Young man, I observe with satisfaction that, unlike others in your position, you are no stranger to hard work!"*

The business, limited to men's suiting material, occupied a single office adjoining Dad's office suite. The cloth was imported from England. In London, Dad was represented by an agent and much of the correspondence went through Maurice's hands. At the end of 1929 Maurice graduated with the degree of Bachelor of Commerce. To mark the occasion, Dad offered him a nine-week trip overseas on one of the annual NUSAS[37] tours. I was excited for him but he rarely showed his emotions! Neither of us had ever been abroad! I envied Maurice for the wonderful gift he had won. He chose the tour of Britain and wasted no time getting his application in. The tour fee was fifty pounds!

For me, 1930 was an important year. I was faced with the challenge of the R. I. B. A.[38] Intermediate examinations for which I was registered. I knew it to be a critical barrier to overcome. I was apprehensive!

Scanning the notice board in the quadrangle one morning, I spotted a NUSAS notice. It listed various tours planned for December and indicated that the tour of Britain was fully subscribed. "Lucky Maurice," I thought, "he had put his application in, in time!" I read on. There were others tours all leaving at the same time. One was a nine-week 'Art & Architectural tour'! The schedule showed that several days would be spent in London and Paris, 18 in Italy, 3 in Switzerland and 2 or 3 more in London before returning home! What flashed to my mind were visions of many of the famous buildings that I had studied, sketched and become familiar with in 'history of architecture' - St. Paul's Cathedral in London, St. Peter's in Rome, the flying buttresses of the Gothic cathedrals in Paris and Milan! "Would I ever see them – other than on paper?" What a dream! "If only I had graduated with my brother! Maybe my chance will come in 2 years time?" I dismissed the thought as quickly as it came.

As Student Demonstrator, much of my normal working day was spent helping first and second year students. My own set design subjects took me to the University studio three or four nights a week, often to return home well after midnight! The work became more and more absorbing. The Intermediate exams, with the exception of "Design', took place in June. The 'Design' exam took place toward the end of the year.

Days later the mid-year exam results appeared on the studio notice board. I had passed them all but that was something I had come to take for granted. What concerned me was the important 'Design' exam! That had still to come! That evening, I waited till my father got home before mentioning the results. As they did not include 'Design', I felt that they would not be considered of much significance. My parents obviously did not see them in the same light. Mother got up and hugged me. Dad's eyes lit up! "I knew you'd do it! Congratulations!" I tried to tell them that the important 'Design' exam had still to come! But they did not appear to be listening. Suddenly Dad said: "Phonsque, how would you like to join your brother at the end of the year?" I could not believe my ears! Was I dreaming? I was flabbergasted! I explained that his tour was fully subscribed. Mother responded: "There must be others!" "Yes," I said, trying hard to control my emotions. "There's an Art and Architectural Tour leaving at the same time!" "Well, that's it," said Dad, "make sure your name goes in first thing in the morning!"

I could not believe my ears; my excitement was intense. *'I will be abroad in Europe for the first time!'* My excitement was soon tempered by mixed feelings! Maurice looked glum! 'Was he displeased with what he had heard?' The thought flashed to mind: He had waited until he'd graduated before winning his prize. I had not yet completed my Intermediate – another two years had yet to pass before I could be in that position! I felt a brief sense of guilt! It did not last too long! It vanished that evening when Dad handed me a check. It was for fifty pounds and made out to NUSAS. "Take it in first thing in the morning; don't be late!" I thanked him profusely. He put his arm around me and said: "You deserve it, Son. I am proud of you." I began to cry.

Maurice displayed no emotion! "Was he aggrieved?" I wondered. He made no comment to merit that thought, but his general demeanor convinced me that he was displeased. Maybe he felt that I hadn't 'earned' the prize or that I might spoil his fun.

In due course in October all the lads in my class passed the design examination with the exception of Morrie Friedman. I felt sorry for him. He had struggled hard throughout the three years. I was so pleased to hear that he, too, had put in for the tour as had my friend Max Dembitzer. Max was in his second year architecture having switched from another course of study. For me it meant that the important R. I. B. A. Intermediate Exams were behind me! I felt a sense of relief and hoped 'now perhaps Maurice would not feel so bad!'

SAXON CASTLE

One Friday afternoon in December 1930, Maurice and I joined more than 300 students from all over South Africa aboard the *Saxon Castle* to start *the* adventures of our lives! Signboards indicated where the several tour groups were to assemble. Maurice and I joined our respective groups. There were only 14 students in our group[39], seven boys and seven girls. (NUSAS tours traveled 3rd Class) We were shown to our cabins (six per cabin - near the stern), unloaded and went up on deck to wave fond farewells to families and friends on the quayside. The gangways were lowered, sirens sounded and the ship slowly moved away from the quayside. Within minutes we were at speed steaming out of harbor. Our 17-day voyage to Southampton had begun.

By Sunday, most of the passengers had gained their sea legs. In the Third Saloon that night the captain welcomed us aboard and announced

that 'it was our good fortune to have on board the famous Scottish come-
dian Harry Lauder! He has graciously consented to entertain the students
two or three times a week!' Each of us received a printed "Programs of
Sports and Entertainment, commencing Monday, December 8th, 1930".
Time aboard passed quickly. Students of the various tours intermingled. I
met the Marais sisters: Dirkie and Pietertjie - the latter referred to as
'Pieter'. She was an attractive girl, about my age, perhaps a little more
mature than I. Together we played deck quoits, deck tennis, swam, sun-
bathed and occasionally danced together. A warm friendship ensued.

Most of us were crossing the equator for the first time and participated
in a traditional 'initiation ceremony'! It entailed a series of short pillow-
fights on a slippery cross bar above a large canvas pool. The 'fights' were
short, lasting only until one or both competitors were driven, or had
slipped, into a canvas pool that had been rigged-up on deck. Winners and
losers were presented with the traditional 'Certificate of Enrollment' to the
"Disorderly Court of His Oceanic Majesty King Neptune".

We had been at sea for ten or eleven days when the ship cast anchor
outside Madeira. Passengers were taken ashore by tug. Some were happy
merely to tread 'terra firma' again! Others, who spent the day shopping,
returned laden with gifts - principally embroidery-work for which the
island is famed.

In Southampton harbor we were met by a number of NUSAS representatives and divided into our different tour groups. I said farewell to
Maurice and the new friends who were not on our tour. Pieter and I
promised to look out for each other on the return voyage! Soon entrained,
we were speeding our way to Waterloo station.

LONDON

From the station, we were taken by bus to a small hotel near Oxford
Street. We each received a copy of our itinerary, small pocket maps of the
city's bus and tube routes and were left to our own resources for the rest of
the day. Max and I ventured out together. At Oxford Circus we stopped and
gazed in amazement at the massive crowds, dense traffic and countless red
double-decker buses all efficiently controlled by red, yellow and green
lights! We walked the length of Regent Street and remarked on the elegant
consistency of the architecture. We watched the lights, milled with
the crowds in Piccadilly Circus, strolled on to Leicester Square and into

Trafalgar Square. We found a bench and rested amidst the fountains at the foot of Nelson's Column. Hundreds of pigeons flew in and out and others came again and again. We spotted several well-known landmarks - the National Gallery, Saint Martin-in-the-Fields by Christopher Wren and South Africa House and other embassies of the British Empire. I think we both felt a sense of awe at the thought that we were at the very heart of the greatest empire of all time and our country was part of it.

During the following days we visited the Houses of Parliament at Westminster, and the Tower of London; we crossed London Bridge and walked along the Thames embankment; we strolled through Hyde Park along Park Lane; and at Marble Arch we listened to soap-box orators vehemently condemn the government for alleged misdemeanors. We watched the 'changing of the guards' outside Buckingham Palace, spent a night at one of the many ornate Victorian theaters, visited the Haymarket and lunched in the Latin Quarter. For many of us, the highlight was the visit to Saint Paul's Cathedral, the Wren masterpiece (familiar to both of us from our 'History of Architecture'). I recall gazing upward at the magnificent dome that I knew was 100 feet in diameter, then the second largest dome in Christendom! A passing padre joined us. Recognizing us as a group of strangers, he kindly offered assistance. He asked where we were from. On hearing: "South Africa!" he responded: "Well, I never – I thought you were all black!" It astonished me that an educated person should be so uninformed! His remark made an impact on my childlike vision of "my great country"! I began to see South Africa in a more realistic perspective!

The next morning we went by train to Dover and joined hundreds of other passengers aboard a ferry to cross a turbulent English Channel.

PARIS

From our Hotel Carpentier on the Montmatre, we had a glimpse of the domes of the Basilica of Sacré Coeur. Two of us, having no scheduled plans for the afternoon, decided to walk there. We were confronted with a large imposing white stone structure, Byzantine in style, all in white marble. In scale it completely dominated the area. An aspect that astonished me was that marble, a hard stone, had been chosen for the construction of the domes. It meant that the inner and outer faces of each course of stones had to be cut and curved to different radii horizontally and vertically, both internally and externally. That, apart from the general design complexity, was an extremely exacting challenge to both architect and mason.

During my three years of architectural study, I subscribed to architectural journals from Europe and the United States. I became familiar with and admired the contemporary works of architects Dudok of Holland and Frank Lloyd Wright of the United States. To my eye, their designs were original, logical and consistent with advanced constructional methods. In my judgment, too many buildings of recent vintage were the product of preconceived commitments to one or other particular architectural style (often of a past era). They appeared to be inconsistent with our time and age, often lacked amenities and seemed unnecessarily costly. I felt that the Basilica of Sacré Coeur fell into that category! Interesting and ingenious in many respects, it seemed incompatible with advanced technology and out of place in a contemporary environment. That reaction was entirely absent when I was confronted with historic examples of period architecture that were built in their own respective eras.

During our three days in Paris we walked and walked, crossed the Seine on the Pont Neuf, watched artists on the embankment working in a variety of media, visited Notre Dame Cathedral and marveled at the magnificent flying buttresses. We spent time in the famous Louvre, strolled past the Paris Opera House and dined at an open-air restaurant on the Champs-Élysées. There we sat and gazed at the seemingly endless lines of traffic! The countless red lights in one direction, we were told, were the 'rubies', the white lights in the other, the 'diamonds'! We walked to the Arc de Triomphe[40] and paused by the 'eternal flame' glowing in tribute to the soldiers of France who fell in the First World War.

WORLD WAR I

A day was spent at the historic Palace of Versailles. We stood in the Hall of Mirrors where we remembered that only twelve years had passed since the world's chosen leaders gathered to sign the 'Treaty of Versailles' – one that was designed to *'disarm Germany and put an end to all wars for all time'!* We were blissfully unaware that that Treaty produced the seeds that were to produce the greatest disaster ever to confront mankind. Few realized and no one wanted to believe that the crimes being perpetrated by Hitler's 'Brown Shirts' would force President Hindenberg to resign and bring the Weimar Republic to an end!

DISARMAMENT

A significant by-product of all the horrors of World War I was the great "disarmament" ideal - one to which the Allied nations readily committed themselves! They were happily oblivious to the fact that that 'ideal' would render them powerless in the face of threats from nations less idealistically oriented. Thus it was that the great democracies could do no more than hold countless public meetings protesting against the horrors perpetrated by the Nazis prior to and after the dawn of the Third Reich. Protests fell on deaf ears. Heinous Nazi crimes inside Germany continued with ever-increasing terror. Hitler's Germany pursued a relentless rearmament program, flaunted the terms of the Versailles Treaty and treated all protests by the civilized world with unmitigated contempt.

Max and I spent a morning together. We visited the Eiffel Tower, lunched on the Montmarte and joined the rest of our group for a night of cabaret at the Moulin Rouge. We enjoyed the delightful, colorful dancing and song and were entertained by the famous Maurice Chevalier. The night was very special! It was close to midnight when taxis brought us to the hotel. The girls in our party went off to bed. It was our last night in Paris. Four of our lads felt it was 'too early for bed'! They decided on a 'night club' (of a kind very different from the one we had just left) and kept back one of the taxis. They urged me to join them. I declined. I was worse than tired. I was hot - felt I had the 'flu'! With 2 aspirins from the obliging night porter, I took myself to bed where I spent the next morning. However I was up in time to accompany our group to the station en route to Milan.

MILAN

Early the next morning we were in Milan. Mario met us at the station. He introduced himself as chairman of the Italian Fascist Students Union and said that he had been delegated to be 'our guide and friend' to look after our needs and that he would be with us for the duration of our visit to Italy. A good-looking man, about 23 years of age, he spoke excellent English. He explained that as our itinerary gave us only one day in Milan, he would defer our welcome to Italy to the following day. He assumed that we would wish to spend the short time available at the Cathedral for which Milan was famed and said that unless any of us had other plans, he would take us there forthwith.

Like the Notre Dame Cathedral of Paris, the Milan Cathedral is a Gothic landmark. Until then, I knew it only from my 'History of Architecture'. I had no idea of its massive scale, or the magnitude of the towering stone pinnacles that taper and terminate with sculptured human figures that are larger than life. No pictures can portray the boldness of the flying buttresses, the intricate stonework or the refinement and delicacy of detail! The edifice dominates the entire landscape. Its pinnacles cast shadows across the roofs and domes of buildings on the opposite side of adjoining streets.

BOLOGNA

At our hotel, Mario gathered our group together for a brief chat. He said that we would be on our own for the rest of the afternoon and urged us to 'take it easy' as that night we were due to attend a welcoming banquet and ball in the City Hall - a reception by the University of Bologna. He explained that it was the oldest University in Italy. With a twinkle in his eye, he added: "Bologna is famous for another reason! It is said to have the most beautiful women in the country - men take care!" He went on to say that although our itinerary was pretty full, he had been directed to ask if there were any particular wishes we would like to be included during our stay in Italy. He would try and arrange that they be met. We each had a copy of the itinerary. I could not imagine that there was room for more. Morris Freedman thought otherwise. He asked: "*Could we meet Mussolini?*" That, I thought, was a pretty 'tall order'. Mario replied: "I don't know if that can be arranged, but I will certainly try!"

The center of the large lofty hall had been cleared for dancing. Seated at two rows of tables around the room were many guests - all complete strangers to us, many of them elderly! The boys in our group danced with the girls in our group! Dancing with Elma, she asked: "Why are you not dancing with one of those Bologna girls we've heard so much about?" I said I hadn't met any. "You're slow!" she answered. That was a bit of a challenge. When the music stopped, I found Mario and asked him: "Are we not going to meet any of those beautiful women you spoke about?" "Come with me!" He smiled, took my arm and hastily led me across the hall. I asked: "What if she doesn't speak English - what on earth do I say to her - how would I thank her for the dance?" He rattled off something that I would certainly never remember. I asked him to write it down. He took my dance card, wrote on the back of it and quickly ushered me to a table where five people were seated. They included a middle-aged gentleman with a pointed white beard, a lady presumably his wife, a young man and two attractive young ladies all about my age. Mario introduced me to the party. He spoke Italian and I assumed explained that I was one of the visitors from South Africa. The men rose. The one with the beard put a monocle to his eye and nodded his head in greeting. (I assumed he was the father of the two girls.) I invited one of the girls to dance. She indicated that she was about to dance with her neighbor, smiled charmingly and offered me her dance card. Save for third and seventh dance, the card was fully booked! I put my name in both vacant places. She smiled graciously, took my card and inserted "Stella" in spaces 3 and 7. A young man arrived, bowed to the other girl at the table and they went off to dance. I excused myself, rejoined our group, watched the dancing and read what Mario had written on my card. It was all in Italian - I could not decipher it.

When the music for dance 3 started, I went across the hall, bowed and claimed my prize. It was a waltz. While dancing, there was no conversation! I assumed she could not speak English. I held my card in my right hand and over her shoulder, quietly rehearsed what Mario had written. When the music stopped, I escorted my partner to her table, bowed and said: "Grazia - Lei e una graziosa signorina!" She blushed - was totally silent! 'Had I offended her in some way?' I looked for Mario, told him of my misadventure and asked him to translate precisely what I had said. He laughed: "You merely thanked her and added *'You are a very beautiful lady'*- no harm in that!" Said to a stranger without due emphasis, it was probably totally inappropriate! Mario seemed to enjoy his little joke. I asked him to please write down a more appropriate "thank you" as I had booked another dance with the same lass. This time he wrote: *"Grazia - kei belle oche!"* I assumed it meant something like *"Thank you – it's been most pleasant!"* Mario added: "Don't rush it. Say it slowly - pause a little - as though you meant it!"

I joined some of our group in the banqueting room. We sat at a long table; it was colorful with a variety of fruits and refreshments. My attention was drawn to the man sitting diagonally opposite me. He glared fiercely at me! I realized that he was the young man who had danced with Stella when I was first introduced. 'Had I offended him in some way?' I wondered how! His showed his teeth - seemed to growl! Suddenly he put his right hand under the lapel of his jacket. For a moment I thought he was about to draw a stiletto! I followed suit as though to indicate that 'I too have one!' Fortunately it was only a handkerchief that he drew! He wiped his brow; it did not erase the glare! The music started up; the seventh dance had begun and

I went in search of Stella. She was at the same table with her family. Again the men rose and I bowed! Stella got up, smiled graciously, took my arm and we were back on the dance floor! All went well despite our inability to converse. She danced beautifully. Again while dancing, I studied Mario's new directive and remembered his advice. The dance over, she again took my arm and we strolled to her family table. As she sat down, I smiled and uttered very slowly: *"Grazia – kei belle oche!"* She gave me a half smile and replied slowly in English: *"You are a very naughty man!"* Later I learnt that I had commented on her beautiful eyes and realized that my demeanor hardly matched the remark! When I confronted Mario about his mischief, he laughed heartily and said: "She was probably sorry you didn't ask for her address!"

ROME

Rome was of course the highlight of our Italian venture. On our first day there Paul, one of our guides, introduced us to seven or eight male students from the University of Rome who had volunteered to accompany us as guides. Formalities were quickly dispensed with. They soon became friendly - some seemed readily attracted to our girls - mostly blondes! We broke up into several small groups. Mario had a list of famous buildings which he knew would interest us. We scanned the list and I and three others decided to accompany him. The others scattered with their student guides in different directions. I felt quite excited as I realized that many famous buildings, hitherto objects of remote study, were soon to become three-dimensional realities! We would be able to touch and 'feel' architectural forms that we had copied and drawn during the previous three years. We were to witness the unmatched cultural splendor bequeathed to us by the Greeks and Romans centuries ago!

Mario found a place to park his car. Together we walked into St. Peter's Square and planned to spend the entire morning in and about the Basilica. I knew the story. It was the work of six great architects three hundred and fifty years ago and took more than sixty years to build! I was aware of some of the salient features but had no conception of its scale or composite grandeur. I had no idea of the array of sculpture that adorns the walls internally. The Baldacchino with its twisted bronze columns, at the heart of the nave, reaches up 100 feet towards the whispering gallery on the perimeter of Michelangelo's famous dome. Spellbound, I took the elevator up the height of 10 floors, to emerge onto the gallery and walk around the circumference of the dome. I counted no fewer than 180 paces! I then climbed up to the lantern and from there into the ball where ten other people had already entered. That was as far as I could go! There was no visible access to the cross above. Through small apertures in the sphere I could identify some of the many historic buildings of 'the Eternal City'. My memory of that moment is one of wonderment - I was one of eleven people inside a copper ball above the lantern and below the cross at the apex of what was, and will long remain, one of the World's greatest architectural gems of all time.

EXCAVATIONS

In the afternoon Mario took us to a large open site several acres in extent, on the periphery of the city. Men were working, some sitting on their haunches, some on stools scraping the ground. Others were gently chiseling pieces of sculptured marble that they had unearthed. The head-man came to meet us. Mario introduced him as the 'senior archaeologist on the site'. He explained that in the course of excavations for a large complex of commercial buildings for which building and other contracts were entered into, priceless objects of antiquity were found. It became increasingly clear that they were working on the site of ancient ruins. "Mussolini intervened! He ordered the proposed development be stopped, all contracts cancelled and the site taken over by the State in order '*to preserve for eternity yet more examples of past achievements of the nation!*'" He stopped - stared searchingly at each of us, and slowly recited (entirely without emotion): "*That could never have happened, were it not for the timely intervention of our great leader - Mussolini!*"

His change of tone and manner caused me to question his sincerity! Why? - I could not explain! The answer came weeks later!

SPORTS COMPLEX

We were then taken to a large newly built sports complex. The manager took us round and proudly showed us a large arena with tiers of seats overlooking a gymnasium. It was sparkling new and seemed to contain every conceivable form of equipment. From there, we were led to a magnificent enclosed swimming pool surrounded by tiers of seats capable of accommodating thousands of visitors. Pointing to diving boards at different levels and an array of swimmers' equipment, he attributed it all to the efforts of Mussolini and concluded: "No one has ever cared so much and done so much for the health of the nation!"

Such were the praises showered on Mussolini (the Dictator) at every conceivable opportunity. I became wary! My impression of the man was that of a ruthless tyrant! "Could I have been so ill-informed?" We had yet to be enlightened! Before leaving us that evening, our ever-attentive Mario informed us that we were due to meet Mussolini at noon the next day! (Mario had seen to it that Freedman's Bologna wish, had been granted.) He told us where we were to go and urged us to arrive 'well before 12 - not to be late!' None of our group seemed very enthusiastic at the prospect of meeting Il Duce! I certainly was not keen! I had an innate dislike of the man, but I admired Mario's tenacity. To Freedman I said: "You owe Mario a 'thank you'!" He shrugged his shoulders saying: "I really couldn't care less. It was a 'challenge' - I could think of nothing else!"

THE PANTHEON AND THE SISTINE CHAPEL

The morning was 'free'. I had a pamphlet of historic sites and an illustrated map and decided to walk the city on my own. It was fascinating to 'find' one historic building after another. I made my way to the Pantheon, a beautiful circular temple! I read that its dome was 142 feet in diameter and was built way back in the second century. I then paced through twelve centuries - to the Vatican to spend far too short an hour in the Sistine Chapel. The indescribable beauty of the frescoes by Michelangelo and Botticelli left me spellbound!

Situated in the heart of the Vatican, the Sistine Chapel houses Michelangelo's incredible masterpiece – a ceiling fresco ten thousand square feet in extent with countless figures each exquisitely executed. It took the master four years to complete.

Reluctantly, I had to leave and rush by taxi – not to be late for the midday appointment!

MUSSOLINI!

We all arrived at Mussolini's headquarters in good time. Mario was there to meet us. An attendant led us by elevator to a waiting room on an upper floor, saw us seated and left us saying that we would be called presently. Mario departed and we sat chatting and paging through magazines. We waited! Half an hour passed! I became impatient and was suggesting to the others that we should leave, that there was too much to be seen in Rome, to waste our time in a waiting room, when an attendant entered and said: "Ladies, Gentlemen, please follow me." He ushered us into an enormous room! It was more like an assembly hall! With a sweep of the hand, he pointed to a white line on the floor indicating that was as far as we should go. He nodded courteously and left. The room was exceptionally large – more like a banqueting hall! It was empty save that in the far left-hand corner Mussolini was sitting at a large desk, obviously undisturbed by our presence. He was in conference with a tall smartly bearded younger man who was standing at his side. They continued their conversation as though no one else was present! It was only when the man turned towards us that I recognized him. He was Count Ciano[41], Mussolini's son-in-law. Suddenly Mussolini rose from his chair. He was incredibly small! He braced his shoulders, threw his chin and chest out, and marched briskly towards us. I uttered to myself: *"What a showman!"* As he approached, I noticed his heels were unusually high! I murmured: *"He's even smaller than I thought!"* He faced Angus, the first in line, and asked: "How did you enjoy the journey through Tuscany?" Leaving no time for a reply, he stepped to the next in line, and then the next. When he faced me and asked: "Did you like Florence?" I had no time to tell him that we hadn't been there yet when he confronted Elma and then the next! To fourteen questions, he received no answers! He stepped back, chin out, he clicked his heels, gave the Fascist salute and said: *"Arrivederci"* (Good-bye). He turned swiftly and marched from the room. Downstairs, as we stepped into the open courtyard, a car was leaving the building from another exit. In the car sat Mussolini! As he passed us, he delivered another Fascist salute! "What a showman!" flashed to my mind! That concluded our visit to the Dictator!

I was not impressed! In fact, I felt irritated. The meeting lasted barely five minutes but it consumed more than an hour - time that was all too precious! There was so much to see in the 'Eternal City'- more than we could possibly manage in the time available! That, I realized much later, accounted for only a small part of my annoyance. I knew little about the Dictator and less of what he stood for, yet I had an innate dislike of the man. I did not know then that eight years earlier, twenty-five thousand of his black-shirts marched on Rome, threatening civil war! King Victor Emanuel III, fearing the consequences, refused to declare a 'State of Emergency', enabling Mussolini to form a coalition and become Prime Minister although his Party held only 35 of the 365 seats! I was aware of his seizure of Albania in 1928! I was unaware that within a year of committing that heinous crime, he had talks with the Pope - talks that culminated with the Lateran Treaty declaring Roman Catholicism the state religion and giving the Vatican full autonomy - freedom from State, in recognition of its support of the government! Thus it was that Mussolini's personal power and Fascist rule in Italy were entrenched!

That knowledge and the grim events of succeeding years put our student meeting with the Dictator in a new and balanced perspective! Perhaps it is as well that I was ignorant at the time of so much of Mussolini's past! Had it been otherwise, I doubt if I could have exercised the restraint necessary to ensure our continued safe journey through Italy!

THE ROMAN FORUM

We wandered among the ruins of the Roman Forum at the core of ancient Rome. It took one far back in time! I fingered the stones of the Temples of Saturn and Concord which were built during the rule of Augustus! I marveled at the skill and exquisite craftsmanship of the architects and masons who operated more than 1800 years ago! For sheer sensitivity and refinement, I doubted if there had been any advancement in all those centuries. In the distance I caught a glimpse of the Colosseum! It was there that we spent the rest of the morning.

COLOSSEUM

Viewed from afar, one has no conception of the magnitude of this remarkable edifice which defies any sense of its height - 160 feet! Our guide spoke fluent English and certainly knew his subject. Inside the vast arena, he told us that we had come through one of no fewer than eighty entrances! It was built in A. D. 80 - nearly 2,000 years ago, and could seat fifty thousand spectators. Pointing to the large holes in the ground, he explained that they were the cells in which prisoners, slaves and persecuted Christians were accommodated before being fed to the lions – "for the amusement of the audience!"

The cells were normally covered by heavy wooden floor panels that were removed by the slaves from time to time so that the cells could be filled with water for staging mock sea battles which was a popular form of entertainment in those days.

One could write chapters on and on about the many important Renaissance landmarks we visited over the next few days. That would be inappropriate in a book of this kind. However, brief reference to a few that made an unforgettable impact on my memory cannot be avoided.

BERNINI'S COLONNADE

The colonnade is in the form of two arcs of Doric columns encompassing St. Peter's Square. It is four columns in width and provides a unique and fitting approach to the famous basilica.

I looked for and found the focal points from which the arcs were scribed. From them, I scanned the entire perimeter of each arc. They are built to such perfection that it was impossible to see more than one of the four columns at any point of either arc! In every instance the remaining three columns were completely hidden!

VICTOR EMANUEL MEMORIAL

This comparatively new structure in white marble, classical in style, was completed in 1911. Rich in treatment, it has been referred to by some as the "wedding cake"! It is a monument to the first king of a unified Italy, and contains the nation's Tomb of the Unknown Soldier.

FLIGHT OVER ROME!

Italy (an Allied country during World War I) gained a reputation for having 'the finest pilots in the world'! That was still the position when we were there. One morning our ever-thoughtful Paul announced that for those of us "who are venturesome enough", short flights had been arranged for our last free afternoon in the city! In those days, commercial flying had barely begun. Ten of us felt it was an opportunity not to be missed! When the day came, intense excitement accompanied our drive to the aerodrome. We were allotted to two airplanes and told that each flight would last about 10 minutes. The airplanes were two-seated single-engine biplanes. I was given a helmet, introduced to one of the pilots who led me to his airplane. In no time we were air-bound. The pilot pointed to landmarks but the roar of the engine made conversation impossible. The pilot turned towards me, grinned broadly, and turned his forefinger turning in the form of a circle! I thought he meant he was going to encircle the city. Not so! The airplane turned skyward - the land below disappeared completely! I felt giddy! The blood rushed to my head. He had decided to 'loop the loop'! Within seconds, I was back to normal. The pilot was laughing! Suddenly the airplane turned upward at great speed and down again! The land revolved and disappeared from view! My pilot had decided to do his stunt a second time! I thought I was going to faint - quickly recovered - did not think it at all funny! Seconds later we were gliding along the tarmac after a perfect landing! Others appeared to have been similarly treated. For all of us, it was our very first flight – a little nerve-wracking but memorable and very different from the 300 passenger jetliners that we were to enjoy decades later.

Rome was an unforgettable experience. We had seen a great deal! I knew there was more that would bring me back – one day! We were grateful to our Italian student companions. In our free time they took us wherever we wanted to go and made sure we were never idle. When the time came for us to depart, a few of them seemed as sorry as we were! Some were quite distressed! I recall our last night in Rome! It was shortly after nine when I returned to our hotel. Approaching my room on the second floor, I passed two of the lads outside the closed doors of the rooms occupied by the girls of our group! One was on his knees talking through the keyhole! As I passed I heard his slightly accented words: "Patsy – I love you!" I have no idea what followed but there was little doubt that our girls - especially the blondes, had made a considerable impact on our young Latin friends in Rome and elsewhere! That indeed was the case in each place we visited when a new group of students would take over guide duties.

POMPEII (via Naples)

During our travels, we spotted many posters that read: "*See Naples and die!*" Approaching Naples by train, we knew not what to expect! Obviously those words were not intended literally! As we stepped out of the train in the Naples station, I began to question that conclusion! The atmosphere was putrid - the stench unbearable! The sewers of all Italy seem to have concentrated on Naples! Fortunately we were not there long enough to learn the cause of the problem. Unfortunately perhaps, our schedule gave us no time even for a glimpse of the Naples that allegedly was worth *dying* for! Soon we were breathing clean fresh air again - on the road to the once buried city of Pompeii.

My memory of the visit is the distant view of Mount Vesuvius. It was still smoldering. True to the many pictures we had seen, a white cloud hovered above the apex. One of our two guides told us that it first erupted in A.D. 76, that volcanic ash spread over a vast area and covered the prosperous city of Pompeii and buried two thousand of its citizens!

Pompeii was rediscovered in 1748. Relics, still being unearthed, bore testimony to the advanced civilization that thrived there 2,000 years ago!

Very soon, we discovered that there was infinitely more to be seen and learnt among the ruin, than was possible in the single day available to us. There was evidence that the city had running water, wealthy homes decorated with life-size frescoes, public buildings with fluted columns, flour mills, public bars and countless examples of sculptured ornament - some exquisitely beautiful! Hot ash once covered the land for many miles burying many people. The ash turned to rock. The bodies decomposed leaving voids that were perfect casts of the victims.

In the heart of the ruins, one of our local guides paused and said that we were about to separate, the ladies to go with him, the men to follow Paul (the other guide). He added: "We will meet again later." Strange as it seemed, we parted with each group going in different directions. Our guide explained: "Gentlemen, we are about to enter a venue frequented by our illustrious ancestors at the turn of this era. You will see that human nature has not changed in all those years!" He led us into the hall of a large building, thence into a loftier chamber. "This," he said, "was once the principal brothel of Pompeii!" He pointed to several large decorative murals, faded with time yet still rich in color. "They depict a variety of human postures. Clearly there is little we could teach our ancestors!" He paused and added: "Please do not misunderstand me! I'm referring to the pigmentation skills - of which those artists were masters!"

Outside the building my attention focused on a white marble figure of a boy! It was about half full-size, mounted on a four foot high undressed stone pedestal. It was unidentified and appeared unrelated to anything around. The lad carried a pitcher on his left shoulder, supported by his left hand. The tilt of the head and subtle posture of the body made it an object of exquisite beauty! It revealed a level of artistic sensitivity rarely seen.

Our cobbled road ended at a crossroad. Immediately opposite were the ruins of what was once a public building. The central feature of its façade overlooked a low flat rectangular paved marble surround to what was once a pool or fountain. The composite symmetry of the arrangement was evidence that town planning was among the highly developed arts practiced two millenniums ago. In the center of the pool was another sculptured gem - a statuette of a nymph about two feet high, dancing on tip-toe, her legs crossed, arms raised and waving; it was sculptured *grace* such as I have never seen before or since. It was in black marble (or possibly weathered bronze), undoubtedly the work of a skilled artist – blissfully unaware that she was shaping a priceless bequest to posterity.

I pause now to ponder over what I have written! Have I given undue rein to events and emotions long past? I wonder...! I realize that if I am to produce a balanced account of my life, I must curb my enthusiasm for youthful impressions! I realize that I have already allowed the story of my very first visit abroad to occupy a disproportionate amount of space! In contrast, I fear the brief references that follow will do scant justice to some very wonderful places we were yet to visit or to the experiences they produced.

FLORENCE

From Pompeii, we journeyed to Florence. On each of our few days in the city, four guides, (of whom two were senior female students), joined us. They were both knowledgeable and attractive, and presented aspects life in their extremely interesting city that may otherwise have eluded us.

My memory turns to Michelangelo's *David.* Sculpted in Carrara marble, it was completed at the start of the sixteenth century – three hundred years ago! Serenely poised, *David* stands upright with a slingshot over his shoulder before killing Goliath. My eyes scanned every muscle, every tendon from neck to toes. Technically it was the most exquisite example of the human form I had ever seen. More than that, the entire posture was of incomparable grace. I have never seen anything like it before or since.

Of particular interest and fascination was the Ponte Vecchio on the River Arno. It is a covered bridge built in 1565. The ceiling and walls are massively decorated with historic pictures in gold and yellow. Years later I learnt that it was the only bridge in Florence that survived the disastrous bombing of World War II.

Here I offer my readers an apology! I am aware that, in many instances, my brief references to places and objects do scant justice to their importance. I remind myself that my purpose in commencing this book was to give a balanced review of my life of which I have covered only the first two decades! There are more than seven to follow! Clearly I must not dally if I am ever to complete the story. Nonetheless, I want to acknowledge with affection Ivy Ottino. She was one of the guides who made my visit to Florence memorable! We corresponded for a while after our return to South Africa until time and distance took their toll.

VENICE

The next day we were in Venice! Until then, for me, it had been a kind of phantom city - the setting for Shakespeare's "Merchant of Venice" - one of our set-works in my last year at school. Venice appeared again two years later during 'History of Architecture' as the site of the famous church *Santa Maria della Salute* - a prototype of Byzantine architecture. Suddenly that morning, the city became a living reality. The streets were waterways crossed here and there by covered pedestrian bridges; gondolas, once a romantic novelty, were the popular means of transport that took rich and poor alike, about their daily business. Live pigeons[42] in their thousands made their daily landing on the slate and marble paving of St. Mark's Square - there to receive their rations of corn supplied by the city hall authorities.

Overlooking the Square and the Grand Canal is the Doge's Palace built in the 14th Century. The facades, exquisitely delicate in detail, comprise two floors of open arcades of pointed arches for their entire length of some 500 feet. Internally, one is awe-stricken by the vaulted ceilings and corridors paved in marble in a variety of ingenious designs.

All too brief were our visits to other structures of great historic interest. Crossing the Rialto Bridge and the Bridge of Sighs is lodged in my memory. The latter linked the Doge's Palace to the prison. We were told that the bridge obtained its name from the sighs made by the prisoners when made to cross after being interrogated in the palace.

The next morning we traveled by bus to Chiasso on the Swiss border where we were to bid farewell to Italy. Over the past weeks we heard Mussolini's praises sung with incredible frequency. It was often accompanied by the anthem "Giovinezza". It had an appealing lilt, so much so that at idle moments, we often found ourselves singing the song or humming the tune. Such was our mood as we strolled up and down the platform, waiting for our train to Lucerne. Mario was with us. He never joined us in song. Suddenly he stopped in his tracks! He seemed quite solemn as he gathered us around him.

He gazed into the eyes of each of us and said: *"In a few minutes your train will be here."* He looked down to the paving on which we stood, pointed to a white line on the paving and stated: *"That line marks the Italian border. The tune you've been humming is the anthem of the Fascists;*

singing or humming it implies support! For God's sake do not murmur it on the other side of the border! Many of Mussolini's enemies escaped to Switzerland. They only wait to get even. The sound of it could attract a bullet at the back of your head. Take care." He shook his head and repeated: *"Never, never sing or hum it outside Italy."* He paused and continued: *"By the way, don't believe all the 'praises' you've heard! Among strangers, Italians are scared of the presence of Fascist spies! They cover their emotions by lauding Mussolini - he's hated and feared by millions!"*

The train steamed in. Mario had been a great guide and friend. We thanked him profusely. He shook each of us by the hand. *"I feel I've made many friends. Travel safely. Come back again!"*

On the train, we compared notes and reviewed some of our experiences. Our weeks in Italy had been a tremendous success and for some of us, an invaluable extension of our architectural studies. For me it was all that and more. Mario had been a splendid guide and we were all grateful to him. He had been tireless in his efforts to meet our every need and wish. His farewell talk at the Ciasso station was intended as a timely protective warning. It was more than that! It explained why a ruthless Dictator was widely acclaimed - frequently out of context! For me it provided an insight into the political morass into which Italy had sunk and was a grim warning of the dangers confronting Europe and the free world!

LUCERNE

We had only one full day in Lucerne. Some of us went skiing. Others, I included, preferred to spend the time tobogganing down the lower slopes of the Sonnenberg. It was a refreshing enjoyable day. It also provided a measure of relaxation after weeks of intense exposure to many of the most wonderful architectural and cultural achievements of all time.

ENGLAND AGAIN

Back in London for two days, I visited the National Gallery, watched the Changing of the Guard, walked across London Bridge, dined with distant relatives and spent time buying gifts for family at home. At the hotel, we met students from the other NUSAS tours who had gathered there prior to entraining for Southampton to commence the 17-day homeward voyage. One of them, Max Schneier from the Witswatersrand University of Johannesburg, told me that he was staying on in London for two weeks and that he had run short of cash and wondered if I had a pound to spare that I would care to lend him! The pound (which went a long way in those days!) was repaid immediately when Max returned to Cape Town. I mention the incident because it was a prelude to an interesting friendship that developed two years later. Aboard *R.M.S. Balmoral*, friendships that commenced on the outward voyage were rekindled. I looked for and found Pieter and her sister and enjoyed sharing each other's experiences in Europe. Aboard there was no one like Harry Lauder to entertain us night after night as he did on the outward journey. I saw a little of my brother Maurice. He and his friends were of another age group but we mixed at deck tennis, quoits and cricket tournaments and at night there were Bridge drives, treasure hunts and informal dancing. I also watched the popular game of Bridge[43] and occasionally participated. Slowly I learnt the rudiments of the game. Everyone was kept happily entertained on what might otherwise have been a long monotonous voyage.

I spent many hours with the Marais sisters and occasionally danced with Pieter. Unquestionably she was the more attractive of the two but she was ever watchful never to leave her sister unaccompanied. Despite that, we spent precious moments together. She was a happy personality; there was always laughter in her eyes. Of course she knew that I was attracted but it seemed her intuition told her it was a passing fancy! Towards the end of the voyage, she commented: "Wait till you meet my friend Greta - you'll fall in love with her!" - an interesting comment in light of developments months later.

CAPE TOWN

The seventeen days on-board passed quickly. At the crack of dawn on the Monday of our arrival in Table Bay, passengers gathered on deck to witness the splendor of the crimson granite escarpments of Devil's Peak and Table Mountain aglow in the light of the rising sun - a breath-taking experience!

Soon we were in the harbor. Sirens sounded. Powerful tugs pushed the ship towards the quayside. Excited students were rushing in all directions bidding fond farewells with promises to meet again. Pieter said that they were to be in Cape Town for a few days; she would telephone me before returning to the farm! Maurice and I, on deck with our bags, spotted Dad among the crowd below. The Vauxhall was parked nearby.

A hired uniformed driver relieved us of our baggage and within minutes we were skirting the city on our way to "Longwood" and home!

That evening, some of our cousins joined the family and gathered round the large breakfast room table to hear about our adventures. The table was covered in photographs. For nearly an hour Maurice and I answered countless questions and told our stories. Maurice told his in his usual quiet manner without emotion. He had been to many parts of Britain that I had never heard of but hoped one day to visit - but I had no regrets at not having joined him. Too excited to control my emotions, I described and relived countless experiences in Britain, France, Italy and Switzerland. They became entrenched in my memory. For many years they remained *the* adventure of a lifetime!

True to her word, Pieter called a day or two after our arrival. Their train was due to leave for home at noon! They joined me for an hour's chat at Makhams Café prior to their departure. We reminisced a little. Pieter and I promised to 'keep in touch'! Before leaving she gave me a happy smile and said: "I haven't forgotten - Greta will contact you!"

GRETA

We had been home about ten days when Greta Van Zyl telephoned. Her 'very dear friend Petertjie' had asked her to call. We arranged to meet at Cartwright's Corner, a well-known Cape Town meeting spot, at 11 the following Saturday!

I was there a minute or two ahead of schedule. Punctually a light-footed, fair-haired, bright-eyed, very attractive young lady approached me. With a happy captivating friendly smile, she exclaimed: "Alfred!" as though we were old friends. There was no mistaking who she was. Pieter's reference to her 'bright fascinating personality' was as accurate as it was appealing!

Over tea, we chatted about our respective activities and interests. I learnt that she usually returned home to Porterville for the weekends 'unless there was something special ...like today'!

CHAPTER 10

STUDENTS' PARLIAMENT

1931 was a year filled with memorable experiences! The Intermediate examinations were passed and an important hurdle on my road to the Royal Institute of British Architects was behind me. I was now a fourth year Student; my appointment as Student Demonstrator was reaffirmed and I had been abroad - into the heart of the civilized world! I was now 21! I had the uncomfortable feeling that my carefree youth was behind me; my boyhood had passed!

It seemed that my sister Sybil also reached that conclusion! She was six years my senior - always steeped in study and until then, I had been her 'kid brother'! Now, she actually asked me to accompany her to a meeting - a meeting of the Fabian Society of which she was a member! I went. It was my first experience of anything of that nature. The meeting took place in a small building in Hatfield Street near the center of the city. Forty or fifty people attended. Among them were many senior students, lecturers and one or two professors. I heard the name of Professor Farrington mentioned, but I never met him. The general discussion concerned the 'various steps' to be taken to advance 'Communism' which many speakers claimed was "the only solution" to the many social and economic problems confronting society! Most of those present seemed to regard Trotsky and Lenin with awe; some referred to them as the "revolutionary heroes of the century!"

I left the meeting feeling disturbed! I knew of some of the atrocities committed during the Russian Revolution and very recently Mario in Italy had drawn attention to those committed by the Fascists! It puzzled me that my sister, a quiet non-aggressive personality, should belong to an organization that seemed to justify or condone such inhumanity! When I confronted her with my concern, she seemed able to rationalize and accept that such ghastly conduct was "inevitable in any great social revolution!" She averred that the one in Russia was destined to "spread throughout the world", would "free the down-trodden masses from the shackles of capitalism!" I could not go along with that! I told her that I felt convinced that attempts to change social conduct were doomed to fail if they relied on terror or any form of conduct that violated the accepted norms of humane behavior. Sybil felt I was "not well informed," shrugged her shoulders and said: "I give up!" I think she wrote me off as unrealistic and immature!

STUDENTS' PARLIAMENT

Away from the main campus, I often felt cut off from the main student body. One of those occasions was when I was reading a poster on the notice board that gave prominence to the impending elections for the "Students' Parliament" to be held in Bloemfontein later in the year. Every few years the National Union of South African Students (NUSAS) organized a Students' Parliament representative of all the universities in the country. The number of seats allocated to each university was proportionate to the number of its registered students in relation to the number in the entire country. The Universities of Cape Town (UCT) and Witwatersrand, the two largest in the country were each allocated 14 seats and each student was given 14 votes which they could distribute as he or she saw fit. The principal political parties were the South African Party (SAP)[44], the Nationalist Party (NAT) which mirrored those at the national level and the Socialist party which took the place of the Labor Party. There was no doubt in my mind that the forthcoming election would generate a great deal of activity and excitement on the main campus in Rondebosch! I was sorry not to be there and felt somewhat cut-off!

One evening a senior student called me and said he was asked by the 'head committee of the South African Party (SAP) - General Smuts's Party' to ascertain if I would allow my name to go forward as a candidate for election.

I said that I was very interested but questioned the wisdom of having a candidate from a faculty that was isolated from the main campus - one who was not known to the majority of the student electorate. He said that the point had been discussed exhaustively at the meeting and was considered to be without merit! I accepted the invitation.

In due course, notices appeared on the boards of all faculties. They contained the names of the candidates (about 24 in all). The majority were

SAP members; my name and that of friend Berry Malan were among them. Other SAP names known to me were Caradoc Davies, Coventry and Cunningham. There were five Socialist candidates of whom I knew three personally: Harry Snitcher, Sam Kahn and May Berold. Harry had a reputation for brilliance; he and Sam were both Law students. Peter Neehaus, the only Nationalist on the list, and I had never met. Another notice gave a list of pre-election campus meetings which included a *"Debate between the South African and Socialist Parties"* to take place the following week - Subject: "The Japanese Trade Treaty"[45]. Caradoc Davies and I were delegated by the United Party, to support the Treaty against Snitcher and Kahn who would oppose it on behalf of the Socialist Party.

The debate, attended by a few hundred students, went off well. I had made myself familiar with several aspects of an extremely contentious issue. I was pleasantly surprised that I felt in no way inhibited by Snitcher's reputation or by Kahn's attempt to ridicule the arguments that he anticipated would be made by us. Several members of the audience participated. In the end, it was the splendid summing-up by Caradoc Davies that gave our team a resounding victory.

Before my trip to Europe, I had developed a friendship with Moira Goodfellow. She was a BA student, lived in Tamboers Kloof, off the Kloof Nek Road some distance from "Longwood". I had dined at her home and occasionally accompanied her and her parents on pleasant Sunday drives into the country.

A day before the election, I was chatting with Moira in the Hiddingh Hall quadrangle when my sister Sybil appeared. She did not know Moira and did not wait to be introduced! I knew that she disapproved of my membership in the *"capitalist South African Party"* but I only realized the intensity of her displeasure when she commented: "I warned you - tomorrow you will learn a lesson - and you're not going to like it!" Without another word she walked off! I felt embarrassed, not so much for what she said, but because it seemed rude to slight Moira's presence. That seemed deliberate and totally unacceptably abrupt. Moira commented: "Wasn't that your sister?" I responded: "Yes, of course. I'm afraid she has the Socialist bug!" Moira took my hand and said: "I am sorry! That has earned you all my fourteen votes tomorrow!" With that she rushed off.

The Election hustle, such as there was, was confined to the main campus. Our city campus was relatively quiet. It served only a small part of the student body and had only a single polling station in the foyer of the Hall.

The day passed without incident. Excitement mounted at about nine that night, when the election results were announced on the main campus from the steps of the Jameson Hall. Of the fourteen elected candidates, nine were S.A. Party, 4 Socialists and 1 Nationalist: Percy Neehaus. The successful SAP candidates included Carodoc Davies, Coventry, Berry Malan and me. The successful Socialists were Harry Snitcher, Sam Kahn, Jean Duthie and May Berold. Two of the candidates polled over 1,000 votes. To my surprise (and to Sybil's concern!), I was one of them! I was, of course, delighted, as were my parents. Sybil made no comment! She disapproved of her family's political leanings and remained silent when matters political were discussed at home!

My memory of the 'parliamentary' session in Bloemfontein is vague. I recall a luncheon at the historic Polley's Hotel hosted and addressed by General Smuts and a visit to the Haartebeespoort Dam by the entire body of student parliamentarians.

BACK TO THE DRAWING BOARD – (not entirely!)

As the work at college continued, challenges increased. Design problems presented to architectural students were less and less 'academic'! They included 'realistic' planning and design and began to appear more like 'architecture', as I understood it. Advanced building mechanics included vector diagrams and the design of roof trusses and complex long span lattice girders. It was all increasingly interesting. My work as Student Demonstrator now embraced first-, second- and third-year students. With less time for my own work, I returned to college after supper two or three times a week and enjoyed working non-stop for three or four hours. Mother often lay awake waiting for my return! Once or twice I missed the last tram home and had no choice but to make the long up-hill trudge on foot! That had happened a few times when my dad came to the rescue! He offered me the car for my nightly sessions in the studio! That made it all much easier! It also provided an occasional opportunity for diversion - unrelated to my work!

One night, I had been at the drawing board 'for hours', and felt that I 'had enough'! My thoughts turned towards Greta. We had met a few times in the afternoons after lectures. Now I decided to telephone her and asked if she cared for a spin. She liked the idea. We drove to Sea Point, strolled along the waterfront, sat and watched the moonlight streak across the ocean! Such outings were repeated. She was always happy and light-hearted and I liked that! The night drives grew more frequent. We would drive to Clifton or Milnerton to enjoy the sea breeze and, when the tide was low, we strolled along the beach, alone - sometimes bare-footed - all cares abandoned. We fell in love! So I thought!

At vacation time, Greta returned to her home in Porterville - a pleasant village about 100 miles northeast of the city. Before the year-end, I was invited to spend a weekend with her family. Happily, I accepted. I met her widowed mother, her brothers Bertie and Jack and her married sister Mollie. There was little to do in the village other than to golf on a 9-hole 'green-less' golf course and visit friends for coffee. The village was entirely Afrikaans speaking! Unlike my father, my knowledge of Afrikaans was limited! My English accent was a source of good-hearted mirth to all I met! Courteously they always addressed me in English! That was not easy for Mrs. Van Zyl, Greta's mother, but she tried! She seemed to like me and must have thought that a fourth year student of architecture was sufficiently qualified to design a house! She showed me a vacant level plot overlooking the town and asked if I would design her home. I had done a number of sketch plans but never one from which it was intended to build! I wanted to tell her that, but hesitated before doing so. She wanted a 'cottage-type' house and told me her limited needs. She produced a site diagram that she had taken from her title deed. I made a copy, noted the North point and the direction of the prevailing wind, and said: "I'll do my best!"

Back home I began sketching whenever I had an 'odd moment'! It became clear that was no way to go about the job. It required concentration and time! Preference had to be given to my college work so many weeks went by 'sketching and discarding' before I came up with anything that I felt was worth developing. I finally completed the drawing, had a blueprint made and mailed it to Mrs. Van Zyl. My covering letter explained that it was a 'preliminary proposal', that she should let me know the changes she wanted and I would be glad to prepare the final drawings. I received a nice 'thank you' letter written in English that one of her family had helped her write!

That was 1931. Months later, Greta mentioned that the house was built. After that, I never heard of it again – until for fourteen years when, under very different circumstances, I was given a remote glimpse of it! That is part of another story! I will tell it later.

POTFONTEIN

A letter from Pieter invited me "to join some friends who are coming to the farm for the 10-day June vacation." I showed the letter to my mother. She commented: "It will be a nice break - you've been working hard." Of course I was delighted and accepted the invitation - wondering if Greta would be among the 'friends' to whom Pieter referred. 'Had Greta told her our friendship had developed?'

Seventy-three years have elapsed since then! I wrack my memory for details. The farm, hundreds of acres in extent, was a few miles from the Potfontein railway siding in the heart of the Karroo. It was some 25 to 50 miles from the important De Aar junction where I had strolled a year earlier, on my way to Keetmanshoop. Pieter and her father Mr. Marais were at the station to meet me. They drove me to their farm, a large homestead with many outbuildings nestling in the shade of gum and willow trees - quite an oasis!

Greta was there gleeful as ever! She had arrived a few days earlier and seemed oblivious to the embarrassment I felt at our being together in Pieter's presence! However, with a measure of 'strained aloofness' by the two of us, and perhaps tactful discretion by others, all went well.

Pieter mentioned that they had been horse-riding and asked if I would care to join them in the morning. I liked the idea. I was by no means an experienced horseman but had enjoyed riding on an occasional Sunday morning on Milnerton beach and in the Tokai forest with Maurice and a friend. Next morning after an early breakfast, one of the stable-hands was waiting for us at the rear of the homestead. He held the reins of three horses - all freshly groomed! The three of us mounted our horses and the two girls took off. I sat in my saddle wanting to follow. My horse would not budge! I shook the reins, tapped the horse's side with my heels, talked into its ear - used every means I knew! There was no response! The animal was rigid - would not budge! I looked ahead - feeling very embarrassed! The girls had stopped on the crest of a hill 500 yards away and were waiting for me. They looked back, saw my predicament, and returned immediately. I felt stupid! Pieter said: "Let me try!" I dismounted; she took over and in a flash she was up and away! My ego thoroughly deflated, I mounted her steed and quietly followed – Greta at my side. For an hour or more the three of us rode single file through the scrub, up and down the 'koppies'[46]. We stopped at a spring in the middle of nowhere and returned home in time to escape the intense heat of the mid-day sun.

Early morning rides became a regular and enjoyable exercise for the rest of the week. The embarrassing first morning experience never recurred. Very politely, the girls never referred to it again.

On Sunday, visitors came from a neighboring farm. Among them, to my surprise, were two whom I knew from Cape Town – one an old school acquaintance and Sam Weinberg, a final year medical student at UCT - a friend of my brother and sister, Maurice and Beatrice, and a fairly frequent visitor to "Longwood".

The rest of the week was fairly quiet and relaxing. Turning-in by 9:30 at night was a novelty for me. It made my visit a period of relaxation to which I adapted readily. It also gave me a glimpse that was not displeasing of the life of a farmer on the desert-like expanse of the Karroo! Before leaving, Greta suggested that I should plan to come to Porterville for a few days during the September vacation when she would be home! I jumped at the idea!

BACK AT WORK

At Varsity I found myself under more pressure than usual. 'My students, preparing for their annual exams, kept me pretty occupied during the day. Of course I had my own fourth year exams to contend with in addition to the set 'design' drawings that I had yet to complete. It was obvious that I would have to continue my nightly visits to the studio - perhaps more frequently than before. The moonlight drives with Greta soon became a thing of the past! I saw no reason however, to call off my planned visit to Porterville!

I took the train to Gouda, the nearest station to Porterville. Jack was there to meet me and drove me the 20 miles to his home. It was near midnight when we arrived and it was not until the next morning that I saw Greta and the rest of the family. After breakfast, the others all went their ways and left me alone with 'my girl'! She was her old naturally happy self - warmer perhaps than ever before! She took me on a short drive - I know not where! We returned home for tea when she told me she had completed her course at the Training College and would not be returning to the city! Then she added: "Darling, you will have to come here more often!" She seemed distressed when I told her that I had taken a job in an architect's office for two months and thereafter my final year work-load would make such visits few and far between. She shook her head and said: "I'll wait!"

Apart from my duties (as Student Demonstrator) and one or two fourth year studies I had yet to complete, my final year at Varsity was about to commence. That year was to be devoted to preparing for the final design exam at the end of the year. I had also to prepare preliminary thesis proposals that required official approval. The months that followed proved to be busier and far more significant than I had imagined. As I recall, I saw Greta twice during that time - once when she came to town and once when I drove through Porterville. More of that later!

CHAPTER 11

1932: TRAGEDY AND DESPAIR!

My final year at Varsity was about to commence, as arranged, with a two month's session in McConnell's office. Working under him had been a tremendous inspiration for me! I looked forward to a recurrence of that experience. Immediately after the New Year holidays, I reported to McConnell's office for duty. Terence Orpen met me at the door. He looked grim! "Is Mac here?" I asked. "No," he said, shaking his head. "He never came back!" He took my arm, drew me in and stared! He tried to speak but could not find his voice! A tear ran down his cheek. He was in a state of shock! It was a while before he uttered: "Mac - home in Queenstown for the holidays, swam in the pool and drowned!" I was dumb-founded! He added: "That is all I know!" The telephone rang. Terence answered. He spoke briefly and said: "That was Elsworth! He's coming over - wants you to wait." When Elsworth arrived, he, too, was deeply distressed. He explained that he had been directed to take over the practice and said that I should remain to help Terence complete projects that Mac had commenced.

Leonard Forbes McConnell was 35, in the prime of his life, when the tragedy occurred. We had lost a brilliant architect, a great human being! He was widely loved. For me, he was a fond and resourceful inspiration!

Such were the thoughts - such the mood that accompanied the start of my third job as a student. Orpen and I prepared many detail drawings. It was not an entirely happy task as I was wondering at every turn 'how Mac would have done it?' However, under Elsworth's direction, it was an invaluable experience. Orpen had been with Mac quite a while and was of considerable help to me. Our friendship grew

Back at college, most of my time was spent assisting first and second year students. As far as my own work was concerned, my thoughts were focused on my final "Design" exam and the thesis that I had not yet commenced but was a prerequisite to qualifying as an Associate of the Royal Institute of British Architects. All other exams were happily passed. I submitted a resume of proposals for my thesis. The theme I chose, "A Residential Public School for 500 Boys", had been approved. I compiled a list of the essential buildings and facilities. They included the main school building with assembly hall, laboratories, staff rooms, etc. The list included several different types of building such as boys' residences, gymnasium, swimming pool, chapel and library, as well as playing fields with pavilions, ablution facilities, etc. Several attempts to produce a coordinated Layout Plan were discarded. By the time I came up with one that I considered adequate, I realized that I was committed to a thesis of considerable magnitude, that it would take far longer than I had hoped. There was not the remotest possibility of completing it before leaving for Johannesburg!

OUDEKRAAL

A call from Morrie Walt invited Maurice, my brother, and me to join him on a hike the following Sunday. About ten of us met at Kloof Nek at 8 a.m. Accompanying Morrie were his two charming sisters Freda and Janie. It was a gorgeous day, sunny but not too hot! Single file we walked along the narrow stony contour path at the foot of the Twelve Apostles to a point beyond Camps Bay. We made our way down onto Chapman's Peak Road and hiked two abreast to Oudekraal, where we rested and camped on the beach between the massive boulders characteristic of that part of the coast.

At the time, the country, and indeed the whole world, was in the throes of an economic recession - one that developed into the worst depression the world has ever known! Poisoning the atmosphere were reports of Nazi activities in Germany! Very occasionally for diversion, I would stroll down the Avenue to listen to a debate in Parliament. There I heard depressing references to Hitler and the ongoing unrestrained activities of his 'Brown Shirts'! The economy grew progressively worse! I began to wonder what the prospects were for young architects! Building activity had declined; there seemed little prospect of conditions improving! I pictured myself applying for a job as an electrician's assistant!

DILEMMA

Continued reports of increasing unemployment and economic duress all over the world distressed me! In a few months time my life as a student would be over - I knew of architect's assistants who had lost their jobs and wondered what was in store for me! One day in June, depressed by such thoughts, I decided to discuss matters with my dad. I put down my pencil, left the studio and walked to my father's office in Dominion House, Long-market Street. Miss Robins (Dad's secretary) explained that he was in con-ference - didn't want to be disturbed! I waited. Minutes passed. Miss Robins rose: "I'll tell him you're here." She was back within seconds and said: "He wants you to go in!" Dad introduced me to his interviewer "Her-man Kallenbach - architect from Johannesburg!" and asked me to join them to lunch. I was not about to discuss my concerns in the presence of a stranger but I accepted the invitation. At lunch Dad addressed his guest and said: "Herman, I am sorry my schedule prevents me from being with you this afternoon, but," he added, turning to me, "perhaps, if Alfred is free, he could drive you wherever you'd like to go."

I jumped at the opportunity. Of course I was free. Mr. K. said he too was free until 5:20 when he had an appointment in Kloof Street. That gave us more than four hours. He asked me to suggest an itinerary! I decided to make for the new University campus in Rondebosch which, I felt sure, would interest him. We walked to the car parked in Greenmarket Square. On the way, I drew attention to the Michaelis Art Gallery – a "beautiful 18th Century building that housed a famous collection of Dutch Masters." Mr. K. seemed eager to be on our way! We drove eastward along De Waal Drive and down to Park Road adjoining the Rondebosch Common to obtain a distant but comprehensive view of the Campus. I drew attention to the Jameson Hall at the center, directly below Devil's Peak and explained that architect Soloman used the peak as the central motif of the composite design. Kallenbach was silent. I asked him if he knew of any other archi-tectural design in which an element of nature was the dominant influence. He said: *"No, I do not - it is a remarkable conception!"* We then drove up, around, onto and through the campus, stopped at the entrance to one of the student residences to admire one of the carved teak fanlights - the work of my friend and tutor Vladimer Meirowitz. We walked to a central point in front of the Jameson Hall where my visitor pointed to a thin white pole at the head of the pediment and uttered: *"It is focused precisely at the Peak - quite amazing!"*

We went to the nearby Rhodes Memorial. As we passed through the gates, wild deer scattered, stopped and gazed, to the delight of my passen-ger! At the Memorial, he was deeply moved by what he saw. He had never been there before. Staring at the bronze bust of Rhodes he read and murmured: *"His brooding spirit... Cecil John Rhodes 1853 – 1902"* and remarked: *"An imperialist, yes - but he did a great deal in his short life; he put his diamond fortune to great purpose. Today, hundreds of scholars all over the world are grateful to him!"* We walked down the granite steps flanked by bronze lions and paused beneath the larger-than-life equestrian statue of "Energy" by Thomas Watt[47] - a remarkable manifestation of 'power' and 'vision' that characterized the life of Rhodes - the last of the empire builders!

Our next stop was at the Groote Constantia in the heart of the rich wine-land valley. The manor house, a fine example of Cape Dutch architecture, and the pediment above the wine cellar at the rear of the house are the works of Anton Anreith - part of the Cape's rich heritage from the eighteenth century. The pediment depicting the story of the Ganymede is but one of Anreith's many sculptures with which the city is richly endowed.

We drove up the valley, stopped at a rustic restaurant on Constantia Nek. Over a cup of tea, our visitor mentioned that I had taken him to places he had never been before and he wondered, "how many people realize how fortunate they are, to live in an city so endowed by nature - so enriched with a bounty of cultural attributes!" Then, out of the blue, he said that he understood I would be graduating shortly and if I was interested, he had a job for me! ("Was I dreaming?") He continued: "We'll be building a new synagogue in Benoni. It is a unique structure with extensive cantilevered galleries that will not be counter-balanced at foundation level as is customary, but by transverse beams above the ceiling." He added: "If you can make it by September 1, the job is yours!" 'That, Sir, would be wonderful!" I exclaimed. Excitement surged through my veins – only dampened by the thought that my final Design exam was scheduled for mid-November! We crossed the Nek and drove down to Hout Bay, a delightful fishing village on the Atlantic seaboard. I wanted to show my guest the harbor, to stroll on the beach but "time was running out, we must be on our way if I am to have you back by 5:20!" We drove round Chapman's Peak, past Llandudno, Oudekraal to Camps Bay. We got out of the car for a glimpse of the Twelve Apostles. "This," I said, "is the western face of Table Mountain. I would like to have shown you Clifton and Sea Point but there is no time for that!" We drove up through the Glen, passed Lord Charles Somerset's shooting box to Kloof Nek and down into Kloof Street and arrived at our destination in good time. Mr. K. thanked me and said: "Please thank your father. You've been a splendid guide. Let me know about the job as soon as possible – not later than the thirtieth!"

My dilemma was intense! Eagerly I wanted that job! 'What was I to do?' The depression was getting worse by the day. Jobs were scarce! The last and most important of all my exams was 'DESIGN', a 5-day effort that would take me into November - two months after 'D-day' for the job! I lay awake grappling with my problem! 'There was also my thesis to complete, but that would take many months and, in any case, I had planned to do it during the long vacation and in the new-year!

The next morning, I called on Professor Wheatley and explained my predicament. He sent for Mr. Gregory, head of the architectural branch. They talked for awhile. Addressing me, Gregory said there was to be a special final design exam early in August. It was primarily for past students who had not made the grade previously. He said: "They have since gained considerable experience working in architects' offices; the standard expected of them is likely to be higher than usual." He added: *"But, if you would like to 'chance your arm', the professor has agreed that you could enter - instead of waiting till November!"* To me, that sounded like a warning! It was certainly a challenge! Thoughts of the Depression and prospect of a job weighed heavily! 'If I fail, I could try again - if I'm lucky, the hurdle will be behind me!' I decided to enter! I immediately wrote to Johannesburg accepting the appointment!

The following weeks were spent delving into the plans and technicalities of as many building types as I could lay my hands on: town halls, law courts, museums, gymnasiums, conference halls, hospitals, schools, theaters, churches, art galleries, you name it! I made notes pertaining to acoustics, air-conditioning, projection rooms, floor gradients, lines of vision etc. and put as much as I could to memory!

Candidates were informed that the examination would extend over a period of 5-days each of six hours; the first day to be devoted exclusively to the preparation of preliminary eighth-inch sketch plans, sections and elevations of the project on a single sheet of drawing paper; the drawings would be collected at the end of the day and returned the following morning in a sealed transparent envelope - they were 'not to be altered'! The following four days would be devoted to the preparation of full working and detail drawings. Candidates were reminded to bring their own instruments and were encouraged to bring a lunch package for at least the first day as they would not be permitted to leave the premises. It troubled me that the time for the initial design was limited to the first day! I had never been asked to design a building within the space of a single day!

In due course, I was one of twelve candidates who assembled at the examination studio. My friend Terence Orpen was among them. The subject set: - A repertory theater (plus cinema) to seat 1,000 people (site-dimensions, etc. were attached).

It did not displease me! My pre-examination studies proved useful. I had memorized a good deal about 'angles of vision', 'floor gradients', etc. and could thus apply a fair amount of practical data. My concern and tension gave way to a sense of enthusiasm and relaxed comfort with the importance of the task on hand. The five days passed by quickly. My drawings were completed early on the fifth day enabling me to spend the last few hours adding minor refinements. I handed in my drawings and specification notes feeling that I had fully completed the allotted task! However there was no way of knowing if my effort had reached the level needed to justify a pass!

When the Design exam results were posted, only three candidates were shown to have been successful. They were: D. Andrews, T. Orpen and A. H. Honikman! Of course I was delighted as were my family. It seemed that the biggest of all hurdles was past! I felt enormously relieved and relaxed - free of a prolonged tension! Of course there was still my thesis to complete! I had committed myself to a large project entailing a great deal of work; but there was no particular target date and I was content to think that it could be completed at night and at weekends during my sojourn in Johannesburg!

My impulse was to share my news with my family and with Greta! It was a several weeks since I had spoken with her. My calls to her were always from an outside public booth on a corner opposite our house. I had no desire to share my conversations with members of the family who might be within ears' distance. That evening I was back in the booth - only to be told that Greta was away for a few days. Days later I received a call from a man I did not know! He said: *"My name is Kurt[48]; I work for a bank in Porterville. Greta and I, with a group of young people, spent the week-end together on a nearby farm. She and I became engaged!"* I was speechless! He went on to say: *"Before all present, we took a pledge over the bible, to remain ever faithful to each other!"* I could not believe my ears! I asked: *"Why are you telling me all this? Did Greta ask you to call me?"* He answered: *"No - I knew you were close friends - I asked her your number."* I thought: *"Was I dreaming - it seemed only days since I felt captivated by utterances of her affection!"* I pondered: *"Could this be true or was I dreaming?"* I was flabbergasted!

A few days went by. Greta called. She sounded as cheerful as ever - as though nothing had happened! She wanted to know how 'things were going - could I manage another visit before leaving for Johannesburg?' I was speechless. Then I asked: *"Do you know that Kurt telephoned me - told me about your week-end on the farm - and your pledge?"* She replied: *"Darling, you don't understand - it was in front of everyone - all very awkward!"* I told her that I was leaving on Monday – that there will be no more calls! A long silence followed. I was heart-broken. I heard myself saying: "Good bye, Greta!"

The event disturbed me for a while! In time it became a distant memory. Slowly I seemed to experience a sense of 'relief'. I realized how different were our backgrounds, our values and our beliefs and no doubt also our loyalties! They were root-differences that could never have been reconciled!

There was no question - what had happened was for the best!

CHAPTER 12

A NEW LIFE IN A NEW CITY

A few days before the end of August 1932, I left home. Mother prepared a hamper for the two-day train journey! I do not remember any emotional impact associated with my departure. My parents were too self-controlled to show any and I was too excited at the thought of what lay ahead! On my behalf, they had made a temporary bed-breakfast arrangement with my aunt Leah who lived with her family on the Berea in Johannesburg. Until I found suitable accommodation, I was to pay her nine pounds a month. I gathered that her husband was not working!

As the train puffed its way through Paarl, my thoughts went back to our car accident on the Hex River Pass! I pondered: "How much younger was my dad when he left home - a natural scholar - his education in Liverpool radically curtailed, he was denied the advanced education! That, he made sure, would not be denied his six children!"

I wondered what lay in store for me in my new environment - would I be equal to the challenges that lay ahead? Whom did I know in Johannesburg apart from family? Very few! I thought of lads at school and at the Students' Parliament! I remembered Max Schneier whom I met on board the *Saxon Castle* nearly two years earlier; Dina Malkin in Muizenberg and again at a tennis party in Oranjezicht! Those were all!

In the dining saloon on the train shortly after noon, I sat at the only empty table. Looking outward, oblivious to the brown barren earth fleeting by, I felt a hand on my shoulder. I looked up at the friendly smile of Jean Duthie! "May I join you?" she asked. I was only too pleased to have company. I remembered her immediately - we had met a few times in Bloemfontein a year earlier; she was also a candidate to the Students Parliament and I rather liked her! She was a member of the Labor Party, but we had got on well! We chatted through the meal and well into the afternoon. She said she lived with her family in Johannesburg, that her father was a keen member of the Labor Party, had actively participated in the General Election when Smuts was defeated! My response was that I thought 'Labor' had entered into "an unholy alliance with the Nationalists to obtain their first important victory" which I feared would cost the country a heavy price! We shared our political differences entirely without rancor. I sensed that she was not an ardent political 'animal' and did not appear to resent convictions that I had expressed a little too vigorously! We met again that evening. I enjoyed her company and asked if I could call her when I was settled. She replied: "Please do! You may like to meet my father!"

My cousin Joey was at Park Station to meet me. We took a tram to my Aunt Leah's home on the Berea where I was welcomed by my aunt, Uncle Elkin and by Cousin Elsie. Her younger sister Beattie, of whom I was fond, had married and was living in Benoni. She had two children Maurice and Jeanette.

My aunt showed me to my room. It seemed adequate - except that there appeared to be little room for a drawing board! I thought of the thesis and all the many drawings it would entail! I put it at the back of my mind thinking: "maybe somewhere else in the house!"

MY FIRST REAL JOB

The offices of Kallenbach, Kennedy and Furner were in Sacke's Building, Joubert Street, in the heart of downtown Johannesburg. Punctually at 9 a.m. on September 1, 1932, I reported for duty. Confronted by two clerks at the front desk, I was shown into Mr. Kallenbach's office. He welcomed me, made no reference to our previous meeting and proceeded to refer to my main task as 'Clerk of Works'. He said the site was being cleared, that it was in the residential area of Benoni about 'seven or eight minutes from the railway station'; they would be taking me there tomorrow to meet the builder. He took me to meet the rest of the staff. In the front office I met the head typist, Mrs. Stratham, and a second typist whom I had met on entering. In the adjoining room I met Mr. Furner. He was introduced as "our principal designer." He was at the drawing board. Seemingly distracted by our entry, he got off his stool and with a congenial smile, welcomed me to the staff. He was much younger than Kallenbach - probably in his early fifties. I liked his manner - pleasing and friendly. He explained the duties of 'Clerk of Works' that were to occupy much of my time for the next 9 or 10 months, "but not all the time - for the rest you will be at the drawing board working under me." He led me to an adjoining room: "This is your office!" It was small but sufficient. On the drawing table was a double-elephant drawing board covered with a clean white ground sheet, tee-square, set squares and a set of instruments all neatly prepared for my arrival. "Let me know if there is anything you need," said Mr. Furner as he led me to yet another office where I met Mr. Kennedy, *"our quantity surveyor-in-chief."* His room was untidy, table clotted with drawings with many more rolls on racks in front of him and above his head. His manner was dour and rather curt - obviously 'very occupied'! In the next- door room I met his head quantity surveyor Robert Law. In the large drawing office, I met four others and in the room adjoining two more. They included architects Pat Duncan and Wagner, both senior officers. Furner turned to me and said: "If you have any problems, Duncan or I will help you!"

Thus it was that I learnt for the first time that the post to which I had been appointed was not exclusively that of a 'Clerk of Works'!

THE SYNAGOGUE SITE

The next morning Furner drove me eastward along Commissioner Street to Benoni on the East Rand - about 15 miles from the city. We stopped at the railway station. Furner explained that he came there to give me 'direction for your daily calls'. Pointing ahead, he said: "The site is about half a mile along Park Road. They can't have done much - only started on Friday!"

It was a large level site. Three newly erected temporary structures were on the east boundary. Introducing me to the builder and foreman, Furner said: *"Meet your Clerk of Works; he will be in contact with me on a daily basis and will convey our requirements from time to time - please regard his directives as coming from the Architects!"* That was my introduction to the nature of the job to which I had been appointed and for which I was assumed to be qualified! The builder led us to the adjoining shed. The door was newly posted: "Clerk of Works". He opened it, gave me the key, nodded and took his leave.

Mr. Furner handed me a roll of drawings and the Bill of Quantities saying, *"You will want to become familiar with these - take them home if you like, and feel free to discuss them with me!"*

Outside six or seven African laborers were digging trenches. Furner remarked: *"There's no purpose in remaining here. To-morrow you'll probably be asked to test the trenches before they pour the concrete; make sure there are no loose pockets!"*

From the site, we drove to the office of Rennie & Nestead where I met Mr. Barney Nestead. He was introduced to me as: *"The Mayor of Benoni and Chairman of the Benoni Hebrew Congregation!"* He gave me a congenial welcome saying: *"We're all excited that work has started at last. We're looking forward to a fine building. It should be a great asset to Benoni!"* As we were leaving, a gentleman entered. Mr. Nestead introduced him as *"my friend, Mr. Harrison"*[49]. Furner then drove me out to Nigel - a new mining town about 25 miles east of Benoni where he wanted me to meet a new client. He said it was a small job – they were still busy on the sketch plans but that it was an opportunity to show me the site. The new client was away but we visited the site before returning to Johannesburg. On the way, Furner referred to "another potential Benoni client" and said: *"If that materializes, you will not manage it all by train; you'll have to have a car!"*

Back in the office, I was handed a hard-covered diary labeled "Benoni Synagogue!" Furner suggested that I spend the mornings in Benoni and, before leaving the office in the afternoons, I should be sure to collect any drawings or directives that may be available for the job.

That became my routine procedure over the following weeks.

My first afternoon in the office was spent examining the roll of drawings that I had been given. It consisted of some thirty plans and detail drawings! I remembered what Kallenbach had told me in Cape Town about the cantilevered galleries and my attention focused on related framework details. At home that evening, with drawings spread across my bed, I took particular note of the foundations, the trenches for which were to be the object of my inspection the next day. In the morning, I took a tram down town, called at the office and made for the new Park Station. I bought a weekly return ticket to Benoni.

The site was about an eight-minute walk from the station; lorries were loading and carting away soil. The foreman greeted me and said: "The excavations are ready, Sir!" He obviously wanted my approval! I watched bare-backed African laborers form a ringed mound of sand about 15 inches high and six feet in diameter. Alongside was a pile of 2-inch stone and a heap of brown paper pockets of cement obviously in preparation for the mixing of concrete. The foreman noticed me counting the pockets of cement! He intervened adding, "To each mound, Sir, there are five of stone; three of sand - that applies to all four mounds!" He was assuring me that mix: 5:3:1, was as specified! (Three similar groups of sand, stone and cement having been formed at different points alongside the excavations). I got down into the trenches and tramped my way along; the foreman followed behind. This was, of course, all new to me. I felt self-conscious - wondered if I was making a spectacle of myself! I thought: 'How else could I know there were no loose pockets - how else could I make it clear from the start that there was to be strict compliance with the conditions of contract?' I stepped into a hole deeper and wider than the rest of the excavations. There the foreman explained: *"I had to remove a refuse pit - it was tamped solid!"* I continued to pace through the entire length of the trenches. Stepping out of the trenches (and not wanting to show that I felt a little unsure of myself), I faced the Foreman with the comment: *"Looks good - nice job!"* He replied: "Thank you, Sir!" I stepped into my shed and made my first entry in the job diary.

That afternoon, Mr. Furner showed me two prints of a perspective drawing of the Synagogue. *"It will all be faced in two-and-a-quarter-inch semi-glazed golden-brown facing bricks - – please reject any that are chipped. The window reveals and arches are lined in light cream-colored pre-cast stone - – also the cornices and the caps to the gate piers."* It was a fine drawing! I thought: "A splendid example of contemporary architecture." and I commented to that effect! Furner responded: "Have a shot at rendering! Take these - use one to try out the colors!" He handed me both prints and with them, his paint box and brushes! I was glad of the opportunity. I had done several watercolors at art classes with Mrs. Du Toit and quite a bit of rendering under McConnell. I thought: "This is my first job in the office - it had better be good!"

Uninterrupted, I was 'at it' for the next two hours. I drew in the shadows, mixed the colors and put 'all I knew' into the rendering! I took it to Mr. Furner. He commented kindly: "That's splendid. Come with me!" He took it to Mr. Kallenbach. Shaking his head approvingly, he said to Furner "Have it framed. Nestead will want it for his Committee!" I thought: "If it was good enough to present to the client, it was OK!" I felt vindicated!

FRIENDS!

I had been in Johannesburg for more than a week and felt it was time to meet friends! I called Max Schnier whom I had met aboard the *Saxon Castle*. I last saw him two and a half years earlier when he returned the pound I had lent him in London! He sounded pleased to hear from me and asked if I could join him to a picnic the following Sunday. I accepted gladly! He called me back later and asked if there was a girl friend I'd like to bring with! I said I had not, to which, on hearing that there was no one whom I cared to ask, he responded: "Not to worry - We'll bring someone for you! - and don't worry about food; we'll have hampers - enough for all."

At about ten on Sunday morning, two cars turned up, Max driving one. He got out, gave me a warm welcome and introduced me to his 'two buddies': Felix Heyman and Bob Pollock. They were about my age - possibly a year or two older. "Why two cars?" Max explained: "We plan to go to Vereeniging - will pick-up the girls on the way!" In another part of the city I met their "old friends - Alice and Kay." Alice took my seat next to Max and Kay sat with Felix. Minutes later, I was introduced to two other girls whose names I do not remember. One jumped in with Bob, the other with me and we were off!

The drive was about 35 miles. Apart from idle chatter, conversation was minimal! I found nothing attractive about the two girls in our car! They on the other hand were by no means shy! To me, their manner seemed coarse to say the least! We hadn't traveled far when the girl next to Bob had moved - I thought - dangerously close! I heard Bob chuckle and comment quietly: "not while driving!"

STRANGE BEHAVIOR

The surrounding landscape - unlike the Cape Peninsula to which I had grown accustomed - was bleak to say the least! Relief came when the water of the Vaal River and the surrounding greenery came into view. We turned off the road, drove along a narrow track and parked under some trees. Max and Felix, obviously familiar with the area, took hampers from their car and walked us through the foliage to the riverbank. A short stroll brought us to a pleasant opening among the trees. Two blankets were spread across the grass and weighted down with stones. We all sat on our haunches. "Here," I thought, "we would chat and I would get to 'know' the company

I met for the first time that morning." That was not to be! Soon Max was up helping Alice to her feet. They wandered off and disappeared into the bushes. Minutes later, Felix and Kay followed suit. They went in another direction! Soon Bob and his girl friend were up and gone! Their purpose seemed obvious! Nothing could have been more brazen! What astonished me was the cool manner in which all six seemed to take matters for granted. I was left there with the girl who had accompanied me in the car! She was probably about twenty years of age. Her occasional comments, shallow and lacking in substance, suggested a low level of education. I felt out of my element - totally 'cold'! I wondered if she had sensed my feelings. She got up and walked around. Glances across her shoulder made it pretty obvious that she expected me to accompany her! I am no prude, but in no way could I bring myself to comply! I stretched out, shut my eyes, and lay wide awake - feeling like a duck out of water!

In due course Felix and Kay returned from their secluded retreat followed soon after by Max and Alice and then by Bob and his friend. The hampers were opened! They sat and chatted over refreshment, as though we had never parted company!

We returned to Johannesburg divided up precisely as we had come. To my companion, my behavior probably appeared strange and off-hand! On the way back, my attitude had not changed. Indeed I felt repelled!

The girls were dropped at their respective destinations and the three of us made to Phillips - a popular Greek restaurant down town. At dinner Max apologized, said he "felt sorry about that girl." He said they had never met her before - wanted a partner for me and Bob and asked his girl to bring a friend!

OTHER FRIENDS

That night I lay awake thinking about the day's excursion - so unlike our outings on Table Mountain, at Muizenberg and Oudekraal! I felt nauseated. The girl that was assigned to me and the one who had partnered Bob - were so 'different' from my friends at home! I had no desire to see them again! That prospect made me shudder!

My thoughts turned to Dina Malkin whom I had met twice in Cape Town and had found attractive and intelligent. I felt 'That was the kind of friendship I wanted!' I telephoned her the next morning. She remembered me and appeared pleased that I called and accepted my invitation to dinner in town the following Thursday!

DINNER AT THE CARLTON

We dined at the Carlton Hotel – reputed to be the best restaurant in the city. We had been there over an hour and were chatting idly over coffee when a tall gentleman appeared. He nodded! His manner appeared assertive, somewhat curt! My guest seemed undisturbed by his presence. They obviously knew each other. Uninvited, he pulled up a chair and briefly joined in the conversation. I knew the face! Suddenly I remembered I had met him before! It was at that tennis party in Cape Town - it was Dr. Penn, a young plastic surgeon now practicing in Benoni! He had not been there for more than minutes when he looked at me and in a brusque voice said: "Do you mind if I take her home!" It was more a statement than a request! Dina seemed by no means surprised by his presence or his remark. Clearly it had not occurred by chance! It had been arranged and I was not informed. I felt slighted. Staring at Dr. Penn, I replied: "Not at all, you're welcome!" I said good night and took my leave.

Dina Malkin married Dr. Jack Penn. I was invited to the wedding.

Two years went by. By then, the Carlton incident had taken on a new perspective! My sojourn in Johannesburg was drawing to a close when I decided it was time to telephone Dina Penn and wish her well! I did so. She invited me to tea. Jack, in fact, called for me and drove me to their home. I was struck by the boyish enthusiasm with which he demonstrated a device that he had recently acquired! It was a new gadget that enabled him to operate and open his garage door from the car as he approached the house!

We reminisced for an hour. Dina, then the wife of a very successful surgeon, performed most graciously. Our paths never crossed again. (Thirty years later I heard they were at their holiday home at Clifton on Sea).

BENONI

The Synagogue building continued apace and with increasing interest. My job as Clerk of Works became routine. One afternoon, Furner informed that as I would be supervising other work on the East Rand, I would need a car! The firm had decided on a new Austin 10 and one was provisionally on order. He asked me to see it immediately and if I felt it would serve my needs, they would confirm the order! I was delighted. I was aware that the office had been adversely affected by the ongoing depression. The purchase of a new car seemed to suggest that conditions had improved. That was a comforting thought!

MEMORIES REVISITED!

Weeks after my arrival in Johannesburg, my mail included a letter stamped 'Porterville'! It was from Greta! What could it mean? She had been out of my mind! She wrote that she and her mother would be in Johannesburg for a few days, that 'it would be nice' if I could meet them at Park Station and, if that was not possible, she would call me at the office! The letter gave the time of their arrival two days hence! In the past, the prospect of seeing her never failed to stir me. This time, it made absolutely no emotional impact! Indeed I was a little concerned that my routine was about to be interrupted! On the other hand, I had been a guest in their home more than once! To meet them was a courtesy I could not shun!

Waiting at the platform barrier as the train steamed in, I spotted Greta's blond head among the passengers alighting. As they approached, she stepped out ahead of her mom, dropped her bag at my feet and, with a smile - that was once magic - threw her arms around me! She must have felt my welcome was not as warm as it had once been - or perhaps she thought I was showing restraint in the presence of her mother whom I greeted with the usual courtesy! I drove them to their hotel. They were to be in the city for three nights. As my days were fully committed, I invited them to dinner that night. Mrs. Van Zyl said she was sorry she had an appointment and added: "But Girlie[50] is free!"

I called for her at seven. We went to a small restaurant off Eloff Street. It was not a happy occasion. I was uncomfortable and I guess she felt the same. I thought of asking her why she had written and why she'd come! That seemed a little blatant. Instead, I asked if she was married. She chuckled and said: "Married - heavens no!" I asked: "What happened to Kurt? I thought you were mutually pledged?" She answered simply: "I told you. I was in a spot - It was difficult…"

I took her back to her hotel, kissed her brow and said: "Travel safely!" There was an embarrassing silence. As she took my arm, I commented: "That all belongs to the past! It was fun while it lasted and I'm grateful for it. We're in different worlds now. I hope yours will be kind to you!"

That was towards the end of 1932. I never saw her again!

Years later, (circa 1948/9) I had a call from Mollie - Greta's sister. She was in town and wanted to see me 'urgently'! She came to my home and explained that Girlie was very ill - diagnosed cancer! She said the family did not want to rely on their local doctor and wondered if I could put her in touch with a reputable physician. I immediately telephoned Professor Foreman whom I knew personally. He offered to see her without delay. She made an appointment and left. I heard no more until months later when I heard that Greta had passed away. She was 36 years of age!

NEW FRIENDS

I had moved from the Berea to 'Stemler's Boarding House' in Parktown, a far pleasanter residential area. I soon learnt that Wagner, another assistant in the office, also resided there. My room was extremely small but I liked the setting. It was also near Max's home. He and I had become friendly and saw each other often. Max worked at his father's firm 'Schneier & London' – well known timber merchants. Mr. London was deceased and Max's father was the sole owner.

Frequently after office, Max and I went swimming at the Houghton Baths. His friends, Felix and Bob, often joined us there. We also met occasionally for weekend outings when I became acquainted with their friends Alice and Kay. I was a fairly frequent dinner guest at Max's beautiful home in Parktown. His mother was a charming attractive hostess. His father, very short, was not very communicative! I also remembered to telephone Jean Duthie, dined at their home in Parkview and spent a pleasant few hours chatting with her family and particularly with her father. His political leanings were staunchly 'Labor' but he made a point of telling me that he was no supporter of Communism. When Mr. Schneier's name cropped-up, I was surprised to hear that he was a strong adversary of General Smuts and had 'harbored Communists' during the Rand[51] uprising in the twenties. That, I recalled, was the occasion that Smuts called out the army to quell the riots - an act that cost him his first defeat at the polls.

I lost touch with Jean and her family - never saw them again.

Such were my social activities in the months following my arrival in Johannesburg.

THE JOHANNESBURG PUBIC SPEAKING CLUB

Max was a member of the Johannesburg Public Speaking Club. One night, I accompanied him to one of the monthly meetings. We were seated in the front row among an audience of about fifty members and their guests. At a table about 10 feet in front of us was the Speech Master and his secretary. The Speech Master welcomed the guests and described the evening's program. He said that the evening would be devoted to three-minute speeches, that he would announce the topic of each speech and would nominate the speaker by pointing to him from the chair. He explained that, in his experience, there was no better training in public speaking than for one to be called upon to deliver an impromptu speech on a topic of which he had no prior warning. He added: "Tonight I will start with one or two club members but participants will not be limited to members. Guests and members will be pointed to at random!" He pleaded with the guests to cooperate, to step forward and speak to the nominated subject for three minutes - if possible without hesitation. "In that way," he said, "you'll be contributing to what should be an interesting and enjoyable evening. HAVE FUN! - Let's start."

Pointing to a young man in the second row, he exclaimed: "The first subject is: 'Taken unawares!' The man, a member of the Club, stepped forward and said: "Mr. Chairman, like Hitler, you've attacked me entirely unprovoked!" The audience started to laugh. He went on: "Like most victims, I am unprepared for such assault! Of me, you've made an enemy. Hitler's technique was quite different. You, Sir, will have to visit Germany to learn the technique…" He could not go on. The audience was in hysterics. The speech master made notes. He then pointed to a man in the front row and exclaimed: *"Disarmament"*. The man got up, scratched his head and said: *"That, Mr. Chairman, was a great ideal – a dream designed to rid mankind of war! A gullible public, sickened by the horrors of World War I, enabled ambitious politicians to lead it to the altar, to witness a slaughter unprecedented in the history of…"* . Applause drowned the rest of his words. I pondered, thinking how appropriate his words were to what had been happening in Europe, when I saw the chairman's finger pointing at me! It was my turn! Slowly he pronounced the word: "Cosmetics". I jumped to my feet! The word 'cosmetics' was not unfamiliar to me but for the moment I was in shock! Its meaning escaped me. I was in a dilemma! 'What was I to do?' I was on my feet - had to speak! I heard myself saying: "Cosmetics is a dangerous medium - It has confounded me and my kind for ages! It confuses and leaves one dumbfounded." (I was of course talking about my own dilemma). I went on: "It is like a weapon that remains shrouded in mystery. We are lost; we need help and know not where to turn. Reluctantly we turn to women! They alone can provide the answer…" Loud, sustained clapping drowned whatever I might have said after that. The noise made it unnecessary for me to continue. I bent down and whispered to my friend: "Max - what the hell are 'cosmetics'?" He laughed! Others shook my hand. I was dumbfounded! I had been on my feet for minutes and had made an exhibition of myself - but nobody seemed to care. Other speakers followed but I could not concentrate - too embarrassed by my folly! Refreshments were served. The speech-master thanked all for their contribution to a joyful evening. He added, "I think you'll all agree – to-night's 'special award', goes to the 'Cosmetics' speaker!"

On the way home, Max commented: "Alf, that was great!" He refused to believe that the meaning of the word had eluded me. For my part, I felt appalled that a public speaker could get away with such rubbish!

IN THE OFFICE

A telegram arrived from my dad. It read: "Your friend Mr. Sonnenberg has purchased the old library site in Johannesburg for a branch of Woolworth's." I concluded that Dad had not passed on this information solely for its news value! That he sent it by wire obviously meant that he considered it more important than that! "What was I to do?" My dad's crack-of-dawn visit to the incoming mail-ship and his initiative flashed to mind! I decided to show the telegram to Kallenbach! He read it and commented: "Very interesting! …"A long silence followed. I broke in: "By the way, Sir…" But Mr. Kallenbach was not interested in what I was about to say! He rose, telegram in hand, and ushered me to the door saying: "Come back later!"

Half an hour later, Mrs. Stratham was at my door. "You're wanted … the boss!" I returned to Mr. Kallenbach's office. He handed me a sheet of paper saying: *"Tell me if you have any suggestions."* It was a Post Office telegraph form. On it was a typed message addressed to Mr. Max Sonnenberg. It read:

> *"Forgive my thus unceremoniously approaching you. I have been induced to do so by your friend Alfred Honikman, an esteemed member of our staff. He has informed me of your purchase of the library property in the heart of this city. It is a site ideally suited to a major departmental store. We congratulate you. If we can be of service, we would be honored."* (It was signed Kallenbach. Kallenbach Kennedy & Furner, Architects.)

The thought flashed to mind: "The telegram was a skillful attempt to circumvent the code of professional practice that denounced any form of canvassing." Obviously I was in no position to ventilate such thoughts! I handed back the form: "No suggestions, Sir!" Kallenbach gave the form to his secretary and instructed her to 'send it!' He turned to me: "When you gave me your father's telegram, you were saying something when I interrupted - what was it?" "Nothing important, Sir. I was about to mention that my friend Max Schneier had asked me to join him to Umhlangha Rocks for ten days over Christmas. Of course I declined and explained that I've only been here for far too short a time to consider leave." Kallenbach raised his eyebrows and beckoned me to be seated! "Is your friend not of Schneier and London?" I confirmed that he was. "You must go on that trip! - Your friend's father is probably the largest single property-owner in this city – always building! His work has never come our way. Maybe with you here, he may relent. See what you can do. Give your friend a call - tell him you have changed your mind!"

I did just that. Max was pleased and I looked forward to the break. I had heard so much about Umhlangha Rocks[52]. The idea concerning Mr. Schneier senior and his building interests, made me apprehensive! I seldom talked with the man; how could I ever broach the subject of his personal business interests! Such an opportunity was extremely remote to say the least!

CHAPTER 13

NAZI RUMBLINGS!

A neo-Nazi Greyshirt organization formed in 1933 was said to be gaining considerable support among Afrikaners in the rural areas. When a Jewish cemetery near Johannesburg was vandalized, a number of young Jewish boys formed themselves into a vigilante body and stationed groups at potential Grey Shirt targets! Waiting in watch outside a synagogue, they saw four Grey Shirts step out of a car and stealthily approach the building. One was carrying a can of gasoline, the others, logs of wood. They stopped at a side window. One was unscrewing the can cap when the vigilantes emerged from the shadows and pounced on them. The would-be arsonists abandoned their plot, ran for their car leaving behind the gasoline can and logs. Little damage was done! For a while the incident appeared to mark the end of Grey Shirt activity on the Rand!

In 1938 Afrikaners commemorating the Great Trek[53] formed themselves into the Ossewabrandwag (Oxwagon Sentinel). It was a Nazi inspired paramilitary organization aimed at inculcating a "love for fatherland" with the object of instituting (by armed force if necessary) an Afrikaner-controlled republic in South Africa. (By 1939, its membership had grown to 250,000 out of a total Afrikaner population of a little more than 1 million.)

In Germany, Nazi atrocities were unabated, violent and cruel! Protests from the capitals of the free world were numerous and persistent! A public meeting, advertised to take place in the Johannesburg City Hall, was to be addressed by the Mayor and other notables. In the office, Wagner asked me if I intended going to the meeting as Mr. Stemler had kindly offered us a lift. I wrongly assumed that they felt as outraged by the German atrocities as I did and I was glad to accept the offer of a lift.

THE GREYSHIRTS

A neo-Nazi Greyshirt movement called the 'New Order' was formed within the Nationalist Party in 1933. Public protest meetings against Nazi atrocities in Germany were followed by a formal warning by Prime Minister Hertzog telling the public "not to interfere in foreign matters of which they were not fully informed!" It was not generally known at the time that the 'New Order' was founded by Oswold Pirow, Hertzog's Minister of Justice. He remained in that position until September 1939. The 'New Order' drew widespread support among rural Afrikaners. Its fascist program was designed to 'remake' the South African society along Nazi lines. Fortunately, in the 1939 'war debate' in Parliament, Smuts prevailed. He won the support of a majority of the cabinet and of the House. He succeeded Hertzog as Prime Minister and led the nation to side with the Allies in the long struggle against the Nazi terror. Hertzog resigned. Pirow disappeared from the public scene. Hertzog died months later but not before he had joined with Dr. D.F. Malan[54] in forming the Hereenigde (Reunited) Nationalist Party (HNP). Many of its members longed for a Nazi victory! Some were responsible for disastrous covert activity at home, and a few spent time in prison. A few actually left the country to join the Nazi espionage network.

THE CITY HALL MEETING

The nearest available parking spot was some walking distance from the Hall. By the time we got there, the hall was crowded. We could find only standing room in the upper gallery! Stemmler, Wagner and I stood and listened! Speech after speech by the Mayor and other prominent citizens were unremitting in their condemnation of the Nazi atrocities. One of the speakers said something to the effect: *"Nazi Germany encourages the unspeakable Brown Shirt activities! The time has come for the civilized world to take concerted action - to completely isolate that country from every form of contact - economic, cultural, political! Anything short of that makes a mockery of these protests!"*

At that point, Wagner, who stood next to me, had become restless! He blurted: "I can't take this any longer!" He turned and made for the exit. Stemmler looked to me, shrugged and said: "We better see what he's up to!" In the street, Wagner, referring to the comments he'd just been listening to, said: "They don't know what they're doing!" He was seething! 'Did his manner simply indicate a natural resentment of criticism levied against his country?' - I wondered! Stemmler took his arm, tried to appease him and said: "Let's go and have a drink!" We walked to the German Club[55]. It was sparsely occupied. We sat in the lounge - ordered beer shandies. Wagner's anger persisted – left me in no doubt that he was a Nazi supporter! Suddenly a steward rushed through the lounge, with a hose reel under his arm; two other stewards hurriedly closed the shutters! Noise from the street grew louder! Crowds from the City Hall had gathered to pursue their protests outside the German Club! I felt as though I was entrapped inside an 'enemy camp'! The noise outside sounded aggressive! It was time for us to leave. I got up. Stemmler and Wagner followed. In the entrance hall, the large double doors, barred and bolted, bulged under pressure from the crowd yelling outside. A steward with hose reel nozzle pointed at the doors stood at the ready! Clearly we could not leave the way we had come. We found our way to the kitchen at the rear of the building - made our exit through the back door. We traversed a long service lane that exited into the street some distance from the entrance to the building! Looking back we saw the crowd! It was beginning to disperse!

The following morning the Rand Daily Mail carried news of the City Hall meeting but no reference to the protest outside the German Club! I was in my office about to leave for Benoni when Kallenbach sent for me. He asked if I had seen Wagner. He knew that we stayed at the same boarding house. I said I had not seen him since the previous night! Kallenbach remarked: "He's usually very punctual. It's after ten - there's no sign of him. Please telephone - let me know if there's something wrong!" I called Stemmler. He too hadn't seen him – said he would go to his room and call me back! He telephoned ten minutes later: *"There's no sign of him. The room is empty – his possessions gone!"* I reported to Kallenbach. He asked if Wagner was OK when I saw him the previous night. I told him what had occurred and referred to Wagner's reaction to the meeting. Kallenbach responded: "I often wondered where his sympathies lay!" Wagner was never seen again. It was rumored that he had returned to Germany - for what purpose - one could only guess!

THE NATAL COAST

It was early morning when Max called for me and together we drove down to Natal. It was about 400 miles and took the best part of a day. On the road, Max said that neither Alice nor Felix could make it but that Kay would be coming two days later. I was unaware that he had asked them. I was glad I went. It was a splendid break - especially enjoyable were the long walks along the beach in the breeze off the Indian Ocean. On a few occasions a young attorney, Hymie Epstein, accompanied me. He told me that his family lived in Springs, a town on the East Rand and that he practiced there. We got-on extremely well! A friendship developed. I had heard about the Springs mine. It had been 'in the news' and was referred as "one of the richest gold deposits on the Rand"! My friend said that he had been handling an ever-increasing number of title-deed transfers and felt sure they were a prelude to building activity. "In fact, I expect a 'building boom' in the immediate future!" When he heard that I was in architecture, he said: "Why don't you set up practice in Springs - you won't regret it!" The idea excited my interest only to be dimmed by the thought of my thesis! I wished that I had completed it! Instead I had not touched it in the three months that I had been in Johannesburg. I realized I would have to do something about it!

When Kay arrived, she joined us on our strolls along the beach. I got to know her as a bright interesting person - so different from my reaction to the girl who was chosen to partner me when we first met on our picnic trip to Vereeniging. Apparently Kay had been equally appalled! We never referred to that event again. I learnt that Kay had separated from her husband and was fending for herself as manageress of a small china shop in Eloff Street in the heart of Johannesburg.

After dinner on my last night at Umhlangha Rocks, I had joined three others at Bridge and we were playing in a quiet corner of the lounge. It was close to nine when Kay appeared, greeted us, quietly handed me a note and said "good night." I opened the note! It read: *"Room 157 - see you later!"* My heart was pounding as I put the note in my pocket! Ten minutes later we stopped playing. The bridge group dispersed. I looked for and found Room 157, tapped on the door and heard Kay's voice: "Come in, Alfred!" She was in bed!

BACK TO REALITIES!

My vacation had been a vacation full of new experiences! Mr. Schneier's property interests had not been mentioned. That, I thought, would not please Mr. Kallenbach! Uppermost in my mind, however, was my unfinished thesis! It concerned me! I was still unqualified, painfully aware that I was not in a position to grasp at practical opportunities - such as the one Hymie had suggested either on behalf of my firm or on my own behalf! 'I must do something about it!' My room was so small - not enough room for a small bedside table, let alone a drawing board. I was reluctant to move again! The months slipped by. I had been in Johannesburg for over a year before I faced the fact that unless I took concerted action, the thesis would never get done and my dream of ever practicing architecture would be aborted! The realization shook me! I scanned the 'bed and breakfast' advertisements and found a room in Hillbrow with an adjacent covered stoep almost as big as the room itself! In it was a table large enough to take a double-elephant[56] drawing board. The rent was slightly more than I had been paying at Stemlers - that was no obstacle! My salary had been increased to 30 pounds a month and when payday came, I always had a few pounds to spare! I took the room. In my new 'digs', all was set to resume my neglected thesis! Now there was no excuse! The job had to be done and I planned to give it about 18 hours a week and still have a night off and hopefully, the best part of the weekends!

Trying to prepare an 'off-duty' work schedule was difficult! My thesis entailing several different types of buildings, had inherent problems that had to be confronted and analyzed before satisfactory planned solutions were possible. I was committed to the several building types shown on the approved site layout. They included the main school building with assembly hall, science laboratories and ablutions, the residences, gymnasium, swimming pool, change rooms, sports pavilion, an inter-denominational chapel, as well as the sports fields - all interrelated and far more challenging than I had imagined! However, there was no turning back! The job had to be done! Working day and night became habitual. I tried to stick to my schedule but I often found my nights off and 'free' weekends had been trimmed - sometimes ruthlessly!

BAD NEWS, HIGH HOPES!

Soon after my return from Natal, Duncan commented: "Things are bad!" Two projects on which he and others had been working had been deferred indefinitely and another canceled and "two of our chaps are on notice"! That was depressing news and I wondered when my turn would come! When Kallenbach sent for me, I feared the worst! Then I thought 'perhaps he wants to hear if I had made any progress concerning Mr. Schneier's building ventures!' To my surprise when I confronted him, he said: "I have to thank you and congratulate you! We have been appointed architects for Woolworth's new building. You have brought us luck! How was the holiday?" I was delighted with what I had heard - particularly as Duncan's remark seemed to bring the depression right to our door! I went on to tell of the meeting with my attorney friend, his remarks about the many transfer deeds that he'd been handling and his anticipation of a building boom in Springs! Kallenbach listened intently. "I think he's right," said Kallenbach. "We should open a branch office there - and you should run it for us! How would you like that?" I tried to quell my excitement. "I'd be happy to do that, Sir!" He added: "Of course, when the time comes, your place is in Cape Town; you'll be opening our office there - in the meantime, you'll do well in Springs! Don't be impatient - it will take time." He called his secretary and asked for "Fridjohn's agreement"! He handed it to me saying: "Look it through. It should be suitable for Cape Town. Let me have any suggestions!" Klem Fridjohn was a young architect three or four years my senior whom I had met on a few occasions over the years. He ran the Durban Branch. The agreement roused my interest. It was for 3 years, provided for 25% of all fees on work handled by the Durban office to accrue to him. A clause provided for a handsome guaranteed monthly minimum. A few days later when I returned the agreement to Kallenbach, I said that it seemed adaptable to Cape Town, that I had made notes and looked forward to further discussions when the time was considered opportune. Kallenbach responded: "Keep those notes; we may need them sooner than we think!"

I telephoned Hymie Epstein, told him what had happened and asked him to look out for two small offices centrally situated.

On my first trip with the new car, I drove first to the job in Benoni and from there to Springs for a lunch appointment with Hymie. It was a nice reunion. His delight in the decision to come to Springs was most encouraging. He took me to see two offices that he had provisionally reserved for me. They were quite suitable and were situated near his own suite.

That night, in a letter home, I referred to the Woolworth's project, thanked Dad and told him how pleased we all were that his very thoughtful telegram had borne fruit – most welcome especially in the light of Duncan's remarks! Of course I wrote also about the Springs proposal and Kallenbach's reference to Cape Town. I lay awake thinking about the thesis and the importance of 'breaking that barrier'!

In his reply, Dad told how pleased he was with my news. He said that he had never met Mr. Sonnenberg personally but 'the latter had proved both his friendship and his confidence. No doubt you'll make sure it was fully justified!' The letter went on to say "potentially there is more good news!" His Hotel Assembly partner Mr. Allswang (whom I had met once or twice at home) who was also a director of Lutjes Langham Hotels Ltd. had spoken of 'possible extensive additions to their Johannesburg hotel'! Dad inquired if an architect had been appointed and was told that the idea was still under review, that the appointment of an architect had not yet arisen. Dad's response was that when the time came, he would like them to bear my firm in mind and Mr. Allswang answered that he would gladly do so.

I wrote a personal thank-you letter to Mr. Allswang, and told him a little about my firm and some of the projects for which they were responsible. About ten days later he replied saying that they were going ahead with the job and would be writing to my firm direct!

The New Year started well. There was an air of optimism in the office - so different from the preceding month. The Woolworth's building contract was signed. It was for the sum of forty-five thousand pounds[57] - then a very substantial amount!

My daily visits to Benoni continued. Work on the synagogue was on schedule I was well aware that the post 'Clerk of Works' carried with it a measure of authority which in my case, was not backed by practical experience! My past five years had been devoted almost exclusively to 'theory'! I often felt it was not enough and hesitated to assert myself unless it seemed absolutely necessary. Some minor matters might well have gone uncorrected. Fortunately, they could not have been many, as the general standard of workmanship was high - consistent with the builder's reputation!

The new car was a boon except that, after a day or two, it was tending of its own accord to pull towards the left! The condition became progressively more pronounced! There was obviously something radically wrong! I reported the matter to Furner. The car was returned to the dealer. Apparently the chassis (on which all cars were mounted in those days) had been made of steel that had not been adequately tempered! It was slowly bending toward the left causing the front wheels to follow that direction. The chassis had to be replaced. I was without the car for several days. I had no choice but to revert to the tram and train for my daily visits to the East Rand. Days later the dealer advised that another chassis was not available, that an entirely new car had been ordered and would only be available in a week's time.

AN UNTOWARD INCIDENT!

For two weeks, I had no choice but to revert to tram and train for my daily visits to the East Rand. In Eloff Street one morning, on my way to Park Station, I noticed that my fly was open! I felt it was not inconspicuous! I walked a short distance holding my brief case in front of me! I was embarrassed – felt I could not continue like that all the way to Benoni! 'What was I to do?' Suddenly I remembered I would soon be passing Kay's porcelain shop! I decided to call on her. Maybe she had a needle and cotton and would not mind lending them to me - I could do the necessary on the train in the restroom. I was soon entering the shop - my briefcase as inconspicuous as possible! Kay was alone, behind a low glass showcase; the door behind her slightly ajar. "Alfred! What a nice surprise! - Looking for a gift?" "No, Kay dear. I thought maybe I could borrow a needle and cotton - and perhaps a button?" She beckoned me to her office and placed my briefcase on her desk! Smiling broadly, she remarked: "You have a problem!" She opened the drawer of her desk, looked below my waist and exclaimed: "It's gray – Alfred, you haven't to be shy with me." She took out a reel of black cotton and some buttons, pulled up a chair, unbuttoned the rest of my fly and proceeded to sew on the missing button - as though it was nothing unusual! She stood up. "That's it!" she said tapping me on the tummy. As I made my exit, I thanked her and said that she had saved me 'a headache!' "Any time!" came her parting response!

A HAPPY SURPRISE!

Invariably on my return from Benoni, I reported to Furner. This time, I had a lot to report! In addition to information concerning the Springs offices, I had decided share the Langham news with him. I proceeded to tell him about the proposed hotel extensions and said that the firm would be receiving a letter from Lutjes Langham Hotels, Ltd. "That sounds promising!" said Mr. Furner. "We've only just signed-up for Woolworth's and now this! You've turned the depression around. Thanks to you, the office has sprung back to life - we're all very grateful. It's been a difficult time!" Furner went on to say: "We've been discussing your position; all agreed as a matter of course "that you should surely share in the fees on the work that you introduce" and he added: "on work on the East Rand where you'll be in charge of our new office." He explained that he was asked to discuss the matter with me. I was delighted and surprised particularly as I had been with the firm for less than four months! Of course, I concurred. "Well, come with me; let's tie it all up right now!" Furner led me into

Kallenbach's office. Addressing his partner, he said: "Herman - Honikman was telling me of another job that he expects will be coming our way. I took the opportunity of telling him of our discussion regarding his position here - the proposal that he should receive a quarter of the fees on the work he introduces and of course on any East Rand work that comes our way!" Kallenbach replied: "That's great. I'm glad it came from you! I was beginning to wonder if I'd been pushing this young man too much!" "Very well," said Furner, "I'll call the attorney and have him draw up the agreement." Kallenbach interrupted: "That can wait till we finalize on Cape Town. For the present, the understanding is simple enough" and he repeated: "Honikman will receive a quarter of the fees on all East Rand work and on the work he has introduced, and may yet introduce. That is clear enough - no need for an attorney at this stage!" With two fingers pointing heavenward as though to make a pledge he declared: *"If we can't trust Honikman, he's no good to us - if he can't trust us, we're no good to him! No written agreement would help!"* Furner turned to me and asked: "Honikman, does that satisfy you?" and of course, I answered: "Yes, Sir!" I was not only satisfied, I was elated!

Soon after that, the firm was commissioned to do the Langham job! It was a large project - the contract amount: eighty-five thousand pounds!

A MIXED PERSONALITY!

A busy morning on the East Rand was followed by my usual visit to head office. I recall sneezing heavily when Mr. Kallenbach appeared. "Young man," he said "you have a touch of flu? You shouldn't be around. Take the afternoon off. Go up to my home; relax there - have a sitz bath and you'll feel better. I'll see you later!"

Apart from the break at Umhlangha Rocks, I had not missed a day from work since my arrival in Johannesburg. I was glad to have the afternoon 'off'! Kallenbach was a bachelor. His home was on a hill in a rather remote spot on the outskirts of the city. There was no one at home except for an African manservant. He stood at the open front door, greeted me with a radiant smile and said: "I am Conrad! It's all ready, Sir!" Kallenbach had telephoned him and I relaxed for ten minutes in my first sitz bath! I returned to the front stoep. Conrad brought me refreshment and made sure that I was comfortable.

MAHATMA GANDHI

Conrad also handed me a batch of many letters: "Master says you may enjoy reading these. They are all personal letters from India - from his friend Mahatma Gandhi." All were addressed: "My dear Lower House". I read several of them by the time Kallenbach returned home. They were all personal - much of their contents beyond my comprehension! I thought it strange, however, that the letters were addressed in terms that I thought referred exclusively to one of the two houses of parliament. Kallenbach explained that for several years, he and Gandhi had lived together on a farm in the Northern Transvaal. They named the farm "Tolstoy" and ran it successfully in terms of an understanding by which Kallenbach was referred to as the "Lower House" and was responsible for all matters material; Gandhi was described as the "Upper House" and was responsible for "all matters of conscience". For a long while after Gandhi's return to India, they corresponded – never failing to address each other in those celebrated terms.

We had a light supper together. It consisted of beetroot soup, mealie[58] and fresh fruit. Kallenbach explained that he and Gandhi were strict vegetarians and that it was part of their faith not to partake of any flesh! I asked if he was a Buddhist. He replied: "Much of the philosophy is to be admired - however I do not subscribe to any formal religion!" He added that he was at his best in the early morning – 'usually rose before the sun' and to make that possible he 'shunned night-life' - 'invariably turned in early!' That seemed to be a signal for my departure! I thanked him for an 'interesting thought-provoking few hours' and took my leave.

It was about nine when I got to my room. My sneezing had stopped completely. I seemed free of 'cold' and wondered if that was attributable to the sitz bath! I turned-in early and lay awake recalling the events of a promising, unusually interesting day. I thought of Kallenbach and Gandhi - 'their correspondence - both vegetarians - philosophers - idealists!' I recalled also Kallenbach's references to Mr. Schneier, his telegram to Mr. Sonnenberg, his reaction to my East Rand comments when I returned from Natal – 'all so shrewd – inconsistent - complex!' I fell asleep – my thoughts conflicting and confused!

In later years I became aware that way back in the thirties I had a remote glimpse of the character of a man who was to change the world - that Ghandi's journey to his fatherland was probably motivated by an innate idealism that was to impact the entire world. I had yet to learn that *"passive resistance"* could be more than a match for *imperialism,* that the destiny of mankind was not dependent solely on the sword! I believe it was that kind of thinking that characterized the sequence of developments in South Africa after the bloodless revolution of 1994. In 1996, the United States of America paid tribute to the memory of Mahatma Gandhi with the erection of a monument to his memory in Union Square Park in the heart of New York.

I LEARN A LESSON!

My daily visits to the East Rand continued. The synagogue was taking shape. The light buff pre-cast stone lining to the window reveals and parabolic arches at the main entrance looked particularly neat. They provided a delicate relief to the semi-glazed golden-brown bricks that faced the rest of the building. All looked particularly attractive! I was up on a narrow scaffold above the arches watching the face-bricks being laid to the rest of the entrance tower. I observed a badly chipped cut brick that had just been laid. Anxious that the work would not be marred by faulty brickwork, I asserted my authority. "That," I thought "cannot be permitted!" I removed the brick and took the bricklayer's trowel to demonstrate just how (I thought) a face-brick should be cut! The brick was harder and heavier than I imagined. To cut it clean would require considerable force, so I reckoned! I raised the trowel above my shoulder and brought it swiftly down - a little too swiftly! I lost my balance, dropped the brick and was on the verge of falling when the bricklayer grabbed me, pulled me back and stopped what might have been a disaster! The drop was about 20 feet! A very embarrassed Clerk of Works thanked him profusely. I felt an awful fool! It was I, not he, who had learnt a lesson! Never again did I dare assert myself on a matter for which I was untrained and totally unskilled!

CHAPTER 14

FAMILY MARGO

A letter from my brother Maurice told of a SACS Old Boys dance where he had met a charming Johannesburg girl whom he thought I would like to know. Her name was Deena Margo! He had told her that I had left home and was on my own in Johannesburg! She in turn promised to contact me when she returned. Later, I had a call from her brother Lionel Margo saying that his sister had been in Cape Town, had met my brother Maurice at a dance and had promised to contact me. He said he'd like to meet me and kindly invited me to 'dinner at home'! The following Friday, I made my first visit to "Berloga," the Margo home at 9 Elm Street, Houghton. I met them all: Deena (referred to by the family as 'Dickie'), Lionel (Acko), Max, Cecil (Ces), Harold (Hal), Golda and their parents Saul and Manja! My first thought: 'six kids - like my own family – except that there are four boys and two girls!'(We were 3 & 3.) Phyllis Herzfeld, a friend of Max, joined us and we dined on the spacious veranda that extended for the full width of the house. After dinner I sat in the lounge with Lionel, Deena, Golda and their parents. The others had dates to keep. We chatted. I learnt that Margo senior was a practicing architect, Lionel, a structural engineer, Max, a medical graduate, Cecil, a graduate lawyer and barrister-to-be, and Harold, a student of architecture. I learnt also that Deena had been selected as pianist to Leotine Sagan's visiting theatrical company and was participating in a play, "Madchen in Uniform"[59], that was being produced in Johannesburg at that time. The evening went by quickly and pleasantly. I was delighted when I was asked to join Lionel and Deena at tennis on 'Sunday a week'. I looked forward to that - not unaware that it would encroach on my 'thesis time'. Saying 'good night', Mrs. Margo said very kindly: "Come whenever you like - make yourself at home!"

A day or two later I telephoned Deena. We went to a show together. On the way home we spoke about our respective interests. I recall telling her how much I missed Table Mountain and adding 'that it was just as well, as my would-be free time was now committed to my thesis!' She replied: "Surely you're not 'at it' all the time - you need some respite and, by the way, Mother meant it when she said you should make yourself at home!"

Working at the thesis at night and on weekends became a routine. I missed out only if something really worthwhile cropped-up. I enjoyed the Sunday tennis at "Berloga" and found the company happy and congenial. I stayed on for supper, my conscience clear, having worked at my thesis till past mid-night the day before!

DEEP CONCERN!

A day or two later, I called Deena again. Her mother answered. There was no greeting! She was unusually brief: "I'll call her," she said and put down the receiver! 'Something was wrong!' It was a while before Deena came to the telephone. She said: "I can't talk now - Acko's in hospital!" She was crying! I drove over immediately and met Cecil on entering. Deeply distressed he explained: *"Acko had an accident on his motor bike - badly hurt! I'm taking Dad to the hospital."* I asked if I could help - or should I leave? He shook his head and murmured: "Try to console Dickie!" In the hall, Mrs. Margo, deeply distressed, showed me to the study and left. It was a while before Deena appeared. She gazed at me through sodden eyes. Slowly she shook her head and uttered: "Poor chap, he's in such pain - thank you for coming!" She was struggling to hold back the tears. I took her arm and said: "I am so sorry! Come, let us walk!" We went out into the garden. The telephone rang. Deena ran inside. Her mother had answered the call. She put down the telephone and said to Deena: *"Dad says 'he's unconscious'; the doctor said 'he's struggling' - it will take time!"* Again I took Deena's arm. We returned to the garden.

Round and round we walked. Neither spoke! I remember breaking the silence: "Deena, this is no time for gloom! He's asleep and fighting! We have to fight with him and think for him! If we do that positively - he will win through! There is not time for doubt!"

Lionel awoke two days later. The doctors were optimistic. More days went by before the crisis passed! Finally Lionel was brought home, his face heavily scarred. He used a crutch until his leg healed. From then on, his recovery was rapid! Despair had lifted and "Berloga" quickly resumed its joyful spirit.

During that worrying period, my return to "Berloga" each day immediately after work seemed to occur as a normal, natural sequence of events. Everyone in the house was under great stress. Even Phineas, the young African male servant, so much part of the family was in a state of sorrow - his ever-radiant smile was gone!

Deena's attachment to Lionel was deeply moving. I found myself sharing her emotions and the ordeal that she and her family were suffering!

I was in love with Deena!

I told her about my thesis. She sensed its importance, and understood that it would take many months to complete and would consume much of the time that I would otherwise want to be with her. To that end, she helped me plan my 'free time' and together we prepared a schedule allocating five nights a week and a weekend (morning or afternoon) to thesis! That left two nights and half a day every week that was totally uncommitted! 'That time,' I thought, 'would be exclusively Deena's!'

Deena and I became engaged. Both our families were delighted. Deena was the first in her family to take that step. My eldest brother Ephraim was already married and Maurice was engaged to Lily Jowell and it seemed likely that Max and Phyllis would soon follow suit. More and more my thoughts turned to 'future plans' and obligations - but everything served only to emphasize the urgency of my thesis objective!

Dinner at "Berloga" was a frequent Friday night event. Once or twice a week I met Max, Felix and Bob for a swim immediately after office. With very few exceptions, I stuck religiously to the planned schedule.

MOTHER-IN-LAW: TO BE!

On my way to work one morning, I called at "Berloga". I had arranged to take Deena to an appointment in town. On entering the house, I met her mother in the hall, greeted her and said I'd come for Deena. She responded: "I want to talk to you!" She ushered me into the lounge, closed the door in a manner that seemed unduly stern! Obviously she sought privacy! "Young man" - her manner seemed aggressive - "What are your plans? How long is this going on!" It was clearly a rhetorical question! I asked: "How long is what going on?" Angrily, she replied: "What are you doing about Dickie?" I replied quietly: "We intend to get married one day, when my...." There was fire in her eyes! She interjected: "What do you mean 'one day'!" I wanted to say '.... when my thesis was completed and we were in a position to plan our future'. Mrs. Margo - anxious for her daughter's well-being was seething and in no mood for a quiet amicable discussion! It was getting late for office! I thought I had better leave and looked to the door! She turned, stood, arms spread, her back against the door as though to bar my way. 'What was I to do?' I had no desire to force my way past her. I turned towards the window and eyed the couch below! There seemed my only option! I pounced onto the seat, then onto the sill and out through the open window!

I sat in the car for several minutes hoping that Deena would appear! I thought of returning to the house, but to risk another confrontation seemed unwise. I drove off alone! From the office, I called the house. Phineas answered. Cheerful as ever, he said: "Miss Dickie not at home!"

Back at "Berloga" that evening, everyone including Mrs. Margo was in good spirit as though nothing had occurred! Phineas's characteristically happy smile reflected the family mood. The morning incident was never referred to again!

FEELING GREAT!

My job became increasingly interesting. As the building developed, I learnt the importance of architectural detail as was reflected in the drawings that lined the walls of my job office. Of particular interest was the original form of the parabolic arches in the face-brickwork at the main entrance to the building and the manner in which they were lined with pre-cast stone. The stonework had been detailed with the narrow end projecting forward of the adjoining brickwork thereby articulating the attractive arches with a sharp thin delicate 'white' line. The stonework served also to conceal the rough edge of the cut bricks. Similar treatment was used to line the deep reveals framing the windows to the main hall. The upper and lower windows were conjoined to produce an element of verticality that relieved what might otherwise have appeared too massive a building. The observation recurred repeatedly during the course of my work as Clerk of Works. For me, it served to emphasize of the importance of *detail* to the success of an architectural design and proved to be an important factor in my architectural education. It was an invaluable asset that served me well throughout my architectural career. The Synagogue, completed in just under a year, was widely admired. It was considered an architectural asset to the city of Benoni.

FAMILY!

During my daily visits to Benoni, I often called on my cousin Beattie. She, her husband Philip Kahn and son Morris lived within walking distance of the site on which I worked. Philip had a bicycle shop in the town and was rarely home when I called. Jeanette was born a few days after I commenced working in Benoni. The baby seemed to consume Beattie's attention - a situation to which Morris was not immediately attuned. He seemed always pleased when I appeared and I enjoyed being with him. (Four years later, after I had returned to Cape Town, Deena and I were surprised and delighted that he, his parents and grand-parents had come to Cape Town for our wedding.)

During 1934, the working drawings for both the Woolworth's and Langham Hotel projects were under way. They, and a few new projects in Springs, Nigel and Benoni, small as they were, kept the firm busy! In addition to my customary architectural duties, I was required from time to time, to prepare Statements of Estimated Cost, Revenue & Expenditure of proposed new apartment buildings. That was an important and realistic aspect of my work that was not ever touched upon during my five years at college. It was an invaluable experience.

When I was asked to defer my annual leave, I was not disappointed! On the contrary, I was elated because the request was accompanied by an explanation that it was in part due to the success of the East Rand office and to the work that I had introduced! Particularly pleasing to me was the fact that two assistants who were on notice had their notices lifted! Not least gratifying, of course, was the awareness that considerable benefits were accruing to me in terms of my agreement! I was glad that I could let them accumulate! My monthly salary was more than sufficient to meet my daily needs.

MR. KENNEDY

My contacts with Mr. Kennedy, the third principal of the firm, were infrequent! It was early in 1935, on my return from the East Rand that he asked me to join him to lunch. It was at a small restaurant on the first floor of Sacke's Building. He spoke of the "dire effects of the prolonged depression" and remarked: "We were lucky last year - thanks to you - to add the Woolworth's and Langham projects to our work load and now it seems that the East Rand work is ongoing!" I found the remark very pleasing! It was an acknowledgment from the third principal that my contribution to the firm's interests was not unimportant!

WEDDING BELLS!

Early in 1935 I received a letter from my brother Maurice telling me that he and Lily had decided on November 25 as their wedding date. They were to be married in Cape Town and they expected me to be present. They had invited Deena to be one of Lily's bridesmaids! A thought of our own marriage flashed to mind! Quickly I put it aside. 'My thesis hurdle had to be surmounted first!'

There was a gap in Maurice's letter! It suggested an interruption. The letter continued: "*I'm sorry to tell you, Grandma passed away during the night! Mother went to her room this morning; found her on her back smiling - but not breathing*"! I thought 'how characteristic of her. She was in her hundredth year. For us, her grandchildren, she was always smiling; she would not have left us otherwise!'

I wanted to be home. In a call to my mother she urged me not to come –"not until the wedding!"

Apart from the five days in Natal over Christmas 1932, I had taken no leave in all the time I had been in Johannesburg. More than five weeks leave had accumulated and I decided that October/November would be a good time to take it! I put the idea to Mr. Furner. His comment was: "Absolutely - it's about time. You've been here over three years without leave – far too long!" He suggested that I start my leave at the end of September and added: "In that case, we'll expect you back mid-November!" Furner asked me to make sure that Mrs. Stratham had a note of the exact dates. I informed her immediately!

I planned to submit the thesis to the University during October. That, I thought, would be an appropriate time to look for a suitable investment for the funds that were accumulating in terms of my agreement with the firm. It occurred to me: "There must be quite a nest egg by now!" Based on the value of the relevant contracts, I reckoned the amount due to me would be in excess of three thousand pounds[60]. For me, that was a substantial sum! I thought of the flats that my dad had built behind the Volks Hospital! I reckoned that with suitable loan facilities, I would be in a position to contemplate a property investment of about ten or twelve thousand pounds! That, I felt, was the kind of financial security I needed - something additional to my profession, the success of which seemed to be so much dependant on factors beyond my control - such as the general economy! It was the kind of security that I felt was missing at the time I ventured to ask Deena to share her life with me! It was that (in addition to my uncompleted thesis) which stood in the way of fixing a date for our marriage!

The time had come to implement the agreement - to realize the fruits that had accumulated thus far! I would put the matter to Mr. Kallenbach without delay!

CHAPTER 15

THE GREAT DENIAL!

First thing next morning I interviewed Kallenbach. I told him my plans for Cape Town, and said I would like to draw on the agreement. I reminded him that I was engaged to be married and explained my intentions while in Cape Town. He stared at me, shook his head and said: "What agreement are you referring to? I don't know of any!" I could not believe my ears! Briefly I outlined the terms as initiated by Mr. Furner and reiterated by him - particularly those that entitled me to a quarter of the fees on the work I'd introduced. At that point, Kallenbach interjected: *"And what work have you introduced, young man?"* My blood was boiling! I kept my calm and said: "You can't have forgotten: Woolworth's, Langham..." He shook his head and said: "Woolworth's! - I've known Mr. Sonnenberg for a long time!" That was the last straw! I resisted swearing at him - remembered the telegram that he drafted and, with all the calm I could muster, replied: *"This, Sir, is incredible! The idea of an 'agreement' had not come from me but from Mr. Furner and you, Sir, confirmed it! Please look at the file."* Kallenbach pressed the bell. Mrs. Stratham appeared. He asked her to call Mr. Furner and, turning to me, he said: "And, Honikman, you mentioned a 'file'?" I turned to the secretary: "Yes, please – Woolworth's!" She returned within minutes: "Mr. Furner's in consultation; he will be here presently." She handed me a bulky file. It started with letters to the contractor. The telegram to Mr. Sonnenberg was not there! I stepped into the general office and asked if there was an earlier file. Mrs. Strathan asked: *"Do you want the preliminary file?"* "Yes, please!" At that moment Mr. Furner passed by. I followed. Kallenbach addressed him: "Honikman wants to draw on 'some agreement' that he's been dreaming about. Do you know anything about it?" Mrs. Stratham entered and handed me a smaller file. Furner looked flabbergasted and puzzled! He replied hesitantly: *"I do not remember - either negatively or positively!"* I was dumb-founded! I realized that Kallenbach was the senior partner and had a forceful personality but could not believe that he held such sway as to obscure the integrity of his partner! I was seething - had difficulty in controlling my anger! I rose and stepped out of the office! I was trembling! In my office, I put the file down. My impulse was to walk out of the office, never to return! Mr. Furner appeared at the door: *"Honikman"*, he said, *"Please don't do anything hasty! I was taken by surprise; my thoughts were elsewhere. Of course we discussed an agreement - for the moment I could not recall how it all ended! We will sort things out. Please be patient!"* His comment did little to allay my disgust! I knew Kallenbach was shrewd but never expected him 'to stoop so low' - 'No way could he have forgotten'! His posture when Furner suggested the agreement, with 'fingers pointing to high heaven', loomed large in my memory! By his references to 'mutual trust' he had skillfully dismissed the idea of formalizing the agreement! I thought: 'Was that a mere ruse to provide scope for a subsequent denial? Had he deliberately pulled the wool over my eyes?' I could find no plausible explanation for his behavior. I knew then that I could not work for or with such a man! The references from time to time by both partners that I should one day represent the firm in Cape Town - an idea that once appealed to me - had become meaningless! Furner, I always thought, was open and honest! Now I questioned my own judgment! 'Was his independence so dominated - his integrity dimmed, by the overbearing personality of his senior partner! Had he really been caught off guard?' Such thoughts persisted!

I opened the small Woolworth's file. There, sure enough, was the typewritten draft of Kallenbach's original telegram telling Mr. Sonnenberg that I had 'induced' him to send it! I immediately took it into Kallenbach's office and showed it to him. His response was that he had 'known Sonnenberg for a long time'! That seemed nothing less than an unscrupulous attempt to hide the truth! I returned the file to Mrs. Stratham and asked her to make three copies of the telegram, one for me and one each for Kallenbach and Furner.

DAD'S COUNSEL

The following day, my dad was due in Johannesburg on a brief business visit. I decided to take no action until I had discussed the matter with him. 'His counsel would be wise and worth waiting for!' Early next morning I was at Park Station, waiting at the platform barrier as the train steamed in. I watched the passengers alight. I had not seen my dad for three years! Suddenly, I spotted him through the crowd! The guard kindly let me through. Excitedly, I ran forward. As I approached, Dad looked towards me and exclaimed: "Phonsque"! In an instant, we were locked in a warm gentle hug. Dad looked tired. I took his suitcase. Walking to the car, his first comment was: "How is Deena?" I said she was fine and "waiting to meet you and they expect you for dinner tonight!"

In his hotel room, Dad and I chatted briefly about the folk at home. Dad explained that he was on a tight schedule with morning, afternoon and dinner appointments and was leaving for home the following evening. He asked if he could meet Deena after office and if I could join him for lunch.

That lunch hour was the opportunity to share my concerns with him. I had previously written about Kallenbach's telegram to Sonnenberg and about the contracts to which my agreement referred. I described what had transpired the previous day and said: "In the light of Kallenbach's comments when the agreement was concluded, I found it impossible to believe that he knew nothing about it!" I spoke of my surprise and disgust, said that "I could not work with such people" - that it was only because of his impending visit that I resisted the impulse to walk out and not go back!

"You will have to see what comes of Mr. Furner's comment - but I am glad you did not walk out! You are employed on a monthly basis. It's bad enough that they appear to have broken their word - don't you break yours! If you have to leave, give them the notice that is due! Do not put yourself in the wrong!"

Dad was shocked at what he had heard! I felt relieved and knew that his advice was the course I would follow! I also knew that my association with the firm was coming to an end!

After office, I drove Dad to "Berloga" where he met most of the family. He was clearly enchanted by Deena! He thanked Manja for the dinner invitation, explained that his prior engagement was in fact a 'dinner meeting' and was the principle reason for his visit to Johannesburg.

I took Dad to his appointment and called for him again the next morning in time for his 9 o'clock departure. At the station well ahead of time, we strolled leisurely up and down the platform.

HIS COUNSEL

There was a moment's silence. Then, before boarding the train, Dad uttered: *"If there is any kindness that I can do for any man, let me do it now. I shall not come this way again!"* It worried me! Dad seldom gave vent to his emotions! This time as the train moved away, he was wiping his eyes. He could not hold back. Something was amiss! I was disturbed and restless!

Back home a while later, I referred to the incident and asked Mother if she could explain the relevance of the quotation. She replied: *"Your father has a heart problem! He feels it could strike at any moment! He was reluctant to go to Johannesburg - worried about the altitude! He missed you a great deal when you were away! He has never been very effusive - probably felt urged to do something for you - and did not know how to tell you!"*

STRAINED ATMOSPHERE

For a few days, my routine visits to the East Rand continued. Inspections and client interviews went on as before except that my interest in the work had dimmed! My heart was no longer in the job! I related my story to my friend Hymie Epstein, told him that my confidence in the firm had been shaken and that I was about to terminate my services. He asked if I would consider setting-up my own practice in Springs. I said that the inducements were great, but that my goal was to practice in Cape Town. I would keep him informed. I shared his wish that the friendship continue - that 'we would not let distance intrude!'

My daily visits to the office were routine and far from comfortable! The atmosphere was strained. For several days I never saw Kallenbach! He may have been away for all I knew! I reported to Furner every day as before expecting to hear from him how they had *'worked things out'*. He never again referred to the issue. It was mid-September when I announced to him that I intended to take five weeks leave from the end of the month! Even that failed to provoke any reference to the impasse! All he said was: "I don't remember your ever taking leave. When last was it?" I said it was "not since Christmas 1932 when Mr. Kallenbach 'insisted' that I go!" I added: "You may remember he thought it may lead to a potential client!" Furner chuckled and said: *"That was hardly a holiday! You deserve a break!"*

The "agreement" was never again mentioned!

I had been with the firm for three years and a month! When I entered the office at the end of September, I planned to confront Furner and formally tender a month's notice. Neither he nor Kallenbach was present. The monthly checks were usually issued a day or two before the end of the month. I had not received mine! As I was to be away for all of October, I was due to receive a salary check covering both September plus a month's accumulated leave! I asked Mrs. Stratham if she had my check! She replied: "You'd better see Mr. Kennedy!" I went to his office immediately, told him that it was my last day before leave and that I had not yet received my check! He commented: "Sorry about that; I'll look into it!" I reminded him that I would be away for all of October, that 'the agreement apart, the check should include at least two months salary'. He asked me to explain! I said that the October check should account for most of my accumulated leave, that I had been with the firm for just over 3 years and had been asked each year to defer my leave! I reminded him that in all that time, I had only 5 days off, and that was in 1932 when Mr. Kallenbach 'insisted' that I join Mr. Schneier on the Natal Coast over Christmas. I went on to say: "To-day I intended to submit the usual month's notice to Mr. Furner. Neither he nor Kallenbach is here. I have therefore to impose this on you! I assume, Sir, you are aware of what transpired about my agreement. In the circumstances, Sir, I will not be back. Your partners are not here. I have no choice but to inform you, Sir that my services with the firm will formally terminate on October 31 – that I will not be back!" Kennedy got off his stool. "What is this - I know nothing about it! Do the others know?" He was referring to his partners. I answered: "Sir, they may have guessed by now! I am sorry to spring this on you - I have no choice! The East Rand files are on my desk with explanatory notes attached; if there are questions, Mrs Stratham has my address." I added: "Please have my check forwarded!" We shook hands and I thanked him for past courtesies.

After office that afternoon, I joined Max and Felix at the Houghton Baths. I felt a sense of relief. I had taken a decisive step but it gave little satisfaction! Since Mr. Furner's remark *"We'll sort things out"*, I had not heard another word about the agreement. Apparently they had decided to do nothing about it! The next step was up to me!

Back in my room I started to pack my belongings. The thesis was well advanced but not quite finished! Some of the drawings had to be rendered and the Report reviewed, edited and typed. That, I felt sure, could all be done in a matter of days and I planned to tackle it immediately after my return home.

I explained the position to Deena but avoided much of the detail concerning the disputed agreement. I felt it too distasteful a subject to burden her with! However, I told her that I had terminated my services with the firm and intended to complete the thesis in Cape Town and hoped to submit it within of days of my arrival. Thereafter, if all went well, I saw no reason why I should not set up practice in Cape Town immediately! That was a goal I once dreamed of! Now it seemed to be a tangible objective!

Within a week of my arrival, my thesis was completed and submitted to the University. There I was informed that jurisdiction concerning acceptance and approval vested in the University and I would be advised 'very soon'! Thereafter the thesis would be forwarded to the Royal Institute.

The following Sunday morning, Mr. Hirchsohn, an old family friend who lived nearby, was visiting my dad. When he heard that I was likely to commence practice in Cape Town, he turned to me said: "Alfred, we will have to have a talk! Our building in Muizenberg needs to be transformed and modernized." I replied: "Any time, Sir - I'll give it all I know!" And I wondered 'Could this be my first job in Cape Town?'

Word came from the University that the thesis had been accepted, that it had been forwarded to London and that I would be hearing from the R. I. B. A.[61] direct. Wasting no time, I registered as a member of the SAIA[62], a necessary prerequisite to practice. I hired two offices on the second floor of Dominion House - not far from my father's headquarters and proceeded to inform relatives and a few friends of my plans. I decided to approach my old friend Terence Orpen to ascertain if he would care to join me. I hadn't seen him since we worked together for the late Leonard McConnell. I called him! Before I could tell what was on my mind, he spoke of the excellent job he had landed in the Architectural Branch of the City Engineer's Department. He wished me luck in my new venture. We arranged to meet.

In a letter to Deena, I gave her all my news! We agreed to February 4, 1936, as the date for our wedding and that Cape Town would be the most appropriate venue as it would obviate having to leave a young practice so soon after it started. Mother also wrote to Deena inviting her to stay at "Longwood" for a while ahead of Maurice and Lily's wedding and suggested that she might care to remain on until our own wedding in February as that would avoid 'tiresome train journeys to and from Johannesburg'.

CHAPTER 16

MY PRACTICE

Eight years had elapsed since I chose architecture as my career. The large teak drawing table that Dad had made for me and placed in his study for my use as a student had been left unused for the past three years that I was in Johannesburg. Now, it was of greater importance! I had it moved, with all the instruments and equipment collected over the years, to my new offices in Dominion House. For several days, I was there arranging and rearranging furniture, doing thumb-nail sketches of imaginary houses, wondering if all architects started practice that way - idling away time, waiting for their first client! In those days it was deemed grossly improper for a professional man to 'advertise' or to make any public announcement to indicate that he had commenced practice! *'How else was the public to know?'* That thought crossed my mind when a gentleman appeared and said that he had been directed to call, that he was the secretary of a company that owned a pair of semi-detached cottages on the Main Road Rondebosch; a wooden railing to one of the stoeps had collapsed. The property belonged to Cape Peninsula Holdings (Pty) Ltd., a company in which (he said) my father had an interest. They wished me to inspect and suggest what might be done. 'Was this my first appointment?' I wondered. On inspection I noted that much of the timber had rotted. The railing was beyond repair. I reported back suggesting that the only long-lasting solution would be to remove it completely and replace it with a brick wall 2 foot six inches high. The Secretary called back to say that they wished me to submit a plan for consideration!

That was indeed my first commission as a practicing architect!

The wall was 12 ft. long and 2 ft. 6 inches high. It abutted an existing cross wall at one end - free standing at the other. I have little doubt it was the smallest commission ever undertaken by an architect! I gave it 'all I knew'! I prepared a drawing to a scale of 1 inch to the foot - large enough to ensure that the clients clearly understood what it was that I was proposing. The drawing showed the wall rounded at the open end, with a 4-inch square red encaustic tile skirting on both sides and a similar 12-inch wide capping. In addition to the elevation and cross-section, the drawing showed details of the planned layout of the tiled capping and a full-size detail of a plaster molding beneath the tiled overhang. At the bottom right-hand corner I attached (for the first time) my stamp! It showed my name and address, the job and drawing number and 'scale'. I had a print made, rendered it in color and submitted it to client under cover of a letter!

In due course, I was instructed to obtain two quotations. The wall was built for the contract sum of fifty-eight pounds[63]. The fee for my services was the handsome sum of 5 guineas[64]. I had made a start!

A TRUE FRIEND!

A day or two passed when my friend Terence Orpen and I lunched together. We chatted about old times. He told me that before I decided to go to Johannesburg, he had been 'toying with the idea of our practicing together!' My departure put an end to that idea and he finally chose 'the security of a good safe job!' He said the purpose of his call was to ascertain if I would accept two assignments that he had been offered! One, he said, was very small - additions to a house in Plumstead for Mr. Thomas, a school principal; (He did not know that the only one I had was much smaller!) the other, a new house in Pinelands for his friends Mr. and Mrs. Dawson. He explained they were both old friends, that he had done some sketches for both parties on an 'honorary basis' and had been asked to carry on with the work on a professional basis. He added that in terms of his City Hall contract, he was not permitted to undertake private work, that he had suggested my name to both parties and they both asked him to approach me and that they both agreed that the standard fees should apply. Terence added: "Dawson, however, asked (and I agreed) that I continue to take an interest and, if necessary, to act as an occasional go-between." I thanked Terence, said I'd be happy to take on the jobs on the understanding that he would share in the fees. His answer was that he was precluded from any such arrangement - "that aspect," he said, "I'd prefer not to discuss - it's entirely for your discretion." He gave me the addresses and asked me to write to both parties accepting the appointments and confirming the fees. His was the gesture of a true friend. I thanked him profusely and added: "Terence, I can tell you now, that when I called you on my return from Johannesburg, it was to discuss the possibility of our practicing in partnership - but before I could get to the point, you told me of your excellent City Hall appointment. I was of course happy for you, but your decision put a damper on my idea." He answered: "Interesting coincidence, Pal - it could still happen - one day!"

ON THE DOMESTIC FRONT

At "Longwood" little had changed in the three years that I had been away. My siblings, now that much older, were seldom around. My eldest brother was married. He and his wife Gertie were living in Sea Point. Sybil, aged 31, an 'avowed spinster', was a teacher of botany at the Observatory Girls High School and was seldom home. Beatrice was in London - a Lecturer in Phonetics at the School of Oriental Studies. Her friend, Professor Uldall, who was once a fairly frequent visitor to "Longwood", had returned to Denmark. My youngest sister Rita had completed an Art and Photographic course and was busy preparing a professional studio that she had recently opened in the city. Maurice and I shared the same room as we had done as boys. Now he was employed as a full-time accountant in Dad's office and of course spent most of his free time with Lily, his bride-to-be. During the weeks preceding their wedding, "Longwood" was agog with visiting families of both bride and groom, among them Lily's widowed mother and her brothers Jack, Abe and Dave.

DEENA ARRIVES IN CAPE TOWN

For me, of course, the highlight was Deena's arrival in Cape Town a few days before the wedding. My dad and Maurice had already met her. The rest of the family, especially Mother, was enchanted by her. Mother had prepared Ephraim's old room for her and as she entered, she was confronted with a bouquet of roses. A card was attached. It read: "*Dear Deena - Welcome home from home - Hetty.*"

Deena was very touched by the warmth of Mother's welcome. She explained that she felt duty bound to return home for the two months preceding our wedding and would be back towards the end of January.

At Maurice and Lily's wedding, Deena looked radiant as she did at the "Longwood" reception that followed. Over the next few days, we finalized plans for our wedding.

PRACTICE PROGRESS

I met Mr. Thomas and the Dawsons, completed their working drawings and submitted copies to the City Council for approval. I also received instructions regarding the Muizenberg property that Mr. Hirchsohn had referred to! It presented quite a challenge! Situated in a commercial area on the West (mountain) side of the Main Road, it was directly opposite the railway station - a four-story structure: 3 shops (one unoccupied) at ground level with a fourth floor attic. The upper floors were occupied by a small residential hotel known as "Hillcote", to which the entrance was from another road about eighty feet back from the Main Road and at a level some 15 feet higher. My instructions (in a letter from the owners) were to suggest ways and means of modernizing the entire building and, if possible, to provide for direct ground floor access to the hotel! Balconies to both upper floors extended over the wide Main Road footpath and covered the entire fifty-foot frontage. The balconies were supported on cast iron columns resting on the footpath. The letter stated that the hotel would be vacated at the end of March, and that, if possible, building operations should be completed by the end of November in time for the forthcoming holiday season.

Obviously 'time' was of the essence! My task started with an inspection of the building (for which I took a train to Muizenberg!). The suggested Main Road entrance to the hotel was clearly a practical idea and would occur directly opposite the railway station. Stair access would necessitate cutting through the second floor concrete slab and would consume some six feet of the adjoining shop. Additional bathrooms to the hotel were clearly needed and the entire building required refurbishing and redecoration. Other structural alterations, however, were of a minor nature. Externally, the Main Road façade called for radical change! Apart from the gable ends at the fourth floor level, the cast iron railings and columns covered the entire Main Road elevation. It was characteristic of many commercial buildings of that era. Such cast-ironwork was widely used throughout the British Empire. It provided a lucrative outlet for the Birmingham foundries! To my eye, it was architecturally distasteful - incompatible with my idea of contemporary architecture! I concluded that the client's wishes (and my ideas) could be satisfied only if the old front was removed completely and replaced by a new concrete structure - one that would give the building an entirely 'new and modern' appearance. A search through the records of the Municipal Building Survey Branch produced the old building plans. I purchased a copy and, within days of receiving instructions, I furnished the client with comprehensive sketch plans, estimates and a report. Within days, I received instructions to proceed.

That was in January 1936. It was at that time that I received a letter from the Royal Institute of British Architects advising that my thesis had been accepted, my formal admission as an Associate approved and would take place at the June graduation ceremony. I was to advise them if I would be in attendance.

THE MOTOR CAR

Apart from week-ends when Maurice or I would take the family driving, my parents had little use for the car. After Maurice's marriage, I was the only driver in the family available for that duty - which I enjoyed. When required, Dad very kindly put the Vauxhall at my disposal. While I had been considering the purchase of a Hillman Minx (the agent had twice brought the car to me to inspect and to trial drive), I was still feeling unsettled and by no means 'flush'! There seemed to be no impelling reason for me to conclude a purchase! I put the matter off indefinitely but I remembered the price - two hundred and seventy five pounds ten shillings (approximately $700) - a considerable sum in those days!

WEDDING BELLS: FEBRUARY 4, 1936

Deena's return to Cape Town and to "Longwood" at the end of January was accompanied by a similar floral welcome to the one she received previously. She looked as lovely and as happy as ever. This time, however, I was feeling less unsettled - more concerned about the responsibilities that I was about to shoulder. I told her about the work on hand and the letter I had received from London. Carelessly, without thinking, I commented how nice it would be if our honeymoon could include the R. I. B. A. graduation! Then, fearing that I may have raised Deena's expectations unnecessarily, I added: "Of course, the practice potentials make that pretty unlikely!" Deena, cooperative and understanding as ever, suggested that we should defer our honeymoon! We finally decided to spend only four or five days in the Cape countryside immediately after the wedding and to postpone the rest of the holiday until some future date when we could be away for longer without concern about the practice. We shared our plans with my parents. Dad seemed pleased that I hadn't rushed into buying a car and kindly offered us the Vauxhall for the short trip.

As our great day approached, members of both families arrived from different parts of the country. They included Deena's parents, Saul and Manja Margo, her sister Golda and brothers Lionel and Cecil. (Max, in London - a recent graduate of the Royal College of Surgeons, had been joined there by his Phyllis, and Harold at the Liverpool School of Architecture was preparing for his final examinations. There were my aunts, uncles and cousins from Johannesburg, Benoni, Port Elizabeth and Keetmanshoop and not least my youngest cousin Morris Kahn, then about six years of age. He was accompanied by his parents, Beattie and Philip and his grandparents - all had come to Cape Town for the occasion. The ceremony, in Cape Town's Great Synagogue[65] in the heart of Government Avenue, was conducted by the esteemed long-serving Chief Rabbi of South Africa, the Reverend A. P. Bender. (He had officiated at my parents' marriage thirty-five years earlier and at the marriage of my two brothers.) The ceremony concluded with the customary breaking of the glass when the groom's (my) foot smashes down on a glass tumbler[66]. After the ceremony, Maurice asked jokingly if I had hurt my foot! He said that I "ended the proceedings with a thunderous stamp that could be heard on another planet!"

The festivities culminated with a great reception - of the kind for which "Longwood", by then, was well known. Families and friends filled the inter-leading lounge, dining and breakfast rooms and large verandah. Guests came and went all afternoon. Finally soon after five, Deena and I were given a great send off. Two hours later we were at the Caledon Baths Hotel - a mineral water spa some sixty miles from the city. There, 'away from it all', we relaxed for five days, walked in fields of flowers, soaked in the hot spring waters and built our 'castles in the air'! The vacation was short - only as long as we thought it prudent to be away from my very young practice.

On our return, we booked in at the Helmsley Hotel in Hof Street. It was near the botanical gardens and a pleasant ten-minute walk to my office in the city.

THE STELLA POLARIS

Paging through the Cape Times one morning, my eye focused on a notice announcing a four weeks' cruise on the well known luxury liner *Stella Polaris*! It was scheduled to embark from Cape Town in April, sail up the West Coast of Africa, touch at Sierra Leone, Freetown, Casablanca

and Cadiz and end at Southampton - ten days before the R. I. B. A. graduation in June. That triggered the thought: "Our honeymoon had been curtailed because of my practice - if the practice became busy (as I hoped it
would) would we ever get away?" I told Deena about the cruise and said
that if I could only find someone to look after the practice for three months,
it would be a wonderful trip for us! I called Terence Orpen. Maybe he knew
of someone who might be able and willing to stand in for me for 3 months!
He said he would like to have done that but his City Hall appointment
made it impossible! He suggested: "Conner Johnston?" I knew Johnston!
He was a colleague three or four years my senior - had met him at 5th year
Building Mechanics classes before I went to Johannesburg. He lived and
practiced in Somerset West about 20 miles east of the City. I called him. We
met the following day. I told him that I was considering a three months trip
abroad - needed someone to look after my small practice in my absence. I
showed him the relevant drawings, explained that I expected to call for tenders for the Muizenberg job before I left, and said that if he was willing, I
would be happy to share fees on a pro rata basis. His response was positive.
He said he had very little work on hand and welcomed the idea. We reached
agreement. I quickly telephoned the shipping agents and obtained confirmation that accommodation was still available on the *Stella Polaris*. I
booked provisionally. Johnston and I proceeded to draft a letter of agreement that we both signed. We made it subject to subsequent confirmation
as I had yet to receive clients' approval!

Johnston had no sooner left when I was on the telephone sharing the
good news with Deena. Together we proceeded to prepare for our great
adventure. We pored over maps preparing an itinerary! We would be in
London for ten days prior to the R. I. B. A. ceremony - then motor through
the south of England, Denmark, Sweden, Norway and Holland for four
weeks, to return to London for a few days before sailing home aboard the
Windsor Castle. Deena made only two modest requests. In England she
wanted to spend time with her brother Max and if possible to call on Arthur
Mee! Mee, a prolific writer, was renowned throughout the English-speaking world. He also edited the *Children's Encyclopedia* dedicated "To Boys
and Girls Everywhere." He founded and edited the *Children's Newspaper*
for which Deena had been his South African correspondent for several
years.

Deena immediately wrote of our travel plans to both her brother and to
Arthur Mee. Our obvious immediate need on arrival in London was a car!
To that end, I cabled particulars to Mr. Stenham (my dad's shipper in

London) and received a reply stating that Rootes of London offered a Hill-man Minx for two hundred and seventy five pounds ten shillings (the same price as in Cape Town) but subject to 10% discount for cash! The car would be 'ready to drive' on our arrival! Days later when our ever keen Cape Town car agent called again, I explained our plans and said that I had placed the order with Rootes of London. I mentioned that the price was precisely the same as his, but that it included a 10% discount for cash! He would not give up and replied: "We can do the same for you here!"

Our next step was to find a home to return to! We chose a new pleas-ant four-room north-facing apartment in Valdora Court, Grotto Road, Claremont, a residential suburb some six miles from the City. We visited the show rooms of several furniture factories, placed orders for our essen-tial needs, and ensured that they would be ready for delivery on our return.

THE OLD FIRM!

More than three months had elapsed since I left Johannesburg. I had not heard a word from my old firm. Their agreement remained unfulfilled and my salary for September and October remained unpaid! Reflecting on all that had transpired, I realized that I had been gullible - too ready to accept Kallenbach's pious references to personal 'trust!' Furner's assurance *"We'll sort things out!"* proved meaningless! He, apparently, was no match for Kallenbach's dominant personality! What was I to do? I felt I had been exploited and decided to consult an attorney - something I had never done before! Who should it be?

In the weeks preceding Deena's arrival, I had spent a few evenings lis-tening to parliamentary debates. Colonel Denis Reitz, a much-admired 'acquisition' to General Smuts's United Party, was receiving considerable press prominence at the time. He was an attorney with an office in Cape Town! I decided to consult him in chambers. He listened intently to my story and expressed disgust that a professional firm should 'resort to such tactics'. "You must understand, however, if you intend to pursue the matter, the case would be heard in Johannesburg; the proceedings could prove costly and it will be their word against yours! - Is it really worthwhile?" He added: "As for your salary - I would certainly pursue that!" I decided to accept his advice! He wrote a comprehensive letter and in reply I received a check for thirty pounds *"being the unpaid salary due to Honikman!"* That, as I saw it, was a final denial both of the agreement and the leave that I had been asked temporarily to forgo!

I pondered briefly - concluded that all the encouraging references to 'my role in the firm's future development proposals' were shallow and meaningless, to say the least! They were folk with whom I could never again pursue any kind of relationship. It was time to relegate the matter to the past!

That is indeed where it ended. It had been an eye-opening experience - of which naught remains other than a bitter memory!

(An interesting development two years later is told in another chapter.)

PRIOR TO DEPARTURE

The first important letter received in my new office was from the client accepting my proposals for the Muizenberg project! It contained instructions to proceed forthwith and to ensure that building operations commenced *'as soon as possible!'* The plans were completed and approved by the Municipality, tenders called for and a building contract signed. I handed Johnston the plans, detail drawings and documents to enable him to appoint the necessary sub-contractors and supervise the work in my absence. The small Plumstead job was all but completed. For the Pinelands house, tenders had also been obtained and a contract signed! Johnston would continue from there and Terence kindly offered to visit the job informally in his spare time and when necessary to refer to Johnston.

Arrangements concluded and approved by clients, I felt free of all material responsibilities! Deena and I were ready for our great adventure! Before departure, she received replies to her letters. Max would meet us at Waterloo and Arthur Mee 'implored' us to visit his home in Kent. He attached a sketch showing how to reach the house. It was 'off the beaten track'.

CHAPTER 17

A GREAT ADVENTURE

The *Stella Polaris* was on a world cruise. It was a luxury cruise ship with every conceivable facility designed to keep passengers interestingly occupied. Our direction was NNW and we were to be at sea, without sight of land, for eleven days! Thereafter, we would call almost every day at a different port on the bulge of Africa. We had both been intensely busy for the weeks prior to departure and looked forward with glee to days of total relaxation and the 'freedom of the seas'!

The Atlantic was calm as a millpond - no land in sight! Deena and I were strolling leisurely on deck when she stopped in her tracks! Her hand shot to her side - a sharp sudden pain! We rested. The pain went as quickly as it came. A day or two later, it occurred again. Again relief came quickly. Deena was reluctant to see the ship's doctor. When we arrived at Monrovia, she was feeling fine. We went ashore, happy to be on land again. The next day following, we were at Freetown in Sierra Leone, and the next at Las Palmas in the Canary Islands. The pain recurred once or twice. At last Deena agreed to consult the ship's doctor. His examination and comment seemed cursory: "Your appendix may be slightly inflamed - see someone when you arrive in England!" It worried me but Deena said she felt fine and was happy to wait till we reached London when we would be seeing her brother Max. She promised to discuss it with him! She was entirely free of pain when we went ashore at Casablanca and at Rabat in Morocco. We both enjoyed the days ashore particularly in Rabat where the extensive contemporary architecture was as surprising as it was interesting.

On our second to last night aboard, the captain made one of his rare announcements on the intercom. He urged us to see Cadiz Bay. It is an exquisitely beautiful sight – not to be missed!

CIVIL WAR!

Next morning at six, Deena and I were up on the crowded deck. We were steaming ahead - no land in sight! Slowly, in mid-ocean, the ship came to a standstill! The passengers looked around in wonderment. Anchors were cast! What could it mean? We waited and wondered! Then came a somber voice on the intercom: "Ladies and Gentlemen, this is your captain speaking. I regret to tell you - we will not be entering Cadiz as planned! Civil War has broken out in Spain! We will be docking shortly in Gibraltar. I wish you good day!"

That was the beginning of the long tragic civil war in Spain! The rebellious forces led by General Franco, heavily supported by the Italian Fascists and by Nazi Germany, wrought havoc throughout Spain. The democracies, shaken to their roots, were totally unprepared! They were committed to the popular ideal of *'disarmament'*- (a concept that gained tremendous momentum and influenced national policy extensively in the years following the First World War). The great democracies were powerless to intervene! They took no action other than to allow volunteers to travel to Spain in a vain attempt to stem the tide of Fascist and Nazi insurgency.

BACK IN ENGLAND

We steamed into Gibraltar and within hours were at sea again heading for Southampton. We docked at daybreak the next morning and took the first train to Waterloo. Max was at the station waiting for us. Some two years had elapsed since he left Johannesburg. He, now a fully-fledged surgeon with the prestigious letters FRCS[67] behind his name, had his sister wrapped in his arms. He listened to our story of her intermittent painful episodes during the voyage, and wasted no time getting us to our hotel. From our room he called a colleague! He said that he preferred not to examine members of the family and had arranged for an experienced and highly esteemed colleague to see Deena. He drove us to the hospital. His physician friend was waiting for us. He too listened to our story and led Deena into his surgery saying: "It won't be long!" Max followed.

A BABY ON THE WAY!

My anxious wait was brief. Max appeared, grinning from cheek to cheek, and declared: "Congratulations - maybe it's a boy!" Then Deena and the doctor appeared. She greeted me with a special smile - one that I will never forget! We embraced. The doctor looked to me and said: "You've heard the good news! All is well - the appendix is fine. Your wife's in good shape. Enjoy your travels!"

From the hospital I telephoned my sister Beatrice. She worked at the School of Oriental Studies and had recently moved from Crosby Hall to Vincent House - a new student hostel in Pembridge Square, Nottinghillgate. She had been 'waiting' for my call and was eager to meet Deena. She surprised me with news that our parents would be arriving the following day. She added: "In time for your graduation. They've hired an apartment in Knightsbridge and will be here for ten days!"

Max drove us to Rootes in Piccadilly to take delivery of our new Hillman Minx. As promised, the car was ready in the showroom, clean and brightly polished! With great pride the manager demonstrated its many features, not least a large tray of numerous tools each one set in its own specially shaped felt-lined compartment in the floor of the trunk! He handed me the keys with a batch of maps of London and of England and an invitation to visit the Humber-Hillman Works in Coventry. When we were about to leave, he introduced us to a uniformed driver. "He's at your disposal for the day - will show you around London; just tell him when you have reached your last point of call and he will find his way home!" For businesslike efficiency and courtesy, there was surely no match!

The driver came with us as far as Vincent House. I thanked him and said that my sister would be our guide for the day and suggested that he could better spend that time with his family! He was delighted and politely took his leave.

Deena and Beatrice were about the same age and seemed to strike a congenial chord. We lunched together and spent a couple of hours in Hyde Park discussing travel plans for the months ahead. It had been a long day. Both tired, we took Beatrice home and made for the 'University Club' where we had booked accommodation for our stay in London.

Next morning we returned to Vincent House. Beatrice met us in the lobby. She had had a call from our parents from their apartment in Knightsbridge. They were on their way and she was waiting for them! They arrived soon after us. There was great excitement! More than two years had elapsed since Beatrice left home. In the lounge, we chatted over morning tea, compared notes and planned for the days that we were to be together in London. News that my parent's second grandchild was on the way produced more excitement! Dad reacted by inviting us all to "celebrate over lunch!" With that I introduced them to my new car and happily we drove through Hyde Park to Dad's favorite restaurant in Knightsbridge.

THE ROYAL INSTITUTE OF BRITISH ARCHITECTS

Graduation day came! A day that was once a vague dream had dawned! A goal that had often weighed heavily on my mind and for which I had burnt much midnight oil over the past eight years was about to climax! Had I been stupidly unrealistic - over ambitious! Such thoughts had recurred time and again! Often, especially when confronted with the great works of Michelangelo, Christopher Wren, Le Corbusier or Frank Lloyd Wright and other contemporaries, I would question my rationale in striving for a goal that was way beyond my reach! Now some of those apprehensions returned! I felt unsure and humble! In vain I tried to share my thoughts with Deena!

That evening Deena and I called for Beatrice and for my parents. We drove down Oxford Street. At Oxford Circus we turned towards the R. I. B. A. Soon after passing the BBC[68] building, a barricade across Portland Place brought us to a stop. A constable approached, saluted and asked for our identity. I showed him our invitation; he immediately opened the barrier, signaled us through and directed us to a nearby parking area. We crossed a red carpet. It stretched across the road and led to the entrance of the Institute which was, of course, our destination - all very impressive! We parked the car, walked back to the red carpet which we assumed we had to follow. Mother's sense of humor took over. As we stepped onto the carpet, she exclaimed: *"Now I know what it's like to be a Queen!"*

Among the early arrivals, we were ushered into the assembly hall and seated in the center of the front row. The hall was soon filled to capacity! Programs were distributed. An announcement on the intercom called on all graduates to proceed to the platform. I stepped forward accompanied by some several others. In a brief address, the President congratulated the delegates whom he said: *'had come from different parts of the Empire'*. He wished them well in their careers. Graduates were asked to step forward as their names were announced. Waiting for my name to be called, I looked toward my family. Deena put a finger to her lips signaling a kiss; Mother smiled broadly; Beatrice looked very serious. I shall never forget the look in Dad's eyes the moment my name was announced! He wiped his eyes! A tear ran down his cheek! (Two decades were yet to pass when, at both my sons' graduations, I sensed the meaning of the emotional surge that overtook my dad at that moment!) The President shook the hand of each delegate and handed him his certificate. The entire procedure (followed by refreshments) was brief, but memorable for more reasons than one!

ARTHUR MEE

Deena and I spent the next few days motoring through the charming villages of Cornwall and Devon. Much as we enjoyed all that London has to offer, we were relaxed and happy to be away from 'the maddening crowd', to come and go and stop as we pleased, to breathe the unpolluted air of the English countryside. On our way back to London we made our way to Kent. With Arthur Mee's annotated map that Deena had kept for that moment, we had no difficulty in finding his home!

Deena's welcome was exceptionally warm. Addressing her affectionately, Mee expressed his gratitude for "all your beautiful contributions!" His gesture embraced me! His love of children and his grasp of language were mirrored in every sentence he uttered! I was in the presence of a great, warm-hearted talented, human being! He told Deena that he recognized her from her photograph that he "kept in a special album of writers all over the world - who have made the 'Children's Newspaper' possible!" His reference to her 'special talent as a writer' was deeply moving. It added color to my endless wonder - that such a person had chosen to share my life!

Meeting and talking with Arthur Mee was an enriching experience that I shall never forget!

CIGARETTES

I was a smoker! On the road back to London I ran out of my supply of "Commando" cigarettes that I had brought from South Africa. I found "Craven A', an English Virginia type cigarette, to my liking and bought only a few thinking they would be readily obtainable while driving in Europe!

SCANDINAVIA

We returned to London with time only to bid farewell to our parents and to Beatrice before driving some sixty miles to Harwich. There we boarded a ferry for our North Sea crossing to Esbjerg, Denmark. We arrived later than planned and encountered a delay before the car was hoisted ashore, but were quickly on the road northward bound to Aarus to renew acquaintance with Professor H.J. Uldall. At dinner, he reminded me that our last meeting was also at dinner in "Longwood" - that four years had slipped by since then. He relished news of Cape Town and said that 'matters linguistic' kept him in occasional touch with Beatrice.

Next morning we drove to Copenhagen, strolled along the Langerline to delight at the sight of "Den Lille Havfrau"[69] - a beautiful full-size bronze mermaid gracefully poised on a granite bolder - so unpretentious, it was as though she had quietly slipped out of the water for a breath of fresh air! For both of us, that 'lady' symbolized the natural friendliness of the Danish people - as we found them. We spent an enjoyable few hours in Tivoli Gardens and dined there. Early the next morning we spent a while at the Frederiksborg Castle before driving through Sjaelland to Helsinger. Waiting to ferry across the Kattegat, Deena remarked how 'at home' she had felt in Denmark! We promised ourselves a return visit – 'one day!'

MY DILEMMA!

On our last night in Copenhagen, I ran out of cigarettes. Unable to find the brand to which I had become accustomed, I bought an unknown local brand! The first one I tried was awful - so loosely packed that dry tobacco dropped into my mouth! I tried a second. It was no better! In disgust, I threw away the pack! Rather than risk a recurrence of the unpleasant experience, and despite the constant urge, I decided against replacement! Slowly the urge diminished and actually ceased after a few days. I had abandoned smoking - so I thought!

SWEDEN

We spent the day driving northward some 300 miles from Helsinborg to Stockholm and did not know what to expect! We were tremendously impressed - handsome buildings - wide spotlessly clean cobbled roads – canals - broad bridges and tremendous animation! We loved Stockholm – spent a day longer than planned and departed reluctantly, after three days there!

Way behind schedule, we decided to by-pass Oslo and to make for the Hardanger Fjord on the Atlantic seaboard. It was early morning when we left; we drove all day more than six hundred miles through countless country roads. There were no freeways in those days! On the road, I again felt the 'need for a smoke' but there was no appropriate place to stop! So I drove on, wondering if I could do without! We reached Bergen in time for a late dinner - both thoroughly exhausted! I was too tired to bother about cigarettes! We regretted having rushed through such exquisitely beautiful country! Our glimpse of those snow-capped mountains and fishing villages mirrored in the emerald blue water of the fjord made a lasting impression!

In later years we often both reminisced to recapture that incredible picture!

Next morning after breakfast, I decided to resist the urge to look for a 'decent' cigarette! 'I must try and do without!' We boarded a fairly large ship in the harbor, watched the car being strapped down to the upper deck and covered with a heavy green tarpaulin. We set sail for Stavanger en route to Rotterdam.

NAZI GAULEITER!

Immediately after leaving Stavanger, we were made glaringly aware of where we were! The North Sea's mountainous waves tossed the ship like a helpless cork! I had never imagined anything like it! Seasick passengers disappeared from deck - made for their cabins! Deena felt awful! I accompanied her to the cabin. I felt queer but found it too close indoors and hurried back to the open deck. I hung onto the rail and moved slowly toward mid-ship in search of a stable foothold! It did not help! Directly ahead, I faced sky - then sea, then sky again! I looked astern towards the upper deck to see if the car had survived the battering! It was totally awash! As the ship rolled, tossed and heaved; the water rushed away and the drenched green canvas re-appeared. Then a mighty splash obscured my view! That went on and on! I wondered how much damage the car had suffered!

I was alone! Not a soul in sight! The sea was wild! When would it end? I glanced toward the sign 'BAR'- resisted the urge to look for a cigarette! Then a man appeared under the sign. He had come out of the bar. Unsteadily, he fumbled, looking for something to hang onto! I wondered: 'Was it the storm or had this man too much to drink?' He made for the rail and clung to it! Slowly he edged his way towards me! I was the only visible soul aboard! As he got closer, the smell of alcohol was unmistakable but he was not intoxicated! He blurted something in German. I shook my head. With my limited knowledge of German, I replied: "Ich verstedt nicht!"[70] He turned to broken English! In a strong guttural accent he started to boast. With one arm, he clung to the rail! Beating his chest with the other, he declared loudly: "Ich bin Gauleiter!" He paused, swept his arm out to sea and boastfully repeated: *"Ich bin Gauleiter uber Holland*[71] *- wen der Fuhrer gives the signal, Holland vill collapse like a pack of cards!"* As he spoke those venomous words, he clenched his teeth and his hand came down like a clustering claw onto the rail!

His words made me wonder: "Was Hitler planning to take over Europe?" Sickened as I was to hear this Nazi gloat over the sinister goals of his *'Fuhrer'*, I realized that he would not have been so loose-lipped had he been entirely sober - he would possibly have exercised some discretion! Perhaps there was more that he wanted to boast about! I looked him in the face and said: "You – - gauleiter fur Holland - what are you doing in Norway?" *"Norvey,"* he declared loudly with a snigger as his thumb tapped his chest: *"In Oslo - I train der gauleiter fur Norvey - a schmart fellow! Ven come den signal, Norvey vil collapse'* - he paused and added: *"Auch like a pack of cards!"* Again his fist pounced on the rail! We parted!

The ship turned shoreward; the sea calmed. Deena appeared on deck and said she felt her old self again. She listened to and was appalled by the story I had to tell! We both felt the implications were extremely grave and decided that we should report the matter to the authorities when back in London.

HOLLAND

We landed in Rotterdam - the car totally unscathed by the pounding it had received on the North Sea! We knew no one in Holland. Our visit there was short. Holland was included in our itinerary because I was keen to see some of the buildings designed by Architect Dudok - a well-known exponent of contemporary Dutch architecture. From Rotterdam we drove to den Hague where I had the addresses of a few of Dudok's buildings - took photographs and drove on to spend the night in Amsterdam.

Next morning, we were to experience another North Sea crossing on our way back to England! We were apprehensive! Were we to experience another such battering? Much to our relief, the sea was beautifully calm! Within a few hours we were in Southampton and on the road again - London bound.

We had only two more days before departure! My parents were already on their way home. Apart from meeting with Beatrice and Max, we planned to drive to Birmingham to meet the Abrahams' and Isaacs' branches of the family. I was keen to meet 'cousin Ester' to whom I once had mailed many of my mother's letters. I was also keen that we should both meet the rest of the family. Ida had been at our wedding but neither of us had met her sister Dorothy (Eden) or her four brothers Harold[72], Sydney[73], Adolph[74] and Lionel[75] all of whom had added luster to the family name.

THAT NAZI INCIDENT

Beatrice and Max were quite shaken by the report of my 'Gauleiter' encounter! They agreed that it was 'important' and should be reported! Anthony Eden, British Foreign Secretary, was thought to be the man to whom I should report and a visit to his office became 'priority one'! With the limited time at our disposal, we would have to abandon our trip to Birmingham. Our intended meeting with the family was deferred to 'some future date'!

AT THE FOREIGN OFFICE

The next morning in Downing Street, we were directed to the Foreign Office where I was informed that Anthony Eden was in the Middle East. His secretary, Mr. Freeman, appeared and said that if I cared to entrust him with the purpose of our visit, he would convey our message to Mr. Eden on his return.

I told him that we were concerned by my experience on the North Sea and that we felt it was a matter that should be brought to the attention of the Government! I described precisely what had occurred. Mr. Freeman thanked me profusely and added words to the effect: - "*The Government is aware of and deeply concerned by much of what has been going on in Europe in recent years! Alarm bells ring relentlessly! For a while Public protest - as, no doubt you are aware - fell on deaf ears! You may well ask what is being done about it! His Majesty's government was convinced that continued verbal protest would be meaningless - unless and until backed by strength! After the War (World War I), Britain, like most of Europe, was influenced by the "dream of disarmament" - an idealistic dream imple-mented prematurely - far ahead of its time - a concept for which the inter-national community is unprepared and ill-equipped to administer! We are powerless to intervene!"* Then he added: *"As things are, we reckon it will take three years before Britain's rearmament program may command the necessary respect! Maybe then, Hitler will think twice before treating protests with the contempt he has shown thus far!"* He concluded: *"Maybe...,"* he paused and added, *"until then, I fear further protests would be meaningless! That, unfortunately, is the situation we are in today! Would that things were different!"*

As we spoke, Italy and Germany were pouring arms and men into Spain in support of the insurgents and in preparation for the catastrophic tragedy that had yet to come! (World War II.)

HOMEWARD BOUND

Aboard the *Windsor Castle*, we were able to relax! For days we lazed on deck recapturing the joyful times we had with our parents, Max and Beatrice in London. We had a good laugh at Mother's remark as we crossed the red carpet in Portland Place before graduation. We reflected on our visit with Arthur Mee, a 'great humanitarian', on the natural friendliness of the Scandinavian people and the exquisite grandeur of the Norwegian fjords! We discussed our several experiences! Our thoughts focused on develop-ments in Spain and my Nazi encounter on the North Sea! The future looked grim! Deena referred to our unborn child that had been making its pres-ence felt and uttered: *"What kind of world, are we bringing our child into - how does one plan for that - are we being fair?"* Her questions were of course rhetorical - neither of us knew the answers! Neither could dismiss the troublesome thought of the 'crisis' that loomed ahead! It worried me that Deena's concern seemed deep and personal! We both realized that the problems facing Europe involved Britain and the Empire, that inevitably South Africa would be involved! Attempting to counter her concern, I tried to rationalize and said: *"The crisis seems pretty imminent! If it lasts as much as three years (*that was the time factor mentioned by Mr. Freeman) *it will surely all be over long before our little one leaves school – let alone become involved!"* My remarks made little impact. Nothing seemed to lessen the load she bore! (Three years had yet to pass before I realized that it was not only the thought of our unborn child that weighed so heavily on Deena! Added to that, was the thought of her brothers to whom she was so deeply attached!)

BACK HOME

It was July when we reached Cape Town! We returned to the Helmsley Hotel for 10 days before moving to our Claremont apartment. That gave us the time needed to take delivery of t he new furniture, to hang curtains and pictures, to find a maid for Deena and, not least, to take over the office work that I had entrusted to Conner Johnston. On the Friday night after our return, there was a large family gathering at "Longwood". Only Beatrice and Grandma were missing! Our cousins Leonard, Percy and Rosalie also put in an appearance. My parents had returned a few weeks ahead of us. They were in their element! Dad, obviously elated, said: "This is like old times!" They were not accustomed to a depleted household! Ephraim, Maurice and I were now married, Beatrice abroad, Rita engaged to Fred Fox, and as usual, Sybil was either out or studying in her room! That night I learnt that our South West African cousins had left Keetmanshoop and were now living in Muizenberg! Uncle Phillip had bought a small guest house, "Sidmouth Hotel", 'on the railway line near the station!'

ON THE HOME FRONT

We soon settled down in our new home and liked it! The practice had gone smoothly during my absence. Johnston presented me with a comprehensive report – virtually free of problems. Dawson's house in Pinelands and the Muizenberg job were well advanced! For the first time I was in a position to cast a critical eye on the limited fruits of my own architectural efforts! The result was not entirely satisfying! I aired my thoughts with both Johnston and Orpen. They brushed them aside – thought I was being over-critical! Of course they were trying to be kind! Unquestionably there were design aspects and details that could have been resolved more simply! Mr. Hirschsohn made a surprise visit to my office soon after my return. He said that he had been concerned that I had left his job 'in someone else's hands' but added: "However, I am pleased with the result thus far - it is looking good!" That was gratifying! All had gone well in my absence! I was more than grateful to both Conner and Terence for their help and not least - their friendship!

THE PRACTICE EXPANDS

Solicitor Joseph Levy called asking for an appointment on behalf of his cousin Boy Leeb! I had met him years back and knew him by reputation. He was a few years my senior, and said to be a very talented! He had worked with my friend Klem Fridjohn in the Durban office of Kallenbach Kennedy and Furner at the time I was with the firm in Johannesburg. When he called he said that he and his wife were staying temporally at the Hotel Atlantic in Muizenberg (owned by his mother) and that he had decided not to return to Durban, but to set up practice in Cape Town. He knew that I was with his previous firm in Johannesburg and was surprised to see from the architect's board on my Hillcote job that I was no longer with them and had set up practice - "ahead of him"! The purpose of his visit was to ascertain if I was interested in 'a joint practice or partnership' and if I felt we could work together. He thought 'it would entail a considerable saving in overhead expenses!' That was certainly an important consideration! The economy was still in the doldrums - building activity was minimal! I explained that I had very little work on hand - insufficient for two architects! His response was that he hoped to pull his weight and that he was busy with a few jobs for a speculative builder friend, that 'although the work does not involve architect's supervision and attracts only half the statutory fees - it appears to be on-going!' After a long talk we decided to meet again two days later.

At the next meeting, we decided to join forces, to enter into partnership as from the following month - the agreement to be on a fifty/fifty basis to apply to everything except current work that each of us had on hand.

My Dominion House offices were obviously too small for both of us! We hired suitable premises in Boston House Strand Street. Leeb's solicitor cousin kindly offered to draw up the agreement which he sent us with his good wishes for a successful practice! Optimistically, we set out on our joint professional journey! Neither of us seemed unduly concerned that there was little evidence of any meaningful work in the immediate future!

The news got around! Members of our respective families and friends telephoned to wish us luck! For days, nothing more than that happened. Work on Dawson's house and 'Hillcote', both nearly completed, filled my time! Boy sat at his board sketching and painting! I observed how exceptionally adept he was at perspective drawing and presentation! I thought: "How useful that would be if only a worthwhile commission was in the offing!"

PROSPECTS?

Long, quiet days waiting and wondering were happily interrupted by a call from my Uncle Phillip! He had heard that I had commenced practice, wished me 'luck' and said I should see him as soon as possible! He was at the Sidmouth Hotel in Muizenberg.

We hadn't met since that memorable car-breakdown on the fringe of the Kalahari Desert! His family had decided to move to the Cape 'to ensure a better education for the children'. Uncle left the Keetmanshoop business in the hands of his two nephews. He explained that the 'Sidmouth' Guest House was a temporary measure, that his principal interest was the Balmoral Hotel on the corner of Beach and Melrose Roads. He had bought the Hotel and the adjoining vacant lot that 'extended to Atlantic Road. It enabled the property to face three streets and overlook the Bay!' He had been under the impression that I was still in Johannesburg and said that he wished that he had known that I had commenced practice in Cape Town! He added: "In my ignorance, I commissioned architect Mac Queen for the Balmoral job - had I known you would be here, I would have preferred you to do it! I could approach you more readily and I'm sure you would give it all you've got!" He went on to say: "Perhaps it is not too late! If you can arrange matters with Mr. Queen, I'd like that. In fact - I would prefer it. So far he has given this - came last week." He handed me a drawing, a covering letter and a brochure. The letter referred to: *"The attached is a preliminary sketch plan for your consideration"* and to *"the enclosed brochure setting out the standard fees for professional services... ."* Uncle added: "I had never met Mr. Mac Queen! I heard that he had won an architectural competition for the new Electricity House in town. I had a look at it - seemed like a nice building, so I called on him there and then and this is the result!" I glanced at the plan. It showed suggested alterations to the existing 3-story building and a proposed new 'Ground Floor' structure on the vacant site. A dotted outline indicated "future extensions" on two upper floors. I asked if the plan accurately represented his requirements. He said it did not; it was a preliminary proposal intended for discussion; there would have to be a number of changes, and he would like to see what I would come up with! He also wanted to have some idea of cost, for both the first stage and for the final building. I asked if he was satisfied with the standard fees as set out in the brochure. He said he was provided there were 'no extras!' He concluded by saying: "It is now up to you! I would very much like you to do the job if you can arrange matters with Mac Queen. Please call on him for me. Tell him what I have told you. See what you can do!"

That was a challenge! Excited at the prospect of a large, interesting job, I was also apprehensive and uneasy! I responded: 'Would I not be taking the food out of a colleague's mouth?' The reply came sharp and firm: "Definitely not! My commitment to Mac Queen will be met - whatever it is! Please see him and let me know the result.

THE MAC QUEEN INTERVIEW

I discussed the position with my partner. He thought Mr. Phillips was being very open - that I should put the position to Mr. Mac Queen and hear what he has to say! I called Mr. Mac Queen, met him next morning and told him all that had transpired. He was most cordial and said he "fully understood" and added, "My work had barely begun - there's no problem! One and a half percent would cover it all - it will dispose of Mr. Phillips' entire commitment!" Graciously, he added: "You are absolutely free to carry on. Good luck. My compliments to Mr. Phillips - seems a nice man! Thank him for having approached me." I asked if he had prepared an estimate of cost. He opened his file and said that his estimate of twenty-two thousand pounds was "very rough" - covered the suggested alterations and ground floor extensions which was all that Mr. Phillips was considering at this stage!

As we parted he wished me luck and handed me a file and a roll of drawings saying, "Take them – you'll find them useful. They're the plans of the existing hotel by Lonstein (architect for the original building)!" I thanked him warmly. He showed no resentment or disappointment at the loss of an appointment. On the contrary, he had been co-operative and friendly. Thanking him, I assured him that the client's commitment would be met and added that if I could assist him in any way in the future, I would regard it a privilege.

Leeb shared my delight! It seemed that we were about to undertake our first major contract! Mr. Phillips also expressed his delight and said he would send Mr. Mac Queen his check and would thank him for his co-operation. He outlined several changes to Mac Queen's plan that he felt were necessary and asked me to submit revised proposals and estimates and to confirm the position regarding fees.

IT NEVER RAINS BUT IT POURS!

On my return to the office there had been a call from Mr. Rosenzweig. He wanted me to see him 'if possible after lunch, at the shop'! I had met him a few times. He and Louis Hirschsohn both worked at the American Swiss Watch Company – owned by Mr. Hirschsohn senior. I knew Louis quite well. He was friendly with my brother Maurice and sister Beatrice who were about his age. I was there at the shop soon after two.

Mr. Rosenzweig explained that he and Louis had bought a corner plot in Hof Street in the Gardens and that they intended to build a block of flats! He said that they 'rather liked' what I had done in Muizenberg for 'the old man' and would like me to tackle their Hof Street project. He wished me luck, handed me a site diagram that he had 'taken from the Title Deed' and asked that I 'please return it for safe-keeping as there is no duplicate!' I was delighted! Two projects in a single day! "Could it be true?"

Before returning to the office, I called at the offices of the Town-planning Department in the 'Old Drill Hall'[76] to obtain particulars of the town-planning restrictions[77] relevant to the Hof Street site - an essential prerequisite to planning! I was eager to get started without delay.

Back in the office, Boy was delighted with the news. Our 'professional teething problems' seemed over! On hand were 'two important projects'! We decided that I should handle the hotel job and Boy the flats, but that we would inter-relate all the way - share problems as they arose to ensure the best possible results!

The two projects were very different! The hotel entailed extensive additions and alterations to an existing building. It was on a 'commercial' site unrestricted by any 'set-back' limitations; the ultimate floor area was to be more than doubled! The other, an entirely new building in a 'residential' zone, was subject to several stringent town-planning restrictions which, when analyzed, led us to conclude that it should not exceed three floors! The regulations required that the building be set back from the site boundaries, a distance equal to three-quarters its height! It was obvious that a height in excess of three floors would leave insufficient area for a building of any substance and would require an elevator, which was not needed in a project of only 3 floors.

From a state of relative idleness, our young practice was suddenly fully occupied. I couldn't wait to get home to share the news with Deena. While describing all that had transpired that day, she gently placed my hand on her tummy as though to say: "I too have news for you!" Indeed she had! I felt the firm movements of our unborn child!

INVESTMENT!

For me, 1936 was a remarkable year! It brought Deena into my life. It took us on our great adventure abroad. It held promise of parenthood and, to my surprise, rekindled the thought of a small property investment although it was barely a year since I had abandoned the idea (when my old Johannesburg firm chose to be 'unaware' of our agreement). Our young practice had blossomed sooner than I dared hope! It seemed that I could afford to allocate about three to four thousand pounds for investment purposes. My attention was attracted to a "For Sale" notice of a 3-story block of twelve 2-roomed apartments on a corner site on the Kloof Road Sea Point. I inspected the property and recognized the style to be that of Architect W.H. Grant (my very first employer!). The building was in a good state of repair and was fully let and the area was fully developed. The price asked was just under thirteen thousand pounds! It seemed a little outside my reach! My dad liked the property and suggested that I discus it with Mr. Le Roux, manager of the South African Association[78]. Mr. Le Roux suggested that that if I could produce four or five thousand pounds, he probably could arrange a first mortgage of eight thousand. I visited the property a second time and inspected two of the apartments internally and made an offer of twelve thousand pounds! The offer was accepted. My contribution was four thousand and the S.A. Association produced a first mortgage of eight. Thus I became a property owner! It proved to be a sound investment. After meeting all expenses including interest, it left me with a return of about 500 pounds per annum which stood me in good stead for several years.

CHAPTER 18

FROM JOY TO FEAR!

In due course, I drove Deena to the Inverugie Maternity Home in Sea Point as was recommended by her doctor soon after our return from abroad. That evening Deena's mother arrived from Johannesburg. She became restless when she heard that Deena was at the Home. Assurances that the doctor was 'pleased with her condition' and thought 'it would be a while yet' before the baby arrived did not seem to calm her!

Next morning on my way to the Home, I called at the American Swiss Watch Company and bought Deena an attractive 18-carat gold Elgin bracelet watch that that I was sure she would like - a small token to mark the arrival of our first child. Louis Hirschsohn served me. Delighted when he heard my news, he produced a beautiful velvet - lined box and commented: "Specially designed for this gem!" I wrote three words, *"Thank you, darling",* on a plain white card and inserted it. Louis had it all beautifully wrapped.

On arrival at the home I was told I could not go in - 'Deena was in labor' - I was to make myself comfortable in the lounge - would be called presently! I became restless! Minutes later I heard two women arguing in the entrance hall. Deena's mother had arrived. She was excited and seemed to resent being denied admission to her daughter. I heard the matron say: "Madam, you cannot go in just now. The doctor is in attendance. All is well. We will call you presently; please be patient!" Entering the lounge, she glared at me and exclaimed: "How can you stand there!" There was fire was in her eyes, reminiscent of our early morning encounter in "Berloga" more than two years earlier! Restlessly, she walked up and down - could not be calmed!

Finally, a nurse ushered us into the room. My heart pounded! Deena was resting against a wall of pillows. She held our baby son at her chest.

She looked up at me. Her eyes were so tired - but they mirrored a precious message - deeply engraved in memory!

The nurse gave me the baby to hold. I handed Deena her parcel and nervously held the child - barely for a minute, when the nurse took him from me and placed him briefly in Manja's arms and returned him to his mother. "She must rest!" said the nurse as she ushered us out of the room. I kissed Deena's brow and said I'd be back shortly.

MOTHER-IN-LAW!

Manja said she was staying with her niece in Kenilworth. I offered to drive her there but she preferred to be dropped in town. Obviously I had displeased her! We had no sooner left the Home when she shouted: "How can you leave her there - with strangers! You don't know what she's been through!", then added with a slur: "And you give her a watch!" On the road towards town she ranted and raved demonstratively. I stopped the car, said: "I cannot drive like this - it's dangerous! There'll be an accident. Please be calm." She was silent! I drove on. She started to mutter, raised her voice and with arms outstretched, she raved, shouting hysterically! We were on the main road half a mile from the city center. Approaching a bus stop, I stopped again, pulled on the brake and said: "Manja, this can't go on! One of us will have to get out." My hand went to the door handle! With that, she opened her door, got out and walked to the bus stop. I pondered for a minute! She boarded a city-bound bus and I drove off.

I called at "Longwood" where I knew my mother would be anxiously waiting for news of Deena and the baby. The car episode with my mother-in-law was never mentioned again!

We named our child Basil Clive. On him, Deena lavished all she had – tirelessly, cautiously and indeed fruitfully! Basil developed into a healthy good-looking child. He attracted attention not only from family but also from children passing-by that we did not know. He charmed my parents! He was their second grandchild - the first grandson! The light that lit up Dad's face as he watched Basil receive his third birthday guests remains ever bright in my memory!

Deena and I enjoyed living in the suburbs. We had bought a quarter-acre north-facing residential plot at the corner of Wood and Mulvihal Roads Rondebosch and began planning our future home. The thought of building in the near future was soon over-shadowed by the ominous developments in Europe!

A TROUBLED WORLD!

In Germany (as elsewhere), the 'great depression' had taken a heavy toll! The Nazis were in control of the streets, pursuing ruthless anti-Semitic atrocities without restraint. Hitler's power in the Third Reich was entrenched. His forces occupied the Rhineland in violation of the Versailles Treaty. The invasion of Czechoslovakia and Austria followed. Alarmed, but apparently still powerless, the great democracies looked on! Some attributed the power crisis in Europe to the complex political situation that had developed and the ruthless savagery under Tzar Nicholas II which was the pretext for merciless savagery that characterized the Communist Revolution of 1917! 'Trotskyism', an extreme brand of Communism, made a profound impact throughout Europe and beyond! The slogan *"WORKERS OF THE WORLD, UNITE"* made a particularly powerful appeal in England. The Labor Party openly supported Communism. Posters throughout Britain carried the picture of Prime Minister Ramsey McDonald with the caption: *"LET US FOLLOW RUSSIA!"* McDonald, a member of the Fabian Society, sought a *'Socialist one world government'*. With the general election defeat of the Labor Party, it seemed that Britain's new rulers were more opposed to Communism than to Nazi Germany, which would explain Neville Chamberlain's timid reaction to the Czechoslovakian crisis. Many in Britain and throughout Europe were captivated by the *disarmament ideal*. Many believed that Stalin's foreign policy was designed to avoid war; others that the military might of the USSR was sufficient to halt Hitler's drive eastward! On September 30, 1936, Chamberlain, Deladier of France, Mussolini and Hitler signed the Treaty of Munich! It virtually handed the Sudetenland of Czechoslovakia to Hitler in response to a promise of peace! To Hitler, the Treaty of Munich was nothing more than a convenient scrap of paper. His advances in Europe continued. Austria succumbed. Poland and Greece were under threat! The Wehrmaght continued to advance!

The fear that Poland would be the next victim took Neville Chamberlain on a flight to Munich to meet with Hitler! Aghast, the 'free world' looked on while Chamberlain negotiated with the tyrant - one who had shown utter contempt for human liberty! On his return to Britain, Chamberlain waived his umbrella and proudly proclaimed: *"Peace in our time"* - words intended to appease a troubled world! It was not long before the

German wehrmacht was massing on the Polish border. At that point the British government announced that an invasion of Poland would produce a declaration of war by Britain! That took Hitler hurrying to Russia where he entered into a non-aggression pact with Stalin - one that secured his eastern front in the event of war in the West. In return for non-intervention, Hitler's forces marched into Poland and, in terms of the pact, Russian forces were free to occupy the other half without firing a shot! Stalin and Hitler had agreed to divide Poland between the two dictator nations!

Stalin celebrated the notorious Pact with a toast to Adolph Hitler saying: *"I know how much the German people love their Fuehrer. I should therefore drink a toast to his health."* The Russian forces focused on the Baltic States and Finland. In Finland they met unexpected determined resistance. The Red army suffered heavy casualties; more than a million men were killed or wounded.

A DIVIDED BRITAIN!

In Britain, 'Trotskyism' had gained tremendous influence! Among the ruling class, many opponents of communism aligned themselves with the Fascist or Nazi ideology! At one time, even Churchill was an ardent admirer of Mussolini.

WAR!

On the first of September 1939, the German army marched into Poland! That same morning Britain sent an ultimatum to Germany stating that unless German troops were withdrawn immediately, the two countries would be at war. The ultimatum expired at 11:00 am. There was no reply! In a broadcast to the nation, Chamberlain declared the two countries to be at war! That night the first air raid warning screeched across London!

France had sent a similar ultimatum and the next day France declared war! Within days Australia, New Zealand, South Africa and Canada had each declared war on Germany!

TOUCH AND GO IN SOUTH AFRICA

South Africa's situation was unique and difficult! Four decades had elapsed since the Boer War! The sad memories of many Afrikaners were exploited for political ends. The division between Boer and Britain widened! The Nationalist Party was in power. Prime Minister J.B.M. Hertzog's strong anti-British sentiments were never appeased! Well before the outbreak of World War II, when public meetings were convened to protest against Nazi atrocities, Hertzog appealed to the nation 'not to interfere in foreign affairs'. Britain's declaration of war in September 1939 was followed by a heated debate in Parliament in Cape Town. Hertzog appealed to Parliament to remain neutral. General Smuts, then Deputy Prime Minister, vehemently opposed! He urged the nation to stand by the Commonwealth and Allied nations, to rid mankind of a 'Nazi monster' and the terror that faced mankind'. Smuts's appeal won the day. South Africa declared war on Germany! Hertzog resigned. Smuts resumed the Premiership to lead the nation through the grim years ahead. Later he was asked to join Britain's War Cabinet, a unique position and one that he had also occupied in the First World War.[79]

FRANCE

A British expeditionary force joined their French allies. French forces were aligned behind the Maginot Line - a heavily fortified, allegedly impregnable concrete barrier on the French border. It was designed to resist invasion. On the other side of the border, Germany manned the Siegfried Line - fortifications intended to counter any possible initiative on the part of the Allies. Months went by without a shot being fired. The expected German invasion did not materialize. Instead there were months of inactivity - a period widely referred to as "the phony war". Light-hearted banter served to preserve the 'spirit' of the Allied forces. I remember some of the words of one of them: *"...we will hang our washing on the Siegfried Line...."* Anxiously, the world waited.

The 'phony' war ended on May 10, 1940. By-passing the Maginot line, Hitler's *wehrmaght* marched (totally unprovoked) into Holland, Belgium and Luxembourg en route to France. Inevitably, the three small countries succumbed. That day Neville Chamberlain resigned as Prime Minister of Great Britain. His handling of the Czechoslovakian crisis cost him the premiership and his place in the destiny of Great Britain!

Churchill became Britain's wartime leader! In his hands lay the fate of the civilized world.

In France, the Blitzkrieg[80] continued on many fronts! In less than a week – on June 17 - Marshall Phillip Petain, the aging hero of World War

I and head of the new French Government, surrendered (It was said - 'to save Paris!'). The battle for France was over! The world gasped! France, renowned upholder of human liberty, a nation that had stood its ground throughout the bitter years of World War I and finally proclaimed victory over the invader, was on its knees 'treating' with the Nazi tyrant! France surrendered. On land and in the air, it seemed that Hitler was in complete control!

The world trembled! Human freedom lay exposed - threatened as never before!

ITALY

Mussolini had been meeting with Hitler! Churchill warned him not to interfere in the war but he had already aligned himself with his Nazi counterpart! On June 10, 1940, within weeks of the French surrender, Italy declared war on Britain and France. Churchill, in a public speech, referred to the Italian Dictator (the man he once admired) as *"that guttersnipe Mussolini!"*

DUNKIRQUE

With France in German hands, British troops that had come there to help defend the nation's freedom faced entrapment! A 'miracle' occurred! Hundreds of ships of every conceivable kind including whalers, trawlers and fishing vessels sailed from British ports to the shallow waters of Dunkirque. There, on the beaches, the men of the British Expeditionary Force had gathered. 338,226 men were rescued.

BACK HOME

Work on our two major projects was proceeding according to plan! By March 1939 both projects were under way. The contractors Buckland & Eaton had won the Balmoral contract. Their tender was the lowest of six very close tenders, all from members of the MBA[81]. S. Nathan, a close friend of my partner, had asked to tender for the Hof Street flats. That concerned me! While his work seemed reasonably sound, he was not a member of the MBA and as far as I knew had never built anything larger than a single dwelling! When submitting our final Sketch Plans and Estimates to clients, I informed them of my concern. They, in turn, inspected Nathan's work and decided that he should be allowed to tender! His tender was slightly less than our estimate and, although competitive prices were not obtained, the clients decided to award him the contract!

AN EXTRAORDINARY COINCIDENCE

After one of my Balmoral inspections, Mr. Buckland asked if I could spare him a few minutes to discuss a private matter that had nothing to do with the job. 'It would take only a few minutes'. He opened up a roll of drawings and explained that he had commenced a small double-story building down the road and was about to lay out the foundations when they noticed that the main staircase - shown clearly on the ground floor - did not appear on the first floor plan. Said Mr. Buckland: "Perhaps we are not sufficiently familiar with planning practices! Could you possibly clarify it for us?" I glanced at the plan and noticed the words "Architect: Dr. Ingber" in the bottom right hand corner. I immediately expressed regret that I could not assist, that it would be unprofessional for me to discuss the work of another architect! I suggested that he refer to the architect concerned. That ended the discussion. I never knew how the problem was finally resolved!

I had not met Dr. Ingber. I had heard that he had obtained a doctorate degree in Italy for his academic study of ancient buildings, that 'although his course of study did not embrace the practical aspects of architecture', the degree entitled him to practice architecture in South Africa.

Weeks went by when I had a call from Dr. Ingber asking for an appointment. I assumed it concerned the missing staircase. That proved not to be the case! In my office, Dr. Ingber introduced himself as the 'Cape Town representative of your old firm Kallenbach, Kennedy and Furner'. He put an agreement before me and said that his 'concern' related to a particular clause to which he pointed. It was to the effect: *'This agreement is subject to termination upon one month's notice, should Alfred H. Honikman decide to represent the firm in Cape Town'*. Dr. Ingber asked if I could tell him what my intentions were in that regard. That, he said, was the sole purpose of his visit. Without hesitation, I assured him that "nothing was further from my thoughts!" I said "that will never happen", for I had long since decided that I would have no further dealings with the firm.

Dr. Ingber thanked me and commented: "I am relieved and grateful." The interview was of little significance for me, save that it took my thoughts back to the unpleasant end of my 3-year sojourn in Johannesburg. It also made me wonder who it was, whose conscience had accounted for the particular provision in Dr. Ingber's agreement - Kallenbach or Furner? That I would never know. I was content to have put Dr. Ingber's mind at rest!

PERSONAL IMPLICATIONS

More and more every day, my thoughts focused on the war and its implications. "What if Hitler's aggression continued unchecked?" In London, my sister Beatrice had been sleeping in makeshift air-raid shelters during the nightly raids. I became increasingly aware of what was at stake. I dwelled over the position. I was not yet 30 - had no right to sit back and watch events unfold. Young men from all walks of life were joining the army. That was the course I had to follow! There was no option.

My partner was away on two weeks annual leave! After an absence of three weeks, his wife called to say he was home but not well! He returned to office some weeks later! He seemed tired but made no reference to health matters or to his prolonged absence! His friend Nathan, delighted to have won the Hof Street contract, produced two new jobs - two houses in Claremont. They kept my partner busy for a while. Our services for Nathan did not include much in the way of detail drawings. Specifications, tenders and supervision were not required. Thus our work for each of his jobs was completed in relatively short time! Boy (he was generally referred to as 'Boy Leeb') had been back for a few months when he took ill again. This time his absence was for several months. Inquiries - to his wife Celia - were not very revealing. She seemed reluctant to discuss the matter. I telephoned his cousin Joe (who had drawn up our agreement) to ask how Boy was getting on. His answer alarmed me. He replied: "I'm afraid it's the old problem." He was surprised to hear that I was unaware of any 'old problem'. He came over to see me immediately! He thought 'everyone knew of Boy's problem'! He explained that it was a 'depressive condition' that involved electrical shock treatment from time to time - that the treatment appeared effective and usually left Boy free of the trouble for quite a while. "This time," he said, "it recurred sooner and took longer than expected!"

The news distressed me. I felt overwhelmed! I had come to know my partner as a natural artist, an exceptionally capable designer. Above all we had become friends. It saddened me deeply that a potentially great career could be so impaired by illness.

I told Joe of my decision to enlist! His response was to the effect that while there was little likelihood of much private building during the war, Boy (my partner) was in no position to run the practice in my absence. He went on to say: "Heaven alone knows how long the war will last! You will obviously be parting company! Shame it's been a happy and promising relationship. I will explain and make it as easy as possible." He added: "Pity it has to end this way. Maybe Nathan's work will keep him busy!" Within days he sent us a document, with a note saying that he hoped we would 'find it acceptable'. It was an agreement to terminate the partnership. When Boy returned to office, he said Joe had explained the position and he had read the agreement. His eyes were tearful! He hugged me and uttered: "I am sorry!" Emotionally overcome, he sat at my desk for a while. Then, without uttering a word, he rose, shook his head and sadly he went home.

Some days later we signed the agreement. It provided for the proceeds of all work on hand to be divided equally. The partnership had ended.

ARMY AND FAMILY!

For Cape Town, army headquarters were at the Castle[82]. There, in the large courtyard, I was confronted with long lines of volunteers. I joined the line heading for the signboard 'ENGINEERS'- the corps that drew my interest. I completed an enlistment form, underwent an exhaustive medical examination and was referred to an ear specialist! After exhaustive tests, I was told that I had failed the medical examination and that I could try again three or six months later and, in the meantime, could register for part-time service! I was of course aware of my hearing problem. It had been with me for a long time. However, I thought it to be slight - never dreamt it could disqualify me from service. At home, Deena was busy in the kitchen. I waited till after dinner before reporting on the events of the day. She handed me a letter she had received from her father. Three of her brothers were in the army! Lionel (he and I shared the same birthday) was a Captain in the Engineering Corps; Max, in England, had joined the British Medical Corps; and Cecil was a pilot in the South African Air Force. He was on call 'liable to be sent overseas any day'. Her other brother Harold (Hal), the only brother at home, had recently returned from the Liverpool School of Architecture and was needed in his father's office. That letter was the source of deep concern to Deena. When I told her the result of my medical examination, she uttered a sigh! It sounded like one of relief rather than sorrow! She wondered what kind of future lay in store for Basil - then only three years old!

I joined a part-time military unit and attended drill at the Castle two nights a week for several months. For a while, Leeb and I continued working side by side from the same offices. All projects that we had commenced together were completed before we parted. The Hof Street flats proved a great success! It drew favorable comment from colleagues and strangers alike. That was most gratifying! We had consulted each other at every stage and on most of the many detail drawings. Particularly pleasing was a letter of appreciation from clients. It was a well-deserved tribute to Boy's architectural skill; he personally had been responsible for the initial design.

I gave up the offices in Boston House and returned to smaller and cheaper accommodation in Dominion House.

MY DAD

On September 1, 1940, my father died. He was only 68 – a massive heart attack! He was a remarkable man. His schooling in Liverpool came to an end when his family migrated to South Africa. He was still a boy when he left home to fend for himself. Largely self educated, he became quite a Shakespearian scholar and frequently quoted from well-known works. He overcame many hurdles and made it his goal to ensure that his six children received all the education (and much else) that had been denied him. He did not leave it at that. His compassion went out to family and strangers, orphans and disabled persons. To them he devoted time, energy and aid. He rarely displayed his emotions. Throughout his life, his actions reflected the lofty standards by which he lived. They were a source of inspiration to his family and his friends. Essentially a modest man, he was unpretentious but immaculate. He never asserted authority nor did he ever flaunt the material success he'd earned and so richly deserved. Today, sixty-five years after his death, I am often confronted with issues that remind me of the lofty principles that were the hallmark of his life, the high standards he set and lived by - never faltering. He was a great man - a truly wonderful father - and I - his grateful son!

WORK GOES ON

To my surprise, despite the war, the practice kept moderately busy. I received instructions to proceed with the second Balmoral contract, embracing several additional bedroom suites and facilities to the second floor and part of the third. The work was to be completed in time for the 'forthcoming season'. That was a challenge! The influx of visitors from all parts of the country was usually in full swing by December 1. That became the dead-line for completion of building operations! Six months would be required for actual building operations; that left me less than three months to complete the plans, obtain municipal approval and call for tenders. With the burning of mid-night oil, the goal was met. Buckland and Eaton were again the successful contractors, which made matters much easier. The work was completed in good time. I had also received a letter from a young Johannesburg firm of architects (Hansen, Tomkin and Finklestein) asking me to undertake the supervision of a new Curzon cinema in Wynberg[83] for which they were the architects. I accepted the appointment and building operations were due to commence. It occurred to me that despite the war, there was a fair amount of building activity! I pondered: '*If conditions improve after the war, as they should, hopefully the practice will really be busy! Will I ever get down to the building of our own home?*' I decided: "Now was the time!" Since I bought the plot, I had done several thumbnail sketches; finality eluded me! Now the need was immediate!

AESTHETICS

After several discussions with Deena, the house plans were completed. During the process, I struck an aesthetic problem. The elevations called for clean sharp lines consistent with my idea of contemporary architecture. My perspective drawings all showed the broad eaves projection as the domi-nant line in the design, but the gutter material presented a problem. All standard gutters involved lapped joints that produced a 'serrated effect' which I felt was 'untidy' and aesthetically unacceptable. To overcome the problem, I felt that the eaves had to be encased. I set about detailing an eaves encasement that concealed both the lapped gutter joints and the pro-truding rafters. Only in that way could I obtain the desired clean sharp appearance. Detail drawings were prepared accordingly. In due course a building contract was entered into with C. J. Champion and Son. They were stationed in Claremont, the adjoining suburb about a mile from our plot. They had successfully completed a few small jobs for me. I liked their work and had got on well with Albert Champion, their head foreman.

At that time, I visited the Curzon site that was being cleared prepara-tory to building operations. Beautiful plants from the old garden were being loaded onto a cart. The demolition contractor was present. He said the load was destined for a refuse dump in Maitland - several miles away! I asked if, instead, he would like to 'dump' the load on my plot in Ronde-bosch - far less distant than Maitland - less than half the distance. He was only too pleased and asked if succeeding loads could be similarly dumped. With that, of course, I could not concur. With that single load, three flourishing plants were delivered to and transplanted in the front garden of our new home. They included a healthy Rhododendron and a rare species of Cycloid. They survived the transplant, thrived in our front garden and were a constant source of pleasure to Deena and the family. In due course, the house was completed. I named it "Ferramee"[84]. It was the family haven for the next 25 years. The transplanted plants flourished.

The Curzon cinema was formally opened and the hotel contract was completed in good time.

THE ARMY

With the completion of other professional commitments, I made a second attempt to enlist. Again, I failed the examination. I felt that was not justified and reported accordingly to Capt. Elsworth[85] who was my Officer Commanding at the Castle. He sent me for yet another medical examination - this time to one of several civilian practitioners commissioned by the army. The one chosen for me turned out to be Dr. Earnest Liberman to whom I was distantly related.[86] He expressed surprise at my attempt to enlist and commented: "I thought you could do better!" It was a strange remark; but I thought it best not to comment! This time, my hearing condition presented no problem!

Enlisted at last, I closed the office and joined the 'Dukes' units, some of whose members were already serving in Egypt. I was sent to Roberts Heights[87] on a six weeks 'officers training course'. With some 30 other trainees I shared one of the several hundred military huts. By 7 a.m. every morning, trainees would be fully dressed and the premises swept and cleaned, each man being responsible for his area. The hut had to be in a neat spotless condition before the arrival of the inspecting officers.

As they entered, we'd hasten to the foot of our bunks and come to attention as the inspecting officers approached. Inspections included a good look behind and below almost every bunk! Woe-betide any man whose bed concealed anything untoward or untidy!

Bugle call at 7:30 every morning would rally more than a thousand men to the vast parade ground. A period of drill followed with orders from the commanding officer broadcast through loud speakers mounted on overhead wires. Off-duty periods on Saturday afternoons and Sundays were usually spent with cousins and friends in Johannesburg.

All went well. I had been at Roberts Heights for four weeks when one morning soon after assembly, my name bellowed from the loudspeakers: "Sergeant Honikman, step forward - fall out - report to your OC immedi- ately." I wondered: 'what possible offence could I have committed. Maybe my suitcase was not neatly paced under my bunk - who knows?' It could be anything! On entering the office of the Commanding Officer, I dutifully clicked heels, saluted and said: "Sergeant Honikman reporting as directed, Sir." The officer's eyes were focused on his desk. Not looking up, he announced: "Honikman, you're an architect?" I replied: "Yes Sir." "Then what are you doing here?" Before I could reply, he looked up, handed me a paper and said: "This is your train warrant. You will proceed to Cape Town immediately." I was flabbergasted. "May I ask what has happened, Sir?" He replied: "Architects are required urgently for special duty. You have been assigned to the Directorate of Fortifications and Coastal Works. Your place is there - not here! Transport will be at your hut in ten minutes. You will be taken to Park Station Johannesburg. The Cape Town train leaves at noon. On arrival, report immediately to DF&CW[88]. Col. Craig will be your officer commanding. Be off - get cracking and good luck!"

The instruction was clear - immediate compliance implicit!

I returned to my hut and packed my belongings. I could not imagine what kind of architectural service could be of such urgency as to pull me away from the course to which I had been assigned.

I was soon to learn the answer in Cape Town.

In the rush, there was no way I could inform Deena of my movements. I left the Transvaal without bidding farewell to family or friends in Johan- nesburg.

CHAPTER 19

BACK IN CAPE TOWN

DF&CW ^(Directorate of Fortifications & Coastal Works) occupied the entire Old Mutual Building in Darling Street in the heart of the City. I knew the building well. It is situated within walking distance but two blocks from the station. There, within minutes of my arrival, I was directed to the office of the commanding officer, Col. Craig. A congenial man, he welcomed me, put me at ease and proceeded to explain what had transpired. The defense of England during the Battle of Britain cost the lives of many British pilots. The War Cabinet was concerned that if British airports continued to be targeted by the German air force, the training of pilots anywhere in the British Isles could become untenable. To meet such an emergency, the War Cabinet decided to build several large, permanent pilot training stations in different parts of the British Commonwealth. One such station was to be built at Langebaanweg near Saldahna Bay on the West Coast about 100 miles north of Cape Town. That task had been allocated to the Directorate and instructions had been received to proceed with the design of the various buildings 'in the shortest time possible'. Col. Craig explained several site plans that were mounted on the walls of his office. They demonstrated the magnitude of the undertaking.

It involved the design and construction of several technical buildings for which the basic plans were to come from Britain. "More importantly from our point of view," he said, "the project entails living accommodation for several thousand men, dining halls, lecture halls, dormitories, and single dwellings for officers, all of which will be designed and built under our direction. In addition, we will be responsible for the sports fields, gymnasium, swimming pool, boat houses as well as the provision of roads, sewerage disposal works, electrical and water reticulation systems. It is virtually a new town that we'll be building from scratch - in addition, current operations remain our responsibility."

It sounded a formidable task. It described the activities that were to keep me occupied for the rest of the war years - something totally different from anything I had ever envisaged.

Major Fox entered the room. He was introduced to me as 'the senior officer' under whom I would be operating. Asked to explain 'the personnel situation', Major Fox said that all seniors on the staff were professional men - architects, engineers, and quantity surveyors. They were commissioned officers and all such posts on the establishment were already filled. He said: "It was never envisaged that we would be confronted with projects of the magnitude of Langebaanweg. When that happened, more professional men were needed than were provided for under the existing establishment. The war office issued a general call - especially for architects - which accounts for your presence here today." He added: "The Establishment has not yet been enlarged and until that happens your rank must remain unchanged. You will be working with other architects who have been here a while. They all hold commissioned rank. Professionally, some are junior to you. I hope you understand."

The conversation continued less formally. He told me that when it became known that I was on my way, one of the officers remarked that he had been one of my students at the university and that I was already in practice when he graduated. He said, in fact, there were 'quite a few' on the staff holding commissioned rank who were junior to me professionally. Major Fox concluded: "I hope that will not cause problems!" I assured him that as far as I was concerned, there was no problem; I realized I was no longer my own master and hoped that my presence would not be a source of embarrassment to others.

HOME AGAIN

The interview ended with a directive from Major Fox to report to him at 9 a.m. the following Monday. He concluded: "Until then, you're on paid leave." That was an unexpected pleasant surprise! I thanked him and asked to use the telephone. In the rush since leaving Roberts Heights, there had been no time to inform Deena of my return to the Cape! When Deena heard that I was back and would be stationed in Cape Town, she commented: "Thank God - Please wait there, I'll be with you immediately."

Half-hour later she and Basil gave me a wonderful welcome - followed by a delightful (unexpected) five-day holiday at home. For weeks Deena had received little news of her brothers - nothing from Max! Lionel was in Egypt and all she had heard was of Rommel's massive advance! "Cecil was due to leave for Britain any day now!" Her obvious concern served to explain her "Thank God" when I told her that I was home to stay! It was one of relief - more than delight!

It was 1941. Basil was four years of age - a bright very good-looking child. I cannot recall ever having spent a happier period. For those five days, the three of us were together totally undisturbed by extraneous demands, professional or military. No holiday could ever have been nicer. It was wonderful to be home again with family - free of the daunting prospect of a prolonged absence! Clearly that had been a problem that weighed heavily on Deena and less consciously perhaps, on Basil.

A CHANGED PERSON

Within days of my return from Roberts Heights, I observed a distinct change in Deena's general demeanor! It disturbed me because it seemed to be deep-rooted. Her joyful disposition had given way to a kind of solemnity that seemed ever present. Concern about her brothers and the dangers they faced may have been the cause. I was aware of that, but it did not allay my concern. The sheer happiness that accompanied my homecoming was short-lived. When I asked what was worrying her, she would brush it aside - did not want to discuss it. For months it was a source of worry. One evening after dinner, we drove to the Table Bay waterfront at Milnerton. We sat facing directly into the long streak of light from the sun settling into the horizon when Deena exclaimed: "I want to have another baby!"

From that moment on, Deena's mood changed. She smiled again; her solemn manner gone, her natural personality restored. Clearly a tremendous load had been lifted from her mind! I felt that she had responded to an overwhelming 'need' - one that she had suppressed. Apparently she felt it was incompatible with the wartime dangers which were ever present in her mind.

AUGUST 5, 1942

This time, Deena had no wish to go back to a maternity home. Her pregnancy was well advanced. She had moved into the second bedroom which she shared with an experienced maternity nurse. I was back home late one afternoon when Dr. Lipshitz was in attendance. After examining

Deena, he thought she would go into labor next morning. He said: "If I'm needed sooner, don't hesitate to call." He lived in Claremont, ten minutes from home. I saw him to the door and returned to the landing up-stairs. Suddenly Deena's door flew open. A tense nurse faced me and hastily exclaimed: "boiling water - the baby's on its way!" I rushed to the kitchen, delivered the water, and called the doctor. He was not yet home. I left an urgent message. Minutes later I heard a baby's cry. When I got to the room, the child was resting on Deena's shoulder. All went well. When the doctor arrived, our second son was half an hour old. The nurse had performed admirably!

SMOKING!

At DF&CW the work was absorbing and interesting but it never extended beyond the normal working hours. To my regret I had lapsed into my old smoking habit! I hadn't smoked for five years, not since that day in Sweden when I discarded the last of those loosely packed cigarettes. In the lounge, we had kept a rather finely embossed ebony cigarette box - one that we had received as a gift and were reluctant to discard. I opened it! It contained two cigarettes. They were old - must have been there for years! I had no inclination to smoke and I wondered what it was about smoking that had attracted me! I decided to 'taste it', took one out of the box and lit it! It was awful - loose tobacco dropped onto my tongue. 'That certainly was not what once attracted me!' I lit the second one! It was better - nothing repelling about it! In fact, I enjoyed it! That was the beginning of my return to the old ugly habit! I became quite a heavy smoker - consumed about 20 cigarettes daily for the next eleven years until 1952 when I finally gave it up! That is another story that I will come to later in these memoirs.

THE REST OF THE WAR YEARS

Our home was some six miles from the city and little more than a mile to the Rondebosch railway station. A regular and frequent train service between suburbs and city was the most economical means of commuting daily to downtown. Routinely, I left home at eight in the morning, cycled to the station to report for duty by nine. I was back home by six in the evening. The Hillman that we bought in London in 1936 was kept mainly for Deena's shopping needs and week-end jaunts with the children to the seaside.

Work at DF&CW was interesting and varied. Over time I was responsible for a variety of structures. They included residential and recreational buildings, dining halls, gymnasiums, single dwellings, a boathouse and a church. My duties included the scrutiny of tenders and not least, reporting on the designs of others - many my seniors in rank. The embarrassment I feared never occurred. The officers concerned graciously accepted the procedure as a matter of routine. Invariably they chose to discuss their proposals in the preliminary stages and seemed to welcome constructive comment. Apart from formal greetings, stern army practices that one might have expected, were seldom apparent at DF&CW. Professional rather than 'military' practices seemed to characterize relationships at all times.

In due course, I was elevated to the rank of staff sergeant and later to that of Sergeant Major. Major Fox then explained that no additional commissioned posts had been added to the establishment and I remained a warrant officer for the remaining three years until the war was over.

LIGHTER MOMENTS!

My job had its humorous moments. As warrant officer, one of my (non- professional) duties was to keep a check on absentee NCO's. They were required to report to me on return to work after absence for whatever reason. Staff Sergeant Allsop had been on sick leave for a few weeks. The report I had received indicated that he had a bad dose of flu and had lost his voice. When he finally returned, he stood before me and clicked his heels and saluted. I looked up and said: "Welcome back, Allsop - how are you feeling?" Slowly, in a hushed husky voice hardly audible, he uttered: *"Sir, my left lung is bad... "* He paused, tapped his chest and, in a firm voice that was loud and strong, he declared: *"but the right's alright!"* A hearty laugh by all around, welcomed Allsop's return to work.

WAR NEWS!

Allsop's humor provided a little relief to prevailing tensions. Within weeks of the fall of France, Hitler's Luftwaffe had turned to England. By July 10, 1940, the Battle of Britain was under way. Driven off by two British fighter squadrons, the Germans suffered heavy losses but the raids continued. British airports and shipping were targeted; time and again the Royal Air Force intercepted and counter attacked. Both sides suffered heavy causalities but the attacks continued. Many airports were rendered unserviceable; night after night screeching sirens took thousands of civilians scurrying to underground shelters. Minefields were laid in the British Channel and elsewhere in an attempt to disrupt the shipping lanes - Britain's lifelines were endangered. Incredible property damage was wrought in England and Scotland and in the heart of London. Hitler reckoned that Britain, like France, would be forced into submission. On June 18, Churchill addressed the House of Commons. These were his words - words that inspired the nation and parts of the world that were still free:

Hitler knows that he will have to break us in this Island or lose the war. If we can stand up to him, all Europe may be free and the life of the world may move forward into broad, sunlit uplands. But if we fail, then the whole world, including the United States, including all that we have known and cared for, will sink into the abyss of a new Dark Age made more sinister, and perhaps more protracted, by the lights of perverted science. Let us therefore brace ourselves to our duties, and so bear ourselves that, if the British Empire and its Commonwealth last for a thousand years, men will still say, "This was their finest hour"

England stood alone to face a major air assault - the first of its kind in the history of warfare. Churchill's words boosted the morale of the people. The nation rallied, as did the RAF[89]. German air raids by day and night faced a determined counter attack. The losses on both sides were heavy! Hitler had miscalculated. He little realized the quality of Britain's resolve never to submit to his terror. Thus it was in the air that he suffered his first defeat! He turned his attention to the eastern front and to Africa. His recent treaty with Stalin, a temporary act of expediency, was to him but a scrap of paper! He attacked the Soviet Union and strengthened his forces in Egypt.

NORTH AFRICA

For a long while, little news filtered through from North Africa. When it came, it was often grim - seldom encouraging. The stakes there were the control of the Eastern Mediterranean, the Suez Canal and the supply of oil. In 1940, a British offensive had driven the Italian army out of Egypt deep into Libya. British troops in large numbers were diverted to Greece. Along that desert strip 30 miles from the Mediterranean, the fortunes of war ebbed and flowed. The Eighth Army, joined by troops from Australia and South Africa, remained heavily outnumbered in both manpower and armor. A massive German attack under the command of General Rommel drove them back to Tobruk. The Allied forces dug in. In the following weeks they were reinforced and reorganized under the command of General

Montgomery. They hit back. Rommel was in retreat! Many regarded the Allied advance as the turning point in the war. During that advance, Deena's cousin Capt. Leo Kowarsky[90] was found in the desert and rescued. He had been seriously wounded in the earlier retreat to Tobruk - his hip partly shattered!

THE UNITED STATES

From the start of the war in Europe, neutrality remained the official policy of the United States. Their support for the Allied cause, however, was never in question. For two years, industrial America had become an arsenal, producing machines and armaments of every kind needed by the Allies. The various shipping lanes to Britain were attacked by German U-boats. Despite the vigilance of the British Navy, the losses were immense but the flow of supplies, continued relentlessly. U-boat activity was not confined to the North Atlantic. Several ships were sunk outside the Cape Town harbor. Nazi spies mingled among the civilian population of the city where countless street placards bore the ominous words: *"Don't talk about ships and shipping."* The German command was acutely aware that the sea lanes around the Cape were vital to the Allies for troops from Australia and for supplies from the West destined for the battle zones in Egypt.

PEARL HARBOR: DECEMBER 7, 1941

In December 1941 cities throughout America teemed with Christmas shoppers. It was said to be the busiest season since 1928! On that Sunday, until darkness fell, there were parties throughout the country. Suddenly, without warning or provocation, hundreds of Japanese bombers attacked Pearl Harbor, the principal naval base of America's Pacific fleet! Bombers came in waves! In the darkness of night, Japanese aircraft carriers had assembled at strategic points in the Pacific. Thousands of American lives were lost. Battleships *Arizona* and *Oklahoma* were sunk; several cruisers and destroyers were sunk or seriously damaged. In manpower and craft, the losses suffered were greater, by far, than in any single event in the history of naval warfare.

Broadcasting to the nation, President Roosevelt referred to 'a Day of Infamy', and declared war on the Japanese Empire!

Hitler chose the occasion to declare war on the United States. Eighteen months after he unleashed his terror on Poland, the war spread to both sides of the Atlantic and Pacific Oceans. No continent was to escape its terror; no country its consequences. Never before had mankind confronted forces more formidable - more evil.

FISSION!

In 1940, Two German scientists, Otto Hahn and Fritz Strasman, discovered nuclear fission - the release of atomic energy. Scientists in the United States and in Nazi Europe pursued a frantic search to harness that energy in the form of a bomb - one capable of a reaction of such magnitude and devastation as to destroy everything in its wake! For five years the search continued - each side fearful that the other might be the first to find the answer!

EUROPE

Hitler dominated all of Europe. His defeat was the Allies first objective. That demanded nothing less than conquest in North Africa and the invasion of the European mainland. It served only .to strengthen their resolve! They set about formulating strategies, combining resources. The magnitude of the task defies description! It would take years to achieve. It entailed coordination of military, naval and air power on a scale never before envisaged. Not least it called for the dedication and dauntless courage of tens of thousands of men willing, if need be, to forfeit their lives in the cause of freedom. Such was the first formidable goal to which the Allies dedicated themselves.

By June 1944 preparations for the invasion of "Fortress Europe" were complete. The actual date for invasion was not determined. That was left to General Dwight Eisenhower to determine. The shortest and most obvious Channel crossing was from Dover to Calais. That, the Germans concluded, would be the chosen route for invasion. Allied strategists took great pains to convince them that they were right. Hundreds of wooden 'tanks' were assembled in Dover and, after midnight on the morning of June 6, 1944, vessels of the Royal Navy raced back and forth offering further evidence that the invasion from Dover was imminent! At 3 a.m. that same morning the invasion began - not at Calais but on the beaches of Normandy. That day 132,700 men went ashore and in less than a week, two million men, 20,000 vehicles and 11,000 airplanes had crossed into Normandy. Another 20,000 men were dropped by parachute or had glided behind the German lines. They faced desperate resistance. The Battle of the Bulge in

December gave evidence that the Nazi might had waned. Boys of 16 were in the firing line. The Eastern and African fronts had taken a heavy toll of Hitler's might. In August, Paris was again in Allied hands. Relentlessly, Allied forces pushed on into Germany. There was no turning back. Germany's might was broken! British and Commonwealth forces under the command of General Montgomery and the United States Army under General Eisenhower headed towards Berlin and in the east. Slowly Nazi resistance yielded to Soviet pressure.

Stalin's 1939 agreement with Hitler over the division of Poland (among other concerns) gave rise to doubts about his intentions after Germany's defeat. The Allies were concerned about his reaction if they were to enter Berlin ahead of him. In Eisenhower's opinion a joint entry was desirable. His view prevailed! The Allies held back until the Russians met up.

YALTA

At last, when Allied victory was beyond all doubt, the Allied leaders agreed to meet to discuss issues concerning the organizing of post-war Europe and the occupation of Germany. Churchill, Roosevelt and Stalin and their staffs met at Yalta on February 4, 1945. They deliberated for a week! Several agreements were reached: Polish independence would be restored; Yugoslavia would elect its own government; Nazi and Fascist leaders would be prohibited. At the time, Russia was not at war with Japan. At Yalta, Stalin agreed to declare war on Japan "in two or three months" subject to several conditions concerning Manchuria, China and islands off Japan. Not all were approved. It was however agreed that Berlin would be divided into zones - the east zone to be controlled by Russia, the other three by Britain, the USA and France. On April 23, 1945, all three armies marched into Berlin.

HITLER'S END

When defeat became glaringly apparent to Hitler, he and a few of his staff took refuge in an underground bunker beneath the German Chancellery in Berlin. His mistress Eva Braun joined him. To satisfy her long felt want, they married in the bunker, entered an adjoining compartment and committed suicide. Thus ended the life of the most venomous of all tyrants - more peacefully, more comfortably than had he faced justice.

On May 7, 1945, Admiral Doenitz surrendered. VE Day[91] had come at last!

THE REACTION AT HOME

In South Africa, and certainly for those of us stationed there, VE Day produced an understandable sense of relief. News from all the war fronts in Europe and in the Pacific had been sparse. Unprecedented enemy espionage imposed strict censorship of all news. We, who were remote from the actual theaters of war, knew little of the grim events that took place in Europe and less of those in the Pacific. In retrospect, it is difficult to comprehend that there *were* spots on this planet where one could live in tranquility, while drama of unprecedented magnitude was unfolding elsewhere.

In the Cape, we soon became aware that the sea route around our coast had ceased to be a target for German U-boats. We understood also that for Britain, the training of pilots abroad was no longer a matter of urgency. Our work at DF&CW lost all urgency and was virtually at a standstill. Indeed, many of us hopefully imagined that discharge from the army was imminent! That, we were told was not to be - not while additional manpower could be needed in the war with Japan. That, more or less, represented the extent of the information reaching us about the many grim and momentous events that were happening in extensive areas of the South Pacific.

We were required to report for duty every day as before, but the need for the Langebaanweg air training station appeared to have lost all urgency. Our work came to a virtual halt! Most of the architectural staff were idle - left to our own resources. That extraordinary situation continued.

IN THE PACIFIC

The war with Japan entailed problems vastly different from those in Europe but no less grim or tragic. In January 1942 the Japanese attacked Bataan in the Philippines, invaded the Dutch East Indies and Dutch Borneo and advanced in Burma. On the 27th of January, the first Japanese warship was sunk by a U. S. submarine and the following month, airplanes from U. S. carriers attacked Japanese bases on the Gilbert and Marshall Islands. Days later the Japanese invaded Singapore and Sumatra, conducted a raid on Darwin in Australia, and invaded Bali. On February 23, they sank a U. S. aircraft carrier and the largest U. S. warship, the *Houston,* and attacked the U. S. mainland near Santa Barbara. In Singapore, the British surrendered! In the U. S., despite the internment of many Japanese American civilians, 17,000 Japanese Americans signed up to fight for the U. S.

From Bataan came a report of the notorious 'Death March'! 76,000 Allied prisoners of war, including 12,000 Americans, were made to trudge sixty miles exposed to the glaring sun. Five thousand men died! Conditions were grim!

In April 1942, U. S. bombers raided Tokyo and a month later Japan suffered its first defeat at the Battle of the Coral Sea off New Guinea. Meanwhile, Japanese forces captured Burma. On June 4 and 5, fifteen months after Pearl Harbor, the Battle of Midway was a turning point in the Pacific war. U. S. squadrons from carriers *Enterprise*, *Yorktown* and *Hornet*, destroyed or sank four Japanese carriers, two cruisers and two destroyers. The *Yorktown* was sunk. On land, at Guadacanal and the Solomon Islands, the U. S. Army under General Macarthur, together with the Australians, took New Guinea. U. S. forces continued their advance. A political crisis in Japan and the fall of the Japanese government was followed by a massive air battle in mid-June in which the Japanese lost 400 airplanes – the U. S. 30. The Battle of the Philippine Sea followed. The hazards of war in the Pacific continued. Then Japan lost the carriers *Luzon* and *Okinawa*. That marked the end of Japanese sea power. The U. S. had gained control of several island bases that would be required for an assault on the main Japanese islands. Such a venture, it was reasoned, would demand incalculable resources and would entail hazards that could cost the lives of a million men. It was an unthinkable proposition! On April 12, 1945, Franklin Delano Roosevelt died. Harry S. Truman became U. S. President. On him vested the destiny of the United States and in his hands rested the reins of human freedom.

ATOMIC BOMB

Soon after the outbreak of war in 1939, the search for the atomic bomb continued with ever-increasing intensity. The Manhattan Project, a massive industrial research program under the direction of Dr. J. Robert Oppenheimer, unlocked atomic power was unlocked for the first time in history. Predawn - on July 16 - the Trinity test took place at Alamogordo in New Mexico. "The gadget", the first nuclear device, was detonated. The explosion made an awesome visual impact. The sky turned orange to mark the beginning of the Nuclear Age.

At 8:15 a.m. on Monday, August 6, the first atomic bomb exploded over the city of Hiroshima! Three days later, August 9, another much larger fell on the city of Nagasaki! Accompanied by a blinding flash and followed by an awesome expanding mushroom cloud, the bombs resulted in the indiscriminate slaughter of 250,000 men, women and children - all innocent non-combatants, punished for the crime of war that they did not commit! Thousands more were burned, tortured and maimed. Homeless infants writhing in agony groped aimlessly through the streets; their parents, their homes and their hopes all gone. The air was poisoned - the cities reduced to rubble. The devastation, the horror, defies description.

On August 15, Japan surrendered. World War II was ended.

WHERE DO WE GO FROM HERE?

Mankind took a deep breath! Lives lost in World War II, greater in number than in all other wars combined, have been estimated at 75,000,000[92]. The millions maimed and suffering were found impossible to estimate.

One ponders! The process by which Man lives at peace with fellow Man is a natural, seemingly simple one - obviously a very desirable one! Why then, is that freedom in constant danger? Generation after generation, human life and liberty are forfeited in ever-increasing numbers to assert that *freedom?* Why? Why have we failed, thus far, to devise a system by which to live at PEACE with fellow Man? Man (the only known species capable of rational thought) has to his credit an array of incredible achievements of vast benefit to his kind. He has revealed sources of energy capable of prolonging life, enriching it and simplifying it. He has reached the threshold of yet greater discoveries that hold promise of a life ever more glorious! Alas, despite such promise, he has failed to produce a FORMULA by which to live at *peace*! Instead, he has acquired the ability, at the turn of a switch, to destroy all life, to reduce all his aspirations to dust. That FORMULA is civilization's vital need at this hour. Two World Wars in the past century and continuing life-consuming strife make that glaringly apparent! Ninety-one years ago, in an attempt to find the answer, world leaders came together in the Palace of Versailles in France. They deliberated for days on end; they formed the League of Nations but their combined 'wisdom' failed to produce the answer. It was too lofty a challenge! Two decades later, the entire world was again enmeshed in war - more bloody, more painful, more costly and infinitely more tragic than ever before! The need for that FORMULA loomed larger than ever. To that end, our leaders broadened the scope of the League. They called it '*The United Nations*'. They deliberated. They argued - but the answer eluded them! The most powerful nations were unwilling to yield their will to that of the majority! Instead they chose a right to VETO any resolution including those that were seen by many to be necessary to preserve PEACE! The sought-after FORMULA eluded them—-They had become oblivious to the enormity of the price that had already been paid for PEACE! It was not enough, not grim enough to justify their submission to the will of the people of the world! The price paid was apparently not a deadly enough ransom to produce the elusive FORMULA FOR PEACE.

Now, at the dawn of the new millennium, the problem remains unsolved. The unthinkable prevails! Civilization, indeed all life on this planet, remains threatened and would-be tyrants and terrorists remain undeterred!

We, ordinary men and women, look on, vainly believing that:

> *Every individual, every nation has the right to live in peace! It is a sacred right that demands universal protection such as only a world authority can provide. Thus far our leaders have failed to produce the answer. Threats to violate that right, large or small, need to be confronted with penalties so formidable as to render violation unthinkable. To be effective, such penalties need to be spelled out! They include economic and/or military sanctions against would-be pirate nations and personal penalties against would-be individual perpetrators of such magnitude as to render violation unthinkable.*

That is the resounding silent voice that cries out for action by a world authority whose every member is irrevocably bound - never to violate or abandon the sacred trust vested in him. Such are the rights of every man, woman and child of every nation. Such rights are thus far denied - because there were nations and individuals unwilling to bow to the will of the people. Such is the nature and such the magnitude of the challenge that confronts mankind at this hour.

Dare we ask ourselves: *"What is it that so contaminates our thinking as to deny us the remedy of which we are all in dire need?"* Is it 'lust' or 'fear' or 'suspicion' or other of the negative forces that mold man's thinking? What is it that has denied us the right to a *Formula for peaceful co-existence?*

Without it, Mother Earth, despite its vast potential, is destined to become another lifeless planet - an inglorious monument to human enterprise.

Such is the nature of our prime need at this hour. Obviously it is one that demands of all nations and individuals that they conduct their affairs according to clearly defined civilized procedures - or face unthinkable consequences.

Such then is the nature of the franchise pledge to which every adult should be bound. Without such commitment, no one should have the right to participate in the election of lawmakers and national leaders. Such is the duty of all communities seeking lawful recognition - and such the challenge that confronts us all.

PART 2

CHAPTER 20

FROM WAR TO PEACE

Thirteen weeks elapsed between VE Day, May 8, 1945, and August 15, when World War II, waged for five-and-a-half death-ridden years, finally ended.

It was an end not all wrapped in glory! Man had found the means of splitting the atom - gaining access to the formidable hitherto hidden power that had rendered the atom indivisible - nuclear *power!* Zealously, tirelessly, he sought to harness it - to confront an enemy with the most devastating weapon ever conceived.

To achieve peace - the obvious and only basis on which human relations can be reasonably conducted - man knew no way other than to perpetrate a crime more evil, more painful, more ruthless than ever before conceived.

That crime overshadows and dwarfs the countless achievements gained throughout time. It marks the level that 'civilization' had reached at the start of the second millennium!

That then is the measure of the challenge that confronts us all at this hour.

Dare we forget.

CHAPTER 21

TRANSITION

Far from the Pacific, I was of course untouched physically by the momentous events of that time. Those 13 weeks, however, were not free of problems. The building of Langebaanweg - originally motivated by the threat to British airports during the Battle of Britain - was no longer a matter of urgency. At DF&CW, work was virtually at a standstill. I was among a group of architects, engineers and quantity surveyors with little to occupy their time. A few were allocated sundry tasks of relatively little importance. Others were idle. I was restless - eager to get back to civilian life and private practice. A few would-be clients had telephoned me. One Mr. Baraitser said he had seen my house and wanted me to design his. I felt flattered! Another, Mr. Pasvolsky, introduced himself as Chairman of the Golden Arrow Bus Company. He said they required the services of an architect for building a large new bus depot and inquired if I was in a position to accept the appointment. Those were encouraging signs but I had no choice other than to express thanks and explain that I had not yet received my discharge from the army, that it was due any day, but until then, I was not free to undertake private work. Both very kindly asked me to contact them as soon as I was free. I became concerned that the would-be clients may not be able to wait. Two unexpected incidents occurred. Both widened my horizons and, in effect, changed the course of my life.

AN UNEXPECTED VISITOR

Stella Van Hoogstraten called for an appointment and visited me at home. She introduced herself as the Secretary of the Rondebosch Ratepayers Association (R.R.A.) and said that she had been asked by the Executive Committee to try and enroll me as a member. She explained that the R.R.A was one of several civic bodies in the seventeen municipal wards of greater Cape Town and that their function was to be watchful of the interests of the city's ratepayers. She digressed saying that I knew her brother Capt. Harold Van Hoogstraten who was at school with me. I remembered him. She went on to explain that there was concern throughout the country about the activities of an Afrikaner movement known as the 'Ossewabrandwag'[93]. It had been active during the war and was said to have been the breeding ground of German spies, some of whom had been responsible for the sinking of several Allied ships off the coast. "Today," she said, "they are more active than ever; vehemently anti-British and anti-Smuts, they have generated strong inter-racial cleavage - their goal - nothing less than the overthrow of the Government and the severance of all ties with the British Commonwealth!" She added: "They are supported by a secret society known as *'Die Broederbond'!* Their insidious activities have penetrated deep into Afrikaner society." I had heard about the Broderbond but never in so 'cool' a manner as to rouse concern about potentially grim consequences. She went on to explain that the *'Torch Commando'* had been formed in an attempt to counter the influence of the Broederbond, that thousands of ex-servicemen had already joined - including her brother Harold. She added: "No doubt you too will be contacted!"

My visitor reverted to the R.R.A., produced an application form and said that her initial purpose was to enroll me as a member. I joined. From then on, I regularly attended their meetings in the Rondebosch Town Hall at 8 p.m. on the first Tuesday of every month.

KILLING TIME!

At DF&CW, with so much time on my hands, my mind turned to a technical problem that I had encountered when I was designing our home. It related to the eaves construction. The solution I had adopted met aesthetic considerations but was technically complicated and costly - such as I would hesitate to impose on a client. I started to look for a simpler answer. I found myself sketching a gutter with concealed laps - one that would dispense with the repeated 'lap projections' and so produce the flush, 'sharp line' effect that I was after! Major Fox, on one of his occasional rounds, asked what it was that I was doing. When I explained, he remarked: *"Interesting - you should develop it. You have lots of time. Nobody is likely to disturb you - I doubt if that will be necessary!"* With that, I got down to the drawing board and tried to visualize the various problems that could arise when putting such a gutter to practice. The answers proved simpler than I had imagined. Asbestos seemed to be the most suitable material for the purpose. I prepared 2 sheets of detail drawings illustrating the different elements (eight in all) that I thought would be required to adapt the gutter to every possible circumstance. The drawings included an isometric sketch to show the visual effect of a fully assembled gutter and were headed: "Honikman Patent Flush Gutter - Sheets 1 & 2".

I showed the drawings to a visiting asbestos-roofing manufacturer (one of the DF&CW contractors). He was interested and said that if I registered the gutter as a patent, he would offer me an agreement to manufacture and market it on a royalty basis. I consulted Mr. C.W.A. Coulter, M.P., my one-time neighbor and family friend (he was the only attorney I knew person-ally). It was a long while since I'd seen him. He gave me a hearty welcome, listened to my story and undertook the documentation and registration of the patent. Finally an agreement with the Asbestos Company provided for a royalty payment of 10% on all sales. That gave me quite a boost! My time had not been wasted after all!

OLD FRIENDS

During those quiet weeks prior to my discharge - military duties virtu-ally at a standstill - my thoughts turned to old friends - Afrikaner friends - particularly to those in Porterville. I had not seen them or heard of them for thirteen years, not since the end of 1932 when Greta and her mother came to Johannesburg.

I recalled the happy times we spent together during our student days and wondered how they fared during all that time! What impact had the war made on them? How had they responded to the Nazi influences and to the 'Ossewabrandwag' that Stella Van Hoogstraten had described so vividly. They were "*ware Afrikaners*"[94], that I knew. I wondered how they had resisted the insidious propaganda to which the country had been exposed? I felt impelled to find out! I assumed that Greta was married but did not know her married name. I telephoned Mrs. Van Zyl's home number. Hans (Greta's brother) answered with a hearty "Goeie more!"[95] I replied in English. Hans recognized my voice. When he heard I was in Cape Town, he invited me down for the weekend and added: "Greta will be here!" He obviously thought I needed to know that! His manner, as of old, was warm and friendly and served to lessen my concerns.

It was dark and late when I arrived in Porterville. As I drove up, Hans waived from the stoep. Moments later he, his brother Jack and Greta were at the gate to meet me. Their mother had died; Greta was staying with Hans while her husband was away on business. She had matured but, apart from that, hadn't changed much. We chatted briefly over coffee before turning in.

Next morning after breakfast Greta said she had promised to take me for tea to friends whom I had met years back. As it was still early, she suggested a short drive to 'see the flowers'. Driving through the town she pointed to a house saying, *"That's my home now - remember you designed it for 'ma' soon after we met. You were a budding architect then. We took over when 'ma' died."*

She stopped the car in the shade of a large tree on the fringe of the village. It was early spring! Ahead, the field was a maze of color - wild flowers as far as the eye could see - an unforgettable picture! Suddenly she remarked: "I believe you have a son?" "Yes indeed - two fine boys - they're 8 and 3 now!" She murmured: "Sounds wonderful!" There was a long silence. 'What was she thinking?' She asked: *"Alf - what brought you here?"* Not sure if it was merely a rhetorical question, I answered: "You're old friends; I was wondering how you all fared - how the war and political developments generally had affected you!" "Oh, politics!" she exclaimed. I thought I discerned an air of disgust!

MEIN KAMPF

We drove back to the village. Our first visit was to the home of Mollie Hugo - Greta's older sister. Other visitors arrived - all strangers to me. Conversation was in Afrikaans. Unlike my father, I was by no means fluent in the language. When addressing me, Afrikaner friends usually reverted to 'English'. It was a courtesy I appreciated but it did not allay my discomfort. Glancing at the bookcase, I noticed most of the books were in English. Lying flat on the shelf was Hitler's *Mein Kampf* and with it the bible - both apparently of recent usage! *'The devil and the redeemer.'* That was the thought crossed my mind.

The visit was short. Greta explained to her sister that we had another call to make before lunch. Within minutes, we were at the Versveldt's home. He was a year or two younger than I - said he remembered me from school. There were a few others present. That is all that I recall of the visit save that I spotted among his books another copy of *Mein Kampf*! It made me wonder! When we got back to Hans' home, I went to his study to see if he too possessed that book! Sure enough there it was! It distressed me. Was that the kind of influence to which the Afrikaners were exposed during the war? Had my friends been indoctrinated? Was I in fact among a bunch of Nazis? Such sickening thoughts hammered on my mind. I was disturbed and uncomfortable. When Hans returned, Greta called me to lunch. I asked to be excused - *'not hungry!'* Hans came in. "Are you feeling OK? Can I bring you something?" I thanked him and said I did not feel like eating but would like to see him after lunch! I lay on the bed and dozed off. It was nearly two when I awoke and went into the study. Hans joined me; he brought me a sandwich and coffee and said: "You must eat something! *What's the problem?* Greta tells me something upset you this morning." I took *Mein Kampf* from the shelf, held it up and said: *"Yes. Wherever I've been this morning, I was confronted with this! What does it mean? There was a time when I used to see the bible in every Afrikaner home - now it's this! For six years, Hans, millions gave their lives to eradicate the Nazi curse - a plague that threatens everything we hold dear. It is worrying, to say the least, to come here and find this Nazi hand-book in every home!"* Hans shook his head and reminded me of a conversation we had years past. He spoke then of the anguish of Afrikaner families at the turn of the century when "their women folk were in concentration camps, while the men strove to defend the country against the British. Their suffering should explain much of the anti-war feeling in this country. It certainly accounts for my interest in politics." Then he added: *"We are not anti-Semitic. Hitler taught us an important lesson: the need of a 'scapegoat' to the success of any national movement. Here, we have one on a platter - one that threatens our very survival as a nation - the Kaffir!"* I interrupted: *"I can't listen to this - God help us, if we choose a course so repulsive!"* I felt myself trembling; went inside, packed my belongings. When I returned, Hans, sitting on the rail, seemed deep in thought. I said: *"I'm leaving, Hans. We live in different worlds. I'm deeply shaken by what I've seen and heard; I fear for our country and our children."* I heard him saying: *"My friend, you don't understand...."* I interrupted: *"Thank Greta for her hospitality. Tot siens."* I drove off - a day ahead of schedule!

THE ROAD HOME

The words 'scapegoat' and 'Kaffir' hammered at my mind! I felt repulsed! I realized I was not concentrating on the road! At Milnerton I deviated, turned towards the coast and parked at a favorite spot on the waterfront - one that Deena and I visited occasionally. It was about a half an hour from home. From that spot, on the N/E side of Table Bay, one gained a magnificent panorama of the ramparts of Table Mountain from the eastern slopes of Devil's Peak, to Lion's Head and Sea Point to the west.

Across the 'Kloof Nek' saddle, one had sight of the Twelve Apostles bask-ing in the afternoon sun; faintly on the far left, one could discern the slope of the Muizenberg Mountain where it entered the Indian Ocean at False Bay. It was at that vantage point that memory often took me to the white beaches of Muizenberg where I had spent playful care-free months during my childhood.

My thoughts kept returning to Porterville! I did not want to believe what I had heard! *'Had those folk whose kinship I once cherished, changed so radically? Were they gullible victims, deprived of reason by political opportunists whose lust for power knew no limits?'* Whatever the reason, the impact was marked and grim! Alarm bells rang in my ears! Stella's forebodings seemed all too prophetic!

At home (earlier than expected), I shared my thoughts with Deena. I did not realize how they would affect her! She referred to the Porterville episode weeks - months later. She never ceased worrying about the possi-ble implications for our two boys. One evening, at our favored Milnerton spot, she remarked: *"They were young enough to escape the War; are they to be caught in all this chaos at home?"* I shared her concern!

I joined the Torch Commando - in readiness for - I knew not what!

CHAPTER 22

PEACE - A NEW WORLD!

My discharge papers arrived late in 1945! My release from military duty marked the beginning of a 'new era'. New vistas, new priorities loomed! I seemed to have acquired a new perspective of what life was all about. Before the war, a single objective dominated my thoughts - the building of a sound architectural practice! Now, in 1945, there were new problems at our doorstep; their consequences seemed ominous - unless the racist trend could be halted and reversed! The more I thought about it, the more deep-rooted they appeared to be and the more restless I became. Friends and acquaintances spoke of the *'inevitable consequences'*! Where was the remedy to be found? I became restless! I felt I could not simply sit by and watch disaster approach. I had no right to remain aloof! Clearly the issues facing us were beyond the scope of 'local affairs' - outside the scope of the Ratepayers' Association whose meetings I was attending regularly - they were essentially 'political'! It was a field in which my interests were those of a student - remote and impersonal. It was a field into which I had never thought of entering – but one to which I felt myself being drawn irresistibly! Something (I knew not what) had to be done to combat the vicious 'black menace' propaganda! I joined the Rondebosch Branch of General Smuts's United Party.

END OF MILITARY DUTIES

With my discharge papers came the notice of two material privileges available to professional ex-servicemen. One was a *Government loan* of 2,000 pounds sterling repayable after 2 years, or alternatively an outright grant of one hundred pounds per month for two years. Not wanting to owe so large a sum, I chose the latter. It proved to be the less favorable of the two! After about a year, the conditions were changed. The 'repayment provision' was cancelled and the 2,000 pounds loan became an outright grant! The second privilege was the choice of offices in a new 'controlled' building in the heart of the city. In Cape Town, the chosen building was "Diamond House" at the corner of Longmarket and Parliament Streets. It was still under construction and it would be a few months before completion. The owner was Mr. Hirschsohn who had been my first important client soon after I commenced practice in 1936. I jumped at the opportunity, reserved 3 offices on the (top) 11th floor. Pending completion of the new building, I continued my practice from Dominion House where I had retained a small office to store my furniture, equipment and records during the war.

PRIVATE PRACTICE

Immediately after my discharge, I telephoned and interviewed the two potential clients who had contacted me. I was commissioned to design a large new bus depot for the Golden Arrow Bus Company and a new house in Muizenberg for Mr. Baraitser. My uncertainty and concern as to what might happen to my practice after the war were displaced by a sense of relief - two commissions in the first week! It was a highlight moment - one that Deena shared with me!

The bus depot site was in Klipfontein Road Mowbray (little more than a mile from my home). My instructions were to design a building to accommodate some fifty buses and embrace all ancillary services, work-pits, work-benches, etc. It was emphasized that the roofed-over bus area was to have maximum natural lighting and be free of all internal supports to ensure the unobstructed movement of vehicles in all directions.

HOUSES

In the following months, I received three more commissions - all two-story houses - one for Mr. Sol Green, another for Mr. Martin Brahms, both old family friends, and the third for attorney Shaeffer whom I met for the first time when he and his wife called at my office. All 3 sites were in Oranjezicht not far from "Longwood", my old home. All projects were for 'immediate development'. It was obvious that once the sketch plans were approved, I would not be able to handle everything - the working drawings, details, specifications and supervision, single-handed. Additional assistants were needed - a situation I had never envisaged! The Baraitser site was a long way - sixteen miles from my office! MacIvor, a very able young colleague (whom I knew from college days), was temporally unemployed and agreed to undertake the working drawings. He lived in Fish Hoek, a coastal resort not too far from the Baraitser site. He agreed to do the working drawings and to make weekly inspections on my behalf and so assist with the supervision.

A CITY PROJECT?

The Greens were old family friends. Sol's wife Ester (Manne) had three brothers in Johannesburg all in business together. Sol had joined them and together they ran a chain of successful shoe stores in Cape Town, Johannesburg and Durban, known as Manne Bros. One day, in the course of an informal chat, Mr. Green mentioned that they planned to extend the chain in different parts of the country; their Cape Town store was in rented premises in Adderley Street - the city's main commercial center. They had recently purchased the old Lennons' property - a prominent central city site at the corner of Adderley and Strand Streets.

The Green's home was nearing completion when I received a letter from Mr. Morris Manne enclosing a diagram of the newly acquired site and asking if I would care to 'show them' how I thought it could best be developed. My excitement was intense! The site faced 3 streets with a frontage of about 125 feet on Adderley Street and about 30 feet facing Strand Street and Exchange Place. It was probably the most prestigious site in the city - the envy of any architect! 'Had I landed such a commission?' Intensely excited, I re-read the letter carefully! It contained no specific appointment. It merely posed the question: *"Would I care....."* I replied, congratulated them on a 'splendid purchase', thanked them for approaching me, said that I would immediately ascertain the relevant town-planning and any other site limitations and thereafter would prepare sketch plans to illustrate how I thought the site 'could best be developed to achieve maximum potential'.

IMPLICATIONS!

The next morning I was in the office of Mr. V. Penso, the City's Chief Town Planning Officer. With considerable pains, Penso reviewed the relevant T.P. restrictions. The site was in sub-zone 'A' that allowed for a building floor area of 8 times the site area, a maximum height of 120 feet and a permissible site coverage of 100 %. Mr. Penso explained, however, that there was another important limitation! The Council had in mind the widening of Strand Street for which a substantial portion if the site would be required. He produced a plan showing that the line to which the street would be widened. It would reduce the length of the site by about 19 feet and the site area by about 570 square feet. Thus the value of the property would be radically reduced. It was a situation of which my clients were apparently unaware and one likely to cause alarm.

Mr. Penso said that the idea of widening Strand Street was the outcome of prolonged investigations into the formidable ever-growing problem of traffic influx from the southern suburbs into the heart of the city. He explained that De Waals Drive, recently widened, had absorbed much of the Main Road and Darling Street traffic and was the cause of increasing congestion at the Strand/Adderley intersection. The widening of Strand St. was necessary to permit the construction of a traffic overpass that would take the through traffic from the southern suburbs destined for Sea Point and areas west of the city. It "has been on the books for quite a while," said Mr. Penso. "Its implementation had been deferred as some felt it was inadequate - could not provide a complete answer!" However the proposal was incorporated into the "Final Foreshore Plan" which, in turn, was the basis of the Foreshore Act approved by Parliament and was thus binding on the City and on all property owners affected!

I gathered the impression that the Strand Street widening proposals were binding and irrevocable. Accordingly, I prepared preliminary sketch plans and a presentation perspective drawing of *"Manne's Proposed New Building"*, on the basis of the diminished site. With them, a comprehensive report, including estimates of cost, was sent to the owners. They finally abandoned the idea of an entirely new building. Instead they decided to install 'modern' shop fronts and to convert the major portion of the ground floor to a single shop 'to be their principal store in the Cape'. I received instructions to proceed with the plans 'as speedily as possible'. My dream of building a multi-storied edifice at the very heart of the city was abandoned, with great regret.

GOLDEN ARROW BUS DEPOT

The bus depot presented a challenge. It was an industrial type of structure of a type that I had never worked on before! The site was about 20,000 square feet - not rectangular! It had a frontage of about 165 feet, a depth varying from 103 at the west-end increasing to about 130 feet at the east. I soon became aware that an unbroken area of about 12,000 square feet was required to accommodate 'some 50 buses' and that such area could best be obtained by squaring-off the entire eastern portion of the site for a frontage of 116 feet. That left some 8,000 square feet for the stores, work-pits, offices, rest rooms and open area. To dispense with all internal supports in the bus area, the roof-span of 103 to 116 ft. called for steel lattice girders 7 feet in height. I reviewed the problem with structural engineer Rubin Stubbs whom I held in high esteem. As head of his firm, his services were retained extensively by practicing architects in cases that entailed special structural conditions such as those that now confronted me. I was delighted when my clients confirmed his appointment as structural engineer for the job.

By the time Depot plans were approved, other small commissions had come in - more than I could cope with single-handed. Fortunately, I was able to secure twice the office floor area originally reserved in Diamond House. When I moved there, I was able to accommodate four full-time architectural assistants in addition to Mac Ivor who worked from home. They included three assistants of whom two were with me for many years. They were Jan Greshoff - painstaking, hard working, dependable and loyal - and Madlener who had many novel ideas, considerable initiative and charm. He got on well with clients. A third who joined us later was Louis Kreiner, a senior student who was about to graduate. He was hardworking and ambitious - showed great promise. (Thirty-one years later - in April 1981 after we had migrated, my wife and I returned to Cape Town for the naming of *Honikman Square* in Rondebosch. At a reception in Cape Town's multi-storied Civic Center, Councilor Louis Kreiner, then Mayor of the City, presented me with a plaque - the City's crest.)

MAYOR LOUIS KREINER PRESENTS ME
WITH A CREST OF THE CITY

UNEXPECTED CALL!

One morning the telephone rang. "Good morning, Sir; am I speaking to Sergeant Major Honikman?" The voice sounded familiar! It continued: "I'm Sergeant Sam Lipshitz - remember me - DF&CW"? He said he was in town and would like to visit. As he entered, I recognized him immediately, although in civvies he presented quite a different picture from the one that was familiar to me. He said he had tried to telephone that morning from Durbanville but my line was busy! The purpose of his visit was that his cousin wanted me to design his house and that his brother Charlie wanted to meet me! We fixed an appointment to meet in Durbanville – some 20 miles from the city. When I got there he showed me his cousin's plot and gave me the site diagram with a list of accommodation requirements. I then met his brother Charlie - chatted at length and, before leaving Durbanville, I was commissioned to design a petrol service station *cum* managers flat for Charlie and a house for a cousin - all in Durbanville.

These were encouraging signs. However, they were all small jobs to be completed within a year or so! What then? It was soon after the War; conditions in South Africa were far from stable. It seemed that I was constantly concerned about 'the future' - be it for my family, my country or my practice!

Over the next few years, Charlie would call occasionally at my office. He was keen to build flats as an investment - preferably in Sea Point!

VALUATOR: DISTRICT SIX

To counter my concern, I responded to an advertisement by the Provincial Administration in search of architects, surveyors etc. willing to undertake the 1945 Interim Valuation of City property. The result was a 3-year appointment to undertake the valuation of some four thousand properties in District Six. The fee was four thousand five hundred pounds - a very substantial sum in those days! That, I reckoned, should keep 'the wolf from the door!'

I was provided with maps, valuation forms and records of current valuations. I started by giving two and occasionally three days a week to the task. The area consisted of single-story dwellings with an occasional adjoining shop. It was the City's poorest, most run-down area. Public transport to and from the city was by means of a twenty-minute tram ride along Hanover Street, the District's principal shopping area. The population, primarily 'Colored'[96], numbered approximately ten thousand. My inspections necessitated entering each and every home. Many were in a state of neglect and disrepair! No one seemed to mind my intrusions! On the contrary I was struck by the friendly hospitality encountered every-where and the occasional invitation to join at a meal. I chatted with many of the occupants. All were tenants. Those at home when I called were usually occupied with domestic chores. I gathered that many of the men folk were out looking for work! All were poor - yet proud! I was struck by the amiable good humor that I encountered almost everywhere despite the depressing conditions. It seemed that all had difficulty making ends meet. Some had 'not yet paid the rent'! Inwardly most of the homes were clean and tidy. Externally most were in a state of neglect and disrepair!

The valuation work had continued for nearly two years. Despite my concerns, the practice continued to grow - which of course was what I had had always hoped for! To give more time to the practice, I gave less and less to valuations until the uncompleted valuation work became a source of concern!

One day, I was lunching with Milton Stern (an architectural colleague). He said he was having a quiet time! His eyes brightened up when I suggested that he might be interested to take over the balance of my valuation work - if that was acceptable to the Provincial Secretary. He jumped at the idea. Together we interviewed the Provincial Secretary. The change was approved. To my relief and Milton's delight we entered into an agreement by which he undertook the balance of the valuation work for the balance of the fees that were due to me. My colleagues in the office were obviously relieved and I was grateful that things had turned out so well. However, for quite a while, the valuation episode weighed on me. Many of the people I had met in District Six were poor in terms of material assets - but were always friendly, hospitable, optimistic and proud! They had impressed me deeply! There were times when I felt that I had abandoned them and wanted to go back! Years later, my experiences in District Six came back to mind! They were never forgotten!

THE RAINS CAME

In July 1946 the winter storms were severe and persistent. It had been raining hard all night. The telephone rang unusually early. The caller introduced himself as 'Hugo Kocherthaler'. He said he was a nearby neighbor calling from his home in Sandown Road - less than a mile away. He sounded anxious and explained the reason for his call was that the Black River had overflowed it banks; that his site was flooded and his home surrounded by water! "Could you please come down on your way to office?"

I went down immediately and parked the car outside the gate of the house. (As I recall, it was called "Mafeking".) A heavy flow of water in the gutter along the curb indicated that the road had been submerged. At that point the Black River ran northward along the west-side boundary of the property. I approached the house. The garden was inundated; the paved pathway was sodden but passable. Nearing the house, I glanced up. Through the tall stair window I saw a wide-eyed frightened lady staring outward! Mr. Kocherthaler answered the door, thanked me for coming at short notice, introduced me to his wife Anna who had just stepped down and led me to his study. He said: "An hour earlier, conditions looked grave - Wherever we turned, there was water; the house was an island; my wife felt desperate - she thought we were marooned and became hysterical! We were alarmed that if the rains continued, the foundations would be undermined!" He asked if anything could be done to avert the danger. Mrs. Kocherthaler bought in tea.

I went outside for a closer inspection, crossed the sodden garden and stepped onto the low brick wall that separated the site from the river. I noticed that below the road-bridge were two four-foot diameter pipes - the openings all but completely covered by a massive pile of rubble and tree branches that had been washed down by the river and impeded the river flow. The embankments on both sides of the river were badly eroded. Much of the soil under the foundations of the wall on which I stood had been washed away. I described my observations to Mr. Kocherthaler and said that I thought that the embankments needed protection against further erosion and that the two pipes under the road could not cope with the volume and force of the water. I explained that the root of the problem appeared to be outside the site boundary and called for Municipal action. From a drawer in his desk, Mr. Kocherthaler produced the property Title Deed. The attached diagram indicated that the site boundary was at the gate and that the real problem lay outside the site boundary. I had noticed also that a small part of the embankment on the other side of the river had been washed away as well. It seemed obvious that the four-foot pipes were too small to cope with the volume and force of the river water and that protection of the near embankment was needed to arrest the erosion that had begun to undermine the foundations of his low boundary wall. Mr. Kocherthaler asked if I would pursue the matter with the Municipality on his behalf.

From my office, I telephoned the City Hall, explained the reason for my call and was granted an 'urgent appointment' with the City Engineer

Mr. Lunn. On arrival, I was shown to the office of the Deputy Engineer Mr. Fairweather. He had been delegated to interview me! I described my observations in detail. Mr. Fairweather said that after my call, he 'had a look at the records' and that the pipes under Sandown Road were 'considered adequate'! I replied that I was in no doubt that if he were to inspect - even now that the storm had somewhat abated - he would reach a very different conclusion! He said he would inspect but 'In any event, if Council action is considered necessary, it would be a while before it could be taken.' I felt immediate action was essential to arrest the erosion and asked if there was any objection should the owner decide to take action and consolidate the embankment on his side of the river with a concrete apron? He replied that there would be no objection but that the Municipality could not be responsible for work done privately.

When I reported to Mr. Kocherthaler, he asked if I would take the steps necessary to avert further damage. By then the river water level had dropped appreciably but was not yet low enough for effective action. However, as time was of the essence, I contacted Bakker Bros., a Rondebosch firm of building contractors. Mr. Cuys Bakker met me on the site. I described in detail the nature, thickness and slope of the required concrete embankment. I emphasized 'urgency' and asked for a comprehensive tender. A few days later, Mr. Bakker brought me a tender by hand. It was the detailed document asked for. The price quoted seemed fair. Mr. Kocherthaler concurred, authorized acceptance and within days work was in progress. It was completed within 2 weeks and Mrs. Kocherthaler's 'panic' was ended. Meanwhile, I had written to the City Engineer confirming the interview with Mr. Fairweather and enclosing a copy of the accepted tender 'for the record'.

In due course I mailed my note for professional services. With his remittance, Mr. Kocherthaler enclosed a very kind letter expressing gratitude for the 'expeditious way the matter had been handled and the clean manner in which the work had been completed'.

Several months later, municipal laborers were seen working in the River under the bridge. The 4-foot diameter pipes were removed and 6-foot pipes installed in their place. The Sandown Road flooding problem was at an end.

A FRIENDSHIP BORN

My encounter with Mr. Kocherthaler was the beginning of a long close friendship and a fruitful professional relationship. One day Hugo called, introducing himself as "Managing Director of the Panther Shoe Company" and said that his Company had bought a large property in Maitland for a new factory and had decided that I be appointed architect! He hoped I would accept! Needless to say, I was delighted.

Hugo and I became life-long friends. On week-ends, we walked together in the Sandown Park or the Newlands forest on the lower slopes of Devil's Peak. Occasionally we drove to Muizenberg and swam together. When the tide was low, we often walked for miles along the beach towards Somerset Strand - often followed by a second dip before returning home for lunch.

Hugo brought his friend Phillip Kriwer to meet me. Phillip was the proprietor of the ABC Shoe store at the corner of Plein and Spin Streets in the heart of the city! He and his wife Hertha wanted to live in Rondebosch. They were looking for a plot and noticed that the one adjoining my home was vacant; he wondered if I knew the owner and if it was for sale. I told him that I had bought the plot to ensure that its development would not mar the outlook from our home. I explained that the two plots were precisely the same size (8100 Cape square feet[97]) and that I was willing to sell provided the buyer agreed to observe the same 40-foot building line. He agreed to that; I sold him the plot at the price I had paid, and he asked me to proceed with the design of his new double-storied home. Mr. & Mrs. Kriwer thus became our neighbors and friends. Their house was nearing completion when Philip asked me to prepare plans for the modernization of his city business premises - the ABC Shoe Store at the corner of Plein and Spin Streets. It entailed the construction of a cantilevered canopy over the wide side-walk on both streets to replace an old iron canopy and the supporting 18th century Birmingham cast-iron[98] columns. Technically it was an interesting challenge - the new canopy beams having to be suspended from a very old structure built in the previous century.

The Kriwers had been in their new home for about two years when Phillip asked me to look out for a nearby plot. His wife's health presented problems with the stairs and he wanted a new home with all accommodation confined to a single floor. There was only one small vacant plot in Wood Road - a few hundred yards from his home. It belonged to a doctor who lived nearby. I approached him and he agreed to sell; Phillip bought the plot and I designed a second home for him. It was faced in small, semi-glazed golden brown bricks and built around an internal garden courtyard that the Kriwers found 'very appealing!'

POST WAR!

For me, 1946/7 was a remarkable period. Deena was in her element. Her brothers had survived the war unscathed. Cecil had been remarkably fortunate. Before VE Day he, then a colonel in the Royal Air Force, had flown on seven flying missions over Warsaw. On each, one or more of his crew fell victim to heavy anti-aircraft fire. On one of his flights, he returned to base with all seven members of his crew shot. They were all dead! He was unscathed.

Lionel (the elder brother - my twin) ended his army life in Rome where he married and was now safely home in Johannesburg; Max, preceded by his wife Phyllis, had returned to South Africa to settle in Cape Town. They lived nearby in Glebe Road Rondebosch. Her fourth brother Harold was in Johannesburg; he was his father's sole architectural assistant and had been persuaded to remain at home. Both our boys were thriving. Basil, aged nine, a scholar at the Rondebosch Junior School, was developing nicely. Terence, a bright happy child, attended The Lady Anne Buxton School in Claremont. My practice was in full swing - busier than I ever thought possible!

FORBODINGS!

In Europe and the Pacific, the post-war years were devoted to reconstruction and normal peaceful pursuits. That was not the position in South Africa! The country, free of material damage, was exposed to the activities of the Ossewabrandwag[99]! The insidious 'Swart gevaar!'[100] propaganda took a heavy toll! It produced anger and despair among the African people, concern and alarm in the cities where the bulk of the European population were not ready victims of political tactics of that kind! The Afrikaner Nationalist movement had taken root! It gained enormous ground in the rural areas particularly in the northern provinces. Political repercussions were enormous! The strength of the United Party and the influence of their great wartime leader General Smuts had been undermined throughout the Orange Free State and the rural areas of the Transvaal. The 'black danger' propaganda spread like wild fire and had taken a heavy toll. The situation looked grave! Future insecurity and instability loomed large in the minds of thinking people. "Where would it all lead?" Deeply concerned about their future, young men and women spoke of leaving the country. A few left quietly! Older folk, unable to leave, wondered where to transfer their assets. Some looked north! They felt 'Rhodesia was more British - more liberal - more secure!'

RHODESIA

There was no sense of immediate alarm, yet towards the end of 1947, I felt it would be stupid to ignore the widespread concern. I thought that a small investment in Rhodesia would be a wise precaution. I planned a visit to Bulawayo. On one of my Sunday morning walks, I discussed the idea with Hugo and said that I had in mind a small property investment of about 5,000 pounds. Hugo's response was that he too had similar thoughts and had in mind an amount of about 3,000 pounds. He asked if I would 'keep an eye open' for him adding that he would be interested in a joint venture, if I thought it appropriate and practical. A few days later he came to see me with his friend Phillip Kriwer, who was similarly interested and intimated that he would like to invest about 2,000 pounds – 'jointly if possible'. I explained that I knew nothing about property values in Rhodesia but that I had written to an old 'varsity' friend Ben Baron, a practicing solicitor in Bulawayo, and would probably be guided by him and some local realtor whom I had yet to meet. I had no idea where my interest would take me or whether it would be in one property or more than one. Hugo and Philllip said that if I was willing, they would leave matters entirely to my discretion and would be happy with separate or joint purchases as I saw fit. A few days before I left, they brought me personal checks for 3,000 and 2,000 pounds and both intimated that I should utilize the amounts as I thought best and added that 'if a little more was needed', I should let them know.

On my arrival in Bulawayo, Ben Baron introduced me to Fred Harlen, an Estate Agent. He had no properties to offer but was interested in property administration. He in turn took me to a realtor (with whom Ben had discussed my impending visit). He was expecting me and had available maps and diagrams of a few properties that were for sale. He also had lists of 'recent sale prices' of nearby properties in the different areas. One particular property attracted my attention. It was a tract of land 355 acres in extent situated in Claremont on the road to the north about 15 miles from the city. He said it was near the Matopas - the burial place of Cecil John Rhodes. The asking price was 5,500 pounds. The drive there took about an hour. It was virgin land (with a natural overgrowth) and a gentle rise towards the rear. I walked onto the property for a very short distance. The diagram showed a stream through the center! I did not penetrate far enough to see it; nor did I have a glimpse of Rhodes's grave. It was 'over the hill'. The realtor explained that the land was zoned 'agricultural' and permitted of subdivisions of 15 to 20 acres except that two or three smaller subdivisions of not less that five acres were permitted adjoining the main road. On the way back, he said that there was a fair demand for small subdivisions of agricultural land and, in anticipation of my possible interest, he had contacted a land surveyor to ascertain the relevant procedure, costs etc. which 'were available in the office'. Back in the office, I said I would be interested to purchase the property for my own account at a price not exceeding five thousand pounds (the amount that I had planned to invest). He called the owner. My figure was accepted and I signed a deed of sale.

The following morning I visited other properties on offer. Before leaving I had made provisional offers for two: one a lot of approximately 75 acres five miles out of town where 5-acre subdivisions were permitted. The other, nine acres in extent, was two miles out and there, 2-acre subdivisions were allowed. Both were zoned 'residential'. The cost of these two properties, were 3,000 and 1,900 pounds, respectively, which approximately corresponded with the amounts that Hugo and Phillip had in mind.

On my return to Cape Town, their interest remained keen. They asked if I would join them in partnership. I agreed and we became equal owners of the two properties. Ben Baron attended to all the formalities on our behalves and Harlen was appointed our selling agent. In due course, plans for sub-division of all three properties were approved. Soon after, on a short visit to my sister in London, I carried a letter of introduction to a London solicitor, and from him I purchased Jazzachers, a defunct London based company to which my Rhodesian interests were transferred. Thereafter, my proceeds from the Rhodesian land sales were transferred to Jazzachers and to a London branch of Barclays Bank. For years, sales were extremely slow. Those in Claremont in Bulawayo were on a monthly installment basis spread over a period of eight years. After about two years, Hugo and Phillip had lost interest in Rhodesia and at their request I took over their holdings in the name of the London based company. Nearly 30 years passed before the last of the Rhodesian land was sold. It was the only plot sold on a cash basis and it was to my attorney friend Ben Baron. He bought it 'for his son'.

"EDINGIGHT"

It was about 1948 that my friend and near neighbor Marcus Posniak called on me. He explained that his uncle, Mr. Lewin of Potchestroom, had written saying that he was keen to make a property investment in Cape

Town and, if possible, to build flats, but that he knew nothing about the property market. Marcus had replied saying that he would approach me because, as an architect, I should be in a position to offer suggestions. I said I would scan the property advertisements and come back to him. A few days later I informed Marcus of three properties that were listed for sale - two sites in Kenilworth, one in Rondebosch. All seemed suitable for development. The latter was some two acres in extent, in an area fully developed, near schools and a block away from the railway station. It faced three streets, Duke, College & Gatley Roads, and was partly developed with an old double-story homestead at the south-east corner and three small 2-story units comprising 10 flats in all on the north boundary flanking Gatley Road. I had looked into the town-planning restrictions. The area was zoned for flat development under the restrictions of sub-zone 'C' which would permit the development of about 46 apartments in addition to the existing ten but that the old homestead would have to be demolished. I described the position in a letter to Marcus, pointing out that an added feature of the Rondebosch property was that the existing 10 flats could remain occupied and would be revenue producing during building operations. Marcus passed on the information to his uncle. He purchased the Rondebosch site and wrote instructing me to proceed with the plans as suggested. Sketch Plans and estimates were prepared of a six-story north-facing block of 48 apartments with the entrance at the corner of Duke and College Roads. These were completed and approved. The office was busy on the working drawings when I had a long-distance call from Mrs. Lewin asking me to stop work! She intimated that her husband had had a heart attack - that the doctor recommended no further business worries and that he would be contacting me!

A month went by when he telephoned me to say that he was in Cape Town and was staying temporally in the 'Edingight' homestead and it was there that I met him for the first time. He explained that his health was much improved but that he had decided not to proceed with the building venture. He suggested that I purchase the property at the price he had paid - 32,000 pounds! I laughed and said: "I do not have that kind of money!" Mr. Lewin pursued the matter. He said: "No one was more familiar with its potential than you - I would gladly leave 20,000 pounds on mortgage at 5% interest." (That was the lowest rate available at the time.) He asked: "How much do I owe you for your services?" I had not yet prepared an account and said that it would be about 2,000 pounds. He responded: "Then all you would require would be ten thousand and the property is yours. Think about it!" It sounded very tempting! I said I would let him know. I had never dreamed of owning a property of that magnitude nor could I lay my hands on all that money!

I discussed the matter with my mother and with my brother Maurice. Mother said she would invest three thousand pounds and Maurice offered fifteen hundred. I managed the remainder. Thus it was that we became sole shareholders in Edingight Estates (Pty) Ltd. and I was made chairman of the company.

To proceed with the six-story project already designed would have involved substantially more capital than we had available! I looked for alternative proposals and came up with plans for three 3-story buildings that could be built in stages as and when sufficient funds were available. The relevant town-planning restrictions meant that the 3-story structures would have to be set back from boundaries a distance equal to not less than 3/4 times the height which was only 22 ft. 6 inches instead of the 45 ft. necessary for the six-story scheme. That meant that three new separate 3-story structures could be built instead of the large six-story proposal designed for Mr. Lewin. As with his scheme, the new idea permitted the retention of the 3 existing two-story blocks near the north boundary. They were of more recent vintage than the old homestead. The new proposals would enable all the buildings to overlook a large internal garden court which could be an attractive feature. They also obviated the need for elevators, which of course were essential in the original 6-story project. There was no urgency to proceed as the existing development was financially self-supporting. From my personal stand-point, the new proposals had the added advantage that each new structure could be developed separately in future years as and when available funds permitted.

MY HEARING PROBLEM!

The world had been at peace for four years. The energy, research and expense consumed by war and the preparation for war during the previous decade were now available for constructive peacetime pursuits! An interesting article in the Readers Digest caught my eye! It told of a 'fenestration' operation being performed in London - one that restored full hearing to many people. It described the procedure as one in which the surgeon 'simply mobilized the stapes' that had become locked in the bone aperture in which it was situated; it explained that whereas normally that bone ceased to grow at birth, there were occasions when it continued to grow thereby reducing the size of the aperture. Thus it hampered the vibrations of the stapes and impaired the flow of sound waves to the inner ear. That, I had gathered, was precisely my condition.

The article mentioned the names of three surgeons in London who had successfully performed several such procedures. I selected one of the three - Dr. Terence Cawthorne. It was no longer necessary to spend fifteen days traveling by mail-ship to England. I took an early flight to London and within days was in his chambers. His examination was disappointing. He explained that while the right ear seemed best suited for the 'fenestration', the stapes seemed to have grown to the bone and, in such event, it would not be amenable to much movement and the desired result may not be achieved. He added, however, that the operation was minor - entailing little or no risk, and if I so wished, he was willing to try. Thereafter, if necessary, another procedure, somewhat more intricate, was available but he thought it best to try the 'fenestration' first. I decided to go ahead. With a general anesthetic, I was totally unaware of what transpired. When I awoke, Dr. Cawthorne was standing before me. His beaming smile was most reassuring until he commented: "Movement was minimal - let me know how you're getting on." I returned home. The hearing showed some improvement but it did not last. Dr. Aubrey Schiller, my ear surgeon in Cape Town, said that Dr. Cawthorne had written to him explaining that the alternative procedure mentioned by Cawthorne was a known as a 'stapedectomy' - a 'more delicate procedure with which Cawthorne had obtained considerable success'.

In 1952, I returned to London for the second operation hoping that it would prove more successful than the first. Cawthorne explained that it would be done in the left ear - the stapes would be removed and replaced by a new one to be molded from a vein that would be taken from my arm. He said that the procedure had proved 'extremely successful' but that it depended on my full cooperation - that I would not move my head for 6 days during which time smoking would not be allowed! To ensure compliance, I would have to be in the Clinic where my head would be bandaged firmly to my shoulders for five days to prevent movement - apart from that I should experience little discomfort. He added that I would find my right forearm bandaged to protect a small wound where the vein was to be removed. It all sounded complicated - but I had come a long way and decided not to return home without having tried. I agreed to go ahead! Deena was not with me; she felt the boys were too young to be left to a strange nurse aid. My sister Beatrice who was in London had assured her that she would hold a 'watching brief'.

When I awoke after surgery, I was in the London clinic firmly strapped-up as warned! To look to the left or right, it seemed that I had to turn my entire body! Thus my movements were minimal. However, my arms were virtually free as were the front of my face and the rest of my body. Nonetheless, I was not permitted to leave the bed until the sixth day when the bandages were to be removed. Cawthorne, Beatrice and the matron visited me every day - sometimes twice! I experienced no pain or discomfort and spent my time reading and sleeping.

THE SEVENTH DAY!

I had become accustomed to having my meals in bed. I was entirely free of pain and discomfort but after breakfast, I 'craved' for a cigarette. The bell hung close at hand. I pressed the button hard and long. In popped a young nurse. I had not noticed her before. With a strong Irish accent, she asked: "Is there something I can do?" Pointing to the dressing table, I said: "Yes, Nurse, I'd like a cigarette - in the top drawer is my cigarette case." It was a large aluminum case, slightly cove-shaped, skillfully hand-made and engraved by an Italian prisoner-of-war. I had bought it from him before my discharge. Holding the case in both hands, the nurse stood still, gazed at it - fondled it - and exclaimed: "It's beautiful!" I asked: "Do you like it, Nurse?" Her eyes opened wide. She repeated with emphasis: "It's so beautiful!" (With her strong Irish accent the "beauuu-tiful' sounded prolonged and meaningful!) She stared at me and pressed the case to her breasts. (Apparently she had interpreted my question *'Do you like it?'* to mean *'Would you like it?'*) She shook her head in wonderment and exclaimed slowly: "For me? – ooo thank you so very much!" Hugging the case, she turned and ran from the room. She'd forgotten to give me a cigarette! I lay there thinking - her behavior was strange to say the least but perhaps I had been careless in my comments! I had learnt a lesson - 'to watch my words more carefully – particularly when confronted by a pretty Irish lass!'

My longing for a smoke had not been satisfied. I remembered that in addition to the lost case, I still had the remains of a packet of Commando cigarettes that I had brought from Cape Town. I rang the bell again - determined this time to be more careful in my choice of words. A different nurse entered; I explained my need and asked her to pass me the packet. She questioned whether I was permitted to smoke and said she would have to ask the matron! While she was out, I lay there thinking: "It was in Sweden in 1936 that I last gave up smoking. That was sixteen years ago! Now I had not smoked for a week - maybe this time, if I resisted the urge, I could abandon smoking altogether!" I waited and wondered! I thought: "It is really an awful habit; my nicotine-stained fingers had often told me that!"

The nurse entered. She went straight to the dressing table saying: "Matron says it's OK." She brought me the packet. I asked her if she smoked. She said she did "but not on duty - thank you." I thanked her, handed the packet back and said: "Take it, Nurse. You may like Commando. It's a mild Virginia. I've decided to do without!" I have never smoked since and feel grateful to both nurses.

The surgery was a success. The hearing had improved tremendously and I was able to discard the hearing aid completely - but only for a few years. Slowly the impediment recurred. I reverted to an aid first in my right ear and later in both! That was a shame, but I never regretted the surgery! It had cured me of an ugly expensive habit!

FREDEFORT

A year or two elapsed. An excited Charlie Lipschitz asked me to inspect and report on a site in Green Point that he felt would be suitable for the building development project that he had long dreamed of. My report was that the site was in a dense unattractive area - not conducive to the kind of development which I believed he was interested in. Disheartened by my report, he decided to abandon the intended purchase. Weeks later, however, I encouraged him to buy a site on the Beach Road Sea Point on which there was an old double-storied house named "Vredefort". The site, an important one on the waterfront, was near the pavilion with its large and popular sea pool. It was zoned for flat development, had a bulk factor that permitted a total living floor area equal to two and a half times the site area plus garaging and services. Charlie was keenly interested! He took an option on the site and commissioned me to submit proposals! I burnt much mid-night oil and prepared sketch plans for an eight-story building comprising 24 three- and four-roomed apartments and a penthouse on the 8th floor, in addition to garaging for several cars and a few staff rooms. A very enthusiastic Charlie bought the site and directed me to proceed. At that time, it was the highest and potentially the most 'prestigious' project I had ever undertaken.

When the plans were formally approved by the Municipality, Charlie decided to dispense with the services of a quantity surveyor - a necessary step prior to calling for tenders from Master Builders[101]. He explained that there were a few builders whom he knew personally from whom he would obtain tenders. In due course, he introduced me to a Mr. Altman, handed me his tender and asked me to complete a building contract with him. A substantial sum was involved and I was apprehensive! Mr. Altman was unknown to the building world of Cape Town and I was concerned about his ability to effectively complete a project of such size and complexity. Operations proceeded. Altman was co-operative and painstaking. In due course, the building was completed to my complete satisfaction and to that of a delighted owner. It attracted considerable public interest. Particularly pleasing to me were the gracious comments tendered by a few of my professional colleagues.

BACK TO 'EDINGIGHT'

At "Fredefort" I had got on well with Mr. Altman. His work there was completed meticulously. By then, I was able to increase my investment in "Edingight" and thus in a position to proceed with Block 'D', the first of its development proposals. Sited on a vacant portion of the site, it faced College Road to the south and overlooked the garden court to the north. It comprised twelve apartments: six of 4 rooms, six of 3 rooms. The three existing buildings were numbered: 'A', 'B' and 'C'. I asked Mr. Altman if he was interested to give me an estimate of cost. He took the plans and specification and a week later submitted a figure of twenty-four thousand pounds which, he said, was a 'firm tender'. It was within my estimate and acceptable to my colleagues. A contract was entered into and within a year Block 'D' was completed and all the units leased and occupied.

A year or two later we built Block 'E', a 3-storied building facing Duke Road. It had 3 entrances, each giving access to six apartments. A slight slope to the site permitted the inclusion of 3 garages and a small laundry below the north end. When it was completed and fully occupied, we demolished the old homestead and proceeded with our third contract - Block 'F'. It comprised 12 apartments facing west and overlooking the garden court. The contract included a separate parallel structure of 11 garages along the east boundary separated from Block 'F" by a wide driveway. Above the garages were several staff rooms and bathrooms. As living quarters, they had to be set back 15 feet from the east boundary to comply with the zoning regulations. They were therefore partly cantilevered over the drive and so provided a useful cover above the garage doors.

THE FINAL STAGE

When surveying the site prior to building Block 'F', it became apparent that by demolishing Block 'C', there would be room for yet a further extension at the north end of Block 'F'. Block 'C' was the smallest of the three old buildings. Its demolition meant the sacrifice of 2 apartments, but it made room for the building of six north facing luxury flats and eight additional garages, badly needed in so large a complex. We decided to go ahead. It was the last of four separate development contracts. Like Blocks 'A' and 'B', its entrance was from the garden-court drive. To preserve continuity of numbering, we called the new extension 'C'. Its entrance also provided through access to the garages and staff rooms on the east boundary. The six additional flats included a sunny north-facing 5-room apartment on each of the two upper floors, four 4-roomed apartments and eight additional garages - four accessed from Gatley Road. The last of the 'Edingight' building operations was completed mid-1965. The entire complex comprised 56 apartments. All were fully leased. Deena and I occupied the new five-roomed apartment above the ground floor. It had a large wide sunny terrace and two additional bedrooms in readiness for possible return visits of our sons and their families.

'Edingight' prove to be a successful enterprise - one in which my mother, brother Maurice and our doctor Ruby Lipshitz each retained a small interest until the property was sold at the end of 1980 when I decided to live abroad.

THE POLITICAL SCENE

In the years and decades following the 1948 general election, conditions in South Africa deteriorated. The apartheid syndrome became deeply entrenched. All forms of organized resistance were outlawed. African organizations such as the African National Congress were banned in South Africa but gained increasing support in other parts of Africa, throughout the democratic world and in the Soviet Union. Militant anti-apartheid forces were being trained in countries outside the borders of South Africa - in preparation for the day when they would 'rise against their white taskmasters'. In South Africa, international sanctions tended to reduce the value of the South African currency (the Rand), increase prices of certain commodities and thus affect primarily the lower income group. Many years had yet to pass before any appreciable impact was made on Government policy.

CHAPTER 23

PUBLIC LIFE!

After the war, my attention was drawn more and more to matters extraneous to my personal and professional life. I became increasingly aware that conditions in my country were incompatible with the democratic ideal to which the nation claimed to subscribe. Two-thirds of the population - the entire indigenous population - was excluded from the political process because they were black or because they were thought to belong to a different level of civilization! A powerful political force among the ruling white minority openly and unblushingly labeled them the "Black Menace" and sought to have them further isolated from the social and economic fabric of the country. That force gained tremendous strength during the war years when much of the country's energy and resources were concentrated on the defeat of the Nazi menace that threatened the entire free world. By the time the war ended, the racist propagators had gained control of the Nationalist Party and were swept to power in the 1948 general election!

For me, 'alarm bells' had been ringing ever since my last visit to Porterville! My professional work had ceased to be my sole concern or the only concern outside my home.

AN UNEXPECTED DEVELOPMENT

Early in 1948, Mr. Kaiser, Chairman of the Rondebosch Ratepayers Association, telephoned! He asked if I would receive a deputation from his Executive Committee the following Sunday morning. He gave no notion of the purpose of the visit! That morning Mr. Kaiser and his four colleagues gathered in our lounge. Deena served tea and left us chatting informally. Mr. Kaiser said that the purpose of the visit was to obtain my acceptance of his Committee's decision to nominate me as the Association's candidate in the forthcoming municipal election. He hoped I would accept! Taken aback, I thanked them, said I felt honored but that they were probably unaware that I had recently resumed practice and that my professional work demanded my undivided attention. I told them that much of my free time was already devoted to the Institute of Race Relations of which I was an executive member. I thanked them and said: "With regret, gentlemen, I must decline." I referred to a Mr. Opperman who, at the last meeting of the Ratepayers Association, had informed me of his interest and indicated that he intended 'entering the Council this year'! There was no response! On leaving, Mr. Kaiser urged me to "Think it over. We'll be in touch."

At office next morning, I mentioned the incident to my associates Greshoff and Madlener. Both felt I should reconsider! They assured me that if I would change my mind, they would be able to look after the practice while I attended Council meetings. At home, I discussed the matter with Deena. She was non-committal: "You must do what you think best!" Friends I spoke with thought I should reconsider. Most were more concerned about the political situation, the apartheid propaganda and the rising anger of the African people. That concerned me far more than the local issues dealt with by the Ratepayers Association.

When Mr. Kaiser called a second time, he said his Committee understood my position and understood the demands of my practice, but he added: "Nonetheless - we urge you to accept our nomination. Should you find it too much, you will have our cooperation! I don't think you'll be sorry." I acquiesced. My name went forward as the nominee of the Association. The election passed without a stir. I was elected to the City Council unopposed - the third representative for Rondebosch. The two sitting members were Councilors Bakker and Balsillie.

INITIATION AS A COUNCILOR

A letter from the Town Clerk, Mr. Mervin Williams, asked me to attend an informal Council meeting in the City Hall Library. Before the meeting started, I was introduced to senior officials and to my forty-four new colleagues. One of them surprised me with a warning comment: "Don't open your mouth for six months - it will take you that time to get to know what is going on!" The remark seemed strange and presumptuous, to say the least!

The Mayor welcomed the newly elected councilors and asked the Town Clerk to take over. Mr. Williams explained that the purpose of the meeting was to determine - in advance of the first formal meeting of Council - who were to be the chairmen and seven members of each of the several Committees of Council and who would represent the Council on numerous public bodies. He explained 'for the benefit of new Councilors' that it was an informal procedure that had been in operation for many years and had successfully achieved its purpose which was to expedite proceedings at the first formal meeting of Council - proceedings which might otherwise be unduly protracted. The Mayor took over and asked if all Councilors would agree, "as they had done in the past, to abide by the decisions to be adopted at this informal meeting?" "Agreed," came a chorus of voices! "Those opposed?" asked the Mayor. There was no response and he beckoned the Town Clerk to resume and call for nominations.

Mr. Louis Gradner, a past Mayor, was nominated and unanimously approved Chairman of the Finance and General Purposes Committee. Similarly the Chairman, Vice Chairman and members of sixteen standing Committees and eight special Committees were duly nominated, seconded and approved - as were the representatives on 3 'special' committees and numerous public bodies. For the benefit of the new councilors, Mr. Williams explained how the Council operated: the Committees met once or twice a month; their recommendations were considered by Council on the last Tuesday of the month; etc.

When the meeting closed, all adjourned to the Banqueting room for an informal luncheon. I had been elected a member of two standing committees: 'Plans' and 'Roads' and chairman of the special 'Scholarships Committee', a very minor committee that met only two or three times a year; its sole purpose - to administer the few scholarships granted annually by the Council. I learnt also that the Plans and Roads Committees each met 'not more than twice a month', for about two-and-a-half hours. The information served to allay my concern regarding the time I would have to be away from my practice.

The City Council consisted of 45 Councilors. The City was divided into 15 wards; each represented by 3 Councilors. There was a general election in August each year to elect one of the three to serve for a 3-year term. The system made for continuity of operations - ensuring that not less than two thirds of the members were familiar with what had transpired prior to the election. There were public and press galleries overlooking the Council chamber. I had never previously attended a Council meeting and knew little about its operations other than what I had heard at the monthly meetings of the local Association.

As the months went by, I became increasingly aware of the manifold activities of the Council and of their importance to the community. I became more and more absorbed - particularly in the town-planning and arterial road proposals that were being dealt with at the time. However, I felt somewhat overwhelmed by the multifarious items that appeared on the numerous agendas and reports delivered to me every month a few days prior to the Council's monthly meetings. It was a while before I realized that the committee system was designed to apportion the work-load and obviate the need for every councilor to become exhaustively conversant with every aspect of the multifarious items that appeared on every monthly agenda. For that, there would not be enough hours in the day! It was a while before I learnt to confine my 'exhaustive' interest to matters that appeared on the agendas of the committees on which I served. Other matters were primarily the concern of their respective committees. Generally speaking, they would attract my attention only when challenged in Council and when my vote would be influenced by the arguments advanced in debate. Such, I realized, was the approach of most of my colleagues. Indeed there was no other choice!

VISIT BY DEPUTY TOWN CLERK

A week or two prior to the customary 'informal meeting' at the start of my second civic year, Mr. Gale, the Deputy Town Clerk, called by appointment to see me in my private office. He was accompanied by the Assistant Town Clerk, Mr. Jan Luyt. He asked that I regard the visit as confidential, and explained that it was unusual - some thought improper - for officials to participate in "election matters." On this occasion, the Town Clerk Mr. Williams felt he could do no less than inform me that a few Councilors had expressed the view that, because of my professional background, I should accept nomination as Chairman of the Plans Committee for the ensuing year. He then commented: "Incidentally, senior officials share that view." How such matters were usually handled was not familiar to me. I gained the impression that it was considered 'my duty' to accept. I thought about it briefly and felt that over the past year the two monthly 'Plans' meetings had not encroached unduly upon my professional duties and that the position would remain more or less the same if I were 'chairman'. I knew of no other implications and said I had no objection but was reluctant to 'request' someone to nominate me. "Don't worry," said Mr. Gale, "it will be taken care of." My visitors thanked me and departed.

At the ensuing 'informal meeting' my colleague Mr. Balsillie nominated me and did so again at the subsequent formal meeting. Clr. Albow, the current chairman, was also nominated but immediately withdrew, and I was elected unopposed. At the formal meeting, Clr. Albow ignored my greeting! He turned away. His action was clearly deliberate! I mentioned this to Clr. Balsillie. He said: "Don't worry! He's been at it for many years - didn't like being ousted by a fledgling!" That shook me! I had assumed that he was vacating the chair and had to be replaced. Had I known that I was making an enemy of Mr. Albow my reply to Mr. Gale would probably have been different. It was an aspect of public life that was new to me. I knew Mr. Albow was head of a large public company - a man of prominence in the City with whom I had no desire to cross swords. Subsequently our paths often crossed at Council meetings but he kept cool and aloof. Our relationship remained 'distant'. Several years later, normality was restored - but under totally different circumstances!

CHAPTER 24

CHANGING COURSE

For South Africa, 1948 was a watershed year. General J. C. Smuts, the great wartime leader and his United Party, had suffered their last political defeat. For the first time in the young nation's history, Government was in the hands of a political party whose parliamentary representatives were exclusively Afrikaners - not a single English-speaking member.

GLIMPSE AT HISTORY

To give perspective to my story, let me review very briefly some of the historical events that, in retrospect, influenced my conduct through life. The post-war years were an eventful, formative and troublesome period in the history of the young country in which I was destined and privileged to spend seventy years of my life.

European settlement in the Cape, started by the Dutch in mid-seventeenth century, was followed by an influx of Huguenots escaping religious persecution in France. During the 18th century, Dutch farmers in the Cape sought to escape hard times; they branched out into the countryside in their ox-wagons in search of grazing land for their cattle. Over time, the movement drew thousands and became known as the 'Great Trek'. It continued intermittently until the mid-19th century. Opposition from native peoples (the Xhosa) developed into major wars along the Great Fish River. The trekkers survived to set up independent republics in the Orange Free State and Transvaal. These young countries were democratic in form though suffrage did not embrace the black, Colored or Asian peoples. During that time, immigrants from Britain, with a sprinkling from Germany and other parts of Europe, settled in the Cape and continued through the nineteenth and early twentieth centuries.

DIAMONDS AND GOLD

The discovery of diamonds in Kimberley, Northern Cape, followed by rich gold deposits in Johannesburg (1886), led to an influx of immigrants from Europe and from the Cape to the Transvaal. Limited franchise rights in the Transvaal Republic resented by the government of the Cape led to the Jameson Raid and culminated in The Boer War (1899-1902). In both republics, the franchise was limited to the white population. Only in the colonies of the Cape and Natal were the Colored and Indian population given the vote. The Bantu peoples, comprising some twelve different tribes, were excluded from the franchise. They pursued customs and rituals that the European immigrants considered primitive and inconsistent with the contemporary practices of a 'civilized society'!

THE ACT OF UNION

The Treaty of Vereeneging brought the Boer War to an end. Negotiations followed between Britain and the Boer leaders. In 1909, the British Parliament passed the Act of Union with a view to bringing the two Republics and the two colonies into a single united nation. Racial discord between Afrikaners and British remained a barrier! In search of reconciliation, Britain invited Louis Botha, leader of "Het Volk" (the People), the principal political Party of the Transvaal, to head a provisional government until a general election could be held. Botha, an esteemed Boer War general, accepted the challenge. He formed an interim cabinet that included General Jan Cristiaan Smuts[102], his deputy, and members of kindred parties from the two republics and the colonies of the Cape and Natal. His cabinet included General J.B.M. Hertzog of the Orange Free State. Botha and Smuts felt that an end to racial cleavage between the Boers and British was the only road to peaceful progress. That view was shared by a majority of all racial groups. The general election in September 1910 gave the allied parties a clear majority. Botha became the first Prime Minister of the Union of South Africa.

Political calm was short-lived. General Hertzog disapproved the honors that the British government showered on his leaders and particularly on Gen. Smuts. He saw them as the manifestation of an attempt by Britain to impose an 'English' way of life on the young country. He believed it ran counter to, and to the detriment of, an 'Afrikaner' culture which he regarded as the natural heritage of 'his' people. They constituted the majority of the whites who had chosen to make South Africa their country.

Hertzog's sentiments, aired vehemently and persistently at public meetings, produced dissension! He was asked to resign and refused. Botha then resigned. A general election followed. Botha and his South African National Party were returned with 67 seats - a substantial majority. They were supported by a vast majority of both Afrikaans and English-speaking elements. Hertzog, no longer a member of the Government, became the leader of the newly formed Afrikaner Nationalist Party. The principal opposition, however, came from the Cape Unionist Party led by Dr. Jameson. Its members were predominantly British and its primary emphasis was on commerce and industry. A new Labor Party, led by Colonel Creswell and backed by British industrial workers, held four or five seats. Its support was almost exclusively on the Transvaal mines although the railway workers of Salt River - a Cape Peninsula constituency - had chosen a Labor candidate. Eleven independent members were also elected.

ONE UNITED NATION

On May 31, 1910, the Act of Union, passed by the South African Parliament brought into being the 'Union of South Africa'- a single nation and a fifth self-governing Dominion of the British Empire. Cape Town became the parliamentary capital and Pretoria the administrative capital. It was a British- type democracy. The Bantu population, about four-fifths of the total comprised of some 19 distinctive groups, was generally regarded as 'tribal and primitive' and was entirely excluded from the democratic process. Only in the Cape and Natal did the suffrage extend to the Colored and Indian peoples. The European (white) minority were approximately two-thirds Afrikaners and one-third British. Thus from the start, the country was governed by one-fifth of its population - a disparity that was to be the source of increasing trouble over the last four decades of the nineteenth century.

With the outbreak of World War I, South Africa, as part of the British Empire, was at war with Germany. General Smuts led the South African forces to victory in the East African campaign and again in German South West Africa. He became a member of the British War Cabinet. His military successes and the many honors attributed to him abroad were neither acclaimed nor celebrated by Nationalist adherents. They felt that the country was required to fight an enemy against whom it had no grievance. Boer War memories were stirred. Resentment became extremely bitter! Many Afrikaners hoped for a German victory that they believed would provide the opportunity for independence from Britain. Armed rebellion was attempted. It was ill conceived and failed. The country was deeply divided! Cleavage between Boer and British, bolstered by politicians, became intense and continued through the years. After World War I, Botha remained Prime Minister. General Smuts's military successes, his inclusion as a member of the British War Cabinet and his role as one of the architects of the League of Nations, earned him the status of 'international statesman of world repute'.

CLEAVAGE!

Hertzog, leader of the new Nationalist Party, fostered the dream of an 'Afrikaner Republic'. English-speaking citizens were welcomed to his Party, provided they offered 'allegiance to South Africa to the exclusion of all other loyalties'. The new government faced formidable opposition! Racial cleavage divided the nation. Botha died in 1919 and was succeeded by General Smuts as Prime Minister and leader of the South African Party.

The 1920 general election was evidence that the Nationalist Party had made considerable headway. Their appeal for *"South Africa First!"* and *"No more foreign wars"* won them 44 seats - three more than those won by Smuts's South African Party! Another general election followed in February 1921. By then, the South African and Unionist Parties had merged to form a new 'South African Party'. They won 79 seats to the Nationalists' 45, the Labor Party's 9. Thus, Smuts gained what appeared to be a substantial working majority! It was short lived! The world was in a state of economic recession. Labor unrest in the Transvaal led to a strike on the mines, followed by riots that quickly developed into a bloody uprising with all the symptoms of a full-blooded 'red' revolution. (Mr. Schneier, my friend Max's father, was said to have harbored communists in his Parktown home during the riots!) The situation was more than the police could handle. The army was called out! Much blood was spilt before peace was restored. The Nationalists blamed Smuts for bringing out the army, for much of the bloodshed and for a 'lack of sympathy for Labor'. Smuts's support dwindled. The South African Party lost several by-elections. In the 1924 general election, they were confronted by a formidable pact between the Nationalist and Labor Parties! Smuts was heavily defeated. Government fell into the hands of the new pact with General Hertzog at the helm. A brief economic recovery followed. The new government passed the Industrial Conciliation Act, followed a year later by the Wage Act - both designed to avoid a repetition of the 1922 riots.

AUTONOMY WITHIN THE EMPIRE

In 1926, General Hertzog attended his first Imperial Conference. His effort to achieve autonomy for South Africa was supported by the other Commonwealth leaders. A Declaration followed. It gave each of the five dominions full autonomy, free association in the Commonwealth and full jurisdiction over both internal and foreign affairs. Hertzog returned triumphant! The 1929 general election gave the National Party a yet greater victory. For the first time, that Party had a clear majority over all other parties. They won 78 seats; the South African Party, 61; the Labor Party, 8. Three members of the Labor Party, members Col. Creswel, Mr. Madeley and Mr. Boydell, were included in Hertzog's cabinet. Havenga remained Minister of Finance. His reputation for scrupulous integrity transcended politics!

THE GREAT DEPRESSION!

Government solidarity, however, was no match for the 'Great Depression'. It affected the entire world. By 1932, distress had reached unprecedented depths. Britain went off the gold standard! The Wall Street Stock Exchange collapsed! Increased Nazi atrocities in Germany produced ever-increasing concern worldwide. In South Africa, despair was widespread! Tielman Roos, (a judge of the Supreme Court and a moderate Nationalist appointee -at heart, a politician) resigned from the Bench to plead for national conciliation. He toured the country urging Hertzog and Smuts to 'bury the hatchet', 'to come together, and join forces in the nation's interests'! He also advocated the abandonment of the gold standard!

GOLD STANDARD ABANDONED

When Havenga presented his annual budget to Parliament, a contentious debate followed. The budget showed a deficit! Smuts, leader of the Opposition, appealed to the House to reject the budget and abandon the gold standard! In support of his plea, he submitted a fictitious budget which, he explained, was drawn on the basis of the 'gold standard' being abandoned! His 'budget' showed a surplus which he professed was the only reasonable option available to Parliament. With great fervor, he asked Parliament to accept the option and so free the country of a 'shackling' deficit! At the end of the day when it came to the vote, Smuts was victorious! South Africa abandoned the gold standard!

RECONCILIATION!

Negotiations 'behind the scenes' ensued. Dire economic straits coupled with Tielman Roos's strivings, brought twenty-three years of bitter political rivalry (between Smuts & Hertzog) to an end. Reconciliation prevailed! The National Party and the South African Party joined forces. The 'impossible' had happened - Hertzog and Smuts shook hands! The nation 'sighed relief'! In the following 1933 election, the new 'United Party' gained a tremendous victory. They won 144 of the 150 parliamentary seats. The remaining six seats were held by members of the newly formed Dominion Party led by Colonel Stallard and included our friend and neighbor C.W.A. Coulter. They were apprehensive that the new alignment could pose a threat to the country's allegiance to the British Commonwealth. In the new government, General Hertzog as Prime Minister and General Smuts his Deputy. Dr. D. F. Malan, who was Minister of Education in the previous Government, opposed the coalition. He and 18 die-hards had broken away to preserve the old Nationalist Party rivalry.

All that happened soon after I had left home to take on my new job and adapt to a new environment in Johannesburg. I referred previously to Nazi activity inside South Africa, to the Wagner episode in Johannesburg, and to Hertzog's reaction to public protests against Nazi atrocities. It transpired later, that the Nazi movement in South Africa was headed by none other than the Minister of Justice, Mr. Oswold Pirow, and that his 'New Order' had a fascist program with the object of reforming South African society on Nazi lines.

Such were the local events in those days! All were eclipsed by conditions that developed in Europe. Nazi atrocities, Germany's military build-up in violation of the Versailles Treaty, Hitler's threat to Czechoslovakia and the invasion of Austria (1937) posed a threat to the free world.

On September 1, 1939, Germany invaded Poland. Britain, as pledged, declared war on Germany! France followed. A highly contentious debate ensued in Parliament in Cape Town. Hertzog appealed for 'neutrality'! He pleaded that the nation should not become involved in 'foreign wars'! Smuts, on the other hand, contended that South Africa should not abandon its allies - that it was unthinkable that the nation would stand aloof in times of trouble! He referred to the 'wehrmaght's'[103] violation of international boundaries, to persistent Nazi atrocities regularly condoned by the Hitler government and to the magnitude of the threat that confronted all mankind!

'Neutrality' (Smuts said) would imply acceptance of conduct that violated 'civilized standards!' At the end of the debate, Parliament accepted Smuts plea! South Africa declared war on Germany. Similar declarations by the other British Dominions followed.

World War II was under way!

Events in South Africa during and after World War II and prior to the 1948 General Election in South Africa are referred to elsewhere.

POST WAR SOUTH AFRICA

The 1948 General Election witnessed a radical change of direction! Nationalist propaganda had been very active. For the very first time, the nation chose a government that was exclusively Afrikaans speaking. For the first time since Union, the English speaking element that accounted for one-third of the electorate was without a voice in government! Yet more significant was the fact that the indigenous African people[104], numbering 80% of the population, remained excluded from the democratic process, separated - isolated in every way possible - from the white 'master race'! To make sure such situation should prevail, Nationalist politicians persistently referred to the blacks as a "threat to the nation." 'Swart Gevaar' was their theme song. The Colored Peoples, who numbered about 2% of the population and for decades had been part of the enfranchised minority in the Cape, were to be removed entirely from the common roll. Resentment by the African masses gathered momentum. For those of all races who were not indoctrinated by the racist ideology, the future looked grave! The feeling of insecurity, and fear were widespread.

MY ROOTS

I loved South Africa! My roots were deep. Since the war my 'perspectives' had changed profoundly! At the national level there was a marked decline in moral values. My opinion, like countless others, was that apartheid would lead the country to disaster! The future looked grim, the prospect of change, remote. My road ahead was clouded. I was restless - unsure! Simply to 'remain aloof' was no antidote!

POLITICS!

The Rondebosch Branch of the United Party appointed me one of its two representatives on the Cape Peninsula Council. It represented the Party's seventeen Peninsula constituencies. I was in a new environment! At my first meeting of the CPC, Mr. Gay, M.P. for Simonstown, was re-elected Chairman and to my surprise, I was elected vice-chairman.

CONTEMPT FOR WORLD OPINION!

The Nationalist Party success at the General Election far exceeded their expectations! Their members gloated! Their leader, Dr. D.F. Malan, a minister of the Dutch Reformed Church, was regarded as a 'verkrampte'[105]. To him and his followers, the election results were 'proof' that the widespread, persistent, condemnation of their racist policy by their adversaries and by the democratic world, was nothing less than *'meaningless interference!'* They gained all the confidence they needed! All contrary opinion, they felt, could be treated with contempt. 'They claimed that the 'voice of the people' impelled them to pursue their racist ideology relentlessly and (in their view) the 'outside world' could do nothing about it"! - So they thought!

NAZI ALLIANCE!

Nationalist and Broederbond propaganda portrayed the indigenous African people as a threat to the survival of Afrikanerdom[106]. It blinded the nation's rulers to the grim consequences of a policy that was racist and discriminatory - totally inconsistent with civilized standards for fair and decent government! It roused the wrath of the African people, alienated old allies and produced a disturbing restlessness in the country. The 1948 election results gave the nation's rulers a sense of infallibility. Their contempt of criticism at home and abroad was unrestrained. Flaunting their new power, the first act of the new government was to free Robey Liebrandt, a South African Nazi spy who had been recently captured on the coast of South West Africa after having been put ashore from a German submarine!

CHAPTER 25

BIRTH OF APARTHEID

1948 marked the beginning of apartheid - the official policy of the Government and, as such, of the nation! It was a doctrine based on ethnic discrimination. It prevailed for nearly 50 years despite condemnation worldwide. Despite growing unrest among the African people and the threat of international sanctions, the Government pursued its discredited policy relentlessly. They were confident that the inherently strong national economy would counter such threats. In that regard, they confronted a single problem: South Africa's abundant mineral resources did not include oil! To counter a threat of oil sanctions, the Government acted with great speed. They proceeded to line several large underground chambers of old disused gold mines with steel plate - converting them into vast oil containers. A massive search for oil ensued on the country's southern coast. It yielded naught, but that was no deterrent! There was no shortage of oil-rich countries ready, nay keen, to respond to a call for massive oil supplies. Tankers from afar entered the country's harbors. The newly prepared underground chambers were soon filled, - long before sanction could be effectively implemented. Thus the country was never confronted with an oil shortage and the Government was able to pursue its policy with impunity!

BLACK RESISTANCE

The black resistance movement known as the ANC[107] had widespread support internationally! It was no match, however, for the highly trained (and indoctrinated) Government Police force. Would-be revolutionaries of the ANC were being trained in countries abroad, including the Soviet Union, in preparation for the day when it would be opportune to take action. Years had yet to elapse before black resistance and the effect of international sanctions were to make any meaningful impact.

DIVIDED FAMILIES!

Throughout the apartheid era, there was always a nucleus of National-ist Party supporters who were 'uncomfortable' with, and opposed to, the racist ideology. Appalled as many were by the drastic legislative measures taken to enforce its implementation, they hesitated openly to resist and risk being labeled 'traitors to Afrikaner nationhood' - as apartheid was widely regarded. Others felt it prudent not to invoke the attention of the 'Broeder-bond'[108]. All were voiceless! Families were divided! My old neighbor F.S. Malan, well-known member of the United Party and Cabinet colleague of General Smuts, had a brother, S.F. Malan, who was Minister of Railways in the first apartheid Cabinet in 1948. Afrikaner intellectuals and moderates who were appalled by Government policy and sensitive to ever-increasing international condemnation, felt powerless to intervene. A quarter century of apartheid rule had yet to pass before a few 'inspired' Afrikaner Nation-alists found their way into government! Eventually, through their influence, some of the more blatant racist laws were modified or rescinded. Black trade unions were permitted. The Separate Amenities Act and other less effective measures were annulled but the basic concept - *the separation of races* - remained paramount.

BANTUSTANS

Came the time when Prime Minister Verwoerd[109] and his 'race-indoc-trinated' supporters thought it opportune to show the world that 'race sep-aration' was not the discredited policy widely alleged, that it had a positive 'enlightened' aspect that included 'self-rule' for the African people! The Government initiated a 'bold' ingenious 'Bantustan' policy with the estab-lishment of four 'independent self-governing' black states within the bor-ders of South Africa! Separate parliaments were established, each accompanied by all the costly trappings that one might expect with the cre-ation of a new nations. Banquets were held in the finest hotels in Pretoria and Cape Town in honor of the newly appointed black African presidents. It was obvious to those who knew the country well, but not so to the out-side world, that the vast mineral resources and rich agricultural areas of the country were to remain within the confines of 'white South Africa'. The new 'black' states would remain forever economically dependent on and subordinate to 'white' South Africa! The 'ingenious Bantustan' idea proved to be a costly, ill-conceived 'political' flop from the start!

APARTHEID PREVAILS

Despite its bigotry and manifold injustices, apartheid remained national policy for nearly half a century. It was an undisguised policy designed to entrench the power of a section of the white minority. Afrikaners represented only 12% of the entire population! While the policy recognized the franchise rights of the English speaking population (of the same ethnic origin), their numbers were half that of the Afrikaners. Thus the policy would ensure that the destiny of the country would remain forever in Afrikaner hands - a dominance that could be preserved if necessary, by means of influx control!

Apartheid, with all its grim implications, had many young South Africans deeply concerned about the country's future! Many, uninspired by the concept of 'Afrikaner nationhood', left the country. Older people, unable to leave, looked beyond our borders to secure their material assets.

NATIONAL GALLERY

At the start of my second year, I was appointed Council representative on the Board of Trustees of the South African National Gallery of Art. In time, my visits to the Gallery became more frequent - most of them unrelated to my duties as a Trustee. I enjoyed being there. The atmosphere was relaxing - often an 'escape' from troublesome political issues! The 'political intrusions' of senior Provincial officials (supposedly immune to political influence) were a particularly worrisome aspect of my 'political experience' - all so different from what I had expected.

On my retirement in 1980, I had been a trustee of the Gallery for 31 years. I had served as Chairman of the Board of Trustees for 21 years. Before retiring, I was the proud recipient of the Fellowship Award of the South African National Gallery - a treasured honor!

MY CITY

As the years passed I became 'aware' of the extensive land area[110] within the city boundaries. Of particular interest were the several ethnic, religious and social groups that made up the population. I realized as never before the variety of functions performed by the City Council. I found myself being more and more absorbed by town-planning and arterial road proposals. In the beginning I felt overwhelmed by the number of reports that reached me prior to the statutory monthly meetings. It seemed impossible to explore exhaustively the multifarious matters that appeared on the Council agendas and on which I was required to cast my vote! It was a while before I felt comfortable limiting my exhaustive interest to matters pertaining to the committees on which I served and to others that I could readily comprehend. For the remainder, there seemed little choice but to rely on the recommendations of the responsible committees.

The City Council consisted of 45 Councilors. The City was divided into 15 wards; each represented by 3 Councilors. A general election took place in August each year to elect one of the three to serve for a 3-year term. The system made for continuity of operations! It ensured that at least two-thirds of the members were in office long enough to be familiar with what had transpired prior to the election.

UNEXPECTED DEVELOPMENT

In the City Hall, informal discussion at meetings and during periods of recess, appeared to be confined to civic matters. Reference to personal business or professional practices was seldom heard! During the 32 years that I was there, my own practice was never mentioned either by me or by my colleagues. There was a single exception! One morning early in 1949, the Council had adjourned for tea. I was in the tea-room adjoining the council chamber, when Councilor Louis Gradner beckoned me to join him at his table! (He was a senior Councilor, Chairman of the Finance and General Purposes Committee, a past Mayor and, without question, the most influential member of the Council.) His signal came as a surprise! Our relationship though cordial, was somewhat 'distant'. Nine years had passed since my father died. I was only twelve years of age when the Gradner family became neighbors. I remembered that to us as children, their home was 'out of bounds'. Invitations from that quarter were consistently declined. There was cleavage between the two families. At the time, Dad was a first term Councilor. Directly opposite us in Forest Road lived our friends the Coulters. Mr. Coulter was our esteemed M.P. He called one morning, interviewed Dad and drew attention to the terms of sub-division of the Oranjezicht Estate. They precluded the building of flats. He informed Dad that it had come to his notice that Mr. Gradner intended to build flats in the area. He asked Dad to intervene - to urge Mr. Gradner not to pursue his project. He feared that because of Mr. Gradner's 'influential position', the plans might be approved despite the terms of sub-division. That, he thought, could cause dissension and possible scandal! It transpired that

Dad spoke to Mr. Gradner - totally without effect! The plans were approved and the flats were built! Dad was appalled; relations with the Gradner family first cooled, were totally severed. The two families - near neighbors - remained estranged; normal relations were never restored.

Dad was a Councilor for only three years. He never sought re-election. Often I wondered if his withdrawal from public life was occasioned by the Gradner incident! Dad, I believe, regarded it as a 'shady' aspect of public life from which he preferred to distance himself.

Now, a quarter century had passed since the family breach occurred! On this occasion, Mr. Gradner addressed me very cordially, as though it had never happened: "Alf, I've been talking to Mr. Miller of the OK Bazaars. He'll be phoning you! I think you'll be pleased!" The bells were ringing - calling us back to the Council chamber. Mr. Gradner's remark conjured up all manner of possibilities. I remembered Mr. Miller from a holiday boat trip to Durban shortly after the war. I had heard of him - knew him to be one of the directors of "OK Bazaars", a large nation-wide company with departmental stores in many parts of the country! I remembered telling him then that for weeks I had watched with interest the erection of their new Adderley Street building from my dentist's chair[111] and that I was surprised at the number of African laborers that sat idle day after day week after week. Mr. Miller then explained that it was obviously due to the type of contract they had no alternative but to agree to sign. (conditions after the War were so uncertain that Master Builders were able to insist on 'Cost plus 10% contracts' and apparently were not interested in keeping costs as low as possible). A day or two after Mr. Gradner's reference, Mr. Miller telephoned me! I met him that morning in their administrative offices on the sixth floor of the new OK Bazaars building in Adderley Street. I was introduced to Mr. Soloman, his Cape Town manager (whom I had already met at Ratepayers' meetings), and other members of the Johannesburg technical staff who were visiting Cape Town. Welcoming me, Mr. Miller said that his Board contemplated extensive development in the Cape Province starting with a new store on the Main Road Parow. He asked if I was in a position to undertake the commission as architect! Indeed I was! (His remark suggested that more might follow!) "Very well," said Mr. Miller, "we're glad to have you aboard. My Johannesburg office will contact you. Please keep in touch with Mr. Soloman." Then with a broad smile he added: "*and by the way –I've washed my hands of 10 per cent contracts!*" His remark told me that he remembered our meeting on board shortly after the war.

Parow was a rapidly developing town some six miles north of the city. The new store was the first of a number of large O.K. contracts in different parts of the Western Cape for which I was subsequently appointed architect[112]. I never knew whether Mr. Gradner had suggested my name to Mr. Miller or whether he had simply responded to an inquiry by Mr. Miller. In any event his attitude had been positive and I felt indebted. I took the first opportunity to tell him what had transpired and expressed my warm appreciation. Mr. Gradner responded - shook his head and said: "I owe it to you!" (I never knew precisely what it was that he alluded to and wondered if it was that my dad never instituted action for his contravention of the conditions of title? That I will never know!)

Years later I was commissioned to design a new double-storied house in Oranjezicht for Walter, Mr. Gradner's son.
(Years later Walter also became Mayor of Cape Town.)

THE PRACTICE GROWS!

During the fifties and sixties, the practice grew beyond all expectations. It employed nine assistants. Seven were qualified architects; two were juniors. Clients included corporations like the OK Bazaars, Panther Shoe Company, Golden Arrow Bus Company and the Cape Town Tramway Company. Commissions included factories and several large, multi-story apartments and office buildings. Save for several gasoline service stations[113] at which my associate Madlener was particularly innovative, the initial planning of all projects was undertaken by me personally. That is what clients expected and one with which I felt most comfortable. That, and an increasing volume of public commitments, impelled me to take work home - to spend countless nights burning the mid-night oil, preparing sketch plans, specification notes, reports etc., to keep pace with the demands of the practice. It was too late when I realized the extent to which 'family life' was neglected! The countless lonely nights that I imposed on Deena are unforgivable! It is an aspect of my career of which I am painfully conscious and by no means proud!

RHODESIA (now Zimbabwe)

It was about 1950 that I was one of a Cape Town delegation to a town-planning conference in Bulawayo, Southern Rhodesia. I decided to travel by car and was accompanied by Mr. Penso, Cape Town's chief town-planning officer and chief technical member of the delegation. The chosen route was via Welkom, a 'new' town in the Orange Free State. It had sprung-up 'over-night' as it were, following the discovery of gold and the development of one of the richest gold mines in the country. I had suggested that route because I had learned that it was there that my young cousin Morris Kahn (son of my cousin Beatie) had opened a jewelry store. Nineteen years had elapsed since I first met him in Benoni when he was not yet three years old and fifteen years since he, as a boy, attended my wedding. He had since lost both his parents and I was eager to know how he was getting along. I found him a keen, enterprising young man but seemingly worried! I was pleased that I had taken the longer route to meet with him again. I asked what was it that appeared to be worrying him!

CLASH WITH THE POLICE!

He explained that during the previous week he witnessed a native man lying crouched on the ground, being kicked and trounced several times by a young police constable. Morris said: "The poor chap was in pain, screaming helplessly but the constable went on hammering him mercilessly and I intervened! The constable pushed me aside saying in Afrikaans: 'I'll charge you!' He then bent down to hand-cuff his victim." Morris prudently decided to rush off to the police station and reported the matter to the duty officer. He was doing so when the constable arrived with his subdued victim. Recognizing Morris, the constable shouted: "That bug... interfered - tried to stop me arresting this bastard!" The duty officer, who already had the gist of the story, intervened, saying: *"nie so haastig nie Pel - one at a time."* Pointing to the poor victim he asked: "What's he been up to?" The report completed, the duty officer asked the constable: "And why were you kicking him?" He replied, "The bastard tried to resist arrest." With that, the duty officer turned to Morris, signaled with his thumb that he should leave and added: "Forget it, Pal!" Morris explained that was not the end of the story. "Each day after that there was a constable hovering around the house – in the evening and sometimes during the morning - obviously looking for something to pin on me."

I sympathized with Morris and admired his stance! We stayed at Welkom overnight. Next morning before leaving, Penso and I went to the shop to say good bye. Addressing my young cousin, I said: "Morris, you behaved splendidly with that policeman - if you had the best watch in the world, I'd buy it!" "Do you mean that Uncle[114]Alf?" "Sure I do!" Morris opened a drawer and produced a "Rolex". The price: "Thirty-five pounds". That was quite a lot of money in those days! Of course, I bought it. It served me well for several years. My only complaint was that after a few years it started to lose time. When I took it to my jeweler (my client Louis Hirschsohn) he explained that there was nothing wrong but that "these watches need to be cleaned regularly once a year." I decided to put it aside and replaced it with a Japanese 'Seika' that I bought (at about a quarter the price) aboard the *Warwick Castle* during one of my trips up the coast to Durban. Decades later, (we had already migrated to the United States) I responded to a Sotheby advertisement for old "Rolex" watches and sold the long discarded time piece as an antique for about ten times the price I had paid.

BACK ON THE ROAD

The day had all but passed when we crossed the border into Rhodesia and booked into our hotel in Bulawayo. The next morning we proceeded to the Town Hall to attend the opening session of Conference scheduled to last four days. Ahead of the public seating area were individual tables reserved for the delegates. Awaiting us were invitations to different functions. Among mine was a note from May Wolfe. The note said that she was now Mrs. Rogers, living in Bulawayo and would like me to telephone. What a surprise! Twenty-two years had passed since I last saw or heard of her. I called. She had spotted my name in the list of delegates that appeared in the local press. She invited me to dinner the following evening and I was. I glad to accept. She had changed a little but was still the happy lovely person with the same delightful English accent that had so fascinated me when I was a college student. Her husband, a friendly personality, left me in no doubt that theirs was a happy union.

SOUTH AFRICA AFTER 1948

After World War II, South Africa experienced a marked increase in cleavage between the two principal elements of the white population. In my view it was motivated for political reasons. Most Capetonians longed for an end to racial cleavage. Most, I believe, subscribed to the concept of peaceful progress within the framework of an expanding democracy - one that would, in time, embrace all ethnic groups. Nationalist propagandists revelled! The General Election of 1948 gave their Party a substantially increased majority! The new Nationalist Government wasted no time to demonstrate to the world that they intended to implement the *'will of the electorate'*. Expediency enabled them to disregard the fact that the (white) electorate comprised less than one sixth of the population, and that their Commonwealth allies, and the democratic world in general, regarded their racist policy as abhorrent. To them, apparently, it was irrelevant that World War II had cost the 'free world' thousands of lives in an effort to bring racial discrimination to an end! Immune to, and contemptuous of, world opinion, the South African government devised an array of ingenious legislative measures to ensure that racial separation would be implemented and enforced in every conceivable field! Apartheid was pursued with zest and determination. It was the basis of national policy for the next forty-six years. The country's strong economy and mineral wealth encouraged the Government to believe that they were well equipped to counter threats of economic sanctions that were being considered by the democratic world. There was one problem! South Africa produced no oil! In addition to the huge underground oil storage facilities already mentioned, the Government ramped up its SASOL[115] operation which converted the abundant supplies of coal into oil. Thus the Government believed they were in a position to counter all sanctions - even if Apartheid was vigorously enforced.

Succeeding elections gave the Government increasing strength. For more than four decades, racist legislation immersed the nation in an ever-deepening apartheid quagmire. My country became the pariah of the free world!

RACE RELATIONS DISRUPTED

Prior to the apartheid era, civic affairs in Cape Town were virtually free of party politics. Municipal elections and Council debates were confined to civic matters - never conducted on Party political lines. On rare occasions during Council deliberations, the Mayor would call a speaker if he recognized a speaker's tendency towards politics!

All Municipal matters were first referred to the relevant Committee, thence to the Council with Committee recommendations. When the Government sought to involve the Council in implementing apartheid legislation, the Government directives were referred to the General Purposes Committee. There they were discussed, criticized, often deplored and considered unworthy of reference to Council and were often tabled indefinitely.

ENTRY TO POLITICS

In 1952, there was to be a Provincial election in Mowbray - the neighboring constituency to Rondebosch. My name went forward as the nominee of Branch of the United Party. Mrs. Lewis, the sitting City Councilor for Mowbray, was nominated by some of her constituents. An active 'nomination' campaign followed. In due course, I became the official U.P. candidate. The Nationalist and Labor Parties considered Mowbray a safe U.P. constituency and decided not to contest. Thus I was returned unopposed. I then occupied two public offices - City Councilor for Rondebosch and M.P.C. for Mowbray.

MY PRACTICE!

My architectural practice was blessed with a splendid team of professional associates and assistants. It appeared unmarred by the time I devoted to civic interests. I expected that happy situation to continue despite the added provincial duties. Provincial Council meetings were held in Cape Town and would not involve my absence from home! Furthermore, as there were only two Provincial Council sessions a year - one of a month's duration, the other ten days - it seemed unlikely that my added interests would encroach unduly on the practice!

DISENCHANTED

It was my good fortune that opposing political parties continued to regard Mowbray as a safe U.P. seat. Thus I was never confronted with the rigors of an election contest. However, during my eight years on the Cape Provincial Council, I was not immune to aspects of internal party 'disruptions' that I found unpleasant even distasteful.

Soon after the defeat of the United Party in the 1948 General Election, their world-renowned leader General J. C. Smuts attended a meeting of the Party's Cape Peninsula Council. Mr. Gay, M.P. for Simonstown, was in the chair. (I had been elected vice-chairman - a role for which I was totally unprepared.) Addressing the meeting, General Smuts reminded us that while the Party had lost the election, nation-wide it had won the support of the majority of the electorate. He referred to 'current dissension' among the hierarchy of the Dutch Reformed Church (regarded as the back-bone of the Nationalist Party). He saw that as an indication of a 'waning influence - a symptom of their potential defeat' at the General election four years hence. He urged his Party supporters to remain steadfast! Smuts, a brilliant statesman, was a poor prophet. He died soon afterwards - unaware that his Party was never to attain power again - that apartheid was to dominate the political scene more and more for the next four decades.

UNITED PARTY LEADERSHIP

On Smuts's death, the leadership of my United Party vested in Mr. J.G.N. Strauss, M.P. for Germiston, a mining town on the East Rand. An advocate by profession, he became General Smuts's Minister of Agriculture and Forestry in 1940 soon after the outbreak of war. However, he was not widely known and his appointment as Party leader came as a total surprise to many inside the Party and out. Apparently it was a choice that was made in deference to a wish said to have been expressed by Smuts before he died.

Early in his new role as Party Leader, Strauss addressed a number of public meetings in Cape constituencies that were lost to the United Party in the 1948 election. His speeches, as reported in the English and Afrikaner press, indicated a 'leaning' towards apartheid - in direct conflict with official United Party policy! A number of U.P. supporters in my area contacted me. They were seething - wanted to know what I was doing about it! The matter was put on the agenda of the following meeting of the Cape Peninsula Council. As Mr. Gay was away, it fell to me to take the chair. A few delegates, armed with press cuttings of Mr. Strauss's speeches, were angry. Statements reportedly made by Mr. Strauss were read out loud. Someone exclaimed: "He's a Nat. - sent to destroy us." I appealed for order! After a brief silence, someone moved that Mr. Strauss be asked to attend the next meeting of Council. Another said: "he's had lots of time and has repudiated nothing!" A resolution was finally adopted directing me (in my capacity as Chairman) to address a letter to Mr. Strauss to ascertain whether he confirmed the accuracy of the press reports and, if not, was it his intention to request the press to rectify the reports.

It was not easy writing such a letter to the Party leader! I explained, as tactfully as possible, that the reported statements had been discussed at the C.P. Council meeting and that a resolution was adopted directing me (as Chairman) to write to ascertain: "if you, Sir, had been accurately reported and, if not, whether you would request that corrections be published?" I enclosed the relevant press cuttings with the contentious comments underlined. In reply, Mr. Strauss did not affirm that he had been wrongly reported. On the contrary, he asserted that his policy references had won considerable approval and that he believed that the Party had benefited by his remarks. The reply shook me. It implied that to him the apartheid ideology was far from repugnant and that for possible political gain, he (and others members of our party) was prepared to abandon principles hitherto considered sacrosanct.

A NEW LEADER

Months later, Strauss was succeeded by Sir De Villiers Graaf as the Party's leader. That did not strike at the root of the problem. On the contrary, the rift deepened. Marais Steyn, brilliant bilingual orator and popular Transvaal leader, had assumed the national leadership of the Party would fall to him. When that failed, he resigned from the Party, joined the Nationalists and was quickly elevated to cabinet rank. His ministry included 'Indian affairs'!

He, I recalled, was the man whose eloquent condemnation of apartheid had so impressed me that I chose him (of the several Party leaders) to address my meeting in Rondebosch, to dine at my home and meet my family! Had I been unduly gullible or was I only now awakened to the shallowness of the 'political game'? My Party was in disarray! My confidence was shaken!

SEPARATE AMENITIES ACT!

The Act required municipalities throughout the country to provide *separate amenities* for the different racial groups! The matter never reached Council where deliberations remained untainted by politics!

The personal political affiliations of most of the 45 Cape Town City Councilors were known to be anti-Nationalist. Indeed, only one, Councilor Van Zyl, was a known member of the Nationalist Party. He was a good councilor, remained 'aware' of his minority status and discretely refrained from any 'political' activity in the City Hall. In time, he won the confidence of his colleagues, not for his politics but for his restraint and respect for views of his political adversaries. In the seventies, despite his political affiliations, he was elected to the Chair of Van Riebeeck[116].

IMPLEMENTING THE ACT!

As was the general practice, the directive from the Government (requiring the Council to implement the Act) was referred to the General Purposes Committee. On display around the Committee-room were maps and pictures of the several beaches on both the Atlantic and Indian Ocean seaboards. There were seventeen of them on the waterfronts of both the Indian and Atlantic oceans. Some, such as at Muizenberg with miles of crystal white sands unmarred by seaweed, rock or derelict sea-waste, were, without question, the safest, most beautiful, and the cleanest in the world. Others were less attractive and less accessible. To any fair-minded person, it was obvious that there was no way in which such amenities could be allocated *separately* and equitably to the several ethnic groups. There had been no complaints of interference of one group by another. Cape Town, a multi-racial city, was free of ethnic cleavage. Nowhere in the world was there greater harmony between the races. The population of Cape Town was predominantly 'white'. While no 'ethnic' statistics were kept, it would seem that some ten percent of the population were Colored. There were a few areas that were predominantly Colored such as District Six, Athlone, a small area in Claremont and the 'Malay Quarters' on the fringe of the city center. All had developed as a natural consequence of people gravitating towards their own kith and kin. No law or regulation had ever determined their 'ethnic' usage! Nothing was more likely to disrupt that harmony, to cause cleavage, than an attempt to separate and demarcate the City's amenities on ethnic lines as was required by the Act!

It was obvious to Councilors attending the meeting that the bill was discriminative and dangerously provocative! It bristled with potential inequalities! In no way could the Council be party to such an abhorrent measure. The obvious objections to the Bill were well known to the Government. The City Council was not about to 'do the Government's bidding'. It was obvious to those attending the meeting that any recommendation on those lines was unthinkable and would be summarily rejected by Council. The Committee preferred to make no recommendation to Council – to allow the matter to lapse and so remain unimplemented!

In due course, when it became apparent to the Government that the Cape Town City Council (the principal municipality affected by the bill) had no intention to conform, the Provincial Administration was directed to take the necessary steps to ensure compliance. A letter from the Provincial

Secretary to the Town Clerk followed. It was to the effect that if Council 'neglect' continued, the Provincial Administration would have no choice but to 'implement the law at the Council's expense'. Council 'neglect' continued! Finally, the Provincial Administration made the allocations and had notices erected. Needless to say, the most beautiful and most popular beaches such as those at Muizenberg, St. James, Sea Point, Rocklands, Clifton and Camps Bay were all 'zoned' for the exclusive use of 'Europeans'. Less attractive beaches (some remote and outside the municipal boundaries) were zoned for 'Coloreds', others for 'Indians', some for 'Malays' and yet others – far more remote and less accessible - for 'Africans'! Notices such as 'FOR WHITES ONLY' and 'FOR COLOREDS ONLY', etc., became conspicuous features of the Peninsula beaches. The Provincial officials delegated to implement the Act were obviously unaware of the extreme corrosive nature of the salty air on the Peninsula coast. The notices were made of sheet metal (thought to be more permanent than wood). It was not long before many were rusted, fell into disrepair or were vandalized and removed by the beach cleaners! None were replaced!

THE ACT AND THE NATIONAL GALLERY OF ART

The Director, Dr. Bokhorst, showed me a letter just received from the Secretary for Arts and Science[117] calling upon the Gallery to take the steps necessary to provide *'separate amenities' (toilets, etc.)* for the different racial groups - "in compliance with the Separate Amenities Act." I was aware of and I shared Dr. Bokhorst's disgust with the entire apartheid syndrome. His abhorrence reflected in his voice as he handed me the letter saying: "What do you make of this?" The letter was put on the agenda of the following Board Meeting. I reminded members that 'the Gallery was *not* a Government institution; that it belonged to the people'. I referred to the written agreement in the twenties[118] that made it clear that the Gallery was a 'commitment' of the Government and was administered at the *sole* discretion of the Board of Trustees. I added that 'the directive violated the spirit of the agreement' - that I considered it inappropriate and improper for one party to depart from its terms, simply because it was subsequently vested with 'legislative powers'. One member thought it "impudence"; another resented "interference by the Department!" The Director reported that the present facilities were 'quite adequate', that 'unfortunately very few African and Colored people visited the Gallery'. Professors Trumpleman & Louw (representing the Afrikaans University of Stellenbosch) were silent until Trumpleman was asked (by a Board member) how he regarded the matter. His reply was that he considered the Department's letter *'presumptuous to say the least'!* Professor Louw added that 'the Minister should be reminded that his Department was without status in the matter'. The Board resolved that 'the Chairman personally convey the Board's views to the Minister, as soon as possible after Parliament opened in January'.

In January, Dr. Bokhorst and I interviewed the Minister, Dr. Piet Koornhof, in the conference corner of his spacious parliamentary chambers. We were introduced to the secretary who sat at a desk in the background throughout the interview. I had met the Minister previously at Gallery functions. He was one of the 'more liberal', easily approachable members of the Cabinet. He opened the discussion with a friendly comment: "Gentlemen, what can I do for you?" From our letter seeking the interview, he was of course aware that we had come to discuss the directive received from his Secretary. I responded saying that he was no doubt aware that the National Gallery was *not* a Government institution, that the Board of Trustees had full jurisdiction and that Board members regarded the 'directive' from the Secretary, an 'unacceptable intrusion'. I added incidentally that added provisions such as suggested in the 'directive" would be unnecessary and wasteful! The Minister replied that he was familiar with all aspects, that the letter in question was a 'routine directive' sent to all public institutions -'maybe it should not have been sent to you'. He thanked us and concluded: "Gentlemen, you will hear no more. Let us forget about it!" We shook hands and departed. We heard no more!

A MOMENT OF MIRTH!

Humor was a rare by-product of the apartheid regime! One of the exceptions occurred at the National Gallery of Art. It was in the seventies when a few of the less extreme Nationalists - troubled by the inevitable failure of the apartheid syndrome - had advanced to Cabinet rank. Slowly their influence surfaced. While there was no departure from the Government's commitment to apartheid, there was what appeared to be a vague attempt to quell the increasing tide of world opposition. Some of the 'less important' legislative measures such as the Separate Amenities Act were rescinded! When that occurred, the National Gallery received yet another 'routine' letter from the Department of Arts and Science. It stated that the Act having been rescinded, *all notices installed in pursuance thereof, could be removed at the expense of the Department; the relevant bill to be sent to the Department for payment.* An amused Dr. Bokhorst showed me the letter saying: "What does one do with this?" Together we enjoyed drafting the reply. It simply acknowledged receipt and concluded: "We are pleased to inform you that there is no bill! No such notices were installed and thus there are none to be removed."

For nearly thirty years, apartheid had cast an unrelenting shadow over the country before any light penetrated! All manner of racist laws protective of 'white interests' provoked bitter resentment and increasing resistance among the African population. An inhibited news media provided scant news of police action taken in different parts of the country to counter anti-apartheid activity. The news that filtered was grim and often hard to believe!

LIBRARY SERVICES

After the War, considerable progress was made in the provision of free library services throughout the country. Legislation pertaining to education and library services vested in the four provincial governments. The Cape Town library service, however, was run independently by the City Council on the basis of a 50% subsidy from the Province. By 1952, Cape Town's library service consisted of sixteen public libraries of which three were mobile. By that means, reading material was made available to the poorest communities in areas where public transport (to the permanent libraries) was remote or costly. The 1952 general election placed the Cape Provincial Council in the hands of the Nationalist Party for the first time. (That was the year of my entry into politics as a member of the Cape Provincial Council.)

While the Cape Town City Council played no part in party politics, 44 of its 45 members were known to be anti-nationalist and opposed to the apartheid policy. Thus the new Provincial rulers were not very favorably disposed to the City Council! Their mania for 'separating the races' knew no limits! 'Now they would show the City who the new rulers were!' A directive was delivered to the Town Clerk demanding *separate* library services for the different racial groups *'in terms of the law'*! The directive was referred to the General Purposes Committee of which I was Chairman. All Departmental heads and several of the Council's librarians were directed to attend. An unusually large number of non-committee councilors were in attendance. It was by no means clear from the directive what precisely we were expected to do to comply! Reports from the departmental heads left no doubt that compliance in any form would be extremely costly and would take years to implement. More importantly, the enforcement of apartheid in the library services was likely to provoke racial unrest hitherto unknown to the City. Such were the observations reported to full Council. Council adopted the report and decided to send a strong deputation to the newly appointed Administrator Dr. Otto Du Plessis[119]. I was one of a deputation of ten councilors headed by the Mayor. We were accompanied by the City's chief librarian and two committee clerks.

In advance, the Council had sent the Administrator a lengthy memorandum. It described how the existing service was planned to be readily accessible to all areas and to all residents regardless of race. It described the formidable costs that would be involved in any attempt to provide 'separate' services, let alone separate books on racial basis. It also drew attention to the potentially dangerous cleavages that any such attempt was likely to provoke.

DUAL ROLE

A few months prior to the meeting with the Administrator, Councilors Keen, Young and I were the three Cape Town delegates to the annual congress of the Cape Provincial Municipal Association (CPMA) held that year in Port Elizabeth. On the third morning of Congress and before the end of the last session, my two colleagues and I left to return to Cape Town. Days later I received a letter informing me that (in my absence) I had been appointed the Association's representative on the Provincial Library Board. My immediate reaction was that I had too much hay on my fork. I telephoned the Chairman of Congress, Mr. Erasmus[120], to tell him that I was unable to accept. He explained that the Board met only once a year and, as the meeting was in Cape Town, he urged me to reconsider. I agreed! Thus, when the City's deputation met the Administrator, in a sense, I was there in a dual capacity although I had yet to attend my first meeting of the Provincial Library Board.

The Administrator welcomed us with great courtesy. Only one other Provincial officer attended - the Provincial Librarian, Mr. De Vries. Courteously, the Administrator welcomed us in English (it was a gesture - his home language being Afrikaans). He explained that he had read the City's memorandum exhaustively, that he fully understood our problems and wished to put our minds at rest. He said that of our sixteen libraries, there were only three that were of any concern! They were Salt River, Wynberg

and City Center. Those he planned to visit personally and would commu-
nicate with the Town Clerk later. He added: "As for the remainder, there
was nothing to be done - please continue as before!" I immediately
addressed the City Librarian and asked if he was aware of any problems -
racial or other - at the three libraries referred to by the Administrator. He
said he knew of none!

The Administrator thanked us for our attendance and the meeting
ended. We left, pleased with what had transpired and with a considerable
sense of relief!

The Administrator had seemed eager to calm troubled waters. I felt
sure that he had no intention of enforcing apartheid where it was likely to
promote racial cleavage or was otherwise unnecessary. Most of us were
hopeful that after his visit to the three libraries, the problem would cease to
be an issue.

Soon after, the Administrator died.

PROVINCIAL LIBRARY BOARD

I attended my first (and only) meeting of the Provincial Library Board.
Present were five other members including the chairman Dr. Meiring,
Superintendent General of Education. (His brother, a colleague of mine,
was a partner in the well-known architectural firm Meiring and Naude both
of whom were considered moderate fair-minded members of the Afrikaner
community.) The Provincial Librarian Dr. De Vries was in attendance. The
secretary read the minutes of the previous meeting. It included a report on
the City Council's deputation to the Administrator! I could not believe what
I was hearing! According to the report, the Administrator had informed the
City Council that Cape Town would have to comply with the law and that
specific proposals for the libraries at Wynberg, Woodstock and City Center would await the Administrator's personal visit to the three libraries in
question! To me, the report was the antithesis of what, in fact, had
occurred. Obviously I could not let it go unchallenged. Addressing the
Chair, I said that I was present at the deputation and had no choice but to
refute the validity of the report. I expressed concern that what I had just
heard was the opposite of what had in fact transpired! De Vries interrupted! He displayed considerable anger, saying that as I was not present at
the previous Board meeting, I was not in a position to question the

accuracy of the minutes. The Chairman asked if the minutes as distinct from the report were in order. They were approved and signed. "Matters arising from the minutes?" said Mr. Meiring as he looked to me! My response was that it was my first meeting of the Board and I was reluctant to appear contentious but that a report completely at variance with the facts could not go unchallenged. I added that I was surprised that the Provincial Librarian had not seen fit to correct the report and I had no choice but to reach my own conclusions. I went on to say that the Council's strong opposition to the introduction of apartheid in its library services was met with apparent understanding by the Administrator. He was clearly reluctant to provoke racial discord, had said that he intended personally to visit three of the libraries before making a decision in their regard! Mr. De Vries was restless, obviously rattled! I commented that there were nine or ten persons present at the deputation and that it would not be difficult to ascertain which of the two reports was correct. Members of the Board were disturbed! I urged the Chairman to contact the Town Clerk and obtain a copy of the official record of what in fact had transpired at the deputation. My request that my report be included in the minutes of the current meeting was agreed to. De Vries made no attempt to conceal his anger! It was his report that I had challenged. Subsequently, it dawned on me that if the apartheid directive was made imperative and the City refused to comply, the entire Cape Town service would probably be transferred to the Province and would fall under the direction of Mr. De Vries! I was apprehensive of his motive in preparing a report so glaringly false and realized that when he prepared his report, he was unaware of my appointment to the Board or that I would become informed of its contents. The atmosphere was tense. I realized that in due course, I would have to report precisely what had occurred to Congress - the body I represented on the Board.

The following day, I saw the Town Clerk and informed him of what had transpired. At once he called the committee clerk who had attended the deputation and asked him to come to his office with his original notes. The Clerk was asked to read the notes aloud. He said he had completed his report for Council and proceeded to read it aloud. It confirmed my version. The Town Clerk added that that the report I had just heard would appear on the agenda on the next meeting of my Committee and on the subsequent Council agenda and in due course a copy would be sent to the Province Secretary.

MALPRACTICE!

The Cape Provincial Council had been in session for a few days when I had a visit from a director of Juta and Company.[121] He drew attention to an apparent change of policy by the provincial library administration. He explained that in the past, the importation of books required for the many libraries in the Cape Province, was the subject of tenders in which his Company and others had been regularly invited to tender. That practice suddenly ceased and inquiries to the Provincial Librarian produced the answer that the books were now being imported directly by the Department. The result was that the South African book trade was excluded from the tendering process and consequently the Province was deprived the advantages of competitive tendering! He feared malpractice! I was unaware of the position and suggested that his firm (and if possible others similarly placed) should address a formal question to the Provincial Secretary; if the reply was considered unsatisfactory, he should contact me again. I heard no more!

MUNICIPAL CONGRESS IN GEORGE

The following annual Congress of the CPMA took place in the town hall of George - about 250 miles east of the City. Before leaving Cape Town, I called the Board secretary requesting a copy of the minutes of the Board meeting. I wanted to have them available when reporting to Congress. I called the secretarty again before departing. She explained that 'the boss' (De Vries) had instructed her that they were not to be sent out until they were ready to go to all Board members which would be with the agenda for the next meeting!

My report was therefore brief. Indeed there was nothing to report other than what had transpired at the only Library Board meeting that had taken place since my appointment! I submitted my report to the executive meeting immediately prior to the opening of Congress. It related solely to what had transpired at the single meeting of the Board and I was asked to repeat the report when the item was reached on the agenda of open Congress.

As usual some 300 delegates from the different Cape municipalities were in attendance. The Chairman, Mr. Erasmus, was on the platform; seated behind him were guests from the other provinces. Among them was Mr. William Slater, the Cape Provincial Secretary (chief administrative officer of the Province). In due course, when the item was reached, I repeated my report. Of course it drew attention to the radical difference between the facts as I knew them and those recorded in Mr. De Vries's version! I added that I had been at pains to verify the accuracy of my report from the records! There were rumblings and interjections from the floor! Mr. Slater was on his feet at the microphone. He was seething with anger and declared: "I know nothing about this! Clr. Honikman has no right to come here and criticize my Department without first reporting to me!" I might well have reported to him had there been time. In any event I assumed that he had heard from the Town Clerk and must have known, from one source or another, what was going on under his wing. I was surprised at his alleged ignorance of the entire matter! My colleague Councilor Keen was enraged. He jumped to his feet and shouted to Slater: "You forget you're a public servant - we're not answerable to you!" Clr. Keen had resumed his seat and I returned to the microphone and said: "Mr.Chairman, I regret the pandemonium provoked by Mr. Slater's remarks. It would have been more appropriate had he promised to investigate the accuracy of my report! Had he done that he would be better informed of what was going on under his wing!" Slater remained silent. Several delegates from the rural areas rose and declared unqualified admiration for the "wonderful library services provided by the Provincial administration." "Ons moet Meneer Slater bedank...."[122] Remarks of that kind rang through the hall depicting a measure of 'subservience' at the foot of bureaucracy that seemed characteristic of the behavior of several Nationalist delegates.

Congress adjourned for lunch. Delegates returned to their hotels. It was not yet one o'clock. I was chatting with my colleagues in the garden of the Hawthorndene Hotel when Mr. Slater appeared. As he passed, I turned to him and said: "Mr. Slater, you had no right to make a personal issue of my report! You have access to the records and should have seen them by now..." Slater scowled and exclaimed: "I'll drive you out of public life." Angry, Councilor Keen answered him: "Unmitigated arrogance - who do you think you are?" Turning to me, he said: "I wouldn't let him get away with that!"

On my return to the City, I interviewed Clr. Fritz Sonnenberg[123] in his private office, and made it clear that I was interviewing him as an attorney. I told him what had occurred in George and said that I was not prepared to allow Mr. Slater's public slur to go unchallenged. I asked him to write formally to Mr. Slater demanding an apology, failing which I would take legal action. Fritz tried to appease me. He said something to the effect: "That's the kind of rough and tumble one meets in public life - one needs broad shoulders!" I replied that I was not prepared to take it and insisted that the letter be sent. I felt that it might also impel Slater to look into Mr. De Vries's conduct which (I believed) was deliberately false. I questioned his suitability for the responsible position he occupied.

A few days later Mr. Slater made an appointment to see me 'privately' at my office. As he entered, smiling broadly, he advanced with outstretched arm! He thanked me for seeing him at short notice and said that he had come to apologize for his conduct in George. He 'had been taken unawares - felt that his Department was being attacked'. However, he acknowledged that he had been at fault, that there was 'no justification for his loss of control' and asked that I accept his 'sincere apologies!' I realized that his visit was pursuant to a call from my attorney! I responded: "Of course, I accept but that does not take care of the fact that your attack was both in public and in open Congress in the presence of 300 delegates." He replied: "For the record, I will report fully to Mr. Erasmus and will request that my letter be read to open Congress and included in the minutes." We shook hands. In parting, he said: "By the way, I have started an investigation into the De Vries matter. Your concerns appear well founded! You'll be hearing more about it!"

It was not until 1963, after I had resigned from the Provincial Council and was no longer politically attached, that the newspapers carried lengthy reports of a 'public enquiry' into the activities of Mr. De Vries! They described how he had asserted the right to decide on the quantity of books ordered by the Province and that he received a commission of twelve and a half per cent on the value of all such books; furthermore, that he had ordered 500 copies of his own work! Counsel (appearing on behalf of the book trade) stated that he was convinced that "these transactions were in fact a fraud and that the Administration suffered a great deal of harm thereby." Summing-up, the Commissioner said: *"It is my finding that De Vries is not a person on whose evidence any reliance can be placed. "He repeatedly gave evidence that was devoid of all truth and he was prepared without hesitation to twist the truth and manipulate it to suit himself. I find that De Vries has committed grave misconduct and that he has contravened the provisions of Section 17 and 14 of the Public Service Act."*

His services with the Province were terminated. I am unaware if he was tried or found guilty of any criminal offence. The De Vries episode may illustrate the extent to which 'politics' had penetrated the civil service. It shows also how 'politics' could be abused to feather one's nest. Significant as it was, it could not compare with the radical changes that were being wrought by politics at the national level.

AT THE NATIONAL LEVEL

To put my story into some kind of perspective, I will refer briefly to some of the events that were taking place in the country during that period. They were events from which I (like most other white South Africans) was isolated but which were of enormous significance to the entire country and indeed to the world! In 1962, a well-known African leader, Nelson Mandela, was arrested and found guilty of treason. He was sentenced to life imprisonment, hard labor and isolation on Robben Island - a desolate outpost about seven miles off the Cape Town coast. The verdict caused a shudder among the African people and among those deeply concerned at the direction that the Government's apartheid policy was driving the nation. The impact had long-term repercussions internationally! The effect on would-be political adversaries at home was by no means benign!

NATIONAL CONGRESS

In 1959, members of the United Party from all parts of the country gathered in Bloemfontein for their annual congress. The apartheid ideology to which the Government Party had committed the nation - one that attracted universal condemnation - was by then the key political issue facing the country. Within the United Party it was an issue on which attitudes and interpretations varied widely. Dissension was widespread! Office bearers such as Basson and Strauss actually considered it 'expedient'- by no means inappropriate, to offer 'qualified' support for the ideology. They in fact regarded those of us who were vehemently opposed to the concept as 'malcontents'. With a slur, they often referred to us as 'trouble makers' and *'those liberals'*!

Soon after the opening, Congress was addressed by Mr. Mitchell, the U.P provincial leader for Natal. Apparently he had decided to confront the issue head-on. In an attempt to induce support for and 'understanding' of apartheid (which he knew was anathema to many of us), he proceeded to 'inform' Congress that *"in Natal, natives were occupying white farms, and the Government was doing nothing about it!"* That was the first time that any of us had heard of such 'occupations'! It struck most of us as a glaring unforgivable fabrication - designed to whip up anti-black sentiment! There were angry rejoinders from the audience! Mitchell tried to raise his voice above the discordant chatter. Angry members rushed about the hall consulting one another. Zac De Beer[124], sitting behind me, leant over my shoulder and whispered: "Can you beat it - sheer apartheid propaganda! They'll ruin us!" There was pandemonium! Other speeches followed! No one was listening. Someone handed me a note. It was from Graaf asking me to join him to lunch. We were not on close social terms so I assumed that, as we shared the same constituency (Rondebosch), he wished to discuss the situation with me. Just then Helen Suzman[125] appeared in front of me. She and I were personal friends and I shared the high esteem in which she was widely held. She said: "Alf, we're meeting to-night. Please join us?" Vaguely I guessed what it might be about and would certainly have joined them but for an important meeting in Cape Town first thing the following morning - one to which I was committed. I explained that I was leaving that afternoon on the 5:30 plane. (I was Deputy Mayor at the time).

At lunch, Graaf had invited Jan Steytler MP, to join us. Steytler was a strong opponent of the apartheid doctrine and resented members who thought it expedient to tamper 'on its fringe'! Addressing Steytler, Graaf asked: "Jan, what is all this I hear about a meeting tonight?" Steytler replied: "Div, don't worry! Nothing will happen before first discussing it with you." For the rest of the meal, the atmosphere seemed a little strained! The easy informality one might expect among political 'buddies' was absent!

That evening on the airplane to Cape Town, Graaf sat immediately behind me. I was scanning the *Daily Mirror* when a headline caught my eye: *"Can the Catholics and Protestants unite?"* (It was a reference to a forthcoming ecumenical conference in Europe.) Mindful of the day's events, I scribbled *'conservatives'* above the word 'Catholics' and *'progressives'* above 'Protestants'. I handed the paper to Graaf. He chuckled quietly, leant forward and whispered: "Don't worry! They've promised to discuss their concerns with me. I'll keep you informed."

UNITED PARTY IN TURMOIL

Next morning, at the breakfast table, I opened the *Cape Times*! Displayed with great prominence was a caption to the effect:

U.P. Split! Progressives in revolt, form a new Party!

The article referred to the meeting that took place the previous evening at the close of the Bloemfontein Congress. Obviously there had not been time for my friends to discuss matters with Graaf as was intended! I regretted that! My leanings were unquestionably with the Progressives but my disenchantment with party politics had become paramount! I had decided that the time had come for me to withdraw from the political arena!

Days later, Steytler on a visit to Cape Town, called on me at City Hall. He asked if I would be joining them. He was referring to the newly formed "Progressive Party"! I told him of my decision and said it was final.

MY ROLE IN POLITICS!

My active participation in party politics had lasted seven years. It brought me into contact with several interesting personalities - some whose goals were benign and selfless, others not entirely so. It was a great experience but I felt 'out of my element'! At last I realized that the time and energy spent could be put to better purpose - not least to my family where a father's involvement was most needed and to causes more fruitful of the general good. I questioned the 'logic' that took me on the political trail! Basically I guess it was concern about conditions in the country and their likely impact on our two boys at the threshold of their careers. At times, I had experienced a sense of alarm at the ethnic and economic quagmire into which the country appeared to be drifting - a situation that was way beyond my depth but in which I had been 'vain enough to believe that I could make a difference'! It was not long before I observed the extent to which personal interests and personality differences superceded policy issues - the inordinate amount of time and energy they consumed. I recalled an incident that occurred in the early days of Nationalist rule when the apartheid philosophy first dominated the political scene. It was already anathema to civilized communities everywhere and was officially opposed by my United Party. I attended a Cape United Party Congress in the Muizenberg Pavilion. Jack Basson, the sitting MPC for Piquitberg, made an ardent appeal to Party members to be less 'destructive' in their condemnation of apartheid! He went as far as to name a number of Cape constituencies that he claimed the Party would recapture if only we would be "more tolerant about apartheid - less aggressive in our criticism..." I could not believe my ears. Angered by such remarks, my friend Harry Whitehead and other Rondebosch delegates with whom I sat, looked to the platform expecting one of the Party leaders to rise immediately and condemn Basson's 'expediency' - his apparent willingness to forfeit principle in order to win seats! No one stirred! Harry nudged me! It would have been presumptuous of me - then a very junior member - to attempt to contest Basson's remarks.

I rushed to the platform hoping to urge Graaf, the Cape Leader, to denounce the Basson anti-Party attitude. Graaf was not present. Instead I spoke to our M.P., Colonel Pilkington Jordan. I urged him to do something about it! He put his finger to his lips to quell my ardor, shook his head and said: "Don't worry - it will be forgotten by tomorrow!" That shocked me! I began to question whether 'party politics' was an appropriate venue for the fundamental change in national policy. I also wondered whether in 'politics' I had entered a field that was entirely out of alignment with my values!

EXIT FROM POLITICS

The Bloemfontein Congress was the last straw! I decided to leave the political arena! I addressed a carefully worded letter to Sir De Villiers Graaf in which I tendered my resignation from the Party. I explained that I had decided to resign from the Provincial Council and from all political offices. I handed my letter to him personally in his office. He took a while reading it - stared at me, shook his head and tore it up. He said: "You can't do this!" I tried to explain that my decision was not taken lightly, that I was disenchanted with politics, that my decision was irrevocable! Graaf said that my resignation at that point would play into the hands of the National-ists! He explained that the election of the four Executive Members of the Provincial Council would take place immediately the new session com-menced. "We need every vote to retain two of the four seats on the Execu-tive Committee - your absence would give the Nationalists three of those seats and Murray would be displaced." My purpose was certainly not intended to help the Nationalists! I deferred my resignation! King and Murray, the two United Party nominees, were duly elected. The following day I returned to Graaf's office with a new letter of resignation. He said: "I was hoping you would change your mind; apparently I was wrong! How-ever, you owe your old supporters an explanation and I'd like you to attend a joint meeting of all branch committees and explain your reasons - they have been loyal to you over the years – it's the least you can do!" I agreed saying that it would be my last 'political contribution'!

The meeting took place at "Genadendal" - Graaf's spacious country home near Milnerton. There were some fifty delegates present - some were personal friends who had actively assisted me at election time! I was sen-sitive to the delicate situation in which I was placed. I was leaving them and their cause! The 'cool' greeting was in conspicuous contrast to that of earlier days! My decision was obviously resented widely! Indeed I was now among 'strangers'- once warm friends. However, there was no choice but to explain my reasons, to tell them frankly that I had been so repulsed by some of the incidents that had occurred that I was out of my element and had no choice but to sever relations with politics generally and thus with the Party.

Graaf welcomed his guests, thanked them for their tireless, loyal support of the Party and said that he had convened the meeting so that they could hear first hand my reasons for having 'abandoned the ship'!

I thanked him for providing this opportunity for me to address Party members to express my deep gratitude for their support and cooperation over past years. I explained that my decision to leave the political arena had not come easily! It was due primarily to a deep-rooted aversion for the apartheid ideology - a fear that it spelt disaster for the country! I explained that it had become obvious that prominent members of the Party did not see eye to eye with me on the issue. I referred to the Strauss episode, to Basson's fervent appeal in Muizenberg and to Mitchell's contentions in Bloemfontein. "All were apparently acceptable to the Party leadership - all suggested a measure of acceptance, even support of the apartheid syndrome!" I explained that, to me, it represented acceptance of a racist ideology that I found repugnant and to which I could never subscribe. I expressed concern that the Party was tampering with a policy that was reprehensible - scorned by our allies and by the civilized world! For me to remain a member would be to acquiesce and to abandon all conscience! There was simply no choice! I had to go! I turned to Graaf, thanked him for his hospitality and quietly took my leave.

There was not a stir, not a murmur – and, of course, no applause!

That was the last of my political encounters. In addition to disappointment at my Party's apparent 'drift', I questioned whether our political system - exclusively in the hands of a white minority - was capable of producing the radical democratic changes needed to bring 'peace' to the country. African unrest and international opposition to apartheid had amounted to a level fraught with dangerous possibilities.

Once free of all political commitments, I experienced a sense of relief! I was all too well aware that the time and energy that I had devoted to politics had served little purpose and could well have been put to worthier ends.

TURMOIL

By 1980, the anti-apartheid movement had gained momentum within the country, in other parts of Africa and overseas. Three years earlier Ghana had obtained independence! Now no fewer than seventeen African colonies were destined to follow suit. In March, the ANC staged a nation-wide "Freedom" campaign! It started with the burning in public of all passes. It gained the support of hundreds of thousands of Africans through-out the country and culminated with the Sharpeville massacre to which I will refer later. The PAC started a similar campaign. The government's response was to declare a 'state of emergency', to clamp down on all man-ner of civil liberties including the freedom of the press. The turmoil made an immense impact on the vast African population. The rest of the popula-tion in the larger urban areas witnessed little of its devastation and frustra-tion. Restraints imposed on the press kept them largely uninformed and unaware of the dire consequences.

LIFE GOES ON!

Out of politics, I was far from idle. My professional work continued as before. As Deputy Mayor, and as Chairman of the General Purposes Com-mittee and of the Board of Trustees of the S.A. National Gallery of Art, I was kept fully occupied. I was also one of five members of the Foreshore Board responsible for administering the development of the 550 acres that had been reclaimed from the sea to become a significant part of the City's down-town area. I will refer later to the Board's final meeting when control of the area was formally transferred to the City's administration.

APARTHEID IMPACTS MUNICIPAL TERRITORY!

Athlone, a self-contained residential suburb of Cape Town, is about six miles east of the City. It had experienced considerable growth during the war with its own commercial and industrial areas. Its population, predom-inantly of the Colored racial group, included a number of citizens of Indian origin. In accordance with general policy, the City Council had recently completed the building of a spacious new Community Center in the area. Similar centers[126] had already been established in eight other Cape Town suburbs. They were generally well-patronized civic amenities - of increased importance to the Colored people who were now disenfranchised as a result of the apartheid legislation. The new Athlone amenity, a large, attractive facility, was, of course, available to residents of all communities.

It had been open for over a year when my Committee received a report from the manager stating that the new Center was being used on average only twice a week. Disappointing as that was, the report added that public usage was improving slowly as residents became increasingly aware of the many facilities it offered. The disenfranchisement of the Colored people involved the removal of their names from the Common Roll. In addition, they were denied the right to be nominated as candidates for election to any town council even in wards that were exclusively or predominantly Colored. This denial of civic liberties was but one of many of the retrogressive measures for which the Nationalist government was being condemned throughout the democratic world. In an attempt to appease some of the mounting condemnation, the Government introduced an ingenious system of Colored 'Management Committees' to be elected by the Colored peoples! Such Committees were given no legislative or administrative powers! They were entitled to 'review local affairs' in their respective "Colored Areas" and when required, they could 'consult with' their respective 'white' town councils!

A CHANGE OF TONE

The Government resorted to several (cosmetic) changes to the apartheid policy. They thought it opportune to 'woo support' of the Indian community! They addressed a letter to the City urging the Council to build a Civic Center in Athlone for the *'Indian community'*! The Council replied pointing out that the large new Center recently built in Athlone was available to the Indian community as it was to all residents. It was also explained that the new center was in fact being used for only forty per cent of the time and that the provision of another such amenity in the same area could not be justified. The reply did not suit the Government's purpose! They decided to make personal representations to the Council! It fell to the General Purpose Committee (of which I was Chairman) to receive a deputation headed by the new Minister for Indian Affairs - my old Party colleague and one-time friend - the eloquent Mr. Marais Steyn! I had not seen him since he decided to leave the United Party to join the Nationalists! His approach was accompanied by the same 'congenial' manner to which I was attuned a few years earlier when, as a prominent member of my Party, he had dined at my home prior to addressing a meeting of my constituents! This time, his congenial posture was differently motivated. He averred that the Government felt that the Indian Community 'deserved' a civic center and expected the City's co-operation! I explained that the recently built Athlone Center was barely being used, that the Indian community would be more than welcome to use it and any of the many Cape Town civic halls throughout the City - that there was obviously no justification for additional expenditure in that direction! Steyn was not impressed. He pleaded that the Indian community was 'contributing to the national economy and were deserving of the added amenity!' He urged us to reconsider. I emphasized that there were nine Civic halls within the municipal area, all available to the Indian community as to all other groups, that no one group was offered preferential treatment. I warned that any attempt to apply ethnic considerations to the availability of civic amenities would be a provocative highly dangerous departure from policy! Steyn was not impressed! A member of my Committee pointed out that the city had never been asked to provide facilities on ethnic lines and that such a policy was fraught with problems - not least potential ethnic cleavage of which the City had been totally free. Another member averred: "No city could afford such a policy - where would it end?" He asked if the Government was prepared to pay for it. Steyn answered: "Maybe they will. I'll put it to them." To this, I responded: "Think again, Mr. Steyn - it would set a dangerous and costly precedent."

The meeting ended with a congenial comment by Mr. Steyn: "Thank you, Gentlemen. You'll be hearing from us!"

As far as I'm aware that was the last we heard of the proposal!

OPENING OF PARLIAMENT

The opening of Parliament was an annual event performed with considerable fanfare. It was no different in January 1960. A ceremonial procession of cars headed by the Governor General and his staff and those of the Prime Minister and visiting members of Parliament drove down the oak-lined Government Avenue and through the principal streets of the city. An escort of mounted officers of the national police force and their immaculately groomed steeds made a brilliant spectacle. The City's Traffic Police lined the cordoned streets and assumed point duty at the principle intersections. They were well-rehearsed for the occasion. Cape Town's Chief Traffic Officer had been at pains to ensure that the best trained and most immaculate of his men had been chosen for duty.

In Parliament Street, outside the gates of the Senate, as the Governor stepped out of his car, the noon gun struck! With a resounding click of heels, the Governor's Guard of Honor, presented arms - with immaculate precision! The occasion passed without incident.

In the City Hall immediately after the procession (I was Deputy Mayor at the time) it was gratifying to hear tributes to the Chief Traffic Officer for the efficient, smart and courteous manner of his men on duty.

A MAYOR'S REPRIMAND!

A day or two later I had a formal visit by Councilor Doman (one of six Colored councilors). He said that it had come to his notice that the mayor, Mrs. Newton Thompson, had reprimanded the Chief Traffic Officer for having put 'Colored' officers on duty during the procession preceding the opening of Parliament! I suggested that it was probably a mischievous rumor and that it should be dismissed. The next day, the Chief Traffic Officer made an appointment to see me in my City Hall office. (He was answerable to the Traffic Control Committee during my chairmanship and felt that courtesy demanded that he first inform me of his decision.) He placed a letter of resignation in front of me. Alarmed at what I read, I commented: "This is very sudden - what prompts you?" He said he was grateful to the Council for and proud of the recognition he had received - but he had been reprimanded by the Mayor for what occurred on the occasion of the opening of Parliament! He added: "Sir, without the full confidence of the Council, I cannot continue!" Dumb-founded, I asked what precisely had occurred. The explanation alarmed me! He said the men selected for duty during the procession were chosen solely for their efficiency and smartness - no other considerations had weighed with him! They included several 'Colored officers'. The Mayor had sent for him and stated that the Prime Minister had expressed resentment and disapproval that "*members of Parliament and guests of the Government had been subjected to direction at the whim of your Colored police!*" He said that the Mayor feels "I should have 'known better' than to subject members of Parliament to the directives of Colored officers. Sir, she feels that making guests welcome is a priority that must not be overlooked - that I should bear that in mind in the future." The Chief reminded me that my colleagues and I had often expressed aversion to any form of racial discrimination, and he recalled Council resolutions that convinced him that he would have violated Council policy had he acted as the Mayor suggested. He added: "Sir, I stand rebuked by the Mayor! I cannot undo what I have done and would do the same in the future. I have no choice but to withdraw. I do so with deep regret!" I was shaken! I suggested that the Mayor's comments may have been misunderstood, that I personally saw no grounds for criticism - indeed had he discriminated on grounds of race or color, he would indeed have been in conflict with Council policy. I asked him to defer action until I had an opportunity to look into the matter. He agreed.

The Town Clerk Mervin Williams was the senior of six Departmental Heads. He occupied that esteemed office for many years prior to my entering the Council. The Traffic Department fell under his administration. I discussed the situation with him. He too felt that the Traffic Chief had been entirely blameless. We decided to hear the Mayor's version first hand and interviewed her first thing next morning. Mr. Williams told her what had transpired, that the Chief had taken her reprimand seriously and was about to resign! I expressed the view that such a development would have serious repercussions - that in my view the Chief had been entirely blameless. The mayor explained that the Prime Minister viewed the matter seriously - "considered it infra dig - a calculated insult to put Colored officers in a position to direct the movements of members of Parliament - he should have known better." The mayor added: "We have to welcome our visitors - not antagonize them." What was I hearing! I intervened: "Joyce, he was doing his duty - consistent with Council policy! Had he discriminated in the manner suggested by the P.M. - to meet the racial whims of certain M.P.'s - he would have violated a trust and run counter to Council policy." "That may well be," said the Mayor. "We know how they feel; it only required a little tact." She rose from her chair commenting: "Much ado about nothing - don't you think!" That concluded the meeting. The following morning I sent for the Chief, told him of our meeting with the Mayor, that a natural desire to 'welcome' visitors can never take precedence over Council policy and that he would be expected to act no differently on similar occasions in the future. I added the comment that his resignation would constitute a victory for racists and urged him to reconsider. He pondered; then he crumbled the paper in his hand and said: "Thank you, Sir - this is no longer necessary." (It was the letter of resignation that he had shown me the previous day). I was delighted! He accompanied me to the office of the Town Clerk and confirmed that he had decided not to proceed with his resignation. Mr. Williams, obviously very pleased, addressed the chief: "I've had several glowing reports of the meticulous conduct of your men; I compliment you; you did the right thing - could not have acted differently." We all shook hands and dispersed.

An issue bristling with potentially complex repercussions had been quietly resolved.

Later, when I informed Councilor Doman of what had transpired, he muttered: "Good - wish we could rid ourselves of those bloody Nats[127] that easy!"

1960 - A GRIM PERIOD!

Apartheid - the hated policy of South Africa's Nationalist government with all its racist restraints, injustices and police violence - resisted international sanctions and world-wide condemnation for 46 painful years! A significant period that remains vivid in my memory was the year 1960 during my term as Deputy to Mayor Joyce Newton Thompson! The incident relating to the opening of Parliament (already described) was but one of the important events that occurred that year! Ghana became an independent republic and no fewer than seventeen former colonies were scheduled to become republics. Harold McMillan, Prime Minister of Great Britain, visited South Africa. Addressing Parliament in Cape Town, he spoke of *"The Winds of Change"* - a pointer to potential developments in South Africa. His remarks, resented strongly by members of the Government, attracted strong protests in Langa - an African township near Cape Town.

SHARPEVILLE

In the town Vereeniging about 33 miles south of Johannesburg, several thousand P.A.C.[128] members held a demonstration march from Sharpeville - a densely populated African township. They were entirely without weapons - the march was designed to be absolutely peaceful. The marchers surrounded the police station. Panic-stricken, the police, numbering some 75, opened fire. The marchers turned and fled! The police continued firing, left 69 dead and 169 wounded - many shot in the back. News of the massacre spread throughout the world! Repercussions were widespread. The United Nations Security Council blamed the Government and urged racial equality; several nations protested as did the United States State Department! The Johannesburg stock exchange plunged. The P.A.C. leader Robert Sobukwe was hailed "liberator!" The ANC also responded. Their leader Chief Robert Luthuli led a protest march in Pretoria, the administrative capital. He showed his disgust and contempt by publicly burning his pass[129] and urging others to do the same. The Government's reaction was that the Sharpeville riot was 'inspired by communists'! They declared a 'State of Emergency', suspended *habeas corpus* and assumed sweeping powers against any form of subversion - real or imaginary. South Africa was under martial law! Mandela, a practicing attorney and prominent ANC leader, was arrested, charged with treason and confined to filthy conditions in Sophiatown near Newlands Cape Town - before his historic treason trial began.

Those events occurred soon after my withdrawal from politics and immediately prior to my election as Mayor. Soon after I took office, my car was approaching the City Hall. There, a small parking area (reserved for official cars) was crowded with police! They made way as the car slowly entered. "Problems?" I asked the officer-in-charge. "No," he said, "just a few rabble rousers on the Parade!" Minutes later I was in my office. It overlooked Darling Street and the Grand Parade. I glanced out of the window, noticed a man standing on a soapbox addressing a small gathering - about a dozen people. Then I spotted eight or nine police crossing the street. They were from the spot where I had seen them minutes earlier. They halted on the sidewalk not far from the 'orator'! I thought: "Gosh - if they interfere, they'll provoke a riot!" I sent a messenger down to ask the officer-in-charge to come up and see me. Still at the window when he arrived, I drew attention to his men and to the orator whose quiet audience was now about two dozen. I said: "Officer, these orators are a common sight here on the Parade – it's a little like Hyde Park Corner - they're harmless – but if your men intervene, they'll surely provoke trouble!" He saluted, thanked me and disappeared. I watched him cross the road and call his men off! I thought: "Had the police at Sharpeville shown a little restraint, that massacre may have been avoided."

The atmosphere in the country was tense - more so in the northern provinces than in the Cape where we were poorly informed of some of the grim apartheid repercussions up north. The press was to some extent shackled by the emergency regulations following the Sharpeville massacre.

CHAPTER 26

ELECTED TO HIGH OFFICE

In the Cape, it was the practice for the Mayor[130] to be elected by the elected Councilors. They were considered best qualified to assess the quality of his services. In Cape Town, Councilors were elected at a general election in August each year. Their term of office was 3 years. The Mayor's term was one year only. As a rule he was re-elected for a second term but never longer unless something unforeseen occurred. The Deputy Mayor was elected for similar periods. The single exception occurred in the mid-fifties. The then mayor, Councilor A. F. Keen, was nearing the end of his second term when his Deputy, Clr. Balsillie, died. No one was 'groomed' to take over the responsibilities of high office so the Council decided to re-elect Councilor Keen for a third term!

In session, the Council is presided over by the Mayor. He is seated on a raised dais in the heart of the council chamber. His chair, used exclusively by the mayor, is known as the Chair of Van Riebeeck[131]. On September 5, 1961, the honor fell to me. As was customary with the appointment of a new mayor, the election took place at a special Council meeting held in the main hall of the City Hall. It was accompanied by considerable ceremony. The hall was filled to capacity with invited dignitaries from all walks of life, representatives of the different rungs of government, public institutions, universities and colleges and members of the general public. Back-stage were seated the former Mayor's husband, the Honorable Justice Newton Thomson, and family, Deena and my family. The gallery was occupied by groups of scholars from different schools in the city.

As the clock struck eleven the mace-bearer (in his historic garb) entered the Hall, and loudly announced: *"Honorable Councilors - Her Worship the Mayor!"* He proceeded to place the gold mace on its stand at the center front of the hall. Everyone rose. The Mayor, accompanied by the Town Clerk, entered the stage from the wings and approached the Chair of

Van Riebeeck now situated at the focal center above the mace. The Deputy Town Clerk and I followed. The Mayor bowed formally first to her councilors, then to the general public. The Town Clerk and I sat on either side. Then followed a speech by the Chairman of Finance, Councilor A. Z. Berman, lauding the outgoing Mayor for her splendid services. She responded most graciously. Then came speeches by Councilors Goodhew and Bakker nominating me to the office of Mayor to which I was called upon to respond!

THE CHALLENGE

In anticipation of that moment, I had given the matter a great deal of thought. It was a weighty challenge! I had been a councilor for thirteen years! As Deputy Mayor, I became increasingly aware of the magnitude of the responsibilities that I was about to confront. I felt it incumbent to inform the public of the reforms and civic improvements that I considered necessary or desirable and which I would strive to achieve during my term of office. I had no desire to indulge in vague generalities (as had occasionally been the case in the past). I was mindful of the confidence entrusted to me - of the need to ensure that my goals were reasonable and practical.

My thoughts and ideas had focused on District Six. I remembered my experiences when I worked in the area after the war. I recalled the pride of the people despite the depressed, dilapidated conditions that surrounded them - through no fault of theirs. Often I had referred to Cape Town as 'one of the most beautiful cities in the world'. Conditions in District Six tended to refute such claim! The area, situated on the lower slopes of Devil's Peak, was immediately adjacent to the center of the city. It was centuries old - perhaps the oldest residential area in the entire country! Something needed to be done to revitalize it! Something could be done if only I could win the co-operation of my colleagues and of the Directorate of Housing[132]. This, then, seemed the opportune moment! The rehabilitation of District Six was the main focus of my inaugural address. I urged my colleagues to seize the opportunity, to help restore and revitalize the idea, to make it a boon not only to the 3,000 residents in the area but to the entire city and indeed to the nation. I reminded listeners that the area was nearly 300 years old and that its dilapidated condition was a blot on the city and on the conscience of the nation. I urged that it be razed to the ground, redesigned and rebuilt to town-planning standards worthy of the city often claimed to be endowed by nature more abundantly than any other on earth! That, I pleaded, called for an entirely new plan - one that embraced new residential and commercial zones, open-spaces, parks and gardens, new services and amenities, new roads and parking areas. I explained that it would necessitate the construction of apartment buildings and single dwellings developed in a manner as would avoid even the temporary homelessness of any family! It called for nothing less than the complete rehabilitation of the entire District - the largest urban rehabilitation project ever undertaken in the country. There were many obstacles to overcome and I urged my colleagues to accept the idea, to be unrelenting in their determination to see the venture through come what may!

THE BANQUET

The inaugural ceremony was followed by a civic luncheon in the Banqueting Hall, preceded by a small gathering of particular guests in the mayor's parlor. Among them was Uys Krige (Mattheus Uys Krige), a well known Afrikaans writer and poet. He was at the prime of his career. He was my age; we had been at school together and were personal friends. I had invited him to propose the toast to the City at the banquet. His toast, presented with poetic charm, was heartily acclaimed. In thanking him on behalf of the City, I referred to the priceless contribution that he was making to Afrikaans language and to the nation's cultural heritage. I also added a warm 'thank you' to the guests for their encouraging support of the District Six proposals.

DISTRICT SIX: OBSTACLES!

The proposals for the rehabilitation of District Six were approved in principle by the City Council. They were referred to the City Engineer, the Town-planning Department and the architectural branch for review. The result was a comprehensive new plan for the entire District - one on which several branches of the City Engineer's Department continued to work hard and enthusiastically for well over a year. The plan embraced a new commercial center, sites zoned for multi-storied apartment buildings, others for parks, gardens and parking areas in addition to extensive single dwelling zones. The plan was approved by the respective committees and by full Council. When sufficiently developed, the proposals were formally submitted to the Government's Directorate of Housing - the body responsible for financing the nation's housing projects. Within weeks, I received a visit by two senior officers of the Directorate. They said that the purpose of their visit was to inform me that the Department welcomed the proposals but that formal Government approval depended on a single provision! They drew my attention to some six or seven 'pondokkies'[133] which, they said, were visible from the National Road! They explained that Government visitors from abroad were often taken on the National Road and that the 'sight of those slums was offensive to the national pride'! The spokesman asked if the Council would take 'early steps to have the eyesore' removed. He repeated that formal approval of the District Six proposals would await the removal! I explained that it was Council policy to dismantle all slums within the municipal area and that the policy was being implemented progressively as and when suitable accommodation became available for the occupants. I added that, of course, health and hygiene implications were of primary concern to the council and that the visual impact was a secondary consideration. My visitors seemed disinterested in my comments! Their spokesman simply repeated the request that the six huts be removed and that the Town Clerk inform them when that was done. He added: "Until then, approval of the District Six proposals will remain deferred." That concluded the meeting.

The District Six proposals were unrelated to slums elsewhere in the municipal area. Now the six huts 'visible from the National Road' had become a crucial issue! Unfortunately, such huts on the outskirts of the city were on the increase due to the increasing influx of Africans in search of work. It was an enormous national problem and presented all kinds of hazards of which the Medical Officer of Health had issued grave warnings. Now, as far as the Government was concerned, the particular 'six huts' visible from the National Road, had become the crucial issue. Upon their removal hinged the entire rehabilitation proposals for District Six.

The City had several new housing projects under construction and on the drawing board to which slum clearance was directly related. I called the City Engineer (Dr. Morris) to ascertain if any of our current projects related to the six huts in question. He came to my office carrying plans for one of our new housing schemes under construction in nearby Factreton. He pointed out that the number of houses under construction were in excess of those specifically designated for workers in that area - that the excess houses had not yet been designated. He saw no reason why some could be not allocated to the occupants of the six huts in question. I attended the next meeting of the Housing Committee and explained the issue. The Committee agreed that six of the houses nearing completion could be allocated to the occupants of the six huts that so offended the Government's pride (They were no worse than the thousands of shacks that had developed elsewhere on the periphery of the city!) The proposal was approved by Council; negotiations concluded and the Town Clerk wrote to the National Housing Directorate advising that the six shack dwellers would be transferred to the new houses as they were completed whereupon the six huts in question would be removed immediately. Within two months, four of the shack dwellers had moved to their new homes. Their shacks were demolished! Then came a letter from the Housing Directorate stating that *'an inspection of the area revealed that two of the shacks were still visible from the National Road!'* A month or so later, the remaining two huts were demolished and the occupants suitably housed. The Directorate was advised accordingly. For several months, there was no response!

MAYORAL DUTIES

The public duties allotted to a mayor and the functions he is expected to perform are, of course, many and varied. I soon learnt that those delegated to the mayor of a parliamentary capital city are more numerous, more demanding and, indeed, more interesting than I had imagined. My first such duty was to perform the opening of "Settlers' Way" - a new arterial road running eastward across the Cape Flats and linking the Cape Peninsula to the mainland at the base of the Hottentots Holland Mountain range. The opening ceremony took place at its starting point[134] on De Waal Drive. Settlers' Way linked the city with the Cape Town National Airport[135], the town of Somerset West and the Main Road from the city to Somerset Strand and Gordons Bay. It was of particular interest to me as it was one of several important arteries in and around the Peninsula in which I had been actively interested during my terms as chairman of the Plans Committee and Joint Town Planning Committee.

A REPUBLIC!

In 1961, the Government decided to sever the nation's ties with the British Commonwealth of Nations! It was an extremely unpopular move in the country's major cities and particularly in Cape Town where the vast majority of all sections of the population cherished the Commonwealth ties!

The Government had conducted a Referendum! In my view, its terms were tainted! It did not ask if a republican constitution was desired! It asked if a republic was preferred *'within or outside'* the British Commonwealth! The assumption that the nation wanted to be a *republic* was false but it conveniently suited the Government's objective! Significantly, the entire African populace was denied participation in the referendum - rendered voiceless! They, who numbered more than 80% of the population, were known to be loyal to the monarchy[136]! Despite this glaring exclusion, when the vote was counted, *'Outside the Commonwealth'* won by a small majority. Had the Referendum been open to all, there is no question but that the proposed republican constitution would have been rejected overwhelmingly! Despite the glaring anomalies, the Government hastened to take the statutory measures needed to sever century-old ties with Commonwealth allies! South Africa became a republic! The Cape that had been part of the British Commonwealth for more than 140 years was now constitutionally isolated from its allies! Determined to rid itself of every conceivable tie with Britain, the Government proceeded to rid itself of all visible links. All utensils, crockery, cutlery and furnishings that bore the *crown* (symbolizing allegiance to the monarchy) were removed from the parliamentary dining hall, kitchen and pantries. The articles were distributed among the members of parliament and senators! (A Party colleague gave me two such dessert plates - a memento I still possess.)

MY SECOND TERM

A year had passed. In September 1962, my second term as mayor was due to commence. The Town Clerk came to the parlor to discuss my personal wishes and particularly whom I wished to invite to propose the toast to the City at the banquet to mark the inauguration. Prominent among the several national representatives resident in the City was the British ambassador Sir John Maud. I decided that he should be the man. He gladly accepted. His address was a brilliant presentation (one that clearly he had been at great pains to prepare). It revealed a deep emotional attachment to the nation he represented and to the City! It reflected also a remarkable affection for South Africa - unmarred by the recent referendum and the Government's determination to sever the nation's ties with his country. They were ties that had been in place for half a century and went far to promote harmony and goodwill in contrast to ethnic cleavage - a sad, ever-increasing disruptive factor.

A TOAST TO HER MAJESTY THE QUEEN

Months later, I received a letter from Sir John inviting me to propose the toast to Her Majesty at the Queen's birthday celebrations - an annual event that took place at the British embassy residence in Kenilworth. The letter had a footnote to the effect: "I will contact you - please await my call." A few days later when Sir John called, he said that he felt duty-bound to tell me that the Government had decided to boycott the celebrations - that as a matter of policy, they had decided not to attend '*ethnically mixed*' functions! He said: "They may well expect the Mayor of the parliamentary capital to conform!" He felt I should know that before I responded to his invitation and that acceptance by me would be frowned upon and possibly resented strongly by the powers that be! I thanked him for the timely warning and said that that he was probably aware that the Government did not enjoy the confidence of the majority of the people of Cape Town or indeed of the country and that I shared that resentment as I did the referendum! I added that I felt honored by his invitation which I gladly accepted. He thanked me and said that he was delighted but added: "Do not blame me if there are repercussions from Parliament Street!"

The function was a brilliant affair. The spacious lawns of the embassy were aglow with colorful saris and other formal attire of the several racial groups resident in Cape Town. In attendance were many parliamentarians - none were members of the Nationalist Party! One friendly member of the United Party urged me to '*watch your step*' and said that Verwoerd was angry at my decision to 'propose the toast'

Sir John escorted me to a mast on the crest of a small mound in the garden. We stood beneath the Union Jack while several hundred guests gathered around. The band stopped playing. A crisp rat-a-tat-tat of a kettle-drum produced a brief silence! Sir John addressed the gathering: "Ladies and gentlemen, representatives of this great mother city, guests from distant lands, allow me to present the Mayor of Cape Town, Councilor Alfred Honikman." I approached the microphone - somewhat awe-stricken. I recall saying: *"Fellow citizens and visitors, very graciously Sir John honored me with the invitation to officiate today. Only yesterday we were all proud citizens of Her Majesty the Queen! Today, our rulers have chosen to sever the link with our Commonwealth allies! In addition, they declined the invitation to attend this gathering because they prefer to isolate themselves from 'mixed' gatherings of this kind! I'm told that they deplore my presence here - my participation in this event! Ladies and gentlemen, I think they overlook the fact that legislative formalities of the kind they have chosen to impose on us, have little impact on our emotions that are deep and profound – they are emotions which they have chosen to disregard. It would have been dishonest of me to isolate myself from this event and so imply that our regard for the Commonwealth ideal and for the Crown has been impaired by their political machinations! Indeed, I am in no doubt that the vast majority of the people of the nation would wish to resist any implication that their kinship with old Commonwealth allies has been marred! Indeed your presence here today, and mine, is evidence to the contrary, that the sentiments conveyed by your presence here to-day, are widely shared. Thus it is my honor and privilege to ask you all to join me in toasting the health and happiness of Her Majesty the Queen and the well-being of the countless millions she represents."*

The audience raised their glasses and loudly acclaimed: *"Her Majesty!"*

There were no adverse repercussions of which I was aware save that in an informal chat in the lobby of the House of Assembly when reference was made to my toast, Prime Minister Verwoerd was heard to comment: *"It showed contempt for national policy!"* Weeks later at a garden party at the German embassy, I found myself face to face with Verwoerd whom I had met previously. He stared at me momentarily; then, without as much as a nod, he conspicuously looked the other way - a calculated snub! I was amused and a little surprised at his readiness to display his personal feelings.

(Three decades later, when a full democratic state was finally established, South Africa reverted to its old allegiance and was welcomed back - a full-blooded member of the British Commonwealth of Nations.)

THE TECHNICAL COLLEGE

The Technical College, a government Institution, occupied a large central city block immediately opposite the site of the old Drill Hall. The Hall dated back to the days of the Boer War. Only a narrow street separated it from the City Hall. It belonged to the City and was used occasionally for exhibition purposes and had been retained by the City for possible future civic development. Meanwhile the Foreshore Reclamation Project had added 550 acres to the central city area and produced an entirely new approach to prospective civic development. The old City Hall, dating back to the eighteenth century, had in fact outlived its purpose! Both the City Council and the Foreshore Board were eager to encourage private development on the newly reclaimed Foreshore land and, to that end, the Council acquired a large site on the Foreshore for the building of a new Civic Center. From a civic point of view, the Drill Hall site had become redundant. However, it was of great interest to the Board of the Technical College. They were keen to acquire it as it would enable them to increase their floor area in immediate proximity to their existing premises (to more than double if ever necessary). Negotiations for the transfer were under way when suddenly the Government offered the College an exceptionally large site in the heart of District Six! It was a substantial part of the residential land that they had acquired from the 3000 Colored people who were forced to evacuate in pursuance of the contentious Group Areas Act! In form and extent, the land offered was in total disregard of, and in conflict with, the plans already well advanced for the rehabilitation of the area! The magnificent rehabilitation project, a potential godsend for 3000 Colored residents, never received Government approval (despite the removal of the chosen six huts!). Instead came more of the notorious apartheid legislation!

THE GROUP AREAS ACT

From the day in 1948 that the Nationalist Party gained power, ethnic considerations dominated national policy. The Government left no stone unturned in an attempt to isolate the nation's several races from each other and ensure they would remain separated. In pursuance of that policy, the Group Areas Act was passed! In Cape Town, separate areas were 'zoned' exclusively for each of the several racial groups. The most attractive, most amenable areas were zoned 'WHITE'! Unbelievably District Six - an entirely Colored area, was also zoned 'WHITE' - exclusively for 'white' occupation! (Apparently it was considered too near the heart of the city to be occupied by other than the 'chosen' white group!) Thus it became illegal for any of the 3,000 Colored residents to remain in an area that was historically theirs! The Colored people had lived there for generations. All three thousand were informed that they were to vacate the area within a prescribed time - two years as I recall! They had no choice but to comply - no option but to face the obvious hardships that confronted them. Few, if any, owned the properties in which they lived. For them, there was no compensation! Such was the inhumanity, such the outcome of the racist ideology that made it a punishable offence to have been born with a particular skin pigment!

In the course of the next two years, three thousand hapless people had no choice but to move to undetermined destinations - to scattered areas far distant from their places of work and from their centuries-old habitat. Their vacated homes were demolished! Compensation, such as it was, went of course to the property owners (most of whom lived elsewhere).

The rehabilitation project planned to restore a healthy environment for 3,000 people where no one would be rendered homeless proved to be nothing more than a meaningless town-planning exercise! The belief was current that the Government realized that no self-respecting 'whites' would wish to occupy land that had been so ruthlessly taken from the Colored people by an ethnically indoctrinated white government.

A SHATTERED DREAM

My dream for District Six lay shattered! The carefully conceived, exhaustively planned rehabilitation proposals were relegated to the archives - a useless waste of energy, time and money! Naught remained but the rubble of the shattered homes of three thousand people - an indelible scar on the mountainside - visible from the National Road, from the air and from every important approach to the City. Worse than that, it was a scar on the conscience of the nation - a monument to those who saw fit to punish three thousand people for the 'crime' of being been born Colored!

For a brief moment the thought came to me that perhaps I bore some of the responsibility! Had my abhorrence of apartheid provoked a decision to frustrate my plans for District Six? Was my toast to Her Majesty seen to flaunt government purpose at a time when they chose to sever ties with friends and allies in the British Commonwealth? Did the 'non-political' stance of the City Council commit the mayor to utter silence on political issues - even when they imposed unnecessary hardship on innocent people? Such thoughts vanished as quickly as they came! There was no way I could I remain silent on proposals that confounded all conscience!

(In June 2006, Thomas Brennen, a young Rhodes Scholar from Oxford, England, (the son of an old Cape Town friend of my son Terence) attended a conference in Los Angeles. When the conference was over, he and four of his colleagues motored to San Francisco. En route, they spent the night with us here in Terry's home in Santa Barbara. Young Brennen, eager to hear about events in South Africa and particularly Cape Town during the apartheid era, had a long chat with me. When I mentioned the District Six issue, he confirmed that the new Technical College had been built there and he added: "that scar still remains!")

In September 1963, my term of office ended. My Deputy Mayor, Councilor W. J. Peters, took my place - to face the troublesome period that followed.

THE MARCH OF 30,000

Alarm mounted in Cape Town one morning as news spread that some 30,000 Africans were marching on the city from the Langa Township - some 8 miles east of the city center. The marchers were said to have reached the rise to De Waal Drive and were about three miles from their alleged destination - parliament buildings!

News of the march reached me in the City Hall. I walked to the corner of Darling and Parliament Streets and edged my way through the crowd into Church Square. A double line of armed police guarded the approach to Parliament. More police cordoned off the crowds at both Spin Street entrances to the square. Similarly, police were said to be guarding the upper end of Parliament Street. Tension was at a height when the marchers finally reached the Square. They were denied entry. One of their leaders was allowed through the police barrier and was in discussion with a police officer. He informed the officer that a representative group of marchers wished to interview the Minister of Justice. The officer asked him to wait while he reported to the Government. In due course, the officer returned and informed the African leaders that the Minister had agreed to receive a deputation of marchers in his chambers two days later. With that, the leaders turned to their followers, informed them of the Minister's promise, said they were satisfied with what had transpired and urged their followers to disperse quietly and return home. The marchers disbanded. The demonstration was over. The most massive demonstration ever staged in the City had been conducted with decorum and in a very orderly, peaceful manner! Neither a street lamp nor a pane of glass was broken! The damage - absolutely nil! There could never be a more orderly, better-organized mass protest!

Regrettably, the meeting with the Minister never took place! Failure by the Government to follow up on the promise given to the African leaders added tension to ever mounting resentment! Grievances were not confined to the African people. *'How would it all end?'* Apprehension turned to fear!

"CAPE TOWN - CITY OF GOOD HOPE"

In 1963, towards the end of my mayoral term, I felt there was a need for a book that would illustrate, in comprehensive form, all aspects of life in Cape Town, including its varied cultures and its unique topographical grandeur. In my eyes, the scenic grandeur, flora and fauna of the Cape

Peninsula are unsurpassed anywhere on this planet. I pondered: 'Was it possible that such wonders could be reflected in a single volume?' I discussed the idea with my friend Howard Timmins, a well-known city publisher. His reaction was that it was an ambitious goal, *"way beyond my means or yours."* However he thought that it was a goal worth aiming for *"provided you can find sufficient sponsors!"* I decided to try. I wrote to the heads of ten prominent city institutions long associated with the City to ascertain if they would be interested in sponsoring such an undertaking. From each came an encouraging response and a generous offer of financial support. Timmins was delighted and said he 'would be willing to risk' such a publication if I would edit it and undertake its supervision. He added with a smile: *'and provided you're not* too *demanding!'*

Thus it was that I entered a field that was entirely new to me! I soon found that it entailed duties and obligations such as I had never handled before. There was no turning back! I prepared a list of headings representing aspects of the city and city life that I felt the book should cover in reasonably adequate fashion. There were sixteen such headings. A second list carried the names of persons whom I thought best qualified to write about them. Some I knew personally. Most lived in the city. All were lovers of Cape Town and its multifarious attributes. I wrote a personal letter to each. All responded positively. I formed an editorial committee to whom I could refer from time to time. As the articles and illustrations came in, I felt the need of the services of a book designer. I knew no one in that field.

Timmins showed me some of the works of young Willem Jordaan. They were admirable. Jordaan was appointed. He was painstaking and exacting. The level of excellence he demanded took up more and more of my time! It also added appreciably to the cost of production and not least to the concern of the publisher! At one point, Timmins called me to complain: "This book will break me!" To this, I replied: "Friend - excellence breaketh no man!"

Outstanding illustrations in addition to those that Jordaan and I had gathered came from the writers responsible for the different chapters and from members of the committee. Most were of such excellence that few could be declined. We decided to conclude the book with a special 'Camera Section' and to appoint Joy Collyer, a well know Cape Town artist, to design the captions. Apart from editing the book and writing a brief foreword, I agreed to write a short chapter on local government titled: *"For the People, by the People"*. I decided also to dedicate the book to the

University of Cape Town - the institution responsible for my higher education and that of my sisters, brother, two sons, niece and nephew and on whose Council I had served for a quarter century.

Finally, when the book was about to go to print, Jordaan proposed that each chapter be given a different quality of paper! At that point, Timmins made a special visit to my office. In great earnest, he said: *"Alfred, this has got to stop! Your book will break me - the loss will run into thousands!"* I told him that I felt he was wrong, but that Jordaan's request was the last of the demands. He was not satisfied! I tried to allay his concern: *"Howard, if you prove right, we'll face the problem when it comes; but if you're wrong, I want you to promise me that every penny of profit will go to approved charities."* He answered: *"You're an incorrigible optimist! That, I can safely agree to!"*

Jordaan's request was approved. At last, after three years of dedicated effort by all concerned, the book appeared. It was a great success - the object of widespread applause! Timmins lost no money! True to his word, he was able to send substantial sums to several city charities!

TRAGEDIES!

On November 22, 1963, the assassination of John F. Kennedy shook the world! The President of the world's greatest democracy was mowed down, not by a wayward maniac, but by a sniper sent to his concealed perch by conspirators who were never identified and whose purpose remains a mystery. They chose to redress their concerns, not by any normal accepted means, but by murder!

That tragic event took place soon after the end of my term as mayor and I was among those who gathered at the United States embassy to record their sympathy with the American people. That grim tragedy was yet another reminder to the 'free world' that it was not free of terror and that organized society had yet a way to go before it could merit the attribute of *'civilization'!*

In 1966, Senator Robert F. Kennedy and his wife paid a six-day visit to South Africa[137]. His opposition to apartheid was well known! He was the guest of NUSAS, the National Union of South African Students. He was aware that his visit was not one that was welcomed by the Government. His presence was a gesture of sympathy with those South Africans of all races who bitterly opposed the apartheid ideology. It was a commitment to 'brotherhood' - one that was to have enduring impact. On the night of June 6, he gave a memorable, very moving address at the University of Cape Town, which I felt privileged to attend. It was on the day that my book *Cape Town City of Good Hope* appeared for the first time and I presented a copy to him.

Two years later the unbelievable happened! The promising life of Robert F. Kennedy - like that of his elder brother - ended at the hands of an assassin. The world was in shock!

AN AMERICAN ACCENT

The early months of 1963 were an exceptionally busy time socially. My term as mayor was due to end in September. We were dining at home one Sunday evening when Deena commented that it was the first night in weeks that we were spending at home! Cape Town, being the country's parliamentary capital, was the site of many national embassies. At that time of the time of year it seemed that almost every night was occupied with a dinner, reception, or a function at one kind or another! We were looking forward to a quiet evening at home with 'our feet up' as it were, when the telephone rang! I answered. "Hello, Alfred," said a voice I had never heard before. The accent was so strongly 'American' that I thought some friend was trying to pull my leg! It went on: "This is a distant relative of yours. I am Al Levin - my wife is Maxine. We are on a short visit to your city and would like to meet you." Still not convinced that it was not a hoax, I asked if he would identify himself. He then mentioned the name of my cousin Joey of Johannesburg and a Mrs. Cheyney of London, England. The name 'Cheyney' was not known to me, but the reference to Joey satisfied me that the caller was genuine. He explained the he and his wife were in Oranjezicht dining with a doctor friend of ours who had persuaded him to call me and said that we would regret it if he didn't! When I suggested that we fix a date to meet, he explained that they were leaving in two days and asked if we could possibly come there that night! The doctor's wife was a particular friend of Deena's and I was interested to meet this unknown relative.

In a few minutes, we were on our way to the top of Marmion Road - not far from "Longwood". We were given a very warm welcome, met Al and his wife Maxine and, within minutes, Al drew me into the privacy of the doctor's study for a "private chat". He said that the doctor had mentioned that I was 'a busy practicing architect' and that my term as Mayor would be ending in September. He said that he lived in Cleveland, Ohio, and that he was a non-practicing lawyer and, as a developer, he employed a few firms of architects. He said that he would like us to visit them and 'spend a week or two' with them at their home at Gates Mills to see the projects he was building and meet the rest of the family. I said that I would like to do that 'one day' and would keep in touch. His reacted: *"That's a little too vague - I gather you're giving up the Mayor's job in September. Give yourself a break - come then! You'll not be sorry!"* I said we would think about it and let them know. We had been an unduly long time away from the rest of the gathering. It was late and time to leave. With apologies to our hosts, we departed.

Al's forceful personality impressed me as did the earnestness of his invitation to visit Ohio.

CANADA

At the time, I had recently had an interesting chat with Gordon Grey, the newly appointed Canadian consul, the youngest member of the consular corps. He said that he had gleaned from reports that I was 'not entirely happy with current developments in South Africa'! He asked if he could discuss the situation with me. We talked for an hour. From his comments, it became obvious that Canada (a sister Dominion) strongly disapproved of the apartheid policy. I assured him that opinion was widely shared in South Africa. And, notwithstanding that the ruling party had been in power for fifteen years, their ideology was being entrenched and I dreaded the consequences! A personal relationship developed. Gordon asked if I had ever been to Canada. I said I had not but that I was planning a trip to Cleveland in '64. "That's great - it's not far - just across the border! Why not include Toronto, my home-town - you'd be more than welcome." He added that he knew a few architects there whom he thought I may like to meet.

In September 1963, my two year term office as mayor had expired. Initially, I included both Cleveland and Toronto in my travel plans for 1964 but with Basil back in Cape Town, Deena preferred to remain at home; I decided to shorten my absence and postpone the Toronto visit.

CLEVELAND

At the airport I was met by Morton (Al's nephew and 'adopted son').
He explained that Al had guests at the house and had asked him to deputise.
It was a long ride to Gates Mills – over 20 miles. As we entered the driveway, I saw that we were approaching a palatial Georgian residence. Subsequently, I learnt it had been designed in England and that most of the
building materials had been brought from that country and that the site
was more than fifty-five acres in extent! As the car drew up to the entrance
porch, Edward, a smiling well-groomed black man, appeared; he gave me
a friendly greeting and took my suitcase from the car. A moment later,
Maxine was there with a hearty welcome. She explained that Al and his
guests were in the pool and that he would like me to join them - that a
swimsuit and towel awaited me in the pool house. Edward showed me to
my room! It was a suite; it included a study, private balcony and bathroom.
At the poolside, Al emerged to give me a warm (though wet) greeting. He
led me to the pool-house and asked that I join him and his guests in the
water. While undressing, I observed that the walls were papered with old
share certificates! Later Al explained that they were the remnants of scrip
that were rendered valueless during the 'great depression'!

Next morning I awoke late - had not slept much on the airplane. Al had
just returned from his early morning horse-ride that he'd 'cut short' to join
me at breakfast and drive me into the city. We drove via Euclid Avenue,
Cleveland's main street, the longest in the city and about 8 miles in length.
He put the car in a parking garage near the far end of Euclid. Walking to his
office, he was greeted by all and sundry - "Morning, Al," said a policeman
on patrol; "Hi, Al," waved the street sweeper. Everyone knew him - obviously 'a local celebrity!' At the office I met his brother Bob and Bob's wife
Lucille, another brother (a doctor whose name eludes me) and other members of the staff. I was shown to a furnished room: "This will be your office
during your stay," said Al. Later in the morning he took me to a large warehouse nearing completion in an industrial area. "This is for a special client
- let me take you to something more interesting." Back on Euclid, Al
pointed to a very large multi-storied block of shops and offices. It faced
both Euclid and the next parallel street. We walked through its shopping
arcade linking the two streets. Al had recently renovated the entire building, installed new elevators, etc. and it was now fully let - obviously a very
successful investment! From there, I was taken to the offices of Weinberg
and Teare - "one of my architects whom I'd like you to meet," said Al. He
introduced me to Mr. Weinberg as "my cousin from South Africa. He's an

architect - you'll be hearing more about him shortly!" We lunched together in the city. That evening Al took Bob, Lucille, six other guests and me for a sumptuous lobster dinner at his 'favorite restaurant' - from there we went to a pre-election reception for President Johnson. There, I was feted and garlanded by attendants who must have assumed I was a potential supporter! From the frequent attention paid to Al that evening, I was in no doubt that he was an important well-known supporter.

In the office the next morning, Al handed me a specification and a roll of drawings - 'the contract documents I'm about to sign'. He asked me to 'look them over' and 'make any comments you think appropriate'. I read through 'Preliminary & General' of the specification containing reference to the salient clauses to which the ultimate Building Contract would be subject. I noticed that there was no mention of a particular 'condition' (one that I regarded an important feature of all building contracts - large or small). It was one that I was at pains to include in all my contracts and appeared under a heading: *'Extras'*. Its wording was to the effect that *"No claim for 'extras' will be entertained unless supported by the prior written authority of the architect."* I made a note of the 'omission' and presented it to Al. He subsequently informed me that he'd discussed the matter with his architect and that the 'missing clause' had now been included and 'would appear in future contracts!' Then he added: "Alf, I have to confess, I cannot read a plan! What I need is an architect who is "on <u>my</u> side!" You'll have to come to Cleveland! Think about that!" He went on: "Things are not very promising in your country. You owe it to your family and to yourself - broaden your horizons. Come here! You'll not regret it." I was thunderstruck! That evening at home, he returned to the topic and said that he knew of a lovely new apartment under construction - overlooking the Lake – and he would reserve it for me. Al was obviously in earnest. I thanked him, acknowledged my concern about conditions at home but explained that his idea was not easily implemented - that apart from my commitments in Cape Town, 'my qualifications were possibly not acceptable in Ohio in which event I would not be permitted to practice here!' Al responded: "That should not be a problem! Leave it to me. We'll be in touch." Then he said: "Tomorrow night we're having a party at home. You'll meet the rest of the family and a few friends."

That night I lay awake wondering! What did Al mean: *"Leave it to me"? What if my credentials were not acceptable! I loved Cape Town - to uproot could not be easily contemplated! How would Deena and Terry react?*

Next evening, quite a crowd gathered at the house. Among the guests were Bob and Lucille, Leonard and his wife, Martha, other members of the family whose names I've forgotten. Al introduced me to a Dr. Tucker whom he said was a successful medical practitioner. When the guests had departed, he explained: *"Tucker was having a tough time on the staff of a hospital - barely making a living. I persuaded him to try private practice; set him up in chambers down town - in no time he was much sought after - his practice flourished."* Al added: *"Yours will be a similar story!"*

He had me thinking!

BACK IN CAPE TOWN

Weeks later, I received a letter from the Ohio Board of Architects. It listed the several examinations I would be required to pass in order to practice architecture in Ohio. I sent a copy of the letter to Al with a rider that if my Diploma from the Royal Institute of British Architects was not sufficient, I was not willing (at my age: 54!) to *'go back to school'!* I thanked him for all his trouble. Time passed. Came a second letter from the Board. It said that my position had been reviewed - that if I cared to submit an album of photographs of buildings I had designed, it would, if approved, be considered as a possible alternative to the examinations previously referred to. It would, however, be necessary for me to have the photographs authenticated by three Fellows of the Royal Institute and, in due course, to provide evidence that I was conversant with the Ohio 'Code of Professional Practice'. A booklet of the code was enclosed. In many respects it was very similar to the S.A. code with which I was, of course, familiar. At that stage, the likelihood of my ever practicing in the U. S. was extremely remote. I had never considered it a likely eventuality. However, I felt that to be registered there would be a wise precaution - a kind of insurance policy should the need ever arise!

Al had obviously been to a great deal of trouble. I wrote thanking him and informed him of all that had transpired. I prepared the album, had it authenticated by three Fellows (there were only four in all of Cape Town) and forwarded the album to the Ohio Board. In due course, it was returned accompanied by a letter saying that the photographs had been approved. The letter also gave the dates of subsequent Board meetings (to be held in the city of Columbus) at any one of which I could appear in connection with the 'Code'. I chose a date (three months hence), informed Al and suggested that, if it suited him, I would continue from Columbus to Cleveland for a few days.

On the flights from Cape Town and again from London I read through the entire code.

COLUMBUS

The Board meeting took place in Columbus, the state capital, in a hotel conference room. I was due there at 10 a.m. in good time for the meeting. After a short wait, I was ushered in and was confronted by five or six Board members each seated at separate tables around the room. Apparently, I was the only candidate! The chairman welcomed me, regretted 'the need to bring me all that way' and explained that the 'examination' would be in the form of random questions by Board members to whom I was introduced. I don't remember all the questions put to me! What I do remember is that the first was an extremely simple one! It related only remotely to 'professional practice'. A little embarrassed I gave an equally simple reply! After that, the procedure consisted of questions that were irrelevant! They concerned the climate, flora, and topography in and around the Cape - nothing remotely relating to architectural practice! Indeed, the entire procedure was more in the nature of a friendly discussion rather than an examination! It lasted about thirty minutes. The chairman then looked towards each of his members. They appeared to respond with an affirmative nod whereupon he addressed me: - *"Mr. Honikman - congratulations! The formalities are over! Welcome to Ohio. We wish you a happy and successful sojourn in our midst."* I was flabbergasted. I had never faced an 'examination' of the kind. I was also surprised at the brevity of the proceedings and not least at the chairman's obvious assumption that I would be practicing in Ohio!

In Cleveland, Al met me at the airport. He was delighted that everything had gone so smoothly. On the way home, he said: "I'll show you your apartment - Deena will love it!" That shook me! He, too, assumed that I had decided to move to Cleveland! Obviously, I had not made it clear that my decision to go through with the registration was solely a precautionary measure. I was concerned about conditions in South Africa but I had never given 'permanent departure' a serious thought.

Back home, I decided that my next trip would include Toronto. I planned accordingly and informed Gordon Grey. One morning, walking from my office to the City Hall, I had a chance meeting with an old acquaintance, Peter Norton[138]. He said he was leaving South Africa the following day, that he had accepted an appointment with Nielsons in Toronto. I wished him 'luck' and mentioned that my forthcoming trip was to include a first visit to Toronto. He picked up his ears, took down particulars of my travel plans and said he would be in touch. Before leaving Cape Town, I received a letter from him inviting me to dinner at his Toronto home on the night of my arrival. I was surprised (we had never been on visiting terms) but pleased particularly as Gordon Grey had written to say that he had been forced to change his plans and would not be back in Toronto until a day after my arrival.

With Basil back in Cape Town, Deena preferred not to travel that year. I then decided to confine that trip to Cleveland, Toronto and London and to be back home in two weeks. I informed Al and Maxine of my plans.

THE TORONTO INTERLUDE

As planned, I flew to Toronto and taxied to my hotel. A message awaited me - Peter Norton would pick me up at six-thirty! It proved to be a memorable occasion! I met Peter's wife Sheila and six other guests for the first time. It was also the last time I saw any of them - save for two - Tom and Sylvia Scott!

The following night I dined with Gordon and Pat Grey and subsequently interviewed three or four architects whom he had thoughtfully arranged for me to meet. One seemed eager to discuss a 'possible take-over agreement' as he hoped to retire shortly! He urged me to keep in touch should I decide to settle in Toronto!

The rest of my time in Toronto was spent with the Scotts. I met their two daughters and some of their friends. They showed me around the city and took me to a Shakespearean play in a town at the Niagara Falls. They also introduced me to *"The Infinite Way"*, a philosophical organization in which they were keenly interested and which I gathered had branches worldwide. A warm kinship developed! We parted, all expressing the will to 'meet again'.

AN APPEAL FROM JAPAN

In 1967, I received an unexpected letter from Japan! It came from Mr. Takai – who had lived opposite us when I was a boy at "Longwood". On his tennis court, my brother and I were frequent guests and it was from his store, the 'Mikado', that my father bought my first 'man's bicycle'. My memory of the Takai family was a happy one. The letter recalled our 'warm neighborly relationship'. It also contained a profuse apology for 'troubling me'. Mr. Takai had heard that I was Mayor and felt that I could be of assistance to him. He explained that his lawyers had recently concluded a fruitless correspondence with the Government and that it concerned his city property that had been confiscated when Japan entered the war. He added that the correspondence had proved to be fruitless. He asked if I would intervene on his behalf in an effort to obtain fair compensation for the loss of his 'valuable property in the heart of the city'! I was in a quandary! I wanted to help but, aware that there were members of the Government not favorably disposed towards me, I very much doubted if I was a suitable person to make representations on anybody's behalf. How could I to explain that to Mr. Takai? I thought the matter over and realized that it was essentially a financial matter - probably the direct concern of the Minister of Finance, Dr. Donges! Our paths had never crossed. Donges lived in Sea Point, one of the most attractive and best-favored parts of Cape Town! The thought occurred to me that maybe he was not immune to 'Cape Town influences' - that perhaps he was more liberally minded and less racially indoctrinated than many of his colleagues. I decided to write to him. My letter referred to Mr. Takai and his family as 'long-time residents and good neighbors in Oranjezicht', to his children who were 'born South Africans', who had gone to school in the Cape and who would probably inherit their father's assets'. I spoke of the fine business he had developed and of the South Africans he'd employed. My letter concluded with the comment that 'to compensate him adequately for confiscated assets would be seen as a just, humanitarian gesture by one that sought to be fair'. I received a formal acknowledgement but no reply by the time Deena and I left on one of our annual trips abroad. On our return, I received a formal letter from the Secretary for Finance stating that he had been directed by the Minister to inform me that 'due compensation'[139] had been accorded Mr. Takai and that the proceeds had been dispatched to the Bank of Tokyo. There was no indication of the amount involved or that Mr. Takai personally had been informed! I sent him a copy of the Secretary's letter with a personal note of congratulations!

In due course, I received a reply. The letter was 'bursting with excitement' and gratitude! 'Thank you' was repeated in various forms! The letter also told of the expected date of arrival in Cape Town of a Japanese ship, the *Osaka Maru,* and asked me to be sure to meet the ship and to interview the captain as *'he carries an important message for you'*. On the date mentioned, I telephoned the harbormaster. He informed me that the *Osaka Maru* was due at 4 p.m. that afternoon. He gave me the number of the quay at which the ship was to berth. It was about 5 o'clock when I arrived at the ship's gangway. It was guarded and I was not allowed to enter! On deck was a sailor. I waved a signal to him. He responded and took a few steps down the gangway towards me. I gave him my name and said the captain was expecting me! He retraced his steps. Minutes later one of the ship's officers appeared, saluted and asked me to follow him. He took me to the Captain's office and offered me a seat. I waited! An unduly long time elapsed before the Captain entered. He was immaculately dressed! He spent a while on all manner of seemingly irrelevant references! (I thought maybe he was satisfying himself about my identity.) Suddenly he thawed. Amiably he leant over, shook my hand and said that he had been asked to deliver a parcel *"to you personally!"* He opened the bottom drawer of his desk and produced a large box-like brown paper parcel. On it was printed in bold letters: "ONLY FOR:" and below: *"Mayor Alfred Honikman Cape Town"*. He handed the parcel to me together with an open envelope. It contained a list of "Items for: *Alfred Honikman & Family*". A price was set against each item. He also handed me a colored envelope saying: "This is a personal letter from Mr. Takai. He wanted you to see it before you leave here!" I glanced briefly at its contents. It referred to the open list and said 'it contains prices that you may need for the Customs!'

My visit on board took longer than I had planned. It was after six when I departed - with a courteous bow from the captain. Realizing that at the harbor gates I would be asked for a 'customs clearance', I made straight for the Customs office. I tapped on the closed door. A uniformed officer opened it. I explained that I had received a parcel from the captain that required clearance. He put it on a table and asked what it contained. I showed him the list. He stroked his chin and exclaimed: "Pearls, jewelry…you have duty to pay… I don't know the tariffs offhand." Others in the office raised their brows! I was a little concerned! He took a volume from the shelf; he moved his finger down a schedule of rates and uttered: "jewelry - pearls - artificial no doubt - ah, I guess that's it!" He jotted down figures and told me the duty for which I was liable. I don't remember the amount. It didn't sound unreasonable considering the number of obviously valuable items! I paid - in any event I had little choice! He stamped the parcel, gave me a receipt. I was on my way.

At home (late for dinner!), I handed the parcel to Deena and explained what had happened. After dinner we opened the parcel. It contained a lavish array of jewelry - gold and pearls! There were gifts for everyone - for Sybil a beautiful bracelet, for Deena a brooch, a bracelet and earrings (she rarely wore jewelry!), gold cuff links and tie pins, each studded with a pearl, for Maurice and me! There were items for other members of the family - too many to remember! All very embarrassing! There was also a charming 'thank you' letter. It asked if Deena and I would visit him in Tokyo! I replied thanking him for his generosity and said we hoped one day to visit Japan and would let him know. The opportunity occurred in 1968. After our usual visits to London and Santa Barbara, I decided to return to Cape Town via Tokyo, Bangkok, Hong Kong and Ceylon. Deena did not care for so long a trip and decided to take our usual return trip via London. I wrote informing Mr. Takai of our plans and particulars of my arrival in Tokyo.

CHAPTER 27

AROUND THE WORLD WITH
3 KRUGERRAND!

The day before leaving Cape Town my bank agreed to sell me 3 Kruger-rand[140] - two were intended as (investment) gifts for Basil and Terence. (Not wishing to leave the third coin in the house while we were away, I kept the parcel intact and packed it among my belongings.) In New York, a few days after arrival, I learnt that they should have been 'declared' to customs on arrival and later that it was not permitted to bring 'gold' into the country! Not wishing to break the law or render my sons party to any breach, I decided to take the coins back to South Africa. Other gifts were substituted. In due course, when I was leaving San Francisco for Tokyo, I played it safe and informed the customs officer about the coins. I thought that was the right thing to do! He asked me to produce them, which I did, whereupon he again informed me that I was not permitted to bring gold into the country. I explained that I had become aware of that only after arrival, and was therefore taking them back whence they'd come. He said he would have to confiscate them, which he did. At my request, he gave me a receipt. I had no desire to lose 'my precious coins'!

At the Tokyo airport, Mr. Takai gave me a very warm welcome. I told him about my precious coins. He said he had heard about the new Kruger-rand and was eager to see them. Then he pondered, stroked his chin and said "That's a shame - it would have been so nice to exhibit them at the museum during your stay." He then excused himself, asked me to "wait there and please do not wander!" When he returned, he smiled broadly and said that I was not to worry. "The coins are coming here on the next plane from San Francisco - I will collect them at the customs office in the morning." The following day he and his daughter Mariko met me for lunch. He was beaming! "I have them - took them to the museum and will collect them before you leave!" I was relieved! I never questioned him about the details of what had transpired but it was obvious that he was in a position to assert considerable influence.

Mariko had matured beautifully - a very different person from the child I once knew. She lapped up whatever news of Cape Town I could offer. She was married to a consul and at the time was on a short holiday with her father. When I inquired about his wife, Mr. Takai pointed to a large building up on the hill - said she was there - it was a sanatorium. He added: *"In Japan we look after our old people!"* During my three days in Tokyo, he was at great pains to entertain me. He was as virile as I once knew him on his tennis court. I had difficulty keeping pace with him as we walked through the streets of Tokyo. He took me to many interesting spots in and outside the city. I watched men and girls dive into deep (illuminated) water to collect pearls. We spent a night at a nearby hot spring spa that he said would do me good. It did!

At the airport before leaving, Mr. Takai handed me my parcel of Krugerrand and said "the museum was very grateful - my love to Cape Town - come again soon."

We never met again!

BREE CASTLE

Shortly after my term as Mayor expired, my attention focused on an advertisement announcing a forthcoming sale by public auction of a site at the corner of Bree & Castle Streets on the fringe of the city center. It interested me but in no way could I afford such a venture on my own. I felt it would interest a few friends who had occasionally spoken of a 'possible joint enterprise'. I examined the site potential, found it to be highly favorable and decided to make a bid for it. I thought it unwise to appear in person at the auction so I decided to employ the services of an attorney to act for me. I thought of C.K. Friedlander whom I knew personally but decided that he was too busy broadcasting rugby matches! Instead I approached one of his partners, Arnold Kleinman, whom I had met. I knew him to be a personal friend of my brother Maurice. I interviewed him in his office. (As I recall it was in the Colonial Mutual Building at the corner of Adderley & Longmarket Street). I explained my purpose, gave him a maximum figure that I was willing to offer for the property and commissioned him to represent me. Another of his partners actually attended the sale. He purchased the property for me at the precise figure I had mentioned. It was on that site that I finally built "Bree Castle"- a 10-story office block for a group of five friends of whom I was one.

BASIL

In 1960, our elder son Basil graduated in architecture. The apartheid syndrome was an ever-growing source of concern to him as it was to many others. Basil decided to seek his fortune in a less devastating environment. He worked his way aboard a Union Castle liner to Britain. In London he joined a firm of architects and, for three years, worked on War Office projects. I flew to London to attend his marriage to Susan Leeworthy. They then spent a year with a firm of architects in Los Angeles and in 1964 they brought their baby Jessica to Cape Town to meet Deena. Basil joined my practice for little more than a year. During that time he prepared the plans for the "Bree Castle" project. He soon realized that the 'political situation' in South Africa had become more tenuous in his absence. He went back to London, served as a part-time instructor at the Kingston College of Art and in 1966 assumed a full-time position as Senior Lecturer. At the same time, he continued his studies and obtained his doctorate in architecture at the University of London.

In 1971, he was offered an associate professorship at the University of Kansas. The offer, subsequently repeated to include tenure, was accepted. Basil and Susan, now with three children - Jessica, Steven and Joanna - migrated to Kansas. Before leaving Britain, Deena and I joined them at a wonderful family reunion holiday on the Isle of Wight. A year later, we visited them in Kansas. When we returned the following year, we found their relations strained. They had decided to part company! Fortunately, they had the good sense to agree on the terms of the separation and to employ a single attorney to frame an acceptable divorce agreement. Susan returned to England with the children! In 1975, Basil accepted an appointment as assistant Director at the School of Design at the North Carolina State University. He married Linda, a young architect whom he had met as a student in Kansas. Professionally, things did not turn out as expected and a year later Basil accepted an appointment as Chairman of the Department of Architecture at the University of Miami. Linda presented Basil with his fourth child - Jackie. After ten years in Miami, they decided to move to Santa Barbara and the family was united again.

TERENCE

In 1964, Terence graduated as a mechanical engineer at the University of Cape Town. It was soon after Christmas that he informed me that he had made application to pursue the study of aeronautics at Stanford University in California and that his application had been accepted to start in the fall quarter the following September. If, however, he could present himself for admission on January 2, 1965, he could start in the winter quarter and get a six month head start! That was the first I had heard of the application and his intended departure! Within days, all arrangements were made. Terry was packed and on his way.

The absence of both sons (and their friends) produced an 'eerie still-ness' at home that we both found strange and unpleasant. I gathered together some of Terry's model airplanes that he had built over the years. They were left in a box on the workbench in the garage. Some I recognized were those that I had often watched him guide by remote control over the Rondebosch Common. His friends in the neighborhood were happy to have them. Deena, at home all day, felt intensely the void and the absence of young people. "Ferramee" had been a 'lively' home for 24 years. We both realized that at their age and with the interests abroad, our sons were unlikely to return! To continue occupying a home with rooms that contained only echoes of the past seemed purposeless. The fourth and final extension at "Edingight" was nearing completion. We reserved a sunny five-roomed apartment on the second floor and decided to sell "Ferramee". It was not a happy decision. It marked the end of a chapter - one that covered twenty-five wonderful years.

Terry wrote home fairy regularly. He rented a room in a private home in Palo Alto[141]. He had been at Stanford for one year when he wrote saying that he had been appointed as a research assistant to Professor Hoff[142] and that the work he would be doing was an important part of his doctorate studies. He added that the appointment carried an adequate salary, that the monthly allowance from home was no longer necessary and that I should instruct my bank to cease the transfer of funds!

We made annual visits abroad. In Palo Alto, we met Dr. Hoff and several of the Stanford staff. Terry met Jane Israel in Palo Alto. Jane was visiting friends Claus and Liz Jorgensen in Denmark and it was there that their first child Charlotte was born. Jane became seriously ill - so ill that she was unable to care for the child. Her friends arranged for Charlotte's adoption. In time, Jane made a wonderful recovery and returned home - too late to take her child with her.

Terry interviewed potential employers in Detroit, Israel, Pasadena and elsewhere. Then he interviewed with a small company in Santa Barbara and was persuaded by the many charms of that small town. They decided to settle in Santa Barbara and bought a house - in the course of construction - on North Kellogg Avenue. Deena and I visited Santa Barbara before the house was completed.

A HOME IN CALIFORNIA

We both liked Santa Barbara - not least the Mediterranean climate to which we were accustomed in Cape Town. On three succeeding visits there, we rented apartments at "New Horizons" - an attractive two-storied development of some 55 acres. It appeared to have every conceivable convenience including a 9-hole golf course, swimming pool, club-house, gymnasium, etc. - 'an ideal spot to retire - one day!' That day seemed not far off. We considered buying an apartment! There was a problem! South African restrictions precluded the withdrawal of funds for such purpose. By 1975, however, sufficient funds had accumulated in London from the sale of the Rhodesian plots. That enabled me to buy, (for future use), an attractive four-roomed upper-floor apartment at 257 "New Horizons" - minutes from the Fairview shopping center and about a mile from Terence and Jane's new home on North Kellogg Ave.

We returned to South Africa to prepare for the day when we would depart from our beloved Cape Town. By then we had decided to live near our children in a spot less troubled by rampant ethnic discrimination seemingly heading for disaster - possibly civil war! We had taken that decision fully aware that the wrench would not be easy but consoled ourselves in the thought that we would make return visits as often as circumstances would permit.

By 1975, I had practiced architecture for forty years and it was time to retire. I disposed of my practice to a young architect, Basil Conidaris. He accepted the condition that the services of Jan Greshof be retained. Jan - a long-time, loyal and competent professional assistant. He became a partner of Conidaris.

PRIVATE VENTURES

On our return from one of our visits to Terence at Stanford, I realized that financially I was not adequately equipped for retirement! My thoughts turned to possible investment projects. I was attracted to Milnerton, a separate residential municipality east of the city, not far from home. It was experiencing considerable growth and had recently adopted a new town-planning scheme - one that included only three sites in the entire area that were zoned for multi-storied 'flat' development. On one of them a building was in the course of construction. I inspected the other two, became interested and obtained an option to purchase one of them. It was opposite a small attractive well-wooded public park. I designed an 8-story block of 48 apartments *cum* garages which I named "Palo Alto". The project however was way beyond my means, but I anticipated that friends would join me in the venture. I prepared a statement of estimated cost revenue and expenditure and named the new company "Palo Alto (Pty) Ltd". I concluded that the capital I had available (inclusive of the professional fees that would accrue as architect) would be about a fifth of the required capital - provided a mortgage loan of two-thirds would be forthcoming. Four friends, including Deena's brother Cecil, agreed to participate. (Cecil was then a judge of the Transvaal Supreme Court.) The South African Association offered a two-thirds mortgage loan and together we exercised the option to purchase the site. The plans were completed, formally approved and tenders were called for. A building contract was entered into with Bruce Dundas (Pry) Ltd., a firm of 'master builders'. I had decided to adopt what was then a 'new' form of construction - one by which all floors and walls would be in vibrated reinforced concrete to form a homogeneous construction. Brickwork was entirely excluded! Ten months later, the building was completed and within weeks was fully occupied.

Meanwhile, I obtained an option to purchase the last of the three Milnerton sites zoned for flats and designed another high-rise apartment building to the maximum density permitted. It comprised forty apartments and as many garages. This time I was joined by a different group of friends. The Board of Executors provided the bond and joined the group as one of nine equal partners. The new building was to be named Atlantica. On this occasion, I decided to adopt the conventional concrete-frame form of construction. A trial hole was dug to determine the quality of the sub-soil - a prerequisite to determine the depth and size of the foundations. We encountered a problem – there was a water table some 18 inches below the surface over the entire site and beyond! Conventional foundations were no longer possible! In consultation with the structural engineers, an 8-inch thick reinforced concrete raft covering the entire building area was decided on. A building contract was concluded with the Dura Construction Company. The building was completed in record time - virtually without extras! The Board of Executors had a waiting list of potential tenants and within weeks the building was fully occupied!

That was the last of my investment ventures in South Africa.

A NEW CHAPTER

In 1978, Prime Minister John Forster was succeeded by P.W. Botha. Botha was a man whom I had met only once and for whom I had a natural dislike. He was General Secretary of the Nationalist Party at the time of the 1948 General Election. It was he who organized the raid on the United Party offices in Cape Town and the theft of its postal votes. That was the year in which apartheid first became national policy and brought 46 years of ignominy to the entire nation. It was also the year that I entered public life.

For Deena, the American dream was never to materialize! Soon after our 1975 trip to the United States, Deena developed a melanoma on the calf. It was surgically removed and entailed an extensive skin graft that took a long time to heal. All seemed well until months later, when, during a visit to Santa Barbara, (her last), 'secondaries' appeared. The symptoms were grave! Doctors there said there was 'nothing they could do'. They offered no hope - urged us to return home! Back in Cape Town, the condition developed. For months, Deena was treated at Groote Schuur hospital and endured chemo-therapy. She was also flown to Port Elizabeth to a specialized 'heat treatment center'. Signs of improvement were short-lived. The cancer spread to one of her lungs. Surgery added but a few months to her life. Eventually, Professor Sealy said I should send for Basil and Terry. Air-tickets were cabled to them. Days later, both boys were home. They had arranged for two weeks leave. Poor Deena was in great distress. Yogurt was the only food she was able to digest. She fought grave odds, not wanting to 'leave' us while the boys were present. They extended their stay for a week - and then another! Both boys had to leave! They flew off on Friday evening November 30, 1978. That same night Deena collapsed in the bathroom. I carried her to bed. Early next morning I telephoned Professor Sealy. He had her taken by ambulance to Groote Schuur Hospital. I called the Matron, Sister Uys - an old friend. She promised 'every possible care'.

Deena died late that afternoon!

I spent the next few days at the home of my brother Maurice. The sad news awaited Basil and Terry on their arrival. I then went abroad to spend time with them and their families. The return journey took me to friends in Vancouver, Toronto, London and Birmingham. In Birmingham, England I found the site where my mother was born. The house was demolished; the site vacant. I had no knowledge of and could not visualize the conditions of her childhood as I so much wanted!

IRMA STERN

Back home, I was soon immersed in my practice, my civic duties and National Gallery interests. They kept me fully occupied. I learnt that Irma Stern, an esteemed Cape Town artist, had died. Her remarkable ability to depict the unique physical features of the African peoples had won her international esteem and honor! She was one of very few South African artists to have attained that position. She was also a very colorful personality. Deena and I had been occasional guests at her dinner table.

Her personal collection included valuable relics from different parts of Africa. On a visit to Zanzibar she had acquired a unique pair of wooden doors exquisitely carved by a local African sculptor - probably unknown outside Zanzibar! She brought the doors to Cape Town and had them installed at the entrance to her home. To my knowledge, Irma's medium had been exclusively oils. After one of her visits to central Africa, she apparently ventured outside that field! At her home one evening, she presented me with a sculpture of the upper torso of an African woman that she had carved out of a piece of soapstone! It reflects the African features with the same sensitivity for which her oils were renowned. A treasured gift from South Africa's most renowned artist; it accompanied me to the United States and is still with me. I have offered it to and it has been accepted by the South African National Gallery.

Irma Stern's home adjoined the University campus in Rosebank. After her death, the University Council[143] acquired the property and converted it to the 'Erma Stern Museum'. With minor internal alterations, the house was appropriately converted. To-day it exhibits many of her works including her interesting collection of African treasures. The University invited me to take the chair of the new museum committee and to perform the opening ceremony. That, as I recall, was one of my last of my public appearances before leaving South Africa to make my home in Santa Barbara.

CHAPTER 28

A NEW LIFE

After Deena's passing, my civic and National Gallery duties kept me busy. After hours, family and friends were at pains to keep me occupied. Old friends, Dave and Mary Marcus, had come from Muizenberg to live in Rondebosch. Their friendship dated back to 1940 when we lived in Muizenberg while our Rondebosch home "Ferramee" was being built. Then Basil, who was not yet four and a very good-looking child who caught the eye of little girls as they passed by! Terence had not yet arrived on the scene. Dave and Mary now required minor alterations to their new home; I had already retired but they said they knew no other architect and urged me to do the plans. It was the last of my professional duties. Their building work was completed while I was abroad. On my return, they invited to see the result of my efforts and to stay for dinner and bridge. I never dreamt that event was to mark the beginning of a new chapter in my life! There was one other guest - Sylvia Kleinman. She sat next to me at dinner. I felt I knew her but could not recall where it was that we had met. Suddenly it dawned on me that she was the wife of the late Arnold Kleinman and it was she who had entered his office during my interview! Fifteen years had passed since then!

After dinner, her charm (and her proficiency at bridge) impressed me! I gathered that she lived in Sea Point and that she gave private bridge lessons! I offered to see her home and was disappointed to hear that she was spending the night with the Marcus's. A few days later I telephoned her. We 'went out' together - a few times. My visits increased in frequency. One evening, I ventured to suggest that it seemed purposeless to continue our ways separately! She said she had similar thoughts! I told her that I had bought an apartment in Santa Barbara and that I planned to live there. The idea did not seem to disturb her! However, I was concerned because I knew of her love of Cape Town and of the family and friends to whom she was deeply attached, and whom I feared she would not wish to leave behind.

Happily that proved to be no obstacle. We decided to make our 'together-ness' permanent and were married on the eighteenth of January 1980. Fam-ily and friends were not invited. They all understood our wish to avoid festivity and fuss. Only the minister and a single witness (provided by the minister) were with us at the ceremony.

BEFORE DEPARTURE

For me, the thought of migration was not new. I was, however, con-cerned about Sylvia for I knew how much she loved Cape Town. I remem-bered that although she was born in Queenstown she had decided, while still a student at the University of Cape Town, that for her, there was 'no place as beautiful' and that Cape Town was her permanent home. I under-stood her attachment for I realized that there was no place that could offer amenities so bountiful, scenery so awesome and flora so rich as those for which the Cape was famed worldwide! My mind, however, was already set. I dreaded the thought of likely political developments and, in any event, the thought of living near my sons dominated my reasoning. Sylvia and I dis-cussed the pros and cons. We spoke about the landscape, the matchless beaches, the safe bathing on two ocean fronts, the mountain drives, forest walks, the flora and fauna! I had to agree that probably there was nothing to compare elsewhere! As though to make sure we knew what we were con-templating, we decided on a long drive - to compress into a single day as much of Cape Town as we could.

We drove around Devil's Peak to the Kirstenbosch Gardens, then up to Constantia Nek and on to Hout Bay. There we lunched in a harbor restau-rant, continued the drive along the Chapmans Peak road, passed Llan-dudno, and Ouderkraal, and 'neath the Twelve Apostles to Camps Bay. We continued toward Lion's Head, past Clifton-on-Sea, along the Sea Point waterfront, through the Duncan dock and back into the City - all in a sin-gle day! It was glorious! We pondered! While I was long set on moving to Santa Barbara, I was not yet sure that Sylvia was reconciled to the idea of finally leaving her beloved city. However, she agreed to at least 'try it' for a few months and if we decided to make the move permanent, we would surely return as often as circumstances would permit.

We applied for U. S. residential visas and towards the end of the year I resigned from all public offices. They included the City Council of which I had been an active member for 32 years, the National Gallery Board of Trustees and the University Council on which I had served for almost as

long. Reluctantly, I also abandoned the chairmanship of a new special City
Arts Committee that I had only recently been asked to lead to deal primar-
ily with the décor of the newly completed Civic Center on the Foreshore.
All entailed farewells - some quite heart-rending!

Our first flight was to Rome to meet Sylvia's niece Felicity, her two
children and the Italian Judge with whom they lived. We went on to London to spend a few days with Beatrice. We dined with our cousin Leo and
his new wife Dianne and spent time with Deena's Scotch cousin Marilyn
Marco. We enjoyed London! From the Strand, we walked into Trafalgar
Square, on to Piccadilly Circus, along Regent Street to Oxford Circus. Suddenly, in Oxford Street, my old friend Maurice Raphael confronted me. It
had been a close friendship that began at school. What a pleasant surprise
that was! I hadn't seen him since the forties! He and his wife were among
the early migrants from Cape Town and had made their home in Switzerland.

After lunch we found our way to Westminster. There the statues of
Churchill and General Smuts caused us both to ponder! From there we
took an easy stroll along the Thames embankment back to our hotel on the
Strand.

From London's Heathrow airport we flew to Washington, Los Angeles
and on to Santa Barbara where Terry and Jane and my grandchildren
Stephen and Jeanette awaited us. Thanks to Terry's advance arrangements,
we occupied for the first time the apartment at New Horizons that I had
purchased a few years earlier. We decided to buy a car. As we were due to
return to Cape Town in a few months, I bought a second hand car. It served
us well - took us to many spots that were entirely new to both of us. Sylvia
was attracted to Santa Barbara. She enjoyed the many amenities available
- not least the golf course at New Horizons where we were frequent players. At functions in the club-house and at occasional open-air dinners
around the swimming pool, we met many of our neighbors. We attended
the bridge club that met in the clubhouse every Thursday night. We joined
an outside bridge club that met once a month for dinner and bridge at the
Montecito Country Club. Sylvia also joined a ladies bridge group that met
weekly and I was part of a weekly foursome playing alternatively at the
players' respective homes.

We were not far from Terry, Jane and our grandchildren Stephen and
Jeanette! Our time was fully and joyfully occupied. Towards the end of the

year we returned to enjoy the summer in Cape Town. By then Sylvia was completely reconciled to the idea of leaving her 'beloved' Cape Town, to which we subsequently returned twenty times in nineteen years!

During those years we traveled widely - to NewYork, Washington, Boston and to Mexico. On our return flights from Cape Town, we invariably spent several days in London with occasional visits to Cornwall and Devon and on one occasion a few days in Edinburgh. Twice we spent a fortnight in Israel, and on one of the visits were the guests of Morris Kahn who flew us to his fine aquarium in Elat and thence to Jerusalem.

Back in the United States, we took the dome train from San Francisco to the Canadian Rockies, to Banff and Lake Louise. Never to be forgotten were two wonderful cruises - one from Vancouver to the fjords of Alaska, the other from Copenhagen to Stockholm, St. Petersburg, Helsinki and Tallinn on the Baltic. We also had two wonderful holidays, each of a week, in Hawaii - one in Honolulu, the other in Maui. On the latter, we were again the guests of Morris Kahn at the opening of his magnificent aquarium. Memorable were the days spent in Portugal and Spain, the treasures of Madrid and Toledo and the sheer relaxation at Marbella on the Mediterranean. Our retirement years, full and joyful as they were, were burdened by constant awareness of the problems that faced our native land. They were deep-rooted and potentially dangerous and were a the source of unwelcome personal implications.

UNEXPECTED PROBLEMS!

During our first year in America, the South African currency (Rand) plunged steeply and continued to fall[144]. While the capital that we had already withdrawn from South Africa was, of course, unaffected, we were reliant on the income that we were permitted to withdraw. In the months and years that followed, the value of the Rand continued to plunge. By 1993, it was down to less than a third of its original value with a corresponding impact on our income. Inquiries revealed that I was then permitted to withdraw the rest of my capital. I proceeded to liquidate my S.A. assets and withdraw the proceeds. That was completed in 1994. By then, my only material assets in South Africa were an ever diminishing one-sixth share of the proceeds from my late father's estate and a small annuity, the value of which had dropped to the princely monthly sum of sixty-nine Rand fifty[145] - the equivalent then of about ten dollars!

My decision to withdraw all capital assets proved to be anything but prudent! Towards the end of 1987, the capital that was withdrawn from South Africa, was entrusted with an investment manager, Reed E. Slatkin (he was a near neighbor of my son Terence and had handled some of his investments with apparent success.) In 1992/3, as the balance of my capital arrived from South Africa. I put it into my Slatkin account. His quarterly reports continued to be very favorable. Withdrawals were implemented speedily and without demur. 'Meticulously' year after year, he provided all the documentation needed for our tax returns. We had no reason to suspect that anything was amiss - not until April 2001 when we read a front page press report in the NewsPress telling of his bankruptcy! It transpired that he had been conducting a highly organized fraudulent (ponzi) scheme from the start – that throughout the years, funds invested by him were being used for his own advantage and that he was ably and knowingly assisted by his professional book-keeper! Skillfully, he allayed any possible suspicion by remitting detailed quarterly reports and remitting withdrawals speedily as and when required - until one day, when one of his many clients suddenly wanted to withdraw more than he was able to produce! His victims were numerous! They extended from California to New York. Some believed that his ill-begotten gains had been whittled away to anonymous accounts in Switzerland or South America. None could be traced. My account (one of the smallest) stood at $1.2 million when the crash came. My account proved to be valueless. The losses suffered by both my sons were much larger and two of my grandchildren lost all their savings. For my sons, it was a devastating blow. They had been planning for their retirement and Terry had in fact retired in 1998! They had no choice but to put their retirement plans aside for several years! In due course, Slatkin was sentenced to 14 years imprisonment, his bookkeeper to two. His wife divorced him; his son changed his name and many of his clients waited hopefully for the day when they 'might' receive their share of the balance of the funds recovered by the trustees less the enormous expenses incurred in the process.

TAX RELIEF!

In due course, some relief came to Terry and Jane and to me in the form of returned taxes that had been paid on the fictitious profits that Slatkin reported each year. Such profits - if they ever accrued - went to one or other of <u>his</u> personal accounts! Thus it was that the crooked genius was the only one to have benefited from his fraudulent activities!

SYLVIA SHUTS HER EYES

Despite the material setbacks, Santa Barbara was our happy haven for twenty glorious years. It was then that Sylvia became seriously ill. On August 6, 2000, her eighty-second birthday, the ambulance took her to hospital and from there to "Alamar" where, the doctors informed me, she would be cared for, but would remain - indefinitely!

I moved from New Horizons to Wood Glen Hall, a retirement home on the Foothills. It was within walking distance of 'Alamar' and enabled me to be with Sylvia twice a day. From then on, for little more than a year, we walked together in the corridors of 'Alamar'. Occasionally, when weather permitted, we would sit in the garden courtyard - holding hands. Very rarely we would drive to a nearby park.

On July 14, 2001, Sylvia shut her eyes for the last time. Her children, Frank and Lynn, were with me at her side.

Six months later, Terry and Jane graciously urged me to share their home on North Kellogg Avenue. I have been there ever since - in my separate quarter surrounded by art treasures collected over the years - walking in the neighborhood each day, writing memoirs, reliving events of long ago and sleeping more frequently than ever before!

Today, I look back - deeply grateful that the difficult decision taken 26 years ago has proved, notwithstanding drawbacks, to be sound! Those years could not have been spent in a better environment. My sojourn in Santa Barbara has enabled me to be near my family, to watch with glee grandchildren and their parents live their lives and plan for the years ahead, to witness great grandchildren take their initial steps into life. - all that in a Mediterranean climate akin to the one I savored during my first 70 years! I look back on the financial set-backs suffered after leaving Cape Town - particularly to those that my family and I experienced in 2001, and am extremely grateful that they have proved to be little more than 'material encounters'- with little bearing on the quality of our lives, and without impact on the priceless heritage endowed by nature.

CAPE TOWN - MY LAST TRIP!

In 2002, accompanied by Terry and Jane, I made my twenty-first and last return trip to Cape Town - my native city. We had learnt that "Longwood", (my home when I was a boy), was a private residential hotel. For 'old-times sake', we booked to spend a few days there. It was quite an emotional experience! The lounge and dining room with its vaulted ceiling, were entirely unchanged. Each of the six large bedrooms now included a separate bathroom and the upper floor balcony that extended for the full frontage of the house had been removed - was replaced by a pergola over the verandah that extended for the entire length of the house. The study downstairs, which had been my work-room when I was a student (more than seventy years past) also had a separate bathroom and was designated by the proprietor to be 'my' bedroom during our visit. Unchanged (except for the pergola) was the large verandah with its heavy slate paving where Dad used to pace up and down every evening. In the garden beneath the Jacaranda tree, I looked for the horizontal branch from which I used to swing - when I was a boy. Sure enough there it was - only now it was too high to reach and too thick to grasp!

Terry, Jane and I drove to T.K.P.S., my kindergarten school in Tamboers Kloof. Terry parked the car facing the entrance and switched off the engine to give me time to reminisce! From there we went to the nearby spot on the pavement in Kloof Nek Road where I had placed my overcoat when I was 6 years old - where Maurice and I stubbornly refused to pick it up and returned home to receive our well-deserved reprimands - I've never forgotten!

We drove to 2 Kloof Road where I was born. Now it was a vacant plot - our lovely old home "Epherton" had been demolished. Much in the neighborhood seemed unchanged except that everything now appeared so much smaller than when I was a boy! We drove up to Kloof Nek and to the top of Signal Hill where I had taken my grandmother for a drive soon after I obtained my driving license - 85 years ago! In those days it was quite a perilous experience!

We had wonderful visits to our families and friends of long ago; we went to the cemeteries at Maitland where my parents and grandparents were buried. There we were shocked to find (in the very old Maitland cemetery) that most of the tombstones lay scattered - vandalized for the lead content of the engravings. The tombstones of my forebears, however, all remained intact!

My old school and college campuses produced more precious memories as did our visits to "Ferramee" - the home I'd built in 1940 - my family haven for twenty-five glorious years. We drove to Muizenberg – where, as children on the sands and in the surf of the Indian Ocean, we had spent two months every summer. We went on to Simonstown, Cape Point, Kirstenbosch and other memorable spots in the Peninsula and around beautiful Table Mountain which I'd often climbed years past - when limbs were more willing!

A flight to Johannesburg gave me an enjoyable few days with Lynn and Terry Markman and their children Andrea and Kevin – a branch of the family of whom I had grown increasingly fond over the twenty-six years since Sylvia first brought them into my life.

Back in Cape Town, Terry, Jane and I spent five days at a private hotel in Rosebank - a residential suburb adjoining Rondebosch. The particular spot was chosen because of its proximity to the University of Cape Town where Jane attended a four-day conference of P.P.D.[146], an international organization that she founded in Santa Barbara after her unforgettable experiences following the birth of her first child more than three decades earlier. It was there at the University that I studied architecture some 75 years ago and it was the very area that I represented on the City and Provincial Councils during the past century.

From there we visited more family and friends - those that were still alive. They included my fond cousin Rosalie Wolpe, six months my senior, now living in a retirement home in Rouwkoop Road Rondebosch. We dined in Newlands with my nephew Richard and his wife Marilyn. (Richard was now a very busy architect practicing in the city.)

Terry and I lunched at "Hillcote" in Hesseldon Road - the home of our old and very dear friends the Engels. Heinz had passed on. Eva, now a little frail, was as charming as ever. I also spent several pleasant hours with an old friend, Walter Middleman. He was Heinz Engel's partner sixty years earlier. We recalled the occasion when (as a young councilor) I had the unpleasant duty to inform them of the City's decision to expropriate their business site in Buitenkant Street - required for road improvement purposes. Unwelcome at the time, it turned out to be a fortunate decision. Heinz subsequently ran his own successful 'Brakes Super-Service' business and Walter bought a farm where he developed a lucrative business exporting plant seeds to different parts of the world. (He was responsible for bringing the seeds of several species - including South Africa's national flower the Protea - here to Santa Barbara.) He died in 2006.

"Palo Alto" and "Atlantica" in Milnerton, "Fredefort" on the Beach Road Sea Point, "Edingight" and Honikman Square in Rondebosch were still there. We also visited the old Town Hall in Darling Street which I had frequented daily way back in the thirties and the 'new' Civic Centre on the Foreshore for which I - as a City Councilor - was partly responsible more than 30 years ago.

At the airport before our departure, I was walking towards the South African Airways counter when from my side I heard a lady's voice exclaim: "Alfred..." I turned to face a very handsome lady! She seemed about fifty. I stared admiringly and in wonderment! "Whom have I the pleasure of meeting?" I asked. She replied: "Alf - I'm Kay - your niece - Harold's daughter!" Forty years had passed since we last met. She was then a child of Deena's youngest brother. She had developed so beautifully - I could never have recognized her. She and I joined Terry and Jane in the tearoom where other family members had gathered. We reminisced for an hour - until it was time to board our airplane. We promised to correspond - which we did regularly thereafter.

The last of my travels was over! Back in Santa Barbara, I was content and grateful to spend my time near family - in an environment so enriched as to render bearable any longing for the incomparable oasis in which my life took shape. Here, in the kingdom of the mind, I can revisit distant haunts, reminisce and contemplate - perhaps with a more balanced perspective - the remarkable political and humanitarian changes being wrought in my native land. They a are changes which touch on the fundamentals of life itself, but which I feel sure will be wrought in a manner that will glow as an example to all nations and to all mankind.

CHAPTER 29

THE LONG ROAD AHEAD!

Our departure from South Africa and Cape Town in 1980 was anything but a conclusive transition. Attachments to family and friends, to the country and city of my birth, intensified as the years went by. By no means were they severed by our sudden departure, nor were they impaired by any rationale that may have contributed to so radical a step. Indeed, we were drawn back twenty-one times in as many years - just as often as our health and means permitted.

After moving to Santa Barbara, my direct observations of events unfolding in South Africa were reduced to our annual visits. The news media and letters from friends provided scant information of what was happening in my native land. Of great interest are events as portrayed by Nelson Mandela in his autobiography *"Long Walk to Freedom"* published in 1994 by Macdonald Purnell (Pty) Ltd. of Randburg, South Africa.

During all those years that I was absent, conditions in South Africa underwent changes so profound, so far-reaching, as to make the civilized world gaze first in horror as the violence and terror increased, then in wonderment and finally with unprecedented admiration!

By 1980, apartheid had become a way of life that was entrenched. Ingenious measures were applied in an effort to preserve it in perpetuity. Prime Minister Hendrick Verwoerd (often referred to as the 'father of apartheid') was born in Holland. He came to South Africa at the age of 2. Educated at the University of Stellenbosch, he refused an offer to continue his studies in England. In preference, he chose Germany, then dominated by the sinister Nazi concept of 'race domination'! When he returned to South Africa, that concept - compatible with the goals of apartheid - gained tremendous impetus. During his term as Prime Minister, a variety of laws designed to entrench 'white supremacy' were introduced. Slowly, repugnance and opposition by the democratic world mounted. Economic sanctions against South Africa gathered momentum. South Africa became the pariah of the free world. After his assassination in 1966, Verwoerd was succeeded as Prime Minister by the new leader of the Nationalist Party - Advocate P.J. Vorster.

After imprisonment on Robben Island for more than 20 years, Nelson Mandela was transferred to the Polsmoor prison in a suburb of Cape Town and from then on he was the object of negotiation. Numerous interviews took place between him, Ministers of State and with the State President himself. He also maintained contact with the banned ANC (African National Congress) operating abroad. (Letters between them were smuggled by his attorneys).

Despite encouraging signs, several years of discussion, violence and negotiation had yet to elapse before settlement was reached. It was obvious that the Government and indeed all parties were anxious to find a solution. Continued unrest and violence, however, gave the Nationalist Party an overwhelming victory at the General Election (of whites only voters). The official opposition was in total disarray. The United Party (once headed by the renowned General Smuts) had disintegrated. The official opposition was now the Conservative Party - a reactionary group 'to the right' of the Nationalists! Indeed they actually accused the Government of being "too lenient with the blacks"! Now, it was left to the few less-indoctrinated Nationalists within Government to assert the only 'liberal' influence in an exclusively 'white' parliament! In the late eighties, it was they who were responsible for the many private 'talks' that took place between Mandela and Government nominees, Ministers of State, and the State President and with prominent visitors from abroad.

At the opening of parliament in February 1990, De Klerk, who had recently taken over the presidency and the head of the Nationalist Party, announced significant changes. They included the lifting of bans on numerous organizations, institutions and persons including the ANC, the PAC (Pan African Congress), the Communist Party and the freeing of all prisoners interned for non-violent activities. Mandela was formally released a week later. It was a momentous occasion – but years had yet to pass before real progress was made towards a full democracy. That evening, however, Mandela addressed a crowd that had gathered on the Grand Parade in Cape Town and referred to the occasion by saying: *"We will walk the last mile together."*

On September 26, 1992, after two and a half years of sometimes bitter negations, De Klerk and Mandela met for an official summit. On that day they signed a *'Record of Understanding'*. It responded to the demands of the ANC. It enabled *"the government finally to agree to accept a single elected constitutional assembly that would adopt a new constitution and serve as a transitional legislature for the new government."*

The proposal was agreed to by the ANC provided it did not give veto rights to minority parties. In December that year, the government and the ANC began another round of secret bilateral talks. There, it was agreed in principle on a *five-year 'government of national unity' in which all parties polling over 5 per cent in a general election would be represented proportionately in the cabinet; and after five years a government of national unity would become a simple majority-rule government"*. On June 3, the multi-party forum voted to set the date: - *April 27, 1994, for the "first South African non-racial one-person-one-vote election"*. It was an epic moment - a clarion call to the rest of the world.

De Klerk and Mandela were awarded the Nobel Peace Prize.

CONCILIATION!

Subsequent events add a glowing chapter to the long, sometimes painful story of human relations as they evolved in South Africa. They provide evidence that cleavage, however, long and bitter, can yield to dialogue - can be superceded by a durable *peace* - that a seemingly inevitable civil WAR can be averted!

After decades of repression and cleavage, the *peace* plan that followed embraced an organized *reconciliation process*.

It was a tribute to the human spirit - a glowing example to people everywhere!

The history of our kind is the story of an endless search for ways and means to sustain life! We seek land to harvest food! We strive to preserve natural amenities; to overcome dangers; build dykes to prevent floods; provide cures for disease; search the outer space to counter natural and man-made hazards; we train our children to cope with problems that lie ahead. Such strivings - our will to overcome to survive - mirror the human spirit!

Hitherto, our story has also been one of countless wars and a never-ending search for new and ingenious means of inflicting disaster, chaos and death! Some have been deemed necessary to prevent a backward slide of civilization into ages that are too dark to contemplate. All are denials of the human spirit - for which we have failed thus far to find the antidote. Valor, endurance and self-sacrifice, often manifest in times of disaster, are not a monopoly of war! They reflect characteristics that are in dire contrast to all that WAR implies. Yet war has persisted, magnifying our failure thus far to cope with problems of our own creation.

The South African solution - by no means the perfect answer - gave proof that WAR, seemingly inevitable, can be averted - that there is another answer - a humane, nobler solution - however grave and intense the circumstances.

They have paved the way for the rest of the civilized world to follow.

By 1994, conditions in South Africa - to which civil war seemed an inevitable end - had undergone remarkable change! The 'Inevitable' yielded to dialogue. Many of the perpetrators of heinous apartheid crimes were pardoned. They were offered complete freedom provided they co-operated, appeared before a reconciliation tribunal and honorably acknowledged their misdeeds. Many co-operated and, freed from their troublesome past, were able to pursue their normal lives. Some did not do so. President Botha was one who refused! He was unshakeable in his commitment to the idea of an Afrikaner Republic. From childhood he was conditioned in the belief that the 'the black man' could never be party to providing mankind with an answer to one of its gravest problems. He (Botha), however, was allowed to spend the rest of his days in peace - to realize perhaps that his dream lacked numerical reasonableness and could never be equitably realized!

In 1994 Mandela was inaugurated as President of South Africa. In 1996 he signed the new Liberal Constitution of South Africa in Sharpeville and in 2006 ex-president Botha died peacefully at home.

2007

Nearly 13 years have passed since the South African Nation underwent radical change - since apartheid ceased to be the dominant political influence. Since then, how have they fared? Have the African peoples sought retribution for the harm done them during the apartheid years or have they chosen the more humane way? They have chosen the latter despite the odds of circumstance, despite the example set by Zimbabwe, their northerly neighbor, who chose to assert their numerical strength to grab what was not theirs 'while the going was good'! In contrast the South Africans have shown a benign common sense - a patience that will reap its reward as time passes. They have made South Africa a glowing example to all nations. They will show that 'humanity' and 'justice' are attributes that, in the end, will reap the benefits to which mankind aspires.

South Africa deserves to prosper and will do so in time. Temporarily, poverty denies the country sufficient teachers. The inadequacy finds some compensation in the numbers of the more fortunate who come forward to offer their services freely to compensate for the temporary inadequacy. Slowly tribalism will yield to the benefits of an advanced culture. Then, from the shores of southern Africa, will shine a beacon light for the world to imbibe and prosper as time unfolds.

The End

NOTES

¹ The book was presented to me by the South African Government in March 1979. The occasion was the formal transfer of 550 acres of land (reclaimed from the sea) from the jurisdiction of the five-member Foreshore Board to the City. At the time, I was one of the City's two representatives on the Board.

² Stephanus Johannes Paulus Kruger (1825-1904)

³ Honikman and Leeb

⁴ Gen. Smuts, a general in the Boer War, succeeded Gen. Louis Botha, first Prime Minister of the Union.

⁵ These were the first known 'Concentration Camps' - not to be confused or compared with the grim Nazi Concentration Camps of World War II.

⁶ After Union in 1910, General Hertzog served under Generals Botha and Smuts for less than 2 years! His frequent public references to the "undue influence of Britain in the affairs of South Africa" and his resentment of the accolades Britain frequently showered on both leaders were a source of embarrassment to the Government. Hertzog was asked to resign. He refused. Instead the Government resigned and in the General Election that followed, the South African Party was returned to power and Hertzog was excluded from Government. The bitter feud that ensued between Hertzog and Smuts characterized South African politics for the next 25 years.

⁷ In the early morning when the beech was free of crowds, "dirt-carts" and municipal employees were seen removing unwanted sea-weed.

8 Towards the end of the 18th Century, Cecil John Rhodes, Prime Minister of the Cape Colony, commissioned Herbert Baker, a British architect, to build his home - a palatial mansion - on the lower reaches of his estate in Rondebosch. He named it "Groote Schuur" (Great Barn). Baker visited the Cape where he built several homes. Influenced by the unique character of many Cape Dutch homesteads, his work embraced gables of exquisite form! They featured dominantly in his designs. They, in turn, were an important supplement to 'Cape Dutch architecture'. Rhodes endowed "Groote Schuur" to the nation as the home of future Prime Ministers.

9 The shaped vertical profile of a circular column; that is, the tapering line produced by the reduced diameter of the column over the upper two-thirds of its height. It is essentially an aesthetic feature.

10 A beautiful hardwood grown in the forests of Knysna, Stinkwood is indigenous to South Africa.

11 Bema is the central podium which is used throughout the service except when the rabbi spoke from his exclusive podium in front of the congregation.

12 Subsequently I learnt that the building had been designed by Architect Soloman who later was the winner of the prestigious architectural competition for the new University campus in Rondebosch - built immediately prior to my entry as a student of architecture in 1938.

13 Birkby became a popular writer. For a long while, his articles appeared in the local press. They were on a variety of topics - a source of considerable interest.

14 Later renamed to Kloof Nek Road

15 voluntary

16 As I recall there were five dollars to the pound in those days.

17 The South African Party suffered its first defeat in the 1927 General Election. General Smuts as Prime Minister was succeeded by his bitter rival Gen. J. B. M. Hertzog, the first leader of a rapidly growing Nationalist Party.

[18] see Chapter 17

[19] The pier disappeared in the fifties. It was 'consumed' by a massive reclamation project that pushed back the Table Bay coast line and added
550 acres to the downtown area.

[20] Hiddingh Hall was the University assembly hall on the old city campus.
A wash is a method of applying watercolor.

[21] A north-facing replica of St. Pancras Cathedral at Kings Cross, London.
Situated on Wale Street, the portico, pediment and steeple were sited to
overlook the center of St. Georges Street. It was a splendid town-planning achievement providing a handsome terminal to the south-facing
vista down the city's second most important thoroughfare. Not built of
long-lasting materials, it was crumbling and was replaced mid-19th
century by Sir Herbert Baker's handsome sandstone Gothic edifice -
not similarly sited.

[22] Afrikaans for 'verandah'

[23] Now Namibia

[24] Afrikaans for village

[25] track

[26] cattle enclosures

[27] "eyes…eyes"

[28] a then recent car accessory, fitted at a high point under the bonnet

[29] W.H. Grant was responsible for the design of several of the City's largest
buildings.

[30] Wheatley, in addition to his professorship, was appointed first Director
of the new South African Art Gallery that was being completed. His
wife Grace Wheatley, also an accomplished artist, had been entrusted
with the design and execution of the murals to the vaulted ceiling of
the main exhibition hall.

[31] The S.A. National Gallery (now know as the *Iziko Museum*) is an institution that belongs to the *People* <u>not</u> to the Government. It was built
(circa 1929) in terms of an agreement by which the Government
undertook to establish a National Gallery in Cape Town and to provide
the funds necessary to run the institution, in exchange for a valuable
property in Queen Victoria Street (owned by the Fine Arts Guild of
Cape Town) and expropriated by the Government for the building of
the new University of South Africa. Thereafter, in terms of the agreement, the Gallery was governed by a Board of Trustees of 10 persons,
two of whom are nominated by each of the following bodies: Central
Government; City Council of Cape Town; Fine Arts Guild; Universities of Cape Town and Stellenbosch. The constitution was changed in
the sixties to provide for an eleventh member to represent the "Friends
of the South African Art Gallery", a body (established with the Board's
approval) that was doing great work to advance the Gallery's finances.

[32] A nickname derived from Alphonsque which my father ascribed to me.

[33] George the fifth King Emperor

[34] then the equivalent of approximately $2.50

[35] The Huguenots, escaping religious persecution, left France in the 17th
century to settle in the Cape of Good Hope.

[36] The equivalent of 20 U. S. cents.

[37] National Union of South African Students periodically organized overseas tours for the annual year-end vacation.

[38] Royal Institute of British Architects: headquarters Portland Place, London.

[39] Now, 71 years later, those of our group whose names I remember were
(architecture) Patsy Barry, Angus Stewart, Max Dembitzer, Morrie
Freedman, Clarke; (art) Eileen Kreuger, Elma Marquard, and Hen-
drikse (theological student from Stellenbosch University)

[40] 164 feet high, the monument was commissioned by Napoleon in 1806
and completed in 1825. Beneath the arch, a torch burns in honor of
those who died defending France in World War I.

[41] Ciano became Prime Minister; later, for alleged treachery, Mussolini had him executed by firing squad.

[42] The pigeons were said to have been brought originally from Cyprus.

[43] In later years, Bridge was a frequent, challenging diversion from my daily, sometimes stressful, duties.

[44] The South African Party, in power since Union (1910) was in Opposition, having lost the 1927 General Election, to the Nationalist Party under the leadership of General Hertzog.

[45] A Japanese Trade Treaty concluded at the time was a contentious issue

[46] Little hills

[47] Thomas Watt: British Sculptor (1927-1992). *Groote Constantia; historic manor house presented to Simon Van Der Stel, Commander and Governor of the Cape 1679 to 1699. **Anreith: Architect/Sculptor (1754-1822) came to the Cape 1777 as a soldier of the Dutch India Company

[48] The name is fictitious. I have forgotten his real name.

[49] Fictitious name. Head of a timber and hardware firm and prominent citizen of Benoni.

[50] As Greta was known to her family

[51] Abbreviation for an area known as the *Witwatersrand* (literal translation: white water's edge.)

[52] Umhlangha Rocks (pronounced: *um-shlang ha*) was a natural resort on the KwaZulu Natal Coast.

[53] The "Groot Trek" started in 1835. A mass exodus of more than 10,000 Boers (Voortrekkers) in their ox-wagons left the Cape Colony with their families and went north and north-east. The mass exodus was attributed to economic problems, the fear of conflict with the Xhosa, who settled on the other side of the Fish River, and discontent with British rule in the Cape Colony.

[54] D.F. Malan, a Dutch Reformed Church minister, left the altar to pursue a political career. He was not related to the family F.S. Malan who were neighbors in Cape Town.

[55] The building was designed by my firm well before I joined. Wagner had done the drawings.

[56] A large format drawing board measuring 40" high x 55" wide; it was a standard architectural drawing size in the days preceding digital drafting.

[57] Equivalent to 115,000 U. S. dollars - a substantial sum in those days! The South African pound was worth 2.54 dollars at the time.

[58] Afrikaans for corn

[59] "Maidens in Uniform" (German)

[60] As I recall, the pound was then worth 1.58 U. S. dollars

[61] Royal Institute of British Architects

[62] South African Institute of Architects

[63] Pound was then equal to worth approximately 2.54 U. S. dollars

[64] Guinea (one pound one shilling) was equal to 2.67 U. S. dollars

[65] Built in 1903, in the heart of Government Avenue, was (like the UCT campus at Rondebosch) among Solomon's great contributions to the architectural heritage of the Cape Province.

[66] 'The breaking of the glass' – a gesture symbolizing the breaking of all conflicting ties

[67] Fellow of the Royal College of Surgeons

[68] British Broadcasting Corporation

[69] Hans Christian Andersen's "Little Harbor Lady"

70 " I don't understand"

71 "I am Regional leader over Holland."

72 Harold won a "gold" for the 100-meter sprint at the 1924 Olympic Games in Paris. A film, *Chariots of Fire* (1974), depicting Harold's life at Cambridge was shown worldwide over an extensive period of time.

73 Sydney (Solly), also an athlete in his day, was knighted and appointed Lord Chief Justice of Ceylon (1936-39). He was the first Jew to occupy the position of President of the London Athletic Club (founded 1863).

74 Adolphe, an esteemed London physician, was Dean of the Westminster Hospital.

75 Lionel was a well known solicitor.

76 A large hall in Darling Street immediately east of the City Hall, built during the Boer War at the end of the 18th century. There, British received pre-combat training prior to departure for the Transvaal war front.

77 Limitations concerning building type, volume, coverage, height and side-space.

78 The oldest Trust Company ever to have been established.

79 Smuts was the only man in history to have served twice in that capacity.

80 Lightning war

81 Master Builders' Association

82 The Castle, built between 1666 and 1679, is the oldest building in South Africa. Pentagonal in shape, surrounded by a moat, it was built to protect the early Dutch settlers from marauding tribal (Hottentot) nomads. Today, an historic museum, it depicts the military history of the Cape, contains weapons and uniforms from the Dutch and British periods of occupation. It also houses the noted William Fehr Collection of priceless paintings.

83 A suburb of Cape Town some three miles from my home site

84 In memory of my father! When we were very young we had a Scotch nurse. She rolled her 'R's incessantly - to the amusement of my dad. When, in the absence of the nurse, when Dad wanted to curb any bad behavior of his kids, he would shake his head and say *"no fear me!* –in doing so he would playfully mimic the nurse and deliberately roll his 'R's' to the extent that his comment sounded like '*no 'ferrra mee'*. We heard it frequently and as adults often playfully repeated it to Dad.

85 Architect and Partner in the firm Walgate and Elsworth who 3 decades earlier was commissioned to design the alterations to my home "Longwood".

86 He was the nephew of the late mayor and the son of my mother's cousin.

87 Main South African Army Headquarters and training center in Pretoria - later known as Voortrekkerhooghte

88 Directorate of Fortifications and Coastal Works

89 Royal Air Force

90 Months in hospital, Leo made a remarkable recovery and returned to duty. He was appointed Commanding Officer at the Castle, Cape Town, a role he occupied until the war ended.

91 Victory in Europe

92 Military & civilian killed: USSR, 20 million; Allies 44, Million; Axis, 11 million. Military deaths (both sides) in Europe, 19 million, against Japan, 6 million; U. S. deaths in battle 291,131, other causes 115,187

93 "Ox wagon fire watch" was a national movement that attracted large numbers of Afrikaners who sought new homes distant from British rule, many north of the Orange River. The movement became organized and in 1834 developed into a massive migration known as the "Great Trek".

94 True Afrikaners.

95 Pronounced *goi er* with a guttural 'g', and meaning "Good morning"

96 Mixed race

[97] A 100 Cape feet measure is equivalent to 103.333 English feet.

[98] In the 18th century, cast iron was the object of a highly lucrative trade between Britain and cities of her far-flung Empire.

[99] Ox-wagon sentinels or guards

[100] "Black danger!"

[101] All the larger building contractors were registered members of the Master Builders Association

[102] Smuts, of Boer stock, was born in the Cape, a British subject. He was educated at the Universities of Stellenbosch and Cambridge. With the outbreak of the Boer War he relinquished British citizenship to join the Boer forces. Early in World War I, he suppressed a new Boer uprising. As a member of the Imperial War Cabinet (1917–18) he spent much of his time in England. He signed the Treaty of Versailles but averred that its terms would outrage Germany and prevent world harmony – the object of the League of Nations.

[103] German army

[104] Prior to the third quarter of the 18th century, the many indigenous tribes of Southern Africa pursued rural lives untouched by Western civilization. The colonization of Africa by the European powers slowly produced changes. In South Africa, the changes were hastened by the discovery of diamonds and gold in the eighteenth century. Africans in search of work were drawn to the cities from their rural environment. Unfamiliar with and ill-attuned to Western practices, they were totally excluded from the democratic process until well into the 20th.Century when they were given the right to elect 3 white representatives to Senate (Upper House).

[105] There were two elements of Nationalists: 'verligtes" (moderates) and 'verkramptes' (narrow-minded)

[106] Afrikaner nationhood

[107] African National Congress

[108] Literally "Band of Brothers"

[109] Said to be the 'father of apartheid'

[110] The metropolitan area covered an extensive portion of the Cape Peninsula. From the city central (on the shore of Table Bay on the Atlantic seaboard) the city spreads westward along the coast to Sea Point and Clifton at the foot of Lion's Head, and on to Camps Bay beneath the Twelve Apostles. Eastward around Devil's Peak and for 15 miles through the southern, the city extends to the Muizenberg seaside resort on the False Bay coast and onward for another 5 miles along the western shore of the Indian ocean through St. James and Kalk Bay up to the boundary of the Fish Hoek municipality.

[111] My dentist's chair was directly in front of a window that overlooked the site of the old main post office (It had been built in the 18th.century and was to be replaced by a modern Post Office in lower Parliament St.) The Adderley street site had been bought by the O.K. Bazaars for their new Cape Town store and offices.

[112] Wynberg, Claremont, Worcester, Sea Point, Fish Hoek, Salt River, Paarl, Stellenbosch, and Somerset West.

[113] For Texaco and subsequently for the Shell Company

[114] Why he called me "Uncle", I will never know!

[115] South African Synthetic Oil Limited. Initiated in 1927 because of a lack crude oil, the South African government spearheaded the development of an oil-from-coal program.

[116] At all Council meetings the mayor is seated on an elegant old ebony chair surmounted by a large timber anchor - part of the City's ancient crest. The Chair is known as the *Chair of Van Riebeeck* - the first Governor of the Cape when it was founded in 1652.

[117] It occurred (circa 1970) in the midst of my 20-year Chairmanship of the Board of Trustees.

[118] See footnote 30

[119] Dr. Du Plessis was a member of the Nationalist Party. Recently appointed Ambassador to Holland, his credentials were rejected by the Queen because of alleged support for Germany during World War I.

[120] Boet Erasmus was an ex-mayor and veteran councilor of Port Elizabeth

[121] Juta & Company was one of the most prominent publishers and book importers in the country. They had premises in the principal centers with headquarters in Cape Town.

[122] "We must thank Mr. Slater...."

[123] Councilor Sonnenberg, an attorney by profession, was an ex-mayor and an MPC. He sat next to me in the Council chamber.

[124] a brilliant young Cape Town M.P.

[125] M.P. for Houghton Johannesburg – an esteemed, forceful courageous apartheid adversary

[126] Sea Point, Woodstock, Maitland, Mowbray, Rondebosch, Athlone, Claremont, Wynberg and Muizenberg

[127] the Nationalists

[128] The Pan Africa Congress and African National Congress were two active African anti-apartheid organizations.

[129] Africans were obliged to obtain and carry 'passes' to 'legalize' their presence in so-called 'white areas'.

[130] When I first entered the Council in 1948, the Town Clerk explained that the practice was rooted in the belief that the Mayor should be one of the elected Councilors and that Council members were in the best position to assess the capabilities and worthiness of potential incumbents of high office.

[131] Van Riebeeck landed in the Cape in 1652. He was sent there by the Dutch East India Company to establish a victualling station where fresh vegetables could be grown and made available to the Company's ships that passed the Cape on their long journey to the Dutch East Indies. It was a step necessary to overcome the problem of 'scurvy' to

which many of the Company's sailors succumbed due to lack of fresh food. Van Riebeeck succeeded in his mission; he was joined by his wife and became the first governor of the Cape.

[132] A Department of State responsible for the financing of urban housing development

[133] 'Shanties' or slum dwellings

[134] The bronze plaque commemorating the occasion was one of the many subsequently vandalized by petty criminals.

[135] Originally named "D.F. Malan Airport" (the first apartheid prime minister) and subsequently renamed

[136] A fact proven after the establishment of majority rule (1994) when the nation was welcomed back as a self-governing member of the British Commonwealth

[137] They were the guests of NUSAS (National Union of South African Students). At the time Nelson Mandela, Chief Albert Luthuli and other S.A. leaders opposed to apartheid were imprisoned on Robben Island or in exile. Martin Luther King had already identified the civil rights movement as strongly opposed to apartheid. Otherwise, little was known in the U. S. about apartheid or about Kennedy's 1966 visit to South Africa.

[138] Manager of Cadbury's chocolate factory whom I had once represented on the Valuation Court

[139] It was a very substantial sum that was mentioned (I have forgotten the precise amount.)

[140] A large valuable one-ounce gold coin recently produced for the first time by the South African mint.

[141] Palo Alto – the town in which Stanford University is situated

[142] Dr. Nicholas Hoff – world renowned professor of Aeronautics and Astronautics

[143] I represented the City as a member of the University Council for more than twenty years.

[144] By 2003, the South African Rand had fallen from $1.33 to $0.24 and continued to drop to $0.12. In 2004, it started to rise steadily and reached $0.166 by 2006.

[145] By 2003, the value of the Rand had dropped in value to $0.10026

[146] P.P.D. Post Partum Depression

Printed in the United States
92123LV00001B/403-432/A